Socialist Internationalism and the Gritty Politics of the Particular

Histories of Internationalism

Series Editors: Jessica Reinisch, Reader in Modern History at Birkbeck, University of London, UK and David Brydan, Lecturer of 20th Century History and International Relations at King's College London, UK.

Editorial Board: Neil Davie, University of Lyon II, France; Johannes Dillinger, University of Maine, Germany; Wilbur Miller, State University of New York, USA; Marianna Muravyeva, University of Helsinki, Finland; David Nash, Oxford Brookes University, UK; Judith Rowbotham, Nottingham Trent University, UK

This new book series features cutting-edge research on the history of international cooperation and internationalizing ambitions in the modern world. Providing an intellectual home for research into the many guises of internationalism, its titles draw on methods and insights from political, social, cultural, economic and intellectual history. It showcases a rapidly expanding scholarship which has begun to transform our understanding of internationalism.

Cutting across established academic fields such as European, World, International, and Global History, the series will critically examine historical perceptions of geography, regions, centers, peripheries, borderlands, and connections across space in the history of internationalism. It will include both monographs and edited volumes that shed new light on local and global contexts for international projects; the impact of class, race, and gender on international aspirations; the roles played by a variety of international organizations and institutions; and the hopes, fears, tensions, and conflicts underlying them.

The series will be published in association with Birkbeck's Center for the Study of Internationalism.

Published:

Organizing the 20th-Century World, edited by Karen Gram-Skjoldager, Haakon Andreas Ikonomou, and Torsten Kahlert

Placing Internationalism: International Conferences and the Making of the Modern World, edited by Stephen Legg, Mike Heffernan, Jake Hodder, and Benjamin Thorpe

Forthcoming:

International Cooperation in Cold War Europe, Daniel Stinsky

Relief and Rehabilitation for a Postwar World, edited by Samantha K. Knapton and Katherine Rossy

Internationalists in European History: Rethinking the Twentieth Century, edited by Jessica Reinisch and David Brydan

The Human Rights Breakthrough of the 1970s: The European Community and International Relations, edited by Sara Lorenzini, Umberto Tulli, and Ilaria Zamburlini

Inventing the Third World: In Search of Freedom for the Postwar Global South, edited by Jeremy Adelman and Gyan Prakash

Socialist Internationalism and the Gritty Politics of the Particular
Second-Third World Spaces in the Cold War

Edited by Kristin Roth-Ey

BLOOMSBURY ACADEMIC
LONDON • NEW YORK • OXFORD • NEW DELHI • SYDNEY

BLOOMSBURY ACADEMIC
Bloomsbury Publishing Plc
50 Bedford Square, London, WC1B 3DP, UK
1385 Broadway, New York, NY 10018, USA
29 Earlsfort Terrace, Dublin 2, Ireland

BLOOMSBURY, BLOOMSBURY ACADEMIC and the Diana logo are trademarks of Bloomsbury Publishing Plc

First published in Great Britain 2023
This paperback edition published 2024

Copyright © Kristin Roth-Ey, 2023

Kristin Roth-Ey has asserted her right under the Copyright, Designs and Patents Act, 1988, to be identified as Editor of this work.

For legal purposes the Acknowledgments on p. xii constitute an extension of this copyright page.

Series design by Tjaša Krivec.
Cover image: "At the Aswan Dam," Reproduced by permission of the artist's estate and the State Museum of Oriental Art, Moscow.

All rights reserved. No part of this publication may be reproduced or transmitted in any form or by any means, electronic or mechanical, including photocopying, recording, or any information storage or retrieval system, without prior permission in writing from the publishers.

Bloomsbury Publishing Plc does not have any control over, or responsibility for, any third-party websites referred to or in this book. All internet addresses given in this book were correct at the time of going to press. The author and publisher regret any inconvenience caused if addresses have changed or sites have ceased to exist, but can accept no responsibility for any such changes.

A catalogue record for this book is available from the British Library.

A catalog record for this book is available from the Library of Congress.

ISBN: HB: 978-1-3503-0278-5
PB: 978-1-3503-0281-5
ePDF: 978-1-3503-0279-2
eBook: 978-1-3503-0280-8

Series: Histories of Internationalism

Typeset by RefineCatch Limited, Bungay, Suffolk

To find out more about our authors and books visit www.bloomsbury.com and sign up for our newsletters

Contents

List of Figures	vii
List of Contributors	viii
Acknowledgments	xii

	Introduction *Kristin Roth-Ey*	1
1	The School: Schools as Liminal Spaces—Integrating North Korean Children Within Socialist Eastern Europe, 1951–9 *Péter Apor*	21
2	The Airwaves: How Do You Listen to Radio Moscow? Moscow's Broadcasters, "Third World" Listeners, and the Space of the Airwaves in the Cold War *Kristin Roth-Ey*	39
3	The Great Industrial Project: Concepts of Space—Aswan's Distinctive Production Culture *Elizabeth Bishop*	59
4	The Exhibition: Exhibitions as Spaces of Cultural Encounter—Yugoslavia and Africa *Radina Vučetić*	77
5	The Epistolarium: Socialist Internationalism Writ Small—Friendship, Solidarity, and Support Between Women in the Soviet Union and in Decolonizing Countries, 1950s–1960s *Christine Varga-Harris*	97
6	The University: The Decolonization of Knowledge? The Making of the African University, the Power of the Imperial Legacy, and the Eastern European Influence *Małgorzata Mazurek*	119
7	The Expert Community: Expert Knowledge and Socialist Virtues—Czechoslovak Military Specialists in the Global South *Mikuláš Pešta*	139
8	The Military Training Camp: Co-Constructed Spaces—Experiences of PAIGC Guerrillas in Soviet Training Camps, 1961–1974 *Natalia Telepneva*	159
9	The Hospital: Uncomfortable Proximities—Romania's "One Nation Hospital" in Gharyan, 1974–1985 *Bogdan C. Iacob*	177
10	The Trade Union: Kindred by Choice—Trade Unions as Interface Between East Africa and East Germany *Eric Burton*	197
11	The Everyday Space: The Hostel, the Pub, and the Prison—Vietnamese and Cuban Workers in 1980s Czechoslovakia *Alena Alamgir*	217

12 The Travelogue: Imagining Spaces of Encounter—Travel Writing Between the Colonial and the Anti-Colonial in Socialist Eastern Europe, 1949–1989 *Eric Burton, Zoltán Ginelli, James Mark, and Nemanja Radonjić* 237

Select Bibliography 261
Index 267

Figures

1.1	Medical inspection in a Romanian center.	25
3.1	Aswan High Dam workers at work site 5/13/1964.	75
5.1	Gertrude Omog with two Stalinabad schoolgirls, Makhbube and Miroi Zaripov, during a visit to the Soviet Union. *Soviet Woman*, no. 9, 1958, cover.	110
5.2	Guests from Ghana visiting a Moscow crèche: Hannah Kudjoe and Ruby Quartey-Papafio. *Soviet Woman*, no. 9, 1961, 8.	116
6.1	University of Ghana aerial view, *c.* 1950.	124
9.1	A dirt road between newly-built apartment buildings in the town of Gharyan, 1979.	182
11.1	Two Vietnamese workers using a record player in their hostel's lounge.	222
12.1	Members of the Hungarian hunting expedition to Africa before the trip in Budapest, 1959.	247

Contributors

Alena Alamgir is Lecturer and Director of Technical Communication in the School of Materials Science and Engineering at the Georgia Institute of Technology in Atlanta, GA. She earned her Ph.D. in Sociology from Rutgers, the State University of New Jersey, in 2014. Alamgir's dissertation on the Czechoslovak–Vietnamese labor migration program won the 2015 Theda Skocpol Award from the Comparative-Historical Sociology Section of the American Sociological Association, as well as the Anne Foner dissertation prize from the Rutgers Sociology Department. She held postdoctoral positions at the University of Oxford, St. Antony's College, and at the University of Leipzig working on the project "Socialism Goes Global" funded by the UK Arts & Humanities Research Council. Alamgir has published widely on Vietnamese labor migration into Czechoslovakia and, more broadly, on state socialist labor migration and the socialist roots of globalization.

Péter Apor is Research Fellow at the Institute of History of the Hungarian Academy of Sciences. Between 2003 and 2011, Apor was a Research Fellow at the Central European University, Budapest, and an associate researcher at the University of Exeter (2008–2009). In 2012, he was a Fellow at the Imre Kertész Kolleg in Jena. His main research interests include the politics of memory and history in post-1945 East–Central Europe, the social and cultural history of the socialist dictatorships, and the history of historiography. He is the author of *Fabricating Authenticity in Soviet Hungary: The Afterlife of the First Hungarian Soviet Republic in the Age of State Socialism* (2014).

Elizabeth Bishop is Associate Professor in the Department of History at Texas State University. A specialist on the diplomatic history of the Arab world during the 1950s, she wrote "Soviet Policy Towards Egypt: D. S. Solod in the State Archive of the Russian Federation" for the *Maghreb Review* (2020), as well as co-edited *Imperialism on Trial: International Oversight of Colonial Rule in Historical Perspective* (2006). Bishop is alumna of the Merian Center for Advanced Studies in the Maghreb (MECAM) Interdisciplinary Fellow Group (IFG) V "Identities and Beliefs" in Tunis (2022) and co-convened "Arab-Soviet Internationalism" with support from the German Historical Institute in Moscow and Europe in the Middle East—The Middle East in Europe (EUME), a research program at the Berlin-based Forum Transregionale Studien (2022).

Eric Burton is Assistant Professor of Global History in the Department of Contemporary History at the University of Innsbruck. He has published articles and edited volumes on the global histories of socialism, development, and decolonization, including (with Anne Dietrich, Marcia C. Schenck, and Immanuel R. Harisch) *Navigating Socialist Encounters: Moorings and (Dis)Entanglements between Africa and*

East Germany during the Cold War (2021). His first monograph, *In Diensten des Afrikanischen Sozialismus. Die globale Entwicklungsarbeit der beiden deutschen Staaten in Tansania, 1961–1990* (2021), was awarded the Walter Markov Prize by the European Network in Universal and Global History (ENIUGH). In his current research project, Burton focuses on the role of Accra, Cairo, and Dar es Salaam as hubs of decolonization for African liberation movements in the 1950s and 1960s.

Zoltán Ginelli is a geographer, historian of science and global historian, and Researcher at the National University of Public Service in Hungary. His research follows a world-systemic and decolonial approach to a global historical understanding of Hungary in colonialism and the cultural, economic, and political relationships between Eastern Europe and the postcolonial South. Since 2014, he has taught at several universities and at the Milestone Institute in Budapest (2020). Ginelli was Assistant Researcher in the research projects "1989 After 1989" (2015–18), "Socialism Goes Global" (2019–20), "Criminalization of Dictatorial Pasts in Europe and Latin America in Global Perspective" (2020) and "Cold War and Liberal International Order" (2021). He was Leibniz Institut für Länderkunde Visiting Fellow (Leipzig, 2016), Visegrad Fellow at the Open Society Archives (Budapest, 2016), and Leibniz ScienceCampus EEGA Fellow (Leipzig, 2020). Ginelli co-curated the art and documentary exhibition "Transperiphery Movement: Global Eastern Europe and Global South" for the OFF-Biennale in Budapest and for the East European Biennial Alliance in Kyiv (2021). He is a member of the Decolonising Development COST Action academic network (2020–24) and Advisory Board member of the MANIFEST Creative Europe art and research project on the memories of transatlantic slavery. Currently, Ginelli is finishing his book *The Global Histories of the Quantitative Revolution: Tracing the Transnational History of Central Place Theory* and another co-written book on Hungary between the colonial and anti-colonial worlds.

Bogdan C. Iacob is a researcher at the "Nicolae Iorga" Institute of History (Bucharest) of the Romanian Academy. His work centers on the study of Eastern European experts (e.g., historians and physicians) in global contexts during the twentieth century. Iacob has also published on the year 1989 and its aftermath as well as on transitional justice. He co-authored the monograph *1989: A Global History of Eastern Europe* (2019) and edited the special issue "Socialist Experts in Transnational Perspective" for the journal *East Central Europe* (2018). Iacob is also author of "Malariology and Decolonization: Eastern European Experts from the League of Nations to the World Health Organization," for the *Journal of Global History* (2022).

James Mark is Professor of History at the University of Exeter. His research addresses the social and cultural history of state socialism in Central–Eastern Europe and the politics of memory in the area during both socialism and post-socialism, and aims to connect the region to broader global histories and processes through transnational and comparative methods. Mark has been a Principal Investigator on three major research projects: a Leverhulme Research Leadership Award (2014–19): "1989 after 1989: Rethinking the Fall of State Socialism in Global Perspective"; "Socialism Goes Global:

Cold War Connections Between the 'Second' and 'Third' Worlds'" (2015–20); and an AHRC-Labex funded Franco-British project, "Criminalization of Dictatorial Pasts in Europe and Latin America in Global Perspective" (2016–20). His most recent publications are (as co-editor with Paul Betts) *Socialism Goes Global: The Soviet Union and Eastern Europe in the Age of Decolonisation* (2022), the monograph (with Bogdan Iacob, Tobias Rupprecht, and Ljubica Spaskovska) *1989: A Global History of Eastern Europe* (2019), and the edited volume (with Artemy Kalinovsky and Steffi Marung) *Alternative Globalizations: Eastern Europe and the Postcolonial World* (2020).

Małgorzata Mazurek is Associate Professor of Polish Studies at Columbia University. Her interests include the history of social sciences, international development, the social history of labor, and consumption under communism. She has written *Society in Waiting Lines: On Experiences of Shortages in Postwar Poland* (2010), which deals with the history of social inequalities under state socialism. Her current book project, *Economics of Hereness: The Polish Origins of Global Developmentalism, 1918–1968* (forthcoming), revises the history of developmental thinking by centering East-Central Europe as the locality of innovations in economic thought in post-imperial Europe and the postcolonial world. It investigates the role of Warsaw-based social scientists in shaping interwar debates on population and capitalism and further, in transforming the locally produced knowledge into development policies for the so-called "Third World."

Mikuláš Pešta is Assistant Professor at the Institute of World History in the Faculty of Arts, Charles University, Prague. He completed his Ph.D. in 2017. Pešta focuses on the role of international organizations in the Cold War and on contacts between Czechoslovakia (Central and Eastern Europe) and the African and Asian countries in the field of education, cultural diplomacy, and ideology. Furthermore, he is researching the revolutionary violence of the 1970s and the interconnectedness of European extra-parliamentary left.

Nemanja Radonjić is an Assistant Professor at the Contemporary History Chair at the Faculty of Philosophy, University of Belgrade where he teaches courses on Cold War history, and postcolonial studies. His research concerns Cold war interactions and networks spanning Africa, the Mediterranean and the Balkans. He was engaged with several important international projects concerning representation, Cold war history, and national documentation in the past with universities in Berlin, Exeter, and Maynouth. His latest book is titled *Africa in Yugoslavia: Representing and imagining Africa in socialist and nonaligned Yugoslavia (1945–1991)*.

Kristin Roth-Ey is Associate Professor of Modern Russian History at the UCL School of Slavonic and Eastern European Studies. She is the author of *Moscow Prime Time: How the Soviet Union Built the Media Empire that Lost of the Cultural Cold War* (2011), which won Best Book in Literary/Cultural Studies from the American Association of Teachers of Slavic and East European Languages and Honorable Mention for the W. Bruce Lincoln Book Prize from the Association for Slavic, East European, and

Eurasian Studies in 2012. Her current research focuses on Soviet media and cultural diplomacy in the "Third World" during the Cold War.

Natalia Telepneva is Lecturer in International History at the University of Strathclyde. She is a historian of Soviet foreign policy with a particular interest in Warsaw Pact interactions with African elites. Her first monograph, *Cold War Liberation: The Soviet Union and the Collapse of the Portuguese Empire in Africa, 1961–1975* (2022), explores Soviet support for anti-colonial movements in Portuguese colonies. She has also published on the history of Soviet and Czechoslovak secret intelligence.

Christine Varga-Harris is Associate Professor of History at Illinois State University and author of *Stories of House and Home: Soviet Apartment Life during the Khrushchev Years* (2015). Her current research focuses on Soviet cultural relations with developing countries during the Cold War, from the perspective of gender. Specifically, it examines the interactions of the Committee of Soviet Women with women in Africa and South Asia in the following areas: through correspondence, in the discursive and visual realm of its magazine *Soviet Woman*, and through travel and educational exchanges. Her publications stemming from this project include "Soviet Women and Internationalism in Socialist Travel Itineraries in the 1950s and 1960s," which appeared in the June 2022 issue of *Diplomatic History*.

Radina Vučetić is Associate Professor of twentieth-century history at the University of Belgrade. She is particularly interested in cultural diplomacy and the relationship of art, popular culture and politics, with a focus on socialist Yugoslavia. She is the author of *Coca-Cola Socialism: Americanization of Yugoslav Culture* (2018), *Koka-kola socijalizam. Amerikanizacija jugoslovenske popularne kulture šezdesetoh goidna XX veka* (2012, five editions), and numerous articles and book chapters. She was the co-author of the exhibitions "Come Together/Zajedno: 180 Years of UK–Serbia Diplomatic Relations" (Museum of Yugoslav Film, 2017) and "Tito in Africa: Picturing Solidarity" (Museum of Yugoslavia, 2017; Pitt Rivers Museum, Oxford, 2017–18, and The Wende Museum, Los Angeles, 2019). Her research has been supported by grants and fellowships from the Imre Kertész Kolleg Jena, Robert Bosch Stiftung, DAAD, and the US Department of State's Fellowship Study of the US Institutes (SUSI): US Culture and Society (New York University).

Acknowledgments

My first thanks are due to the Arts and Humanities Research Council (UK) for their funding of the "Socialism Goes Global: Cold War Connections Between the 'Second' and 'Third' Worlds" project (AH/M001830/10), which enabled much of the research that went into this volume. Special thanks go to the project's Principal Investigator, James Mark, for his shrewd and sensitive leadership. Many of the arguments in these pages were developed in the context of "Socialism Goes Global" project meetings and email exchanges in 2014–19. I am grateful to all the project participants, including Paul Betts and Steffi Marung, for their many stimulating contributions to these discussions. Martin Thom's expert copy-editing of the original submission was very much appreciated, and I also gratefully acknowledge Maddie Holder and Megan Harris at Bloomsbury for their patient guidance through the publishing process. I am delighted to be able at long last to thank all my contributors for their enduring intellectual engagement and support in what turned out to be a surprisingly long march to publication. Finally, I would like to extend my respect and gratitude to the family of Hamed Ewais, Ola Hamed Ewais, and Tarek Seoudy, for granting permission to use the stunning "At the Aswan Dam" as our cover image, and my thanks to Olga Nefedova for her help is contacting the Ewais family.

Introduction

Kristin Roth-Ey

In 1956, Aimé Césaire resigned from the French Communist Party in an open letter to the party's general secretary. Césaire, at that time not only a major intellectual figure but a deputy to the French National Assembly for Martinique, anticipated arguments against his abandoning a communist movement with worldwide reach. "I am not burying myself in a narrow particularism," he wrote. "But neither do I want to lose myself in an emaciated universalism." The "emaciated universalism" was the party's internationalist politics, he said, which offered nothing to the people of Martinique beyond a subordinate place in its grand world strategy. Césaire's rejection of the party, then, functioned as both a critique of enduring colonialist attitudes within a Eurocentric communist movement and a rallying cry for colonial peoples (he also used the phrase "black peoples") to build a new worldwide community. Although he did not use the term, Césaire's vision was Third Worldist in the original, activist sense of "Third World" coined in the early 1950s by Frenchman Albert Sauvy: the *tiers-monde* as a parallel to the *tiers-état*, the radical Third Estate of revolutionary-era France. "My conception of the universal," Césaire wrote, "is that of a universal enriched by all that is particular, a universal enriched by every particular: the deepening and coexistence of all particulars."[1]

This book had its origins in a series of conversations among scholars of the USSR and socialist Eastern Europe about how to navigate the universal and the particular in histories of the region's linkages with the "Third World" during the Cold War.[2] Césaire's rejection of the international communist movement came at a time when the Soviet Union and socialist Eastern Europe, Sauvy's "Second World," were turning their sights in an unprecedented fashion to the decolonization process and to relations with states, many of them newly independent, in Asia, Africa, the Middle East, and Latin America.

---

[1] Aimé Césaire, "Letter to Maurice Thorez," *Social Text* 28.2 (2010): 145–52 (103). On Césaire, see Robin D. G. Kelley's introduction, "A Poetics of Anticolonialism," in Aimé Césaire, *Discourse on Colonialism*, trans. Joan Pinkham (New York, 2000), 7.

[2] Many of these conversations were connected with the AHRC project "Socialism Goes Global," which also produced James Mark and Paul Betts (eds.), *Socialism Goes Global: The Soviet Union and Eastern Europe in the Age of Decolonisation* (Oxford, 2022). I use the terms "Third World" and "Second World" to mark conceptual categories and political ideals from the historical period under discussion.

In part, this shift in optics related to the momentous changing of the guard in the Soviet Union with Joseph Stalin's death in 1953: Nikita Khrushchev, the man to emerge as the top Soviet leader, was also the Soviet Politburo's "most Third Worldist" member (though the Soviets eschewed the term) and instrumental in prioritizing the Soviet bloc's commitment to promote the Soviet socialist model for modernity in Asia, Africa, the Middle East, and Latin America.[3] As Odd Arne Westad argued, "by the early 1960s, Soviet ideology had already reached a stage where the competition for influence in the Third World was an essential part of the existence of socialism."[4] Yet the shift in the Second World, its so-called rediscovery of the Third, was equally a response to the radical new politics radiating *from* those parts of the globe. Sauvy coined the term Third World "in a manner that resonated with how that part of the planet had already begun to act," asserting the rights of the majority of the world's population in wars of liberation and via new alliances, including the non-aligned movement.[5] The new linkages that developed between the Soviet bloc and Asia, Africa, the Middle East, and Latin America in the 1950s and extended through the 1980s belong to socialist history and to the history of the Cold War, as well as to multiple, complex national and regional histories in both "Worlds," "Second" and "Third"—to the universal of socialism and to a great many particulars, to macro and micro perspectives.

Tension between these two poles is inescapable in all historical work; all historians make decisions about the relative significance of the forest and the trees in the stories they choose to tell. But writing about people who have long been marginalized in (if not absented from) the scholarly record must raise particularly pointed questions about power, or who sets the terms of historical significance. As one historian remarked in a 2013 forum in the *American Historical Review*, "How Size Matters," "there seems to be an inverse relationship between scale and human agency: in other words, the greater the scale of analysis (temporally or spatially), the less room is left for accounts of human agency."[6] To engage in a synthetic analysis of the relations between the Second World with an entity as vast and diverse as the Third is to set the bar for significance so high as to eliminate from our sight all but a few top political agents and, in effect, to remarginalize by generalization peoples across Asia, Africa, the Middle East, and Latin America. Moreover, in a situation where academic history remains overwhelmingly dominated by scholarship on the West (in the UK, to take one example, fully 84% of university-based historians work on the UK, Europe, or North America),[7] there is a strong case to be made for prioritizing small-scale, in-depth studies involving the non-Western world. The point is not apologetics. The point is the trees—great swathes of unknown trees without which any forest must remain a blur.

---

[3] Sara Lorenzini, *Global Development: A Cold War History* (Princeton, 2019), 42.
[4] Odd Arne Westad, *The Global Cold War: Third World Interventions and the Making of Our Times* (Cambridge, 2005), 72.
[5] Vijay Prashad, *The Darker Nations: A People's History of the Third World* (New York, 2008), 11.
[6] AHR Conversation, "How Size Matters: The Question of Scale in History," *American Historical Review* 118.5 (December 2013): 1444.
[7] Luke Clossey and Nicholas Guyatt, "It's a Small World After All: The Wider World in Historians' Peripheral Vision," *Perspectives on History* 51.5 (2013).

In this sense, the perspective explored in this volume is the inverse of some recent moves to write global histories from the Soviet Union/Eastern Europe and reflections on "alternative" globalizations. Reviewing the wave of studies in global history in the early 2000s, Jeremy Adelman, a Latin Americanist, noted the irony of its emphasis on historic cross-border connections and mobility in light of its own limitations, principally, its hyper-dependence on English language sources and publications and on the Anglo-American academy. His point was critical: the exploration of the global proceeded in a very specific framework, then, "and led to some pretty one-way exchanges ... It is hard not to conclude that global history is another Anglospheric invention to integrate the Other into a cosmopolitan narrative on our terms, in our tongues," he concluded.[8] We might also draw a parallel to Africanist Priya Lal's critique of global histories of development that, in overlooking the intellectual trajectories of postcolonial states and their own national development plans, implicitly define the Third World as recipient rather than agent, and present development itself as a static, modular form external to it. They are, Lal wrote, "intellectually imprisoned within the geographic confines of [their] own position of inquiry."[9]

The countries of the Second World have been the object of their own specific othering—as "Eastern Europe," the backward periphery of a normative civilizational ideal, the West.[10] Part of the project of writing Second-Third World histories is precisely to bring Second World ideas, institutions, and actors into the center, subject ground from which they have been excluded. (The forest is hugely underexplored here, too.) But the peripheral position of Eastern European and Russian/Soviet history within the academy does not itself improve its sightlines on Third World histories, nor does it solve the problem of one-way exchanges and arguments. A cosmopolitan narrative on "our" terms, in "our" languages, can have no more analytical reach to the global than any other. Moreover, a global history from Soviet/Eastern Europe, a macro-level view, runs the real risk of distorting the diversity of the Second World itself.

In an influential 2011 essay, David Engerman called on scholars to write a new history of the "Second World's Third World" using what he called the "building blocks" of detailed bilateral and institutional histories.[11] A related 2009 piece in *Diplomatic History*, "Modernization as a Global Project," made a similar methodological point: "Histories of modernization must be written from the local—about specific projects

---

[8] Jeremy Adelman, "What is Global History Now?" *Aeon* 2 (2017). Chakrabarty wrote about an "inequality of ignorance" between scholars of Europe/the US, who can be (and are) ignorant of the Third World, while the opposite dynamic is professionally impossible. Dipesh Chakrabarty, "Postcoloniality and the Artifice of History: Who Speaks for 'Indian' Pasts?" *Representations* 37 (1992): 2.

[9] Priya Lal, "Decolonization and the Gendered Politics of Developmental Labor in Southeastern Africa," in Stephen Macekura and Erez Manela (eds.), *The Development Century: A Global History* (New York, 2018).

[10] Larry Wolff, *Inventing Eastern Europe: The Map of Civilization on the Mind of the Enlightenment* (Stanford, CA, 1996); Maria Todorova, "The Trap of Backwardness: Modernity, Temporality, and the Study of Eastern European Nationalism," *Slavic Review* 64 (2005): 140–65.

[11] David C. Engerman, "The Second World's Third World," *Kritika: Explorations in Russian and Eurasian History* 12.1 (2011): 183–211 (210); David C. Engerman and Corinna R. Unger, "Introduction: towards a global history of modernization," *Diplomatic History* 33.3 (2009): 377, 380.

and individuals," wrote Engerman and co-author Corinna Unger. They counselled "narrowing the scope" in favor of "scholarship using multiple archives and, more importantly, multiple perspectives."[12] Their endgame was unquestionably oriented toward the macro—modernization as a global project—in terms that do not match those of every historian in this book. But the attention to questions of scale, sources, perspective, and agency are very much akin to the approach taken here. The genesis of the volume is in an uneasiness about the pull to "go big" or "go global," with its implicit calling of intellectual rank, as an impediment to understanding—most of all, to understanding agency in Asian, African, Middle Eastern, and Latin American contexts. As (predominantly) historians of the Second World, we are interested in moving in the opposite direction, to the opposite pole on the scale, from the universal to the deepening and coexistence of all particulars. We narrow the scope, in line with a number of other recent studies in this burgeoning field, to take a case studies approach.[13] Several chapters engage with archival and other resources from the Global South—a practice we see as essential to the longer-term intellectual project of writing socialism's global history (and one which needs active facilitation, either by building up the historian's linguistic toolbox or by promoting collaborative, multilingual research teams, or both). And every chapter here seeks out multiple perspectives, rifling through the space between the lines. In this book, we set out to explore the co-constructed spaces of a radically diverse and dynamic Second–Third World encounter.

Space—and *Socialist* Spaces?

The dining halls of a university. The pages of a handwritten letter that traveled 5,000 miles. Hospital wards, museum galleries, shooting ranges, construction sites, the crackling of the airwaves. In these spaces and more, people from the USSR and socialist Eastern Europe and from Asia, Africa, the Middle East, and Latin America interacted.

The concept of "space" explored in this book is, firstly, *social*, and not metaphorical. The spaces we discuss are sometimes akin to Mary Pratt's influential concept the "contact zone." Pratt's work on the literatures of Western European empire defined the "contact zone" as "the space of imperial encounters, the space in which peoples geographically and historically separated come into contact with each other and establish ongoing relations, usually involving conditions of coercion, radical inequality, and intractable conflict."[14] However, Pratt's "contact zone"—fittingly, perhaps, for a

---

[12] Engerman and Unger, "Introduction," 380. Engerman went on to produce his own rich multilateral history, *The Price of Aid: The Economic Cold War in India* (Cambridge, MA, 2018).
[13] Such as, Quinn Slobodian (ed.), *Comrades of Color: East Germany in the Cold War World* (New York, 2015); Patryk Babiracki and Austin Jersild (eds.), *Socialist Internationalism in the Cold War: Exploring the Second World* (London, 2016); thematic issue "State Socialist Experts in Transnational Perspective," *East Central Europe* 45.2-3 (2018); Eric Burton et al. (eds.), *Navigating Socialist Encounters: Moorings and (Dis)Entanglements between Africa and East Germany during the Cold War* (Munich, 2021); thematic issue "Cold War Transfer: architecture and planning from socialist countries in the 'Third World,'" *Journal of Architecture* 17.3 (2012).
[14] Mary Louise Pratt, *Imperial Eyes: Travel Writing and Transculturation* (London and New York, 2007).

concept developed in relation to travel literature and its distortions—does not travel well to all historical contexts, including many of ours. In the cases we explore, cultures do "meet, clash, and grapple with each other, often in contexts of highly asymmetrical relations of power," to quote Pratt again, but without the perpetration of mass violence (or the threat of mass violence) and in situations where the power relations were not always fixed.[15] Many of the spaces our authors discuss are indeed sites of encounter—physical places, like the classroom, where the abstractions of "internationalism," "solidarity," and the "anti-imperialist struggle" became concrete in social terms, as lived experience. In other chapters, the social nature of the space is itself abstracted: there is no place, precisely, or the social relation is itself something imagined. (The airwaves of Radio Moscow, discussed in Kristin Roth-Ey's contribution, are one example of such parasocial spaces.) But throughout this book, the drive is fundamentally ethnographic: the goal is to look at spaces as they are conceived, constructed, shaped, and reshaped by people over time. In some cases, the people involved "speak to" the space: they show us how they understood it and how they connected it to other spatial frameworks—to ideas about gender and space, for example, to the space of the nation, of the modern, of the self. In many cases, they do not or, rather, not in ways easy to detect. On a baseline level, what we seek is to understand how spaces worked—the meeting, clashing, and grappling—and what, if anything, was distinctive and consequential about them.

One possible distinction marking spaces throughout the volume is socialism. Socialism, with its distinctive vocabulary—solidarity, internationalism, the anti-imperialist struggle—is stamped all over many of our historians' Second World sources, including archival records, media accounts, and personal narratives. But to what extent, and in which ways, can we understand the spaces we analyze as *socialist* spaces? Many historians have analyzed how socialist regimes conceptualized space in distinctive ideological terms. "Space was a state project for the Soviets," writes Stephen Lovell, as the Bolsheviks aimed to remake humanity through a total transformation of the environment, including public and private spheres.[16] The Soviet Union, and then the socialist states of Eastern Europe, produced a distinctive repertoire of monumental spaces and shared approaches in mass architecture and city planning. Many of the chapters in this book explore spaces that embodied ideological goals—spaces designed and promoted *as socialist spaces* and explicitly indexed to models in the Second World.[17] Socialist frameworks, though, were far from unitary or exclusive. The great engineering project, the factory, the school, and the hospital were all promoted as paradigmatic socialist spaces. But they were no less paradigmatic modern spaces, and even as Second World institutions promoted their versions as superior to all others,

---

[15] Mary Louise Pratt, "Arts of the Contact Zone," *Profession* 91 (1991): 33–40.
[16] Lovell in David Crowley and Susan Reid (eds.), *Socialist Spaces: Sites of Everyday Life in the Eastern Bloc* (Oxford, 2002),105. The literature on socialist world visions of public spaces is extensive. For shared models, see Elidor Mëhilli, *From Stalin to Mao: Albania and the Socialist World* (Ithaca, NY, and London, 2017).
[17] See Masha Kirasirova, "Building Anti-Colonial Utopia: The Politics of Space in Soviet Tashkent in the 'Long 1960s,'" in Martin Klimke et al. (eds.), *The Routledge Handbook of the Global Sixties* (London, 2018), 53–66; cf. Łukasz Stanek, *Architecture in Global Socialism: Eastern Europe, West Africa, and the Middle East in the Cold War* (Princeton, 2020).

many people had different, and sometimes more meaningful, reference points. This was true of people in the Third World who, as our authors show, brought a wide range of ideas to the table, including different interpretations of socialism and of the modern. Elizabeth Bishop's chapter on the Aswan High Dam project, for example, shows the influence of Anglo-Indian models on the way Egyptian engineers conceptualized modern Nile management. Eric Burton's contribution on the trade union as a space for Second-Third World encounter in East Africa shows it as home to an intricate array of competing reference points and ideals. Although "in East German theories, the affinity between trade unions of the communist camp and labor organizations in the decolonizing world seemed quasi-automatic," he writes, in East Africa, "different understandings of socioeconomic and racial inequalities assigned different roles to trade unionism." At the same time, it is important to recognize that Second World people, too, had other reference points besides (and sometimes intermingled with) socialist ones—including ideas about national and racial identity, to name but two. On these terms, they clashed and grappled not only with their Third World counterparts, but also among themselves. And they collaborated, too, sometimes in surprising ways. It is precisely these sorts of dynamics that can get lost in macro-level analysis and, with them, a sense of spaces as particular, heterogeneous, unpredictable, and historical.

Space and Access: The Universal Meets the Particular

One of the hallmarks of global histories has been their foregrounding of connectivity and mobility, networks and flows. Yet in their focus on macro-level phenomena, global narratives often push the local and the individual into the wings, while those figures who do take center-stage are those who best exemplify the global—that is, those who were connected and on the move.[18] Their stories are not always happy ones: the point is not that taking a global approach amounts to a celebration of globalization, capitalist or otherwise. But the choice to emphasize connection and mobilities can have distorting effects on the way we understand the world of the unconnected and the immobile. It can also skew our sense of the representativeness of certain global stories relative to others.

In this collection, as we explore spaces of encounter between the Second and Third Worlds, we learn about the experiences of teachers, activists, economists, journalists, nurses, students, engineers, soldiers, and many others. The connections between the countries of Eastern Europe/the USSR and Asia, Africa, the Middle East, and Latin America expanded rapidly from the 1950s on and touched many people's lives directly. Thousands of technical specialists and other professionals from the Second World journeyed to the Third every year, and professionals from the Third traveled in the opposite direction, too. Universities in the USSR and socialist Eastern Europe educated

---

[18] Adelman, "What is Global History Now?"; David E. Bell, "This is What Happens When Historians Overuse the Idea of the Network," *The New Republic*, October 26, 2013, https://newrepublic.com/article/114709/world-connecting-reviewed-historians-overuse-network-metaphor.

tens of thousands of Third World students: for 1979–80 alone, the peak year in the USSR, the number reached over 50,000.[19] A further cohort of thousands of Vietnamese, Cubans, Angolans, and Mozambicans traveled to work in the Second World.

Many contemporary historians emphasize that the USSR and socialist Eastern Europe were always connected and global. State borders were "porous" and "airy," more "nylon" than "iron"; traffic in goods, people, and ideas between the socialist states and the rest of the world was constant, even in the dark days of Stalinism, and as it increased exponentially from the post-Stalinist 1950s onward, the Third World took on a new and important role.[20] All this is true, and a necessary corrective to Cold War rhetoric, especially in Western popular media, that did a brisk trade in tales of Soviet bloc isolation and backwardness. But it also is true in particular ways that should command our attention.

The global spaces in this book and the lives lived within them were exceptional, not ordinary. To take the Soviet example, by the mid-1960s, Anne Gorsuch estimates that 500,000 Soviet citizens had traveled abroad as tourists—a large figure, but the overwhelming bulk (roughly three-quarters) journeyed to socialist Eastern Europe.[21] Some 50,000 Third World students studying in the Second World is a large cohort, on the one hand, and about one-tenth of 1% of the population of Africa in 1980, on the other. Even today, over 80% of the world's population has never flown on an airplane. The mobility experienced by the Cape Verdean solider who trained outside Moscow, or the Romanian doctor who worked in a Libyan hospital, two examples from our authors, was something extraordinary. The overwhelming majority of people in the Second World did not have direct, personal experience of the global in any way; they did not move beyond socialist borders in societies where mobility was tightly bound to privilege; they were not physically connected in a culture that glamorized the connected. For them, the experience of the global was, if anything, a mediated experience; it was something to read about in the daily press and in travel literature, to hear about in radio reportages, and to watch on newsreels in the cinema and on television screens— if, that is, they were interested to read or watch or listen at all. It was also, for many in the Second World, something lived in an everyday way in the form of party and trade union activism, things like fundraising campaigns and public meetings in solidarity

---

[19] Constantin Katsakioris, "Soviet lessons for Arab modernization: Soviet educational aid towards Arab countries after 1956," *Journal of Modern European History* 8.1 (2010): 85–106.

[20] Alexander Hazanov, "Porous Empire: Foreign Visitors and the Post-Stalinist State" (Ph.D. dissertation, University of Pennsylvania, 2016); Alexander Badenoch et al. (eds.), *Airy Curtains in the European Ether: Broadcasting and the Cold War* (Baden-Baden, 2013); György Péteri, "Nylon Curtain— Transnational and Transsystemic Tendencies in the Cultural Life of State-Socialist Russia and East-Central Europe," *Slavonica* 10.2 (2004): 113–23; Michael David-Fox, "The Iron Curtain as Semipermeable Membrane," in Vladislav Zubok et al. (eds.), *Cold War Crossings: International Travel and Exchange Across the Soviet Bloc* (Arlington, 2014), 14–39; Anne E. Gorsuch and Diane P. Koenker (eds.), *The Socialist Sixties: Crossing Borders in the Second World* (Bloomington, 2013); Kathy Burrell and Kathrin Hörschelmann (eds.), *Mobilities in Socialist and Post-Socialist States: Societies on the Move* (New York, 2014).

[21] Anne E Gorsuch, *All This is Your World: Soviet Tourism at Home and Abroad after Stalin* (Oxford, 2011), 19. Other Second World socialist states restricted travel beyond the Second World as well. Yugoslavia, which saw travel restrictions lifted after 1961, formed a separate case.

with Vietnam, and, to a lesser extent, in consumer culture.[22] And for societies in Asia, Africa, Latin America, and the Middle East, most with far less developed media and commercial sectors than those in the Second World, the Second World was even more distant. Global mobility was important, but it was a phenomenon of the thousands, not the millions.

Throughout the Cold War era, the threat of "communist infiltration" of the Third World was front-page news in the West and a constituent element in how the Third World was conceived there and policies toward it were formulated. Scholars and journalists alike emphasized economic and military connections, and sidelined cultural and social ones.[23] In recent years, scholars of the USSR and socialist Eastern Europe have moved to correct the earlier emphasis by exploring these previously neglected links—part of an important, wider cultural turn in histories of the Cold War and in the "new diplomatic history." The scope and significance of military engagements, however, now needs to be reincorporated into a broader understanding of socialist mobilities and the global. By any measure, the Second World's commitments in the Third were heavily and, in some cases, predominantly focused on the military sector. In the case of Indonesia, to take one example, the second biggest recipient of Soviet aid (up to 1965) after Egypt, nearly 90% of aid was for military purposes.[24] From the late 1970s to the late 1980s, approximately 46% of all weapons transferred to Third World countries were from the USSR, making it by far the largest supplier in the world.[25] The peak year for Soviet arms sales, 1986, accounted for 25–30% of all Soviet hard currency trade for the year. Defense industry sales oxygenated the feeble lungs of economies across the Soviet bloc.[26] Moreover, Soviet bloc military engagements ran a wide gamut, from weapons sales to technology transfers (e.g. in telecommunications), to construction (such as airfield and port development) and support equipment, to advisers, trainers, and educational programs.[27] The military sector was complex and intertwined with many others: there was significant interaction, and sometimes overlap, in roles among personnel in the military with those in the diplomatic corps, foreign trade, security services, and party elites.[28]

---

[22] James Mark et al., "'We Are with You, Vietnam': Transnational Solidarities in Socialist Hungary, Poland and Yugoslavia," *Journal of Contemporary History* 50.3 (2015): 439–64. On solidarity payments in the GDR, see George Bodie, "Global GDR? Sovereignty, Legitimacy, and Decolonisation in the German Democratic Republic, 1960–1989" (Ph.D. dissertation, University College London, 2020).

[23] Engerman and Unger, "Introduction," 379.

[24] Boden Ragna, "Cold War Economics: Soviet Aid to Indonesia," *Journal of Cold War Studies* 10.3 (2008): 110–28 (121).

[25] Mark Kramer, "The Decline in Soviet Arms Transfers to the Third World, 1986–1991," in A. Kalinovsky and S. Radchenko (eds.), *The End of the Cold War and the Third World: New Perspectives on Regional Conflict* (London, 2011), 46, 56.

[26] Philip Muehlenbeck, "Czechoslovak Arms Exports to Africa (1954–68)," in P. Muehlenbeck (ed.), *Czechoslovakia in Africa, 1945–1968*. (New York, 2016), 87–123; Philip Muehlenbeck and Natalia Telepneva (eds.), *Warsaw Pact Intervention in the Third World: Aid and Influence in the Cold War* (London, 2019).

[27] Gareth M. Winrow, *The Foreign Policy of the GDR in Africa* (Cambridge, 2009), 129, 139; Jocelyn Alexander and JoAnn McGregor, "African Soldiers in the USSR. Oral Histories of ZAPU Intelligence Cadres' Soviet Training, 1964–1979," *Journal of Southern African Studies* 43.1 (2017): 49–66.

[28] See Elizabeth Banks, "Socialist Internationalism between the Soviet Union and Mozambique, 1962–91" (Ph.D. dissertation, New York University, 2019), 67–8.

This volume features two chapters exploring this crucial military space located physically in the Second World and in the Third: Natalia Telepneva examines the two main training camps for Third World revolutionaries inside the Soviet Union, while Mikuláš Pešta looks at the experiences of Czechoslovak military experts sent to teach in the Middle East. Unlike higher education, which had major public outreach functions at the time (and has been very well researched since), military training was shrouded in secrecy. Nearly 80,000 Third World military personnel trained in the USSR and socialist Eastern Europe from 1955 to 1984.[29] Military trainers and advisers located in Third World countries also ran into the tens of thousands and, as Pešta elaborates, formed expatriate communities with sometimes uneasy relations with their hosts. Pešta's and Telepneva's contributions open up new vistas on these important military spaces, and on the conjunction of military and educational spaces, in the Second-Third World relationship. They should also prompt us to consider carefully the kinds of global stories, mobilities, and networks we choose to foreground.

The space of the Second-Third World encounter—the physical, social space—was an ideological universal with very narrow entryways. It is this context of limitation and exclusivity, open to us as we scale down, that helps us understand many of the main themes in this book. It helps us fathom the powerful emotional resonance of parasocial spaces and what might otherwise seem like simple, even banal encounters. Christine Varga-Harris's contribution on the "epistolarium" of *Soviet Woman* magazine, for example, takes a routine, bureaucratic form—letters between women in the Soviet Union and the Third World channeled by an official state organization, the Soviet Women's Committee—and finds within their lines meaningful personal relationships. Eric Burton, Zoltán Ginelli, James Mark, and Nemanja Radonjić explore a writing space of a different sort, Eastern European travel literature, and show it performing complex psychological functions for Eastern European writers and readers alike, offering an opportunity to overcome "a frustrated globality" for the region on its pages. Understanding the restricted nature of Second-Third World spaces also gives context to the anxieties on the part of Second World authorities (and peoples) about social mixing with Third World others, along with the deep sense of European difference and superiority that we see in so many of the chapters. Indirectly, the fact of exclusivity, and the tension between universalist rhetoric and singular experience, may help us reflect on the experiences of the many people left out of, or indifferent to, global visions. The xenophobia and racism of late 1980s and 1990s USSR and Eastern Europe looks less surprising when we understand the particular kind of globality the socialist Second World pursued, with its hierarchies, restrictions, and secrecies.

Second World Social Frameworks and Solidarity Spaces

Across this book, our authors draw attention to the role of individuals as intermediaries or "brokers" between the Second and the Third Worlds. The broker has emerged as a

---

[29] Kramer, "The Decline in Soviet Arms Transfers," 56.

key figure in the history of socialist cultural diplomacy and a focus in the historiography of Second–Third World relations more broadly.[30] Radina Vučetić's contribution reveals the role of two individuals, Veda and Stravko Pečar, in the institutionalization of African art in Yugoslavia. The Pečars' position as functionaries in Africa enabled them to amass a large collection of African art—a fairly predictable scenario of white privilege on the continent. But Vučetić stresses the Pečars' socialist idealism and argues that their work to promote African art was not only effective, but also indicative of a unique Yugoslav state commitment to support Africa on terms of equality. Other chapters show the broker phenomenon at work outside culture and outside, or alongside, socialist ideals. In a chapter on Cuban and Vietnamese workers in encounters with the Czechoslovak criminal justice system, Alena Alamgir finds that interpreters could wield considerable power as cultural arbitrators, not only translating speech for the local authorities, but contextualizing and explaining Vietnamese behavior. Eric Burton's analysis of the trade union highlights the skills of leading East African activists in brokering resources from different partners in the Second World and beyond. Małgorzata Mazurek's contribution offers a counterintuitive tale of Polish economists taking leading roles in Ghana's top university not as intermediaries of Eastern European socialism, but as conduits of Anglo-American economic theory and norms. "Everybody saw me as a representative of a communist country and thought I would lecture on Marxist political economy," she quotes one economist as saying, "but I had no intention of doing that." In each of these cases, the people "in between" are less agents of political forces beyond their control than agents in their own right. Looking only on the macro level can miss out these spaces of nuanced and sometimes surprising interactions.

At a different point on the sociological spectrum, several chapters in this book explore the world of what we might call the Second World's "mid-level" actors—experts, functionaries, teachers, and trainers—and the spaces of Second World expatriate communities in the Third World. Although the everyday experiences of these figures varied widely, all our authors emphasize the extent to which they were bound by strong social norms and by top-down efforts to maintain boundaries between self and other. The expatriate communities were often insular and claustrophobic. Mikuláš Pešta describes pressures to maintain the Czechoslovak community in the Middle East as "homogenous and impermeable"—a model of Czechoslovak socialism for the local population and for its own members, who were seen by authorities at home as vulnerable to moral and political laxity. Iacob shows how similar efforts to control the Romanian community in Libya failed; for him, the Romanians' One Nation Hospital project was a "microcosm" of late Romanian socialism, a portrait in miniature of systemic dysfunction and societal malaise.

---

[30] Rossen Djagalov, *From Internationalism to Postcolonialism: Literature and Cinema Between the Second and the Third Worlds* (Montreal, 2020); Masha Kirasirova, "'Sons of Muslims' in Moscow: Soviet Central Asian Mediators to the Foreign East, 1955–1962," *Ab Imperio* 2011 (4): 106–32; Artemy M. Kalinovsky, *Laboratory of Socialist Development: Cold War Politics and Decolonization in Soviet Tajikistan* (Ithaca, NY, and London, 2018). Cf. the concept of "agents of internationalism" elaborated by Jessica Reinisch in a special issue of *Contemporary European History* 25.2 (2016): 195–205.

Solidarity formed the official framework for the spaces where mid-level actors operated, and solidarity, a socialist key word, meant assistance and cooperation on an equal basis.[31] But socialist ideals rubbed alongside other interests and imperatives, and not always in comfortable ways. Taken at the micro level of this book, the saturation of Second–Third World spaces by financial imperatives becomes plain. For many people from socialist Eastern Europe, the attraction of working in the Third World was financial: the chance to earn foreign currency and buy foreign-made goods, the potential for higher salaries and better living conditions. Economic self-interest played a role in bringing people from Vietnam and Cuba to work in socialist Eastern Europe, too. (The reality of both groups' experiences abroad could fall far short of their hopes.) We know that, for Second World governments, engagement with the Third World had vital financial dimensions: socialist solidarity did mean big business, or aspirations to it.[32] One of the contributions of this volume is new reflections on the everyday dynamics of the business of Second–Third World solidarity and, with them, a fresh take on the experience of the mid-level actor. Iacob's and Pešta's chapters on expert communities show how financial imperatives shaped Second–Third World relationships on the ground. Both describe the spaces of their expert communities as subject to ongoing pressure from the socialist authorities back home to make good on the financial promise of solidarity abroad. The mid-level actor in the story—the teacher, the doctor—figured as both an authority and a subordinate, a professional and a commodity of exchange. In 1968, as Pešta shows, the Czechoslovak experts in Egypt used precisely this language, linked to a reform socialism agenda, to protest what they saw as exploitation by their own government. Iacob's portrait of the hospital space in Libya shows Romanian medical professionals caught between the demands of their own government, desperate for hard currency, and the requirements of the Libyans, who pitted one socialist country against another in negotiating aid contracts. At times in his account, the position of the Romanian staff in Libya looks little better than indentured servitude.

The centrality of financial pressures to the lives of mid-level actors like experts forms a sharp contrast to the experience of cultural brokers like the Pečars, but not the only one. The global was not the same for everyone in the Second World not only because of its very limited access points—the inbred exclusivity discussed above. The global was also stratified by the hierarchies and power dynamics of European socialist societies: they traveled, too. The capacity to shape the space of the Second–Third World encounter, then, was unequally distributed among Second World actors. With macrolevel narratives, we run the risk of treating the experiences of the people who operated on a "macro" level, or who had access to those who did, as representative when the opposite was true.

---

[31] Lorenzini, *Global Development*, 45.
[32] Oscar Sanchez-Sibony, *Red Globalization: The Political Economy of the Soviet Cold War from Stalin to Khrushchev* (Cambridge, 2014); Anna Calori et al. (eds.), *Between East and South: Spaces of Interaction in the Globalizing Economy of the Cold War* (Berlin, 2019); Max Trecker, *Red Money for the Global South: East–South Economic Relations in the Cold War* (London and New York, 2020); Daniela Richterova, et al., "Banking on Military Assistance: Czechoslovakia's Struggle for Influence and Profit in the Third World 1955–1968," *International History Review* 43.1 (2021): 90–108.

Gender and Power in Solidarity Spaces

One dimension of the power dynamics crucial to the experiences of socialist solidarity, in socialist Europe and abroad, was gender. Socialist women's committees, such as the Soviet Women's Committee featured in Varga-Harris's chapter, put into institutional form an understanding common to all socialist bloc societies—that women and men, though equal, were innately different because of women's role as mothers, and that women's interests were often best understood and served by other women.[33] Women's committee work channeled this presumed natural, family focus as a force for peace in cultural campaigns, and it was a major outlet for women interested in socialist internationalism in the USSR as elsewhere in the bloc. It was also smaller in scale and less well funded and prestigious than "mainstream" socialist solidarity work. In the GDR, male union activists showed off female workers to their visiting (male) African counterparts as a sign of Germany's socialist modernity but did not engage with actual African women's issues themselves, hiving that work off to separate women's organizations.[34] At the other pole were the all-male worlds of military training programs, with their commitment to technical excellence, national liberation, and revolutionary transformation—the highest of high-status sectors. The chapters in this book present an especially clamorous set of contrasts—peace/war, emotional/corporeal labor, culture/technology, women/men. Yet they echo, in important ways, the overall gendered division of labor proposed by socialist solidarity.

Across the board, different kinds of solidarity work were available to men and women from the Second World. All of the socialist bloc countries developed extensive programs to train foreign language and area studies experts in light of decolonization, but female graduates of these programs were overrepresented in particular fields (translation, foreign language publishing, the media) and underrepresented in others.[35] The Second World's cultural, military, technical, and political elites were overwhelmingly male, and the elite cadres of socialist internationalism were, too: state and party cadres who traveled globally, the diplomatic corps, first-rank international correspondents, writers, and film directors, and top technical experts.[36] Europe's socialist states varied in their approaches to long-term contract employment in the Third World, with some more, and some less, open to women's participation. The Soviet Union, for instance, did not deploy women to work abroad as diplomats, trade representatives, or foreign correspondents,

---

[33] Christine Varga-Harris, "Between National Tradition and Western Modernization: Soviet Woman and Representations of Socialist Gender Equality as a 'Third Way' for Developing Countries, 1956–1964," *Slavic Review* 78.3 (2019): 758–81; Kristen Ghodsee, *Second World, Second Sex: Socialist Women's Activism and Global Solidarity during the Cold War* (Durham, NC, 2019); Elizabeth Banks, "Sewing Machines for Socialism? Gifts of Development and Disagreement between the Soviet and Mozambican Women's Committees, 1963–87," *Comparative Studies of South Asia, Africa and the Middle East* 41.1 (2021): 27–40.

[34] Eric Burton chapter in this volume.

[35] On the relative lack of prestige of publishing, see Nikolai Leonov, *Likholet'e* (Moscow, 2003), 25; Djagalov, *From Internationalism to Postcolonialism*; Iandolo, "De-Stalinizing Growth: Decolonization and the Development of Development Economics in the Soviet Union," in Macekura and Manela, *The Development Century*.

[36] Bishop chapter in this volume.

though it did send some medical and technical personnel, particularly in husband–wife couples. Romania formally excluded women from management positions in subtropical areas and directed women into traditionally "feminine" and lower-ranking professional roles.[37] All of the countries encouraged, and often required, specialists to travel in a family unit, and wives of male specialists sometimes found work in-country, often as translators and office staff. But a significant proportion of the Second World population that experienced socialist solidarity in the Third did so not as working professionals, still less as high-flying brokers, but as dependent wives and as mothers. We as yet know very little about these lives, although several chapters in this book offer important glimpses. Managing the financial and social pressures of socialist expatriate life in the Third World was, for many Second World households, women's work. It was women, as household managers, who might succeed or fail at the business of socialist solidarity work on a family level—putting money aside or accumulating goods, for example, or employing household staff. It was women who were held primarily responsible for maintaining the image of a proper socialist family and community vis-à-vis the host community.

In that regard, policing Second World women's social and sexual activity was deemed essential. The rich literature on Third World students in the USSR draws attention to the control of female sexuality as a flashpoint: anxieties around relationships between Soviet women and visiting students were common and at times manifested in verbal and physical assaults on visitors. They were also often racially charged—if not openly racist.[38] In this book, Bogdan Iacob and Mikuláš Pešta show how similar anxieties about cross-community relationships and, in particular, Eastern European women's sexual autonomy manifested themselves in Third World spaces. Officially, relationships were off the table for both women and men. But it was women's behavior that stood in for the moral and political probity (or degeneracy) of the community. In the space of Eastern European travel literature, Burton et al. find the instrumentalization of female sexuality in a different vein. Here again, the woman's (imagined) behavior symbolizes—literally embodies on the page—the community, but it is the liberated Third World woman in question, standing in for the liberation of the colonial world.[39] The male heterosexual Eastern European traveler, then, imagined a self-congratulatory place for himself in the Third World as a sexual explorer. Gender was at the heart of the power dynamics of socialist solidarity in the spaces of Second–Third World interaction in ways we have only just begun to consider.[40]

---

[37] Iacob chapter in this volume.
[38] Julie Hessler, "Death of an African Student in Moscow: Race, Politics, and the Cold War," *Cahiers du monde russe* 47.1–2 (January–June 2006): 33–63; Maxim Matusevich, "Probing the Limits of Internationalism: African Students Confront Soviet Ritual," *Anthropology of East Europe Review* 27.2 (Fall 2009): 28–30; Abigail Judge Kret, "'We Unite with Knowledge': The Peoples' Friendship University and Soviet Education for the Third World," *Comparative Studies of South Asia, Africa and the Middle East* 33.2 (2013): 239–56; Monique de Saint Martin, Grazia Scarfò Ghellab, and Kamal Mellakh (eds.), *Étudier à l'Est. Expériences de diplômés africains* (Paris, 2015).
[39] Cf. Anne Gorsuch "'Cuba, My Love': The Romance of Revolutionary Cuba in the Soviet Sixties," *American Historical Review* 120.2 (2015): 497–526.
[40] The literature on the connections between US modernization theory and development policy and masculinity offers an interesting contrast, e.g. Molly Geidel, *Peace Corps Fantasies: How Development Shaped the Global Sixties* (Minneapolis, 2015).

Selves and Others: The Bilateral Vision and its Hierarchies

Bilateralism, as many historians have noted, was the official engine to power the Second–Third World machine. Along with many other elements in the practice of socialist internationalism, such as front organizations, educational and expert exchange programs, and high-profile cultural delegations, state-to-state, bilateral agreements were pioneered in the interwar period and developed further in late Stalin period, both within the new European socialist camp and with post-revolutionary China.[41] Peaceful coexistence and the decolonization process opened the door to an explosion in bilateral arrangements across cultural, economic, military, and other sectors. Readers of the socialist press from the mid-1950s through the mid-1980s got an ongoing celebration of hyphenated (Hungarian-Cuban, Soviet-Mozambican, etc.) friendship and projects. But in truth, the spaces where socialist internationalism operated were always far more crowded and messier than the bilateral vision suggests. Intra-socialist jockeying was often a factor, as was intra-German (GDR vs. FRG) competition in some settings, not to mention the enduring influence of former imperial powers.[42] Mazurek's chapter on the "Africanization" of the University of Ghana in the 1960s deconstructs the notion of bilateral space entirely, showing not only the operation of multiple actors, but the refusal of many of them to take sides—East–West, African–European—in ways that their titular identities might seem to warrant. Moreover, as several of our authors discuss, Chinese Maoism, and Second World anxieties about it, was a key "extra" actor in many Third World spaces—a wrench in the gearbox from the point of view of Second World states. Finally, beginning in the 1970s, socialist bloc countries found themselves increasingly engaged in multilateral deals involving socialist, capitalist, *and* developing economies.[43]

Bilateralism as a way of both organizing and idealizing Second–Third World relations persisted nonetheless—a tenacious self/other vision that all our authors, in a wide variety of contexts, explore.[44] Alena Alamgir's contribution describes workers' hostels in Czechoslovakia as designed to provide parallel, separate national spaces, offering a "combination of physical proximity with social distance" she identifies as typical of state socialism. Péter Apor explores the bilateral vision in his case study of the boarding schools for Korean refugee children that flourished across Eastern Europe

---

[41] Michael David-Fox, *Showcasing the Great Experiment: Cultural Diplomacy and Western Visitors to the Soviet Union, 1921–1941* (Oxford, 2011); Eleonory Gilburd, *To See Paris and Die: The Soviet Lives of Western Culture* (Cambridge, MA, 2018); Rachel Applebaum, *Empire of Friends: Soviet Power and Socialist Internationalism in Cold War Czechoslovakia* (Ithaca, NY, and London, 2019); Elizabeth McGuire, *Red at Heart: How Chinese Communists Fell in Love with the Russian Revolution* (Oxford, 2017); Karl D. Qualls, *Stalin's Niños: Educating Spanish Civil War Refugee Children in the Soviet Union, 1937–1951* (Toronto, 2020).

[42] Young-Sun Hong, *Cold War Germany, the Third World, and the Global Humanitarian Regime* (New York, 2015); Lorenzini, *Global Development*, 83–4.

[43] Sara Lorenzini, "Comecon and the South in the Years of Détente: A Study on East–South Economic Relations," *European Review of History: Revue européenne d'histoire* 21.2 (2014): 183–99. Outside the bloc, socialist Yugoslavia was in a class of its own in this respect. Ljubica Spaskovska, "Building a Better World? Construction, Labour Mobility and the Pursuit of Collective Self-reliance in the 'Global South,' 1950–1990," *Labor History* 59.3 (2018): 331–51.

[44] Karl Qualls makes a related argument in *Stalin's Niños*.

in the early 1950s. Although tasked with the integration of Korean children into local national communities, boarding schools both cultivated and enforced children's separation from those communities as individuals. The focus instead, Apor shows, was on "the contact of collective cultural identities" and on internationalism as something achieved *via* national cultures and national subjects. In the formal settings of student folklore performances—Korean children dancing their Koreanness before their hosts, and applauding Polishness or Hungarianness put on stage for them—we see the bilateral model written in a social script to be replicated across the spaces of the Second–Third World encounter.

On a local level, the tidy spaces of the bilateral vision grew cluttered by human volition. Individuals, not collectives, were drawn together: in fistfights, love affairs, business transactions, as friends. On a systemic level, the bilateral vision for Second–Third World relations was, our authors show, intrinsically hierarchical. Apor indeed argues that the Korean schooling program was foundational in this regard, inflecting the way Eastern Europeans conceived solidarity spaces for years to come. Across the region, he shows, boarding schools for Korean refugees were envisioned as "gateways to civilization," with Eastern European national subjects as gatekeepers, delivering children—vulnerable, unformed—from backwardness to socialist modernity. Socialist experts, like medics, military instructors, and engineers, were encouraged to see themselves in the same light, as gatekeepers with a duty of care toward Third World subjects. Their notions of education, civilization, and the modern were technical, but also behavioral and cultural; they involved not just how infrastructures functioned and economies were organized, but also how people dressed, dined, relaxed, and related to one another at home and in public settings. Telepneva, for example, writes about the centrality of these behavioral factors, known in Russian as *kul'turnost'* (cultured living), to Soviet military training.[45] Military instructors who trained African soldiers thought it important that the men sleep in "proper" beds and have organized outings to the ballet. In Cairo, as discussed by Pešta, Czechoslovak experts brought not only knowledge, but habits of thought and self-discipline they identified with superior socialist education.

Differentiating peoples along national and civilizational lines was fundamental, then, and implied a distinctive "stageist" concept of time. In the eyes of many Eastern European observers, the world of the Third World country was legible as an iteration of the Second World's past. Romanian medics, for instance, saw in Libyan daily life the Romanian village of yesteryear, with all its (to their eyes) pathologies; Soviet engineers saw, or hoped to see, in Egypt's giant Aswan High Dam a reincarnation of the USSR's crash industrialization sites of the 1930s; and Hungarian travel writers spotted their very own ancestors, the heroes of the 1848 Hungarian Revolution, on the streets of 1960s Havana. Within the hierarchical dyad of backward–advanced, the backward must be able to "look up" and to learn—a procedure that mandated division and clear sightlines. And socialist citizens always had a duty of representation in any interaction with foreigners, at home or abroad. Burton et al. further suggest that Second World

---

[45] On *kul'turnost'* in Soviet development programs, see Kalinovsky, *Laboratory of Socialist Development*.

travel literature's framing of difference had an educational role at home: visions of backward Third World nations following in the Second World's footsteps could be used to make the case for solidarity work, by logic and by sentiment, to Eastern Europe's readers.

The intrinsic hierarchy of Second World solidarity, its ineluctable civilizing mission, did not go unchallenged. Césaire's 1956 resignation from the Communist Party derided the "big brother who, full of his own superiority and sure of his experience, takes you by the hand (alas, sometimes roughly) in order to lead you along the path to where he knows Reason and Progress can be found."[46] After the Sino-Soviet split, China made a clear bid to impute a racial hierarchy to Second World activism in the Third as well, arguing that the Soviet Union was a white imperialist power incapable of genuine solidarity with Asia and Africa.[47] It was an argument the Soviets and their allies refuted vociferously on ideological grounds, as anti-Marxist-Leninist, and in practical politics, by attacking white supremacy in the international arena and touting their own societies as free of racial discrimination. The Soviet Union, in particular, showcased the so-called Soviet "East"—Central Asia and the Caucasus—as a model and foregrounded "Eastern" professionals in its relations with Third World countries to drive home the point that socialism was racially inclusive and an empowering, effective route to modernity.

Selves and Others: Race in Solidarity Spaces

Race has been a difficult analytical category for scholars of socialist Europe and the USSR to tackle in part because of its distinctiveness in a context where the history of race in Western Europe and the US has been taken as "the analytical norm."[48] Soviet (socialist) societies refuted racial politics in principle, but not race itself as an intellectual category.[49] Race was "elsewhere," in Alena Alamgir's apt formulation; racial prejudice was officially alien to socialist societies; racial identity was contextually meaningless.[50] And yet, historians of socialist Eastern Europe and the USSR have not had to look far to find evidence of people in the region interpreting cultural differences in racial terms. In the everyday, civilizational hierarchies harmonized with racial ones, and to such an extent that they often formed a single sound. This was true within the Second World, in relation to the populations of "backward" regions and groups (such as the Roma).[51] It

---

[46] Césaire, "Letter to Maurice Thorez."
[47] Jeremy Friedman, *Shadow Cold War: The Sino-Soviet Competition for the Third World* (Chapel Hill, NC, 2015).
[48] David Rainbow (ed.), *Ideologies of Race: Imperial Russia and the Soviet Union in Global Context* (Montreal, 2019), 9.
[49] Francine Hirsch, "Race Without the Practice of Racial Politics," *Slavic Review* 61.1 (2002): 30–43.
[50] Alena Alamgir, "Race Is Elsewhere: State-socialist Ideology and the Racialization of Vietnamese workers in Czechoslovakia," *Race & Class* 54.4 (2013): 67–85.
[51] Alaina Lemon, "'What Are They Writing about Us Blacks': Roma and 'Race' in Russia," *Anthropology of East Europe Review* 13.2 (Autumn 1995): 34–40; Alaina Lemon, *Between Two Fires: Gypsy Performance and Romani Memory from Pushkin to Post-Socialism* (Durham, 2000); Aniko Imre, "Whiteness in Postsocialist Eastern Europe: The Time of the Gypsies, the End of Race," in Alfred J. Lopez (ed.), *Postcolonial Whiteness: A Critical Reader on Race and Empire* (Albany, NY, 2005), 79–102.

was also patently a factor in many Second–Third World spaces, in which Second World interpretations of backwardness came entangled with assumptions of difference connected to racial markers, principally color.

None of this is to argue that every Second World individual was racist, or that the anti-imperialist and anti-racist commitments of socialist states were meretricious. (Nor is it to suggest that race and racism were functionally equivalent in the East and the West.) It is, after all, very possible for people to oppose racism in the abstract without recognizing racism in themselves, on a personal or a societal level. We also need to acknowledge the diversity of the Second World, and the varied experiences of racial identification and racism that people brought to the table when they addressed the Third World. Central Asians came to the issue from a different subject position than did, say, Latvians, and Roma and Jews from others still, to cite a few obvious examples.[52]

But taking the aggregate, what would be notable would be if people in the Second World did *not* have racist views, and if those attitudes did not play a role in how they encountered people they saw as racially other in the Third World. As Burton et al. discuss in this volume, all the national literary cultures of what became socialist Eastern Europe took part in the nineteenth- and early twentieth-century vogue for colonial adventure tales steeped in essentialist racial tropes, and these works underwent a major revival after Stalin. However, they write, "it was not only that a culture nostalgic for a past of European dominance existed alongside an official commitment to liberation movements: colonial culture supplied a fantasy that underpinned it." Many new, socialist-era anti-colonial travel narratives trafficked in the "familiar scripts of expedition, conquest, and mastery"—particularly prevalent, they find, in men's writing about Third World women. Research on other dimensions of popular entertainment fills in the picture further. In popular music, for example, racist tropes connected to jazz in the interwar period did not evaporate after the war, but were instead reworked in Second World socialist cultures as attacks on rock 'n' roll.[53] Moreover, the porousness of the Iron Curtain so emphasized by recent scholars also meant that many people in socialist Eastern Europe had access to Western television and cinema steeped in racist stereotypes.[54] Socialist cultures made the condemnation of racism in the capitalist world their bread and butter, but this, too, offered up a world of static, stereotyped racial imagery. People across the USSR and socialist Eastern Europe were made very familiar with a roster of black, brown, and golden-hued icons—political leaders and cultural figures from around the world who represented the struggle against racist tyranny.[55]

---

[52] Soviet "Easterners" in Soviet institutions of Third World outreach did not necessarily express different views than their Russian (or other white) counterparts. Constantin Katsakioris, "L'Union soviétique et les intellectuels africains. Internationalisme, panafricanisme et négritude pendant les années de la décolonisation, 1954–1964," *Cahiers du monde russe* 47.1–2 (2006): 15–32 (26).

[53] Ute Poiger, *Jazz, Rock, and Rebels: Cold War Politics and American Culture in a Divided Germany* (Berkeley, CA, 2000); S. Frederick Starr, *Red and Hot: the Fate of Jazz in the Soviet Union 1917–1991* (New York, 1994); Maxim Matusevich, "An Exotic Subversive: Africa, Africans and the Soviet Everyday," *Race & Class* 49.4 (2008): 57–81.

[54] Sabina Mihelj and Simon Huxtable, *From Media Systems to Media Cultures* (Cambridge, 2018); Aniko Imre, *TV Socialism* (Durham, NC, 2016).

[55] Quinn Slobodian, "Socialist Chromatism: Race, Racism and the Racial Rainbow in East Germany," in Slobodian, *Comrades of Color*, 32.

They were also well acquainted with media imagery of people of color as the nameless oppressed masses—and sometimes as revolutionary masses—in the US and the Third World. But as Toni Weis argued, solidarity cultures presented people of color "as moral constructs rather than fellow citizens."[56] They invited exoticization and its obverse, alienation, and apprehension, along with a kind of simplistic self-congratulation.

Official race-blindness meant the Second World lacked tools to excavate its own complex relationship to race and racism.[57] It also presents challenges for historians. The combination of racialized categories with socialism's developmentalist paternalism generated a racist substrate for many spaces of Second–Third World interaction, but one not always easy to mark out. Scholars have documented racist incidents most extensively in work on the Third World student experiences. Strewn across the spaces of Second–Third World interaction in this book lies scattered evidence of people from the USSR and Eastern Europe seeing difference in racial terms. The common concern of the expatriate expert communities to maintain self-other boundaries with local communities was sometimes expressed in racialized terms, as in Iacob's analysis of Romanians in Libya and Pešta's discussion of Czechoslovak experts in the Middle East. Racist slurs figured in the pub fights that Alamgir discusses in her chapter about Vietnamese workers in Czechoslovakia. Chapters by Varga-Harris and Vučetić present a different perspective on Second World actors' attitudes to difference, one much more in sync with socialist anti-racist activism (and, in the case of Vučetić's work, advancing an argument about Yugoslavia's particular position as a leader of the Non-Aligned Movement). In Burton et al.'s chapter exploring travel writing as a space of Second–Third world interaction, we find a range of ideas about blackness, whiteness, backwardness, and imperialism that defy easy categorization. Like gender, race was integral to the on-the-ground experiences of socialist solidarity in multiple ways and settings yet to be explored.

Whose Global Socialism? Towards a Conclusion

The capacity of Third World governments to leverage their relationships with different partners has been a theme in much of the recent literature on the global Cold War.[58] Historians have demonstrated that, rather than pawns of superpower conflict, Third World states often found ways to play socialist against capitalist and, indeed, to use

---

[56] Toni Weis, "The Politics Machine: On the Concept of 'Solidarity' in East German Support for SWAPO," *Journal of Southern African Studies* 37.2 (2011): 366.

[57] Several scholars argue that official race-blindness in the Soviet Union backfired, ultimately breeding misconceptions and resentments and manifesting in the overt racism of the late 1980s and 1990s. Alamgir, "Race Is Elsewhere"; Matusevich, "An Exotic Subversive"; Jeff Sahadeo, "Soviet 'Blacks' and Place Making in Leningrad and Moscow," *Slavic Review* 71.2 (2012): 331–58; Anika Walke, "Was Soviet Internationalism Anti-Racist? Toward a History of Foreign Others in the Soviet Union," in Rainbow, *Ideologies of Race*, 13; Meredith Roman, "Making Caucasians Black: Moscow Since the Fall of Communism and the Racialization of Non-Russians," *Journal of Communist Studies and Transition Politics* 18.2 (2002): 1–27.

[58] Leveraging was not a Cold War phenomenon but rather predated it. Frederic Cooper, "Writing the History of Development," *Journal of Modern European History* 8.1 (2010): 5–23 (14).

competition within the blocs to their advantage. The studies in this book contribute to and deepen this understanding. The spaces we explore were not modular units of the Second World transplanted to the Third, nor were they purely bilateral (Soviet-Egyptian, East German-Tanzanian, etc.) The sorts of relationships we describe are not readily characterized in hierarchical terms, such as donor-recipient; they fit uneasily in models of hybridity or union. Many authors write about instances in which Third World people acted in ways that countered the expectations of their Second World counterparts, or simply ignored them. GDR trade union activists saw their East African counterparts as having an unhealthy fixation on racial politics, but there was little they could do about it: their own power in the region was marginal at best, and they knew it, Burton tells us. In her exploration of Yugoslav-African exhibition spaces, Vučetić explains how Yugoslav cultural bureaucrats' assumptions that Egyptian audiences would prefer folklore to high culture met with pushback from the Egyptian authorities, henceforth shaping the contours of Yugoslav cultural diplomacy in North Africa.

At the same time, a number of case studies in this book show spaces of convergence—or, if not quite convergence, of commonalities in goals and values between Second and Third World actors. Reintegrating the history of military engagement into the *cultural* history of Second-Third World connections is an essential move toward broadening this understanding. During the Cold War, the "communist infiltration" story so beloved of journalists often glossed over the fact that many Third World governments valued Second World military expertise above all else and themselves pushed for Second World interventions and assistance. Telepneva's African soldier trainees were no less committed to martial values—discipline, hierarchy, technical expertise—than their Soviet instructors. Moreover, the vision of technological modernity at the heart of the Second World's developmental program was one that resonated loudly across great parts of Asia, Africa, and Latin America. The young people who wrote to Radio Moscow looked to the socialist bloc model as one to emulate, and women who corresponded with the Soviet Women's Committee found common ground with their interlocutors on issues from the arms race to child-rearing. The focus on education and self-cultivation, and social responsibility and collective action promoted by Second World socialism could and did strike chords among elites in the Third.[59]

Yet one thing the chapters in this book also demonstrate is that commonality and influence were not one and the same. The Second World claimed "socialism" as its concept (with nods, often grudging, to possible variant pathways) and asserted rights to leadership. But, in practice, it had no firm grip on either.

Looking close up at spaces of Second-Third world connection, it is, then, their incommensurability that hits you on the head, along with the Second World insistence on the opposite—that is, on universality, consistency, translatability. The institutional archival records from the Second World most of our authors rely on do speak an idiom that frames the spaces in terms of Second World agency ("our work," "our plans") and Second World subjects ("our people"). (The literature of the Soviet/Eastern European

---

[59] Tobias Rupprecht, *Soviet Internationalism after Stalin: Interaction and Exchange between the USSR and Latin America during the Cold War* (Cambridge, 2015), 66; Vijay Prashad (ed.), *The East Was Read: Socialist Culture in the Third World* (New Delhi, 2019).

traveler offers a related dialect, as do media accounts.) But even they provide ample evidence of other dynamics at play, showing the Second World off-center and even in second position, in reaction. They show spaces that were constructed from many sides, not always in harmony, and often with divergent understandings of contexts, methods, and goals. Many of them, marked by their narrow entryways and hierarchical structures, evoked the spaces of "really existing socialism" in the Second World itself. But more important still, in their uses and meanings, in local contexts, all of these spaces remain illegible if we stick to plans and agreements. After all, each of these stories, "our" stories (as historians of the Second World), belongs as much, if not more, to national, regional, and postcolonial histories as to the history of the Second–Third World encounter. The history of socialism "going global" was, importantly, more particular than universal, more singular and original than planned.

1

The School: Schools as Liminal Spaces— Integrating North Korean Children Within Socialist Eastern Europe, 1951–9*

Péter Apor

Years before the socialist states of Eastern Europe embarked on ambitious internationalist education initiatives targeting the Afro-Asian world, they had created special schooling centers for children from war-torn North Korea.[1] Soviet internationalist education programs dated to the 1920s (Moscow's Communist University of the Toilers of the East) and 1930s (the Ivanovo International Boarding School, or Interdom, established for children of persecuted communist and socialist activists). Internationalist education was reinvigorated after World War II, in 1949, when the new socialist governments of Eastern Europe hosted families exiled after the civil war in Greece. But the arrival of several thousand Korean children in 1951 represented the first time experiments with cross-cultural education were undertaken in socialist Eastern Europe. Although the Korean venture was halted abruptly around 1959, when North Korea broke with the Soviet bloc, the experience of organizing schooling and situating foreigners within domestic national cultures continued to have an impact upon the large-scale hosting of students and pupils in the late socialist period.

North Korean children—according to a Soviet military report, more than 2,000 in 1951–2—went first to Poland, Romania, and Hungary, and subsequently to Czechoslovakia and East Germany, to be schooled and taken care of by local personnel.[2] A large proportion of those affected were war orphans, victims of the armed conflict between North and South Korea. Hungary and Poland were the first to host children, accommodating 200 orphans each (in Hungary 158 boys and 42 girls) beginning in November 1951. In 1952, Czechoslovakia, Bulgaria, the German Democratic Republic,

---

* Although the final text is the product of a single author, this chapter is the result of a genuine collaboration. Assistance with archival research and translation was given by Alena K. Alamgir (Czechoslovakia), Bogdan C. Iacob (Romania), and Maria Dembek (Poland). Without their selfless cooperation, this chapter would have looked very different.
[1] Several former classmates and teachers are interviewed in Kim Deog-Young's 2020 documentary *Kim Il Sung's Children*: directed by Kim Deog-Young; produced by LIM, Sooyoung Docustory Production (South Korea, 2020).
[2] Nikolaevich Razuvaev, *Soviet Chief Military Advisor's Korean War Report* (ROK Ministry of National Defense, Institute for Military History Compilation, 2001), 13–16.

and Romania likewise became host countries. While Czechoslovakia, the GDR, and Bulgaria on average accommodated 200 children each, Romania for its part stood out, welcoming some 1,500. In May 1953, another group of 200 pupils arrived in Hungary and a larger group of roughly 1,000 children in Poland, making it a cohort comparable to the Romanian in size.[3]

The children from North Korea were accommodated and educated in special institutions—usually boarding schools with educational, sports, medical, and dining facilities. In Poland, the North Korean children were taken care of in Płakowice near Lwówek Śląski in Lower Silesia, in Szklarska Poręba, Bardo, Gołotczyzna, Świder, Otwock, and Falenica; in Hungary they resided in the Buda hills district of Budapest; in East Germany in Moritzburg, near Dresden; in Romania, most went to Siret; and in Czechoslovakia, to Líšno, Houštka, Liběšice, Valče, Jindřichov u Krnova, Mošovice, and Chocerady na Sázavě. Subsequently, the children from North Korea were sent in smaller groups to ordinary neighborhood schools and taught in mixed classes.

These programs and the spaces framing them were meant to enhance the lives of the Southeast Asian children by offering them proper medical services and education. Given that proper education, however, was understood by Eastern Europeans to include mastering local languages and attending local schools, the hosting of North Korean orphans soon developed into a full-fledged program of social integration. The support provided for the Koreans was a showcase of socialist solidarity with the embattled revolutionary state in Southeast Asia. But the substantial resources that the Eastern European governments allocated to the program, including buildings, services, personnel, and material goods, also demonstrate how seriously Eastern European elites took the integration of the North Koreans into their societies. Often, the commitment to further integration extended beyond party and government officials. For example, the journal of a doctor in the Płakowice Children's Home in Poland reveals how deeply committed he was to saving a Korean child from leukemia, with her lengthy treatment including multiple blood transfusions.[4] Looking back from the vantage point of 1990 to the heroic efforts of the 1950s, Ágnes Nemes Nagy, herself an outstanding poet at the Budapest Sándor Petőfi Grammar School, also remembered how the staff had endeavored to support the Korean children, voluntarily offering them numerous extra classes.[5]

These often sincere intentions were however less important than the actual conditions of integration in shaping the encounter between North Korean children and Eastern European societies. Schools, the traditional spaces of socio-cultural passage, had to tackle a relatively novel challenge for Eastern European societies: making sense of often radical cultural difference. The schools were swiftly turned into laboratories which would influence the nature of the encounter between socialist Eastern Europe and the decolonizing South for years to come. Schooling programs first

---

[3] Mózes Csoma, *Koreaiak Magyarországon az 1950-es években* (Budapest, 2012), 21. Łukasz Sołtysik, "North Korean Children and Youth in Lower Silesia and Masovia in 1951–1959," *Śląski Kwartalnik Historyczny Sobótka* 65.1 (2010): 57–95. Achim Reichardt, *Nie Vergessen! Solidarität üben* (Berlin, 2006), 44.
[4] Jolanta Krysowata, *Skrzydło anioła: historia tajnego ośrodka dla koreańskich sierot* (Warszaw, 2013), 13.
[5] Ágnes Nemes Nagy, "Káin, Ábel, gimnázium" [Cain, Abel, Grammar School], *Vigília* 55 (March 1990): 213.

and foremost saw their task as integrating the Korean children into their respective national societies and, hence, to recast them as Polish, Romanian, Czechoslovak, Hungarian, or East German socialist citizens. This project was largely understood as a "civilizing mission," whereby both biological (illnesses) and cultural (e.g. illiteracy in Eastern European vernaculars) shortcomings would be eliminated.

The conception of socialist integration as a "nationalization" of Korean subjects gave rise to repeated clashes with North Korean officials. It was primarily the Korean tutors and officers who feared a possible dissolution of Korean national identity or, worse still, of loyalty to the Korean state. As a result, they tended to argue for a significant proportion of Korean topics as well as native Korean teachers and textbooks in the curriculum of the East German, Polish, Romanian, and Czechoslovak children's homes. These included classes in the Korean language, identity, history, geography, culture, and arts—the typical elements in the teaching of national identity and the shaping of national subjects since the late nineteenth century in Western primary education. Besides, the Korean officers insisted on the development of a patriotic cult around the leader of their communist state, Kim Ir Sen (Kim Il-Sung).[6]

Space, Difference, and Civilizational Hierachies

Eastern European authorities concerned themselves to a remarkable extent with arranging physical spaces for the Korean newcomers. The Romanian Commission set up to prepare for their arrival proposed that specially designed "pavilions" to suit the Asian children be built.[7] Subsequently, the Red Cross constructed special apartment buildings for the purpose in Păclişa.[8] At the end of 1952, before the actual arrival of the Korean orphans, the Czechoslovak Red Cross and officials at the Ministry of Education spent months locating suitable buildings. On December 18, 1952, the Red Cross submitted a lengthy report with detailed information on the individual buildings they had investigated and explained why they had or had not met the criteria adopted.[9] First of all, it was far from easy to locate property that could accommodate large groups of children. As the Red Cross complained to the Ministry of Foreign Affairs, the original Lišno castle "would hardly be large enough to house half the number of children." New facilities had therefore to be identified, which eventually led Red Cross officials to a former spa in Houštka, which they classified as perfectly suitable "in terms of size."[10]

The quest involved something more than merely a preoccupation with the size of edifices, however. The officials' overriding concern was with sanitary and medical facilities, structures being deemed suitable only if they had heating and adequate

---

[6] Marian Brandys, *Dom odzyskanego dzieciństwa* (Warsaw, 1953).
[7] ANIC, CC al PCR, Relatii Externe, 1/1952, ff. 16–18.
[8] ANIC, CC al PCR, Agitprop, 33/1955, ff. 1–2.
[9] Letter from the Social Affairs Department of the Czechoslovak Red Cross to the Foreign Ministry, December 18, 1952. AMZV [Archive of the Ministry of Foreign Affairs], Korea, TO-T [Teritoriální odbory, tajné] 1945–1954, carton 2.
[10] Red Cross report to the Ministry of Foreign Affairs, August 1952. AMZV, Korea, TO-T 1945–1954, carton 2.

sanitation, by which they primarily meant WCs. Location was also held to be important. As the Red Cross exclaimed, one of the selected sites, the Valeč castle, "is in a beautiful landscape, very suitable from a health point of view."[11]

What is striking even after a cursory reading of the records is the intense concern of the school and ministry personnel with medical issues. The Child Care Department of the Polish Ministry of Health thus reported to the Office of the Minister on February 25, 1954 about the status of the education center for North Korean children in Płakowice. In this document, administrators spelled out the basic responsibilities of the center, setting health as the first priority ("to cure children from diseases [first of all, the epidemic ones] and boost the health of children") and education ("Prepare the children to study at Polish schools and to be placed in children's homes alongside Polish children") only second.[12] Very similar concerns were voiced by the authorities in Romania, where, formally at least, the schooling of Korean children came under the auspices of the Red Cross. In a 1955 report submitted to the Central Committee of the Romanian Communist Party, the Central Committee of the Red Cross explained that just as soon as they had tackled the alarming state of health of the North Korean children, they would be able to broach the less urgent matter of their education.[13] When the Czechoslovak government for its part discussed the imminent arrival, on April 1, 1952, of the contingent of North Korean children, the representative of the Ministry of Health confirmed that they would assume responsibility for the relevant medical issues, particularly the immediate vetting of the state of health of the children upon entry.[14]

So far as Eastern European personnel, teachers, doctors, and political administrators were concerned, then, their initial impression of the unfamiliar children from North Korea was of their ill health. The Korean children, the great majority of whom were war orphans arriving from combat zones, suffered from various, often serious, diseases. Trachoma, lung and heart malfunction, tuberculosis, and mycosis were regularly diagnosed. As the Czechoslovak Red Cross reported to the Ministry of Foreign Affairs in August 1952, "The health of almost all children was not good at the outset. All children came with lice in their hair, about 25% suffered from an infectious hair fungus disease, about 25% suffered from psoriasis, in addition a large number of festering skin conditions, gut parasites, a few cases of TB."[15] The Czechoslovak Red Cross recorded 500 medical interventions in the month of July and a thorough medical check-up of the new arrivals: "All children underwent lung X-rays. Stool samples taken from 150 children. All children underwent a thorough dental examination."[16] The Polish press gave a markedly similar account of the medical examinations of a group of Korean children who arrived

---

[11] Report of the Red Cross to the Minister of Education. AMZV, Korea, TO-T 1945–1954, carton 2.
[12] Ministry of Education, Records of the Childcare Center in Płakowice, 1953–4: Archiwum Akt Nowych, cat. No. 3807, 254.
[13] ANIC, Fund Central Committee of the RCP, Section Propaganda and Agitation, File no. 33/1955. Report from the Headquarters of the Romanian Red Cross, March 28, 1955.
[14] Minutes from the meeting on Korean children at the Office of the Presidium of the Government, April 1, 1952: AMZV, Korea, TO-T 1945–1954, carton 2.
[15] Report of the Red Cross to the Ministry of Foreign Affairs, August 20, 1952: AMZV, Korea, TO-T 1945–1954, carton 2.
[16] Report of the Red Cross to the Ministry of Foreign Affairs, July 1952: AMZV, Korea, TO-T 1945–1954, carton 2.

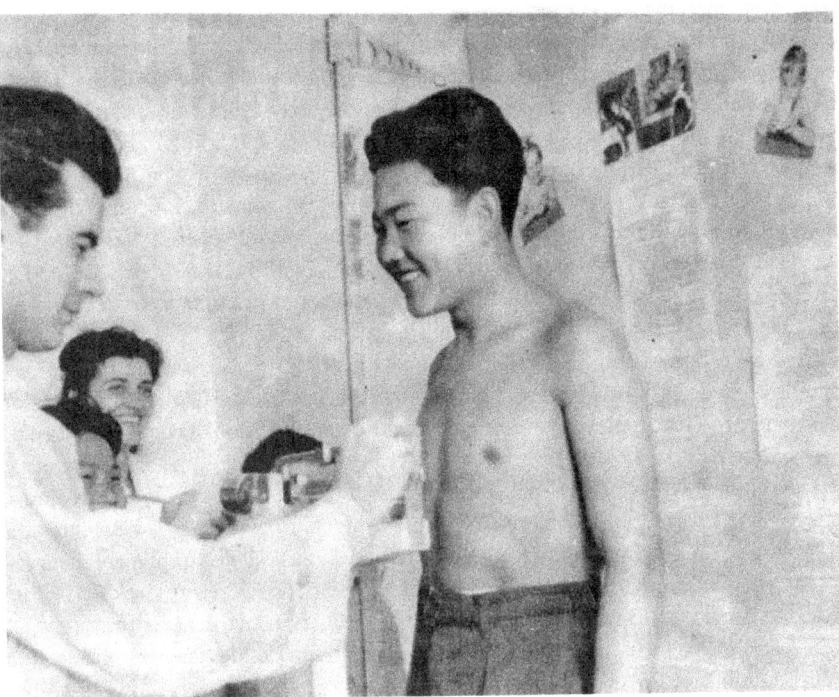

Figure 1.1 Medical inspection in a Romanian center. From a 1953 Romanian Communist Party pamphlet.

in Warsaw on December 23, 1952.[17] The multifarious medical interventions and measures turned these schools, in many ways, into sanitary institutions.

Furthermore, several of the diseases detected, primarily those involving worms and parasites, were unknown to Eastern European doctors. Medical staff often complained about their difficulties combating these illnesses, particularly their lack of knowledge about proper treatment and the sadly ineffectual nature of the medicines they had at their disposal. In a progress report on the Korean children in Czechoslovakia, experts discussed the high incidence of intestinal parasites and their resistance to treatment.[18] These tropical germs were perceived to be the spawn of distant lands, of an alien geography. Given the differences in medical practice, the unfamiliar and exotic illnesses observed and the sanitary nature of the spaces in which the orphans had been placed, it was no wonder that the Eastern Europeans should have thought first of all in terms of biology when addressing cultural difference.

A few of the diseases detected in the Korean children, particularly tuberculosis and parasites, had strong cultural implications for Eastern European observers. In the interwar period, tuberculosis had generally been regarded as a working-class disease

[17] *Służba Zdrowia*, January 11, 1953, 1.
[18] Situation Report on Korean Children and Students in Czechoslovakia, June 8, 1955: AMZV, Korea, TO-T 1945–1954, carton 2.

related to poor living conditions. Working-class children and young parents dying early of TB were typical characters in leftist literature and social criticism. Socialist healthcare in Eastern Europe was thus largely understood in terms of civilization, especially in the postwar and Stalinist period of the early 1950s. The struggle against tuberculosis and parasites was also a quest to eradicate the conditions of backwardness and to elevate a degraded population through the blessings of modern science and technology. Professional medical (in essence, biological) activities were vested with a political and cultural meaning. The biological strangeness of disease was translated into a civilizational difference in culture, thereby acquiring a temporal or stadial dimension. As tuberculosis and parasites in workers and peasants were the physical residues of backwardness, of a previous historical stage, the presence of similar living matter in the bodies of the Korean children all too readily rendered them the subjects of enlightened but drastic intervention. This medical and biological framing could not help but introduce a temporal dimension into the comprehension of cultural difference.

Nonetheless, the new institutions for Korean childcare were not simply sanitary spaces. Taking care of children involved education, and these education programs, moreover, had a special purpose. As the Polish Child Care Department stressed, schooling in the children's home for Korean refugees was designed to prepare them for a swift entry into the host societies.[19] In December 1952, the Czechoslovak Red Cross declared its goal of Korean children starting in ordinary Czech schools the following year.[20] The major focus was, therefore, on language skills. Besides language classes, the Polish authorities for their part favored the integration of the Korean children into mixed classes with local children as well as in extra-curricular activities beyond the walls of their boarding school. By 1956, two education centers for the North Koreans, in Bardo and Płakowice, were teaching the foreign children alongside their Polish counterparts. Cross-cultural education programs such as these were considered the proper route to rapid social integration.[21] Hungarian Ministry officials and Korean Embassy staff held similar views. After the first year of the Kim Ir Sen school in Budapest, 1952, the Hungarian authorities, concerned about the North Korean pupils' slow progress in the Hungarian language, decided to effect a thorough transformation of the school. In the future, it was decided, the school would function as a dormitory and the pupils would be dispersed to study in nearby ordinary state institutions. Ministry officials hoped that the new dispensation would accelerate the language learning process among the Koreans. With this purpose in mind, they limited the number of Korean children to a maximum of ten in each school class and exempted them from compulsory Russian classes.[22] The Romanian authorities likewise realized in 1955 that simple Romanian language classes were insufficient and initiated mixed Romanian–Korean classes.[23]

[19] Ministry of Education, Records of the Childcare Center in Płakowice, 1953–1954: Archiwum Akt Nowych, cat. No. 3807, 254.
[20] Letter from the Social Affairs Department of the Czechoslovak Red Cross to the Foreign Ministry, December 18, 1952: AMZV, Korea, TO-T 1945–1954, carton 2.
[21] Sołtysik, "North Korean Children."
[22] Mózes, *Koreaiak Magyarországon*, 24.
[23] Radu Tudorancea, "Our Comrades Children: The North Korean Children (Orphans) in Communist Romania during the Korean War," *Historical Yearbook* 10 (2013): 33.

The success of the Romanian and the similar Hungarian practices apparently influenced decision-makers in Czechoslovakia. In 1952, Czechoslovak Education Ministry officials in concert with the North Korean ambassador decided to divide the Korean children into smaller groups and integrate them with ordinary school classes in institutions near the children's home in Stará Boleslav and Brandýs nad Labem. As their report argued, "Putting Korean children in regular schools has worked very well in Romania and Hungary."[24] The Red Cross likewise stopped teaching Russian to the orphans, in order to focus on Czech. An April 1954 summary report on the situation of North Korean school children in Czechoslovakia set the quickest possible mastery of Czech as the most important goal of their education. Extra tutoring classes with trained personnel were introduced into the children's homes. Korean children began studying all subjects in Czech, and a huge effort was made to bring on their oral communication skills as rapidly as possible. The need to acquire language skills fast was a matter on which the Czechoslovak and North Korean authorities agreed. In December 1952, the North Korean ambassador to Prague encouraged his Eastern European partners to hire more teaching staff and expressed a wish to see more personal interaction among Korean and Czech children.[25]

Although the generational composition of the Korean groups was diverse, ranging from toddlers to adolescents, Eastern European media typically portrayed them as innocent, helpless little children eager for the care and instruction of their Eastern European peers. The Romanian press published letters from Korean pupils thanking their "Romanian fathers and mothers" and also asking for forgiveness for their "childish disobedience" in the past.[26] A Korean girl, Ra Soc-ran, called the Red Cross personnel "mothers" and "parents" in an interview.[27] To judge by the adjacent photographs, newspaper articles set out to depict the role of women and men differently in the process of administering care and guiding. Women normally appeared as doctors, medical personnel, or daycare assistants. Such visual framings suggested that the proper relationship to have with the Korean children was one that replicated the maternal role. Men, in contrast, were seen as responsible and serious teachers, leading their pupils gently but firmly towards knowledge. As a former teacher at the Petőfi Grammar School in Budapest recalled, one of her male colleagues "became the shepherd [pastor] of the new boys."[28]

Gender differences notwithstanding, the photographs suggest that the boarding schools were constructed so as to provide spaces that encouraged the Eastern European adults to behave like parents.[29] As a 1954 book on a children's home in Poland commented:

[24] Summary report on the education of Korean children and the studies by Korean high school and university students in Czechoslovakia, undated: AMZV, Korea, TO-T 1945–1954, carton 2.
[25] Visit by Korean ambassador Kim Yn Gi on December 9, 1952: AMZV, Korea, TO-T 1945–1954, carton 1.
[26] Letter of eighty Korean orphans sent to Gheorghe Gheorghiu-Dej and Chivu Stoica before their return home, August 19, 1957: ANIC, CC al PCR, Relatii Externe, 44/1957. "Letter of the 500 Pupils at the Kim Ir Sen School before Their Return Home," *Scînteia*, July 17, 1960, 1.
[27] Edmond Frédéric, "Enquête sur quatre continetes a Bucarest," *La Roumanie d'aujourd'hui* 6 (1961): 19.
[28] Nemes Nagy, "Káin, Ábel," 169.
[29] Csoma, *Koreaiak Magyarországon*, 19, 23.

Korean orphans, who came to Poland from [a country in flames], regained their home, childhood, smiles and love in our homeland. They came to our homeland, just as they did to the other fraternal countries of people's democracy, to gain knowledge and the strength to be able to work and struggle, away from the horrors of war. The Polish people accepted them as their own children, the whole of Poland has become their family.[30]

A Hungarian press report on Korean children who took part in sports classes adopted a similar tone: "It is not by accident that even the director calls the Korean boys and girls 'our children.' They are, indeed, our children, [the children] of the entire Hungarian people, which embraces with genuine parental love those orphans of Korean freedom fighters who came to us."[31]

The fact that cultural difference appeared for Eastern Europeans in the 1950s primarily in the guise of children had important consequences for the framing of integration. Integration inside the walls of schools was conceived in terms of training and was understood as the elimination of a sort of illiteracy. Education and childcare authorities imagined the school as a gate which allowed children to cross between two worlds. Outside the gate, they were foreigners, understanding nothing and bringing an alien form of life with them. Beyond the gate, they would become genuine members of the community who could readily understand and participate in its everyday life. It was in the children's home that they were expected to undergo this profound transformation. The school was expected to recast the Korean subjects as Polish, Romanian, or Hungarian socialist citizens. Inside the boarding school, however, the curricula, which combined elements of the Polish, Hungarian, or Romanian national canons with parts of North Korean culture, had already detached them from their native community, without, however, integrating them into the new one. The children enjoyed, and suffered, a liminal status: not-yet true Poles, Hungarians, or Romanians, but no longer authentic Koreans either. These schools were indeed liminal spaces. One Romanian teacher, Georgeta Mircioiu, highlighted in an interview the importance of a preliminary period, focused on proper healthcare and nutrition, for rendering the Korean children fit for further education.[32] It was as if the process of education that proper Romanian citizens normally went through could not be started unless and until a physical transformation eliminating biological difference had rendered the Koreans fit for it.

Since the late eighteenth century, childhood has been predominantly understood as a particular period of human physical and, more importantly, psychological development. Children have been seen as potential but not yet fully-fledged human beings, who grow into mature adults through interaction with, and adaptation to, various social and cultural environments. Supposing this to be true, adults have a responsibility to guide children towards benign and useful influences. Taking this responsibility seriously, a complex of institutional practices was built up around these

---

[30] Marian Bielicki, "Introduction," in Marian Brandys, *Dzieci Gołotczyzny* (Warsaw, 1954), 10.
[31] György Gömöri, "A mi koreai gyerekeink," *Népsport*, July 18, 1952, 4.
[32] Interview with Georgeta Mircioiu conducted by Radu Tudorancea. Radu Tudorancea, *Ipostazele "ajutorului frățesc." RPR și războiul din Coreea (1950–1953)* (Cluj-Napoca, 2014), 104.

concerns, which continue to shape socio-cultural attitudes to children in contemporary European societies, particularly in schools. The fact that cultural difference was institutionalized in schools helped Eastern Europeans in the 1950s to imagine it as a temporal condition and state. Integration, therefore, could be readily understood as a consequence of the elimination of a cultural difference conceived as liminal.

The war in Korea was conducive to modes of encounter between Asians and Eastern Europeans that served to frame cultural difference as a fact of civilization and, thus, of historical time. Eastern Europeans, in their depictions of the outcome of the war in Korea, tended to focus on the shocking devastation of infrastructure and the rapid and precipitous decline in public health. The staff of the Hungarian Embassy in Pyongyang described the collapse in some detail:

> The war erased complete villages and cities from the [face of the] earth ... Urban dwellers built underground lairs, where many thousands of families with children lived for months, often for years. It is only natural that these conditions should have led to the spread of tuberculosis and other mass diseases.[33]

When comrade Ryška of the Czechoslovak Embassy visited an orphanage near the North Korean capital in November 1951, he reported similar depressing details. "Most children suffer from malnutrition, don't have enough clothing, or school equipment. On average 4–5 children fall sick every month due to insufficient nutrition."[34] The horrible outcomes of the war facilitated Eastern Europeans' perceptions of Asia in terms of backwardness and primitiveness.

The boarding schools in Eastern Europe were imagined in many senses as gateways to civilization. As a consequence, Eastern Europeans, who ran these schools or encountered the children either in person or through the media, were led to conceive of socialist integration as in essence a process of civilization. Whether peers, experts, or officials, Eastern Europeans could understand their own roles in straightforward terms: they were to create the material conditions that facilitated civilized modes of behavior. The Asian newcomers' clothing was, for example, routinely changed by their Eastern European hosts. As Rim Zang Dong, a secondary school student in Budapest remembered, "At that time we were wearing Chinese-style clothes. Upon arrival we were taken to the Corvin department store [a central Budapest establishment built in the interwar period], where everyone got a pack of new clothes."[35] The Czechoslovak Red Cross, similarly, reported to the government that all the Korean children would receive proper clothes soon after their arrival. The clothes allotted to each individual, costing 3.5 million Czechoslovak korunas in total, included items that a civilized European socialist gentleman might be expected to possess: three suits including an everyday one, garb for festive occasions, and a Young Pioneer's uniform, jackets, winter coats, and two sets of underwear each.[36] The overview of the educational program for

---

[33] MOL XIX J-i-k Korea, box 4; Csoma, *Koreaiak Magyarországon*, 18.
[34] Report from the CS embassy to the Foreign Ministry, November 14, 1951: AMZV, Korea, TO-T 1945–1954, carton 2.
[35] Interview with Rim Zang Dong conducted by Mózes Csoma, Stuttgart, June 15, 2012. Quoted in Csoma, *Koreaiak Magyarországon*, 88.
[36] AMZV, Korea, TO-T 1945–1954, carton 2.

the Korean orphans in the Czechoslovak children's home stressed the importance of work education. Tellingly, however, this focused on cleaning duties, particularly the bedrooms, classrooms, and communal dining spaces, as well as the upkeep of the garden.[37] The extra-European newcomers also had to be instructed how to eat proper dishes. "But cheese and sausages I could not eat since I had never had anything like these before. Besides, I believed that [Hungarian-style smoked] sausages were raw meat which had to be cooked," remembered Rim Zang Dong.[38]

By polishing the Korean orphans' manners as regards eating and dressing, Eastern European education and medical professionals offered them the conventional routes towards entering civilized society which had been established in Europe since the fifteenth century. The appropriation of modes of eating, dressing, and conduct, which early modern European élites developed to draw boundaries between educated, respectable high society and uneducated, indecorous lower-class people, called for a rigorous disciplining of the body: its movements, gestures, and rhythms.[39] The process of transformation that Eastern European educated élites viewed as integration was addressed by means of technologies that worked on the body. The Eastern European medical and education officials found the body of the North Korean children to be a site of disease and backwardness and were therefore keen to introduce practices serving to discipline and, hence, to transform them. Besides sanitation, vernacular reading and writing, and local habits of eating and dressing, the school authorities considered the shaping of a proper bodily constitution and movement to be crucial both for individuals and collectives. The early phase of education in the Romanian children's home focused on teaching proper modes of gesturing.[40] Czechoslovak children's homes for their part introduced intense physical training in their curricula, including morning exercises, further five-minute bouts of physical exercise during the day, and special group training led by police or army officers.[41] In 1955, the Czechoslovak authorities decided to involve the Korean children in the regional Spartakiad parades.[42] Spartakiads, the Czechoslovak version of the spectacular mass gymnastics performances staged throughout socialist Eastern Europe, were introduced that same year, officially to commemorate the victory of the Soviet Red Army in World War II. Nonetheless, they also drew upon the legacies of Czechoslovak nationalist and working-class gymnastics culture, particularly the Sokol groups.[43] Integrating Koreans

---

[37] Marie Baranová, A short overview. Detailed plan of afterschool activities for the month of April for Korean children in Chocerady: AMZV, Korea, TO-T 1945–1954, carton 2.
[38] Interview with Rim Zang Dong; Csoma, *Koreaiak Magyarországon*, 89.
[39] Norbert Elias, *The Civilizing Process: Sociogenetic and Psychogenetic Investigations* (Oxford, 2000), 109–35.
[40] Interview with Mircioiu. Tudorancea, *Ipostazele*, 104.
[41] Baranová, A short overview. Detailed plan of afterschool activities for the month of April for Korean children in Chocerady: AMZV, Korea, TO-T 1945–1954, carton 2.
[42] Situation Report on Korean Children and Students in Czechoslovakia, June 8, 1955: AMZV, Korea, TO-T 1945–1954, carton 2.
[43] Petr Roubal, "Mass Gymnastic Performances under Communism: The Case of Czechoslovak Spartakiads," in Balázs Apor, Péter Apor, and E.A. Rees (eds.), *The Sovietization of Eastern Europe: New Perspectives on the Postwar Period* (Washington, 2008), 171–80; Petr Roubal, "Politics of Gymnastics. Mass Gymnastic Displays under Communism in Central and Eastern Europe," *Body and Society* 9.2 (2003): 1–25; Petr Roubal, *Československé spartakiády* [Czechoslovak Spartakiads] (Prague, 2016).

into Czechoslovak Spartakiads in particular and Eastern European mass gymnastics parades in general entailed a reconfiguring of bodily movements and gestures to conform to regional, Eastern European, and national structures of corporeal behavior. Physical education and training, thus, were also understood as a means to help the Korean children overcome cultural differences.

The fact that cultural difference in the boarding school setting was perceived to be a consequence of a stadial theory of civilization effectively enabled a gaze to operate in a manner redolent of colonial hierarchies. The colonial perspective usually depicted cultural difference between Europeans and native peoples in terms of stages in a historical process that colonists imagined as universal and normative. To develop themselves, to further historical progress, natives might be required to meet certain prescribed norms, a requirement which, in turn, led Europeans to intervene and discipline them.[44] As the visual evidence from Eastern Europe suggests, the doctor's office and the classroom were the most typical public spaces within the boarding schools where the North Korean children were subjected to the disciplinary and normalizing gaze of white adult experts.[45] Fathers and mothers, doctors and teachers— they all exercised surveillance upon the children with a benevolent, but disciplinary gaze. This gaze observed the physical make-up, gestures, and behavior of the children, intervening and correcting where necessary.

Socialist Integration, Internationalism, and National Identities

When the Czechoslovak government began looking for ideal spaces to accommodate the Korean orphans, it quickly discovered a number of former aristocratic castles near Prague, the Líšno chateau among them. Two years later, Red Cross staff identified a suitable facility in Houštka, near to Stará Boleslav, a former spa. The Budapest Kim Ir Sen boarding school was situated in a villa of the former Forest School in the Buda hills within the city; likewise the Pak Den Ay Children's Home, in use from 1953. These spaces became available by accident, in many respects. Bohemia's aristocratic castles fell into state hands in 1945, the majority of their former owners having fled the country. The East German Moritzburg castle had been the property of Heinz Heinrich, Prince of Saxony, who lost the building when, in 1945, Soviet troops advanced to the Elbe.[46] By 1952, the communist authorities in Eastern Europe had a number of extensive spaces at their disposal, each with gardens and relatively large buildings and with facilities like hospitals in the vicinity. They were all similar in that they could provide opportunities for isolation: they were fenced-off and therefore physically separate from the major residential areas nearby.[47]

---

[44] Johannes Fabian, *Time and the Other: How Anthropology Makes Its Object* (New York, 1983), 37–71.
[45] Helena Cygańska-Walicka, *We are hosting Korean children*, oil painting, 114 x 146 cm, *III Ogólnopolska wystawa Plastyki* (exhibition catalogue) (Warsaw, 1952), 63. "Młodzież koreańska wśród przyjaciół w Polsce Ludowej," *Służba Zdrowia*, January 11, 1953, 1.
[46] Fritz Löffler, *Das alte Dresden: Geschichte seiner Bauten*, 16th ed. (Leipzig, 2006).
[47] Report of the Red Cross to the Minister of Education: AMZV, Korea, TO-T 1945–1954, carton 2.

These large, somewhat isolated spaces not only facilitated a disciplinary and hierarchical gaze, but also encouraged autonomy and self-regulation. "We can barely see any instructors," one journalist visiting an East German children's home for Koreans observed. The report went on to explain that the pupils had created an elaborate system of self-government. Each group of twenty children elected a group elder, as did each class. The formal adult leadership of the school was relegated to an advisory function.[48]

Even if this picture represented an idealization of the Koreans' highly developed socialist consciousness rather than reflecting actual practices, it reveals the kind of space that mainstream socialist discourse imagined as the site of education. A Czechoslovak report stated that children's self-government had been introduced for the collective supervision of order, cleanliness, and discipline.[49] The official regulations for summer activities at the children's home in Siret, Romania, likewise stressed the importance of individual responsibility and of moral motivations arising within the self and extending to the collective: "In these colonies, children must acquire multilateral education, their sense of initiative and responsibility must be encouraged, the love for work and conscious discipline flowing from the sense of social duty."[50] The work undertaken on the self was thus expected to render it transparent. Developing the self was to occur before the eyes of the collective and in the context of the collective.

The methods of disciplining the body and facilitating self-regulation played a similar role in the education of foreign children in contemporary Western Europe and North America, albeit with important differences. In the West, the most salient form of the social integration of children was adoption and not the boarding school. Family adoptions also spurred the creation of intercultural groups in schools instead of ethnocultural segregation and put more weight on private spaces in the processes of developing the self.[51]

In socialist Eastern Europe, the dominance of autarchic and self-regulating spaces fostered the formation of endogenous ethno-cultural communities. In a paradoxical fashion, the spaces that the Eastern European officials offered as sites of integration with Eastern European societies were in fact conducive to modes of separation, thereby reflecting in reality the aims of Korean officials. The children's homes were spaces designed to render tangible the idea of "friendship among peoples." As the North Korean poet Hun Ser Ya, visiting Budapest in June 1953, proclaimed in connection with his stay at the children's home for Korean orphans, "I feel that this school is the true symbol of the unbreakable friendship of our peoples."[52] But cross-cultural encounters and communication did in fact assume a somewhat restricted form. Press accounts of a June 1953 visit by North and South Americans on a peace mission to the boarding school for Korean children in Budapest described a paradigmatic scene: "The

---

[48] Rösner, "Hon Jon Nok."
[49] Marie Baranová, A short overview of the work at the Korean children's homes in Czechoslovakia, Prague, April 26, 1954: AMZV, Korea, TO-T 1945–1954, carton 2.
[50] Guide for the summer work of pupils in colonies for Greek (Korean) children, [issued on July 8, 1953 by the Department of Schools' Administration], SNCR-Serv. Emigranți-Greci, 2/1952. 27.
[51] Arissa H. Oh, *To Save the Children of Korea: The Cold War Origins of International Adoption* (Stanford, CA, 2015), 203–10.
[52] *Magyar Nemzet*, June 20, 1953, 2.

North American, Cuban and Columbian peace delegates sang with the little Korean orphans, their arms around each other's shoulders. After performing a folk song and dance from Korea, the wife of the peace delegate from Columbia sang Spanish folk songs."[53] Thus, the idea of national culture was always imagined as the basis of intercultural encounter and communication. In actual fact, when North Koreans and Eastern Europeans met they normally did so as two distinct groups delineated by strictly drawn boundaries. These encounters represented contact between collective cultural identities rather than a socialist multicultural community.

National identity was, however, effectively reduced to a limited set of artistically recast ethno-folkloric elements and instances of classical high culture. As the official East German party publication declared in an article about the residents of the Käthe Kollwitz Children's Home in Moritzburg, "The young singers cultivate their national heritage, they sing national songs (*Heimatlieder*) and dance folk dances (*Volkstänze*)."[54] The boarding schools in Poland set great store by pupil performance groups. These ensembles typically performed songs and dances that would feature in various political and ceremonial events, such as the August 3, 1953 performance at the Polish Theater in Warsaw celebrating the end of the war in Korea.[55] Illustrations or descriptions of Korean children aimed at Polish audiences would regularly depict them as members of groups performing ethno-folkloric dances and, thus, often altered their image until they came to resemble folk ensembles.[56] In the Płakowice boarding school in Poland, the Korean children were taught Korean folklore and songs with the assistance of a specialist teacher sent directly from North Korea. In fact, the Korean tutors who were residents of the children's home insisted on the rigid separation of Polish and Korean national cultural content in the curriculum. One of them, Kim Te Kuon, was remembered to have vetoed Polish folklore ("Folklore yes, but not Polish").[57]

International in form it might be, yet socialist solidarity was more readily understood if its content was nationalized. The August 1952 official celebration of the liberation of Korea staged in the Warsaw National Theater drew clear parallels between the national histories of Poland and Korea: "The anniversary of the liberation of Korea is dear to every Pole's heart, the Polish nation owing its liberation, just as Korea does, to the heroic Soviet Army."[58] Nascent sympathies and the duty to come to someone's aid were often justified among teachers, doctors, and caretakers in terms of commensurable national experiences. A doctor fighting for the life of a Korean girl suffering from leukemia was mourning a brother lost during the war and had likewise been deeply touched by the death of his teachers' children in the Warsaw ghetto.[59] Polish personnel at Korean schools often recalled the similarities of their experiences in the war and

---

[53] "Amerikai béküldöttek látogatása a Kim Ir Szen iskolában," *Magyar Nemzet*, June 26, 1953, 3.
[54] Rösner, "Hon Jon Nok."
[55] B. Z., "Lud Warszawy manifestuje solidarność z bohaterską Koreą," *Trybuna Ludu*, August 5, 1953, 1.
[56] "Dzieci bojowników o wolność Korei," *Trybuna Ludu*, January 23, 1952, 1. "Children of Korea Accuse," *Życie Warszawy*, June 24, 1952, 1. "Z pobytu koreańskiej delegacji rządowej w Polsce," *Trybuna Ludu*, January 15, 1956, 1.
[57] Krysowata, *Skrzydło anioła*, 98.
[58] *Dziennik Bałtycki*, August 16, 1952, 1.
[59] Krysowata, *Skrzydło anioła*, 13.

the German occupation with the sufferings of the Koreans at the hands of the Americans.

When the Korean children left the precincts of the special schools and mingled with their Eastern European counterparts in ordinary schools, the outcome was very similar to the actual separation produced by the more isolated children's homes. The intention, however, was certainly for them to be integrated into the local national communities. As one Romanian guide employed at summer camps stated, Koreans were encouraged to deepen their knowledge of the "beauties and riches of the Romanian People's Republic."[60] Educational programs designed specifically for the Koreans would normally focus on core elements of the national cultures of each of the host countries, and often stressed patriotic messages. On January 16, 1952, an official Polish newsreel screened a mixed group of Polish and Korean children in their respective national (and socialist) costumes joyfully singing traditional Polish national songs together in the schoolyard.[61] Allegedly authentic national culture, folklore, and customs were by the same token firmly embedded in the curricula for Korean children in socialist Czechoslovakia. The orphans accommodated in the children's home at Chocerady were taken on a walk in April 1954 in order to familiarize them with traditional Czech Easter customs. The Asian children even participated in the whipping of maids and married women with braided pussy willow twigs, a traditional folk custom in Bohemia. A week later, the North Korean children performed the traditional Spring (Morana) ritual alongside their Czechoslovak counterparts.[62]

The Korean orphans were also instructed in Hungary's national patriotic traditions. In December 1952, they were taken to the northeastern town of Sárospatak, the seat of the leader of the early eighteenth-century anti-Habsburg revolt, Prince Ferenc Rákóczi, whom Hungarian Stalinist political culture lauded as a direct forerunner of the socialist popular revolution. In a public performance that same year, they also sang a patriotic song from the 1848 anti-Habsburg revolution, "Áron Gábor's copper gun."[63] Besides history, the Korean children visited the local Museum of Ethnography and the traditional heart of Hungarian patriotic erudition, the library of the Calvinist College.[64] The Korean orphans likewise visited famous Hungarian soccer teams (Hungary won the 1952 Olympics in soccer). "So, do you know anything about Hungarian sport?" a boy is asked. "The boy smiles: Puskás ... Kocsis ..."[65] A widely circulated urban legend in post-1956 Budapest recalled the Korean youngsters who allegedly instructed Hungarian freedom fighters in street fighting tactics against tanks.[66] Some reporters

---

[60] Guide for the summer work of pupils in colonies for Greek (Korean) children (issued on July 8, 1953 by the Department of Schools' Administration): SNCR-Serv. Emigranți-Greci, 2/1952. 27.
[61] Dzieci bohaterskiej Korei. Wojna w Korei, PKF 4/52 from Archiwum Polskiej Kroniki Filmowej, 1952-01-16, 04.15 min., http://www.repozytorium.fn.org.pl/?q=pl/node/7042.
[62] Detailed plan of afterschool activities for the month of April for Korean children in Chocerady: AMZV, Korea, TO-T 1945–1954, carton 2.
[63] "Ünnepi előadás keretében mutatták be az 'Ifjú sasok' című koreai filmet," *Népszava*, June 27, 1952, 4.
[64] *Magyar Nemzet*, December 28, 1952, 6.
[65] Gömöri, "A mi koreai gyerekeink." "Koreai úttörő-labdarúgók a Bp. Bástya öltözőjében," *Népsport*, August 28, 1952, 3.
[66] Mózes Csoma, "North Korean Students in Hungary in the 1950s, and Their Role in the Hungarian Revolution of 1956," *Wiener Beiträge zur Koreaforschung* 4 (2012): 23–30; Mihály Tamás, "A tanárnő," *Holmi* (November 1999): 1437–41.

claimed that Korean pupils of the Petőfi Grammar School had delivered goulash to the freedom fighters in kettles.[67]

The Korean children were regularly allowed, indeed directly instructed, to enter the socialist pioneer and youth organizations in the various Eastern European countries. On April 15, 1953, the North Korean youngsters were officially welcomed into the ranks of the East German Pioneer organization and the Freie Deutsche Jugend, the communist youth alliance.[68] In the autumn of 1953, formally on the initiative of the North Korean Embassy in Warsaw, the Polish Communist Party and the government approved the admission of Korean children into national youth organizations. The younger ones would be called upon to join the Scouting and Guiding Association (ZHP), whereas the older children became members of the Union of Polish Youth (ZMP).[69]

Despite the internationalist language and intentions of the various socialist governments, teachers in ordinary Eastern European schools who seriously addressed the task of promoting North Korean pupils' integration had little option but to turn them into national subjects. Following the communist takeover in the region, the education system had been profoundly transformed. Schools were nationalized and taken into state control, and curricula were largely standardized: geography, history, and literature remained the core of the new socialist curricula and all these subjects focused on the landscape, myths, heroes, and high culture of the nation. But new socialist schools in Eastern Europe also drew on expertise from the interwar and pre-1914 periods. National school systems had emerged during the nineteenth century in Europe as a major vehicle for the production of national citizenship, and thus offered a comprehensive education in national history, geography, language, and high culture. In late nineteenth- and early twentieth-century Eastern Europe, schools often became the sites of contested national identities within the framework of multi-ethnic, increasingly nationalizing states.[70] Schools established in the colonies of European empires offered ways of turning extra-Europeans into proper, civilized Western subjects by focusing on the contents of classical European erudition and national framings of history and geography. While such policies offered many Africans or Southeast Asians paths by which they might journey in between the "Oriental" and "Occidental" worlds, they were also conducive to the emergence of particular ethno-national identities.

Remarkably, the socialist integration of Eastern European schools, though designed to replace the legacies of colonial education, had a markedly similar impact. If the children's homes were spaces designed to open up paths for outsiders to enter socialist national communities, they were also social and cultural spaces that worked to sustain national separation. The North Korean authorities in fact regularly tried to prevent

[67] Katalin Mezey, "A mosógép," *Magyar Napló* 6 (2004): 5–7.
[68] Rösner, "Hon Jon Nok."
[69] AAN, KC PZPR, cat. no. 237/XXII/217.
[70] Joachim von Puttkamer, *Schulalltag und nationale Integration in Ungarn. Slowaken, Rumänen und Siebenbürger Sachsen in der Auseinandersetzung mit der ungarischen Staatsidee 1867–1914* (Munich, 2003). Ingo Eser, "*Volk, Staat, Gott!*": *die deutsche Minderheit in Polen und ihr Schulwesen 1918–1939* (Wiesbaden, 2010).

their citizens from forming personal ties with their Eastern European hosts.[71] The Asian communist government was even reluctant to send very young children to Eastern Europe because, as the Czechoslovak Red Cross warned the political secretariat of the Czechoslovak Communist Party, it feared the potential loss of their original national identity.[72] Eastern Europeans were not necessarily happy to see the forging of close personal ties between their citizens and the North Korean youngsters either. The Romanian authorities, for example, located the activities of Korean children in a way that encouraged physical separation. Although they were sent to mixed classes, they lived and ate apart from their Romanian counterparts and had special clubs allocated for their leisure activities.[73] When children from the Płakowice institution visited the cinema of the neighboring town Lwówek, they took part in an exclusive screening, the intention being to prevent any possible interaction with Polish children.[74] The Polish teacher, Leszek, in Płakowice, who apparently became emotionally involved with one of the North Korean girls, was attacked by her brother and, subsequently, put on trial by the Polish authorities, once the administration had learned of their intimacy.[75]

The boarding school was thus a space marked by secrecy and isolation. Often, forms of solidarity that might involve a physical encounter with members of various ethnocultural groups were not advertised to the public. For example, orphanages for North Korean children were regularly kept secret from local populations. The 1952 internal regulations for employees of the Romanian children's homes prohibited the sharing of information and documentation about the schools with anyone who had no formal links with the institution.[76] The teachers recruited for the education of the Korean pupils were gathered together and kept in isolation until the Koreans finally arrived.[77] The contrast between the reception accorded the 1951 and 1953 cohorts of Korean children upon their arrival in Poland was striking. In 1951, their stay in the country was advertised in the most spectacular fashion in the press and covered at length in newsreels. In 1953, by contrast, almost no press material was published and the film shot by the crew of Kroniki Telewizyjne was never broadcast.[78] If the arrival of Korean orphans could be celebrated as evidence of solidarity between the collective and abstract groups of nations, encounters between real individuals were routinely discouraged.

The solidarity that the Eastern European authorities hoped to establish between national groups was not necessarily viable on an individual basis. Both the Eastern European and North Korean authorities tried to prevent their citizens from forming personal ties with each other.[79] But even when personal encounters did happen, they

---

[71] Charles K. Amrstrong, *Tyranny of the Weak: North Korea and the World, 1950–1992* (Ithaca, NY, 2013), 56.
[72] AMZV, Korea, TO-T 1945–1954, carton 2.
[73] ANIC, CC al PCR Agitprop, 33/1955, ff. 17–18.
[74] Paula Agata Trelińska, "Kim Ki Dok: Korean Orphans in Poland," *PISK*, March 10, 2014, http://pisk.ca/korean-orphans-in-poland/.
[75] Krysowata, *Skrzydło anioła*, 229.
[76] The Internal Regulations of the Colony for Korean Children in Siret, SNCR-Serv. Emigranți-Greci, 2/1952 [applicable for the employees—issued in October 1952], 8.
[77] Interview with Mircioiu. Tudorancea, *Ipostazele*, 103.
[78] Krysowata, *Skrzydło anioła*, 159.
[79] Krysowata, *Skrzydło anioła*, 179.

would often fail to produce a sense of commonality. Although official representations, such as the Hungarian Telegraph Agency's photographs, suggested camaraderie and integration, in fact, sending Korean children into Hungarian schools without language skills and proper cultural preparation resulted in alienation and the rise of xenophobia where local fellow students were concerned. Such sentiments were typically phrased in terms of jealousy and envy. Eastern European schoolmates as well as the local population often accused the Koreans of wearing clothes paid for by the labor and taxes of native citizens.[80] A passage from a novel written in 1964 Hungary that drew upon memories of the Pak Den Ay Children's Home is instructive: "Two old women in black coats jumped out of the snow, the flakes melted on them.—They're Chinese?— No, Koreans.—answered the boy. The old women stopped.—Look, what good clothes they're wearing! They are dressed up ... What 'bout our grandchildren? Why not the Hungarian children? What are these foreigners doing here?"[81]

Conclusion

The methods used to help North Korean war orphans can be considered a prototype for the methods of socialist internationalist aid in general. The modes of socialist global solidarity which the governments of Eastern Europe tried to implement for the first time during the Korean war consisted of two central components: medical aid and education/training support. Aid and support programs were normally interstate actions regulated by bilateral agreements, mostly by so-called agreements of Cultural or Scientific-Technological Cooperation. In the emerging culture of socialist solidarity in the 1950s, firmly linked to the Eastern European responses to the Korean War, solidarity was typically understood to arise between nations. In this context, whereas the children's homes were special spaces in the socialist national and internationalist geography, they were not necessarily exceptional spaces. In many ways, these institutions created microcosmic spaces of the socialist world, which realized in a small but tangible way those strategies and mechanisms that postwar Eastern European elites employed to create a broader socialist international space.

The educational program for North Korean children—boarding schools and integrated classrooms—sheds light on a broader pattern perceptible within the international spaces of early Cold War socialist solidarity. These physical sites of solidarity, most typically hospitals, schools, or construction sites for new urban areas, created the conditions for the division of (Eastern) European and extra-European groups (of color). The two were not necessarily isolated; nonetheless, contacts were encouraged between collectives, between members of two distinct national groups, and discouraged among individuals.[82] The physical sequestration of Eastern Europeans,

[80] Nemes Nagy, "Káin, Ábel," 213. Csoma, *Koreaiak Magyarországon*, 33, 35.
[81] Gergely Bikácsy, "Makacs égitest," *Tiszta szívvel* (November 1964): 78–9.
[82] Young-Sun Hong, *Cold War Germany, The Third World, and the Global Humanitarian Regime* (Cambridge, 2015), 71, 207. Christina Schwenkel, "Affective Solidarities and East German Reconstruction of Postwar Vietnam," in Quinn Slobodian (ed.), *Comrades of Color: East Germany in the Cold War World* (New York, 2015), 267–92.

who from their various centers supervised medical, training, or economic aid programs, encouraged them to translate cultural difference into biological-racist and temporal and stadial attributes. Real, personal, and particular experiences of cultural difference thus dissolved into abstract, generalized, and naturalized collective heritages. In the construction of internationalist socialist solidarity, spaces were developed that enabled the covering over, concealing, and, thus, containing of cultural difference and finally the promotion of civilizational hierarchies.

In many ways, the "civilizing mission" portrayed in the images of childhood that Eastern European doctors, teachers, and politicians developed in relation to the children of North Korea in the 1950s helped them frame their encounter with the Afro-Asian world in terms of assistance and education. The legacies of these early Cold War actions of international solidarity, being encapsulated in an ideal(ized) relationship of teacher and pupil, facilitated the comprehension of subsequent encounters with Afro-Asian peoples in similar terms and also the replication of practices established in earlier decades. Even though many citizens and officials in socialist Eastern Europe sought to dismantle the legacies of colonial hierarchies and replace them with partnerships between equals, in practice they believed themselves to be helping the postcolonial nations by exporting the achievements of an advanced (socialist) civilization. Their criticism of Afro-Asian peoples, who were interested in dialog rather than instruction, led Eastern Europeans to reproduce the early perceptions of radical cultural difference stemming from their encounters with North Korean children. Images of childhood, in turn, facilitated the translation of radical difference into notions of temporal difference between civilizations located at different stages in a process of historic development.

2

The Airwaves: How Do You Listen to Radio Moscow? Moscow's Broadcasters, "Third World" Listeners, and the Space of the Airwaves in the Cold War

Kristin Roth-Ey

Radio took its star turn across the globe in the third quarter of the twentieth century. It was no new technology, of course; in many places, radio listening had become a staple of everyday life as early as the 1920s, and broadcasting figured prominently in the cultures of Depression-era capitalism, fascism, and Stalinism in the 1930s, as well as in World War II. But it was not until the 1960s and 1970s that radio broadcasting became a mass phenomenon worldwide, reaching not only urban populations, but rural ones, and not only in the "First" and "Second" worlds, but across the "Third" as well.[1] And a substantial portion of that reach—in some areas, the lion's share—must be attributed to *transnational* broadcasters: the BBC, the Voice of America, Radio Moscow, Radio Free Europe, Radio Peking, Station HCJB (one of many American evangelical outfits), All India Radio, Vatican Radio, Radio Cairo—a complete list would easily top one hundred, distinct transnational broadcasting operations.[2] For many people around the world in the 1960s and 1970s, then, radio not only entered everyday life, but offered an entrée into a new, everyday, supra-national experience. The airwaves constituted a new transnational space for politicking and preaching, socializing and educating, for sharing and promoting cultural experience.

So far, so global. Certainly, optimism about mass media ran high among modernization school thinkers mid-century in the Anglo-American world. Broadcasting, many thought, had an exceptional capacity to push "backward"

---

[1] The Soviets rejected the term "third world" on principle, although it does appear occasionally in Soviet sources beginning in the 1970s. In this chapter, I use the terms "Third World" and "developing world" as historical artefacts of the era I discuss.
[2] Elihu Katz and E. G. Wedell, *Broadcasting in the Third World: Promise and Performance* (Cambridge, MA, 1977); David Hendy, *Radio in the Global Age* (New York, 2013); Julian Hale, *Radio Power: Propaganda and International Broadcasting* (London, 1975); Donald Browne, *International Radio Broadcasting: The Limits of the Limitless Medium* (Westport, CT, 1982).

populations into the modern world and drive socioeconomic development.[3] "Radio, film, and television climax the revolution set in motion by Gutenberg" enthused the influential American scholar Daniel Lerner in the 1950s. "The mass media [have] opened to the large masses of mankind the infinite vicarious universe."[4] Radio development was destined to spur human development by engendering empathy, extending community, and leveling both hierarchies and borders.

If today, this pacific, communitarian vision of the twentieth-century airwaves has been overshadowed by one of combat, we can thank not only Cold War rhetoric but also the history of broadcasting itself. There was, after all, an inherent tension between the model of radio developed in the 1920s and 1930s and the new realities of a global media age. As historian Michele Hilmes reminds us, radio, "born in an era of nationalisms ... marks a high point in the capture of a technology and a means of cultural production by the organs of the state ... Radio was understood and shaped as fundamentally a national medium."[5] Yet as broadcasting expanded its technical capacity dramatically after the war and decolonization threw new audiences into the ring, radio's moment and the "Third World" moment collided. In an era of imperial collapse and rising new nations, fundamental questions about media's role in development and in promoting national interests on the world stage inevitably came to the fore. Who had the right to speak to whom, and for whom? Was the transnational space of the airwaves one of mutuality or mastery? Or, put another way, whose *space* was the airwaves—the broadcasters' or the listeners'? In the 1970s, it was these vexed questions about media space, voice, and sovereignty that took center-stage at the UN in the New World Information and Communication Order debate that pitched the First, Second, and Third World into conflict.

The Soviet Union's primary international service was Radio Moscow and, in the 1950s and 1960s, it underwent a major expansion to become one of the largest (and, by some metrics, the largest) broadcaster in the world. These years were a boom time for Soviet broadcasting across the board, but even in the context of a boom, the expansion of the international service stands out.[6] Radio Moscow's growth was in both scope (more countries) and intensity (more broadcasting hours), and the decision to pursue it came from the very top; it was at once an important dimension of the post-Stalinist leadership's "peaceful coexistence" policy, foregrounding systemic competition over confrontation, and of its related turn to the decolonizing world as socialism's putative great new frontier. The most prominent changes in Radio Moscow's profile were in its new outreach to Asia, Africa, Latin America, and the Middle East, the subject of

---

[3] Katz and Wedell, *Broadcasting in the Third World*, 3–37; Clare Wells, *The UN, Unesco, and the Politics of Knowledge* (London, 1987), 77.
[4] Lerner quoted in Goran Hyden, Michael Leslie, and Foulu Ogundimu (eds.), *Media and Democracy in Africa* (New York, 2002), 3.
[5] Michele Hilmes, "Foreword: Transnational Radio in the Global Age," *Journal of Radio Studies* 11.1 (2004): iii–vi. Italics mine.
[6] Simo Mikkonen, "To control the world's information flows: Soviet Cold War broadcasting," in A. Badenoch, A. Fickers, and C. Henrich-Franke (eds.), *Airy Curtains in the European Ether* (Baden-Baden, 2013), 241–70; Rossiiskii Gosudarstvennyi Arkhiv Noveishii Istorii (hereafter, RGANI) f. 5, op. 33, d. 177.

multiple party decrees. Although Moscow had already launched multiple new language services in the 1940s, it was in the late 1950s and 1960s that the volume and range of broadcasts to the Third World increased markedly.[7]

The decision to expand Radio Moscow was promoted widely at the time: the fact that Moscow now spoke to so many people, in so many different languages, across such vast distances, was itself a propaganda point of considerable power. The trope of Moscow's great voice breaking barriers, bringing the modern world to backward peoples, had been a war horse of domestic propaganda for decades: "radiofication" had been an associate to "electrification" since the 1920s.[8] With the great expansion of Soviet international broadcasting in the 1950s and 1960s, the old horse got new legs: Radio Moscow demonstrated the Soviets' enlightened/enlightening interests in the Third World. The message could be tailored to the home audience and foreigners alike. The impact of Soviet broadcasting cries out for analysis not only in terms of its content, but also of its identity as an institution and of the connections with listeners it cultivated and advertised—its "brand."

This chapter analyses the Radio Moscow brand from the inside out—that is, by looking closely at how Moscow's broadcasters saw themselves, their work, and their listeners, particularly their Third World listeners. It is story of personal ambitions and professionalization, of ideological commitments and superpower politics. It is also a story of the choices Radio Moscow made about language, style, content, and voice, and the imaginative connections and even intimacy they projected. Across Asia, Africa, the Middle East, and Latin America, the actual audience for Radio Moscow, as for its international competitors, was most often a tiny proportion of the adult population, as I discuss below. Moscow's broadcasters knew this, and they also envisaged and promoted relationships with Third World listeners using a range of methods, the most important of which was a worldwide listener survey program in the years 1967 to 1982. The twinned spaces of radio production and consumption, of broadcaster and listener, developed relationally, imaginatively, and sometimes argumentatively to create a new space: the airwaves. In what follows, I propose to explore this space as politics, as social interaction, as experience. What can the airwaves tell us more broadly about the Second–Third World encounter as experienced in both "worlds" and beyond?

National Voices and Soviet Internationalism

The roots of postwar Soviet international broadcasting were in the pre-war Comintern operation, which relied heavily on political exiles to produce programing. Soviet dependence on foreigners continued well beyond the Stalin era and had certain liabilities. The death of the lone Punjabi announcer in 1943, for example, meant Radio Moscow stopped its Punjabi service. Recruiting politically suitable professionals from India and other developing countries was no simple task; the Punjabi service did not

---

[7] Mikkonen, "To control," 247.
[8] Stephen Lovell, *Russia in the Microphone Age* (Oxford, 2015); T. A. Sherel', *Audiokul'tura XX veka: istoriia, esteticheskie zakonomernosti, osobennosti vliianiia na auditoriiu* (Moscow, 2004).

resume until 1966.⁹ But in other respects, the model of "surrogate" broadcasting had major advantages. The idea behind surrogate broadcasting (Radio Free Europe/Radio Liberty is the exemplar) was to provide a national alternative to audiences living under repressive regimes and to use the airwaves to foster a community of like-minded patriots. This was transnational broadcasting as an open-throated rebuke to state broadcasting services; it was, as the Soviets and their allies complained, inherently oppositional. But the space it offered was not foreign, by definition, but national. In the words of George Urban (György Ungár), RFE director in the 1980s, they were "in effect national 'home' services speaking from abroad."[10] In reality, RFE/RL not only employed many foreigners, but was a foreign operation—funded covertly by the US government until 1971, and openly thereafter. Yet even after its funding was exposed, RFE/RL was able to make a powerful case for its own legitimacy by giving voice to nationals.

In 1957, staff from Radio Moscow's German editorial group wrote directly to Soviet Premier Khrushchev about the surrogate radio model, citing the widespread influence of RFE in Hungary's "counterrevolution" the year before:

> The formal independence of Free Europe from any kind of state power provides it with unlimited discretion and gives it the air of being objective and impartial. Our radio is at a disadvantage in this respect... Moscow radio, being a state-run radio station, does not meddle in the internal affairs of other countries in conducting its propaganda. This deprives us of many opportunities to influence the formation of public opinion in those countries...

Their proposal was to develop a new, formally independent station along the lines of RFE, based in the USSR and in the people's democracies. "When living with wolves, howl like a wolf," they argued.[11]

The German desk's proposal came at a time of not only galloping growth in the Soviet broadcasting system, but also turmoil; radio and television alike weathered an onslaught of critiques for incompetence in the 1950s and 1960s. The problems were extensive and, in many cases, intractable, as the Soviet broadcasting system struggled to marry political demands to popular taste and to meet the challenges of competition in an age of intensifying media globalization.[12] Radio Moscow was repeatedly criticized

---

[9] N. Smetanin, "Radioveschaniia na Indiiu," Gosudarstvennyi arkhiv Rossiiskoi Federatsii (hereafter, GARF f. 6903), op. 3, d. 119a, l. 153. See also L. Belkina and V. Karelina, "Iz istorii sovetskogo inoveshchaniia (ch.2)," Biulleten' inoveshchaniia 6 (1979) in GARF f. 6903, op. 46, d. 53; l. 13; Morten Jentoft, Gud dag! Govorit Moskva! Radio Kominterna, sovetskaia propaganda i norvezhtsy (Moscow, 2013).

[10] George Urban, Radio Free Europe and the Pursuit of Democracy: My War within the Cold War (New Haven, CT, 1997), x.

[11] "Letter to Khrushchev from Radio Moscow Service Urging Creation of Warsaw Pact Station," January 17, 1957, History and Public Policy Program Digital Archive, Archives of the Central Committee of the Communist Party of the Soviet Union. Obtained by Michael Nelson. Translated by Volodymyr Valkov. https://digitalarchive.wilsoncenter.org/document/121544. NB: Translation slightly modified.

[12] Kristin Roth-Ey, Moscow Prime Time: How the Soviet Union Built the Media Empire that Lost the Cultural Cold War (Ithaca, NY, and London, 2011); GARF f. 6903, op. 1, d. 734, ll. 4–5; GARF f. 6903, op. 1, d. 773, ll. 1–17.

in party decrees for its lack of responsiveness, both to listeners' specific needs as they varied by country and to events as they developed in real time. Report from "friends" (foreign communist party leaders) were not reassuring. The general secretary of the Syrian party forwarded a twelve-page dissection of Radio Moscow's faults directly to the Central Committee in 1962.[13] American communists on a friendly visit the year before had commented that Radio Moscow's commentaries were "a little hard on the ear." "It wouldn't be a bad idea to back up your heavy artillery with humor sometimes" to appeal to the American audience, they suggested.[14]

In 1964, the Soviets launched a new station, Radio Peace and Progress, that in some respects patterned itself on the "surrogate" model. With the tagline "the voice of Soviet public opinion," the new station was an arm of the Soviet Peace Committee, the Soviet Women's Committee, the Journalists' Union, and other so-called public organizations and thus officially independent of the state. Factually, Radio Peace and Progress was a division of Gosteleradio using Radio Moscow equipment and supervised (like the public organizations themselves) directly by the Central Committee. With its official non-governmental status, Peace and Progress was seen as capable of being more dynamic and hard-hitting, and there were calls for it to be expanded. Gosteleradio head Nikolai Mesiatsev, identifying responsiveness as the Achilles' heel of Soviet media, argued forcefully for authorizing journalists to comment on news events in real time, rather than waiting for official approval—"in the name of Soviet public organizations"— and cited Radio Peace and Progress publicly in 1966 as the model to develop further.

Radio Moscow remained the jewel in the crown, and like the BBC, the VOA, and many other state-run transnational broadcasters in the Cold War, it was "national radio on a large, imperializing scale."[15] But as the voice of the world's first socialist state, it was also the embodiment of a new culture—socialist culture—and socialist culture designated the people as "not only the creators of all of cultural values, but also their masters."[16] As such, Radio Moscow offered a solid ideological workaround to the question of voice, or who speaks to, and for, whom. The fact that, in the USSR, the means of cultural production were in the hands of the working class guaranteed that all Soviet media, transnational or national, spoke in the people's interest. When Radio Moscow launched its first broadcast in October 1929, the text was in German (and, later that year, French and Spanish), but its message went out "to the workers of the world": the transnational media space it created was itself a perfect embodiment of the dream of internationalism, the borderless, global communion of labor. When four decades later, Radio Moscow spoke Swahili, Vietnamese, Arabic, and sixty-plus other languages, the circle widened in practical terms, but the people's interest remained indivisible, the identification of Soviet national and socialist international, complete.[17] Or, to quote a 1964 Soviet textbook on international relations, "The only true internationalist is he who supports the USSR."[18]

[13] RGANI f. 5, op. 33, d. 206, ll. 63–75.
[14] GARF f. 6903, op. 2, d. 294, ll. 11–14.
[15] Hilmes, "Foreword."
[16] M. E. Airapetian and V.V. Sukhodeev, *Novyi tip mezhdunarodnykh otnoshenii* (Moscow, 1964), 208.
[17] GARF f. 6903, op. 3, d. 579, ll. 1–7.
[18] Airapetian and Sukhodeev, *Novyi tip mezhdunarodnykh otnoshenii*, 73.

The question of voice, however, remained vexed all the same. On the one hand, Radio Moscow's very identity was defined by its mission to project the USSR. On the other, Moscow, as champion of Third World national liberation struggles, prided itself on giving voice to the voiceless, the silenced and oppressed. Tension between these two poles was inescapable. "Only socialism makes the press serve all the people," Khrushchev lectured Third World journalists gathered in Moscow in 1963; it was necessary to seize the means of cultural production.[19] But who best, then, to speak for socialism in the new nations of the Third World? Whose space was the airwaves?

Speaking to and Speaking For

Like all Soviet institutions, Radio Moscow structured its relations with the non-Soviet world in geopolitical, hierarchical terms. The largest editorial groups at Radio Moscow were always those broadcasting to the Soviet Union's Cold War rivals and to friendly socialist countries in East–Central Europe. We might chalk this up to the predominance of English worldwide and to far greater numbers of speakers of European languages in the USSR than, say, Gujarati. But the dominating position of the West was always more than purely pragmatic in nature. The US had, as the Soviets periodically complained (and blamed on American government manipulation), a tiny short-wave radio listening audience, and yet investment in the American operation never wavered.

In more subtle ways, too, Radio Moscow's institutional life revealed its vision of the world. When administrators wrote up reports on their global operations, they not only divided the world into zones—"socialist," "capitalist," and "developing"—but also presented their findings unfailingly in that order. This was also the routine order for all meeting agendas. Memoirs and other first-person sources make it plain that the most prestigious postings for the press and the diplomatic corps were in the West.[20] The geopolitical ranking was clear, and people knew where they stood.[21]

In this sense, to say that the developing world was ever the apple of Radio Moscow's eye is a distortion. Soviet broadcasting to the Third World never matched that of its broadcasting to the West in sheer volume; nor, for the most part, did it match the level of its Cold War rivals. In Radio Moscow's operations, what was more striking and more telling in many ways than either the size of the staff or the number of broadcasting hours was the number of languages it spoke.

Moscow, more than any other transnational broadcaster, committed itself to speaking in the listener's native tongue. The policy was far more than practical; in fact, in some cases, where linguistic expertise was short on the ground, and when many

---

[19] "Comrade N.S. Khrushchev's Talk on Oct. 25, 1963 with Participants in the Third World Meeting of Journalists," *Current Digest of the Post-Soviet Press* 15.43 (1963): 14–20.
[20] See, for example, comments on radio as a "second-rank" placement for graduates in Boris Chekhonin, *Zhurnalistika i razvedka* (Moscow, 2002), 25.
[21] On the intersection of geopolitical and cultural hierarchies, see Rossen Djagalov, *From Internationalism to Postcolonialism* (Montreal, 2019); Eleonory Gilburd, *To See Paris and Die: The Soviet Lives of Western Culture* (Princeton, 2018).

potential listeners were functional in a major Western language like French, it was highly impractical and inefficient. In the Khrushchev era, the files of the broadcasting administration, like those of many other institutions, are peppered with directives to train more language specialists. Only 5% of Radio Moscow employees were members of foreign communist parties in 1961.[22] One Norwegian representative of that group, Morten Jentoft, sent by the Norwegian Communist Party in the 1950s, noted a marked change from the late 1950s on, as new language specialists came to outnumber the old timers. He also detected a demotion of Norwegian in Radio Moscow's attention and a growing emphasis on the new nations and languages of the Third World.[23]

How should we understand the huge premium placed on native tongues, if not native voices? Many of the young people who came to work at Radio Moscow (and other foreign-facing institutions) trained in an area studies framework, and not all of them graduated with strong language skills. One journalist, who later went on to work at Radio Moscow, recalled in a 2016 interview how mightily he had struggled to understand his hosts on his first post abroad—in his case, as a translator in Cuba; he, like many in his cohort, had little exposure to the living language and saw himself as a regional or national specialist first.[24] We might imagine that with experts like this, Radio Moscow was finely tuned and highly differentiated in its approach—one message or genre for West Africa and something very different for, say, Egypt or Finland. This was the image conveyed in the Cold War press in the US, which fretted paternalistically at times about populations in the Third World lacking the sophistication to resist communist broadcasting masterminds. It was also the image Radio Moscow promoted about itself, both internally to radio staffers and externally to domestic and international publics. But the reality of day-to-day broadcasting was rather more routine.

Radio Moscow did sometimes adapt its approach to target audiences, as scholars have demonstrated in relation to specific events, such as the Suez Crisis and the Chilean coup, as well as to more open-ended campaigns.[25] We also have some evidence that editorial groups in Moscow could be responsive to signals from Soviet embassies.[26] Personalities could come into play. The long-term employment of specific announcers, who sometimes enjoyed, relative to domestic Soviet broadcasting, greater latitude to develop their own on-air personas, had an impact on the tone of different editorial groups' broadcasts. Yet while Radio Moscow did allow some scope for variation, it was also well known among media professionals as "the tomb of the unknown journalist." The sobriquet had a twofold meaning. Not only were RM staff unknown to listeners

[22] GARF f. 6903, op. 675, d. 53, also cited in Mikkonen, "To control," 256.
[23] Jentoft, *Gud dag! Govorit Moskva!*, 210–12.
[24] Oral history interview with S., Moscow, March 2016.
[25] Margaret Peacock, "Selling Socialism in Suez: Soviet Radio Broadcasting to the MENA during the Suez Crisis," paper presented at Socialist World, "Third World," Media Worlds conference, University College London, November 2018; Rosalind Bresnahan, "Radio and the Democratic Movement in Chile 1973–1990: Independent and Grass Roots Voices during the Pinochet Dictatorship," *Journal of Radio Studies* 9.1 (2002): 161–81; Peter J. Schmelz, "Alfred Schnittke's Nagasaki: Soviet Nuclear Culture, Radio Moscow, and the Global Cold War," *Journal of the American Musicological Society* 62.2 (2009): 412–74; Margaret Peacock, "Broadcasting Benevolence: Images of the Child in American, Soviet, and NLF Propaganda in Vietnam, 1969–1973," *Journal of the History of Childhood and Youth* 3.1 (2010): 15–38.
[26] Lada Silina, *Vneshnepoliticheskaia propaganda v SSSR v 1945–1985 gg.* (Moscow, 2011), 99.

within the USSR and little known outside it (given the tiny audience size), but much of the work they did was not, to their journalists' eyes, journalistic.[27]

The great bulk of Radio Moscow programing was produced and standardized centrally (it "simply 'came down' from the top" said the Norwegian Jentoft): central editorial groups wrote texts in Russian in set categories, and editorial groups for the different regions translated and recorded them for broadcast. Renata Lesnik, who worked on the Hungarian desk in the 1970s, recalled that she and her colleagues referred to the boxes where they collected these texts as "the feeding trough."[28] According to Radio Moscow's in-house journal, the *Foreign Broadcasting Bulletin*, the role of materials from these central sources increased as of the mid-1960s in response to "increased anti-Soviet imperialist propaganda."[29] For a sense of the themes, we can look to the collection of texts published in the *Bulletin* in 1971: "The leading role of the communist party," "Why does the USSR have one political party?," "Who can become a member of the communist party (CPSU)?"[30] Reports from foreign correspondents were rare, as were interviews and unscripted "talk show" format broadcasts. Looking at the schedules for any given day across the world, a large share is identical. I will return to this theme below, but for now, I want to query again the commitment to native languages. Given the limited resources, why bother?

The fact that the territory of the Soviet Union was itself famously polyglot and had a complex history of language politics is important here. Soviet nationality policy fused linguistic and political identity. Language was understood to be the bedrock of all national cultures, and in Soviet modernization theory, cultural development, grounded in native language, was a critical component of overall economic and political development.[31] In the everyday life of the USSR, all sorts of institutions and attitudes worked to promote Russian-language dominance. But the equation "language–culture–state" remained valid and potent. Language was always about much more than communication; it was about culture, and culture was about mastery (the people as culture's masters) and respect. The identification was mapped out very clearly in international relations textbooks, which cautioned budding diplomats that the language chosen for negotiations held "great political significance." The fact that Bengali had been designated the working language in Bangladesh's negotiations with the USSR, a first "for a young state, fighting for its to international recognition... attracted

---

[27] Vladimir Pozner, *Proshchanie s illuziami* (Moscow, 2015), 236; Arkady Ostrovsky, *The Invention of Russia: The Journey from Gorbachev's Freedom to Putin's War* (London, 2015), 183. Paradoxically, many of the journalists who went on to leading roles in the glasnost' era and early 1990s (particularly in television) began at Radio Moscow. The key factor was not broadcast work itself, but the access it afforded to the extra-Soviet world: to foreign publications and broadcasts and to individuals, including guest speakers in the studio and listener-correspondents. M. Maiofis and I. Kukulin, "Svoboda kak neosoznannyi pretsedent: zametki o transformatsii mediinogo polia v 1990 godu," *Novoe literaturnoe obozrenie* 83 (2007): 599–656.
[28] Renta Lesnik, *Ici Moscou* (Paris, 1982), 90.
[29] Jentoft, *Gud dag! Govorit Moskva!*, 200; Belkina and Karelina, "Iz istorii sovetskogo inoveshchaniia," 28.
[30] *Problemy inoveshchaniia* 1 (1971).
[31] Yuri Slezkine, "The USSR as a Communal Apartment, or How a Socialist State Promoted Ethnic Particularism," *Slavic Review* 53.2 (1994): 414–52.

huge attention throughout the world and especially inside the country itself," one text explained.³²

It is to this kind of language politics that we must look to understand the structures and mores of Radio Moscow. Broadcasting was coded as enlightenment (the electrification of the mind), and enlightenment, or cultural development, was best realized in native tongues. Broadcasting was also, in the transnational context, a kind of disembodied mobile embassy where respect for the culture of the host country was crucial. Respect was best concretized in language. It is a point Frederick Barghoorn, a canny contemporary scholar (and former press attaché in the US embassy in Moscow), made as far back as the 1950s. "Soviets leaders ...," he wrote, "have demonstrated considerable sensitivity to the self-image of almost every kind of national and cultural group. They seem to realize more clearly than Americans or even Western Europeans that one of the most effective ways of flattering an individual is to express appreciation of his national language, literature, and art."³³ Finally, size, or scale, mattered—a point noted by historians of Soviet science and technology, but no less valid, in its own way, in communications and culture. Polyglot Radio Moscow embodied Soviet "gigantomania," or fascination with large-scale, standardized projects.³⁴ The sheer number of broadcasting languages was indexed to the Soviet Union's might on the world stage.

What this meant in practice was that the space of Radio Moscow production was an extraordinary combination of diversity and sameness, cosmopolitanism and monoculturalism. Radio Moscow pursued its audience primarily through language; its linguistic diversity went unmatched and cannot be dismissed. This was the giving of voice, of a kind—the airwaves as a space of linguistic and cultural assertion for populations around the world. Yet Radio Moscow also created a space of great sameness and uniformity, a worldwide monoculture of socialist internationalism. It would be a mistake, however, to conclude that this monoculture was generated automatically, or carelessly, with no thought for the audience. On the contrary, its standardized form was very much calibrated to an abstract, imagined audience.

Exhortations to know the audience and tailor production to the audience were a constant feature in the broadcasting world.³⁵ Broadcasters worked according to plans: take the "Plan to propagandize the decisions of the CPSU September 1965 Plenum" for example. Each of the editorial groups produced a list of programs they planned to produce in conjunction with the plenum—titles and short descriptions—which they then presented to the central radio administration, which presented them to the relevant CPSU department for approval. The plan specified that broadcasts would be "differentiated" into three groups: socialist world, capitalist world, developing world, with the following emphases: broadcasts to socialist countries were to stress the Soviet Union's role in building the material-technical base for communism in the interests of

---

[32] N. N. Firiubin, *Nekotorye voprosy teorii i praktiki diplomaticheskikh peregovorov: uchebnyi material po kursu 'Sov. diplomat. Sluzhba'* (Moscow, 1973), 44.
[33] Frederick Barghoorn, *The Soviet Cultural Offensive* (Princeton, 1960), 20.
[34] Paul Josephson, "'Projects of the Century' in Soviet History: Large-Scale Technologies from Lenin to Gorbachev," *Technology and Culture* 36.3 (1995): 519–59.
[35] RGANI f. 5, op. 33, d. 206, ll. 62–75; RGANI f. 5, op. 33, d. 177, ll. 62–6.

the whole socialist camp; developing countries would hear most of all about the superiority of socialism over capitalism for economic development, and about how the economic development of USSR was in their interests; and broadcasts to the capitalist world would unmask the lie that the Soviet system was moving toward convergence with capitalism.[36] The radio administration discussed these plans at the highest level: Mesiatsev generally approved them, though he worried that they were overly defensive where they should be offensive ("we need to attack and attack, beat, hit") and too far removed from the necessary "historical" approach. What they needed to do, he said, was "demonstrate more widely and more fully to every country, using historical examples from our country, the experience of our country, the experience of building socialism over every year of the existence of the Soviet state."[37] Differentiation was a matter of emphasis or shading, and though it is not uninteresting (more on this below), the fundamental message was the same. It was targeted to the audience, but not about the audience; it was about "the experience of our country"; it was about the USSR.

What else would it have been about? we might ask. (The BBC External Service's mandate was, for a time, "the projection of Britain." The Voice of America was the voice of America.) But we might also remind ourselves of the visionary connection in Soviet history between radio and enlightenment, and between radio and empowerment (giving voice to the voiceless), and, indeed, of the rediscovery of the Third World in the 1950s and all those trained-up area specialists sitting at their desks. We can reclaim our ability to imagine options. The surrogate radio model was one; mass education and mass entertainment were others. Radio Moscow broadcasting to Africa did have the choice to broadcast about Africa, to Latin America about Latin America, or to both about each other, and so on.

Instead, the pattern of coverage of Third World news broadcast on Radio Moscow showed a strong kinship with that of the VOA and other Western broadcasters: when an African, Asia, or Latin American country was discussed, it was in the context of the relationship to the broadcasting nation (what the US, USSR, etc. is doing in X country), of problems (crises, natural catastrophes, etc.), or of East–West conflict.[38] Algeria was unlikely to hear about Indonesia and vice-versa (barring crises), and Algeria and Indonesia heard very little about themselves unrelated to the Soviet world. The Cold War context and the identity and activity of the broadcasting nation, in other words, thematically overrode all other considerations. The Third World nation itself was instrumentalized. The space of the airwaves was not its own.

In the 1970s, it was precisely these issues that gave rise to accusations of Western media imperialism from the Third World nations and calls for a New World Information and Communication Order (NWICO) under the auspices of UNESCO. Here, the Soviet Union joined a coalition of African, Asian, and Latin American states to demand a more equitable distribution of media resources worldwide, meaning not only technical resources, such as radio frequencies and satellite access, but also the resources

---

[36] GARF f. 6903, op. 1, d. 865, ll. 61–2.
[37] GARF f. 6903, op. 1, d. 865, l. 12.
[38] Philo C. Washburn, "Voice of America and Radio Moscow Newscasts to the Third World," *Journal of Broadcasting and Electronic Media* 32.2 (1988): 197–218.

of voice and space. The argument was that the domination of global media by Western corporate and state interests inevitably led to the exclusion and distortion of Third World stories. African, Asian, and Latin American nations had the right to occupy transnational media space on their own terms—to tell their own stories, in their own voices.

On the level of state policy, the USSR and its allies in Eastern Europe were vigorous proponents of the NWICO. The Soviet Union's own transnational broadcasting never embodied its model, nonetheless, and what it did embody was no less universalizing (and, arguably imperialistic) than its Western competitor: the polyglot, monoculture of socialist internationalism. The point was not lost on many policymakers in the Third World who, though making common cause with the Soviet bloc in the NWICO struggle, sought to limit bloc culture in their own countries as much as, and sometimes more than, Anglo-American. Support for stiffer regulation of transnational media flows, in other words, suited different parties for very different reasons. Ironically, Soviet-sponsored initiatives (for example, to restrict direct satellite broadcasting) were embraced by many Third World leaders as protection against Soviet broadcasting.[39]

Radio Moscow Knows its Audience: The Worldwide Surveys

For an enterprise that involved so many thousands of hours of labor, that so preoccupied political authorities and publics, it is remarkable how little is left of Soviet transnational radio broadcasting and, in particular, broadcasting to the developing world. True enough, the archives in Moscow are crammed with the authorized scripts, and thanks to Cold War-era American and British monitoring services, we have an enormous stock of transcribed broadcasts worldwide as well.[40] Determining what was said to whom and when, while not always easy, is not the problem. But radio is more than texts: radio is producing and consuming—both activities embedded in social contexts and also themselves social (or para-social) interactions. At least as important as knowing what was said is how it was said and how it was heard. Scholars have postulated that the nature of shortwave broadcasting technology conditions the kind of space it creates for listeners: because listening very often involves searching for frequencies and coping with interference, the shortwave listener must be more committed and, by extension, emotionally invested.[41]

Simo Mikkonen, a pioneer in the history of Soviet foreign broadcasting, concludes that this important realm of Cold War-era sociability must remain elusive: "any

---

[39] Ithiel de Sola Pool, "Direct-broadcast satellites and cultural integrity," *Society* 35.2 (1998): 140–51; Mark Alleyne, *International Power and International Communication* (London, 1995); Kaarle Nordenstreng, *The Mass Media Declaration of Unesco* (Norwood, NJ, 1984).
[40] Alban Webb, *London Calling: Britain, the BBC World Service and the Cold War* (London, 2014), 81–8. See also the AHRC-funded project "Listening to the World: BBC Monitoring," https://www.iwm.org.uk/research/research-projects/listening-to-the-world-bbc-monitoring-collection-ahrc-research-network..
[41] Alasdair Pinkerton and Klaus Dodds, "Radio Geopolitics: Broadcasting, Listening and the Struggle for Acoustic spaces," *Progress in Human Geography* 33.1 (2009): 20.

far-reaching conclusions about the audience are impossible to make."⁴² He is in good company, given the notorious difficulty of reception studies. Even media ethnographers—people who watch other people watch TV, for example—struggle to come to analytical terms with their observations. They are aware that the questions they ask have everything to do with the audience they "get"; or to put it another way, the audience they can imagine is the audience they find, and not necessarily the audience in a global sense.⁴³ This problem of imagination touches broadcasters, too, and it is evident in Radio Moscow's audience research program. Each of the five worldwide surveys, conducted between 1967 and 1982, show Moscow's broadcasters seeking, finding, and attempting to build relationships with an audience. The data they collected are, as we shall see, overwhelmingly subjective, with a great deal to say of about how Radio Moscow saw itself and the world. Yet for all their subjectivity, they can also help us reconstruct something of a portrait of listenership for Radio Moscow and further our understanding of the airwaves as an interactive social and political space.

Throughout the Cold War, Western broadcasters sometimes went to extraordinary lengths to find out about listeners in the Soviet bloc, while research on audiences in other parts of the world was both more straightforward and systematic.⁴⁴ The BBC, VOA, and other Western broadcasters regularly commissioned market and opinion research firms to conduct listener studies across the globe. A 1988 article by the former Head of International Broadcasting and Audience Research at the BBC summarizing these findings gives a sense of the overall dimensions for the Third World. In Nigeria in 1983, for example, the BBC-compiled data showed regular audiences (as a percentage of the adult population) ranging from 12.9 for the BBC to 1.9 for Eternal Love Winning Africa, an American-funded evangelical Christian service, with Radio Moscow at 2.4. Audience shares did bulge in some regions: in parts of Asia for the BBC, for instance (one-third of Bangladeshi adults for the BBC Bengali service, 1983), or in Dakar, Senegal for Radio France International in French (nearly 40% in 1987). But across the board, region by region, the tables are dotted with single-digit and fractional percentages for all transnational broadcasters. Radio Moscow did not pass the single-digit barrier for a regular listening audience in any region.⁴⁵

In the Soviet Union, sociological research of the type used to produce the BBC's statistics had a checkered history. The time-honored tradition in Soviet media was to rely on written correspondence to assess the audience—in effect, to equate mailbag and audience.⁴⁶ "No matter what its contents and who wrote it, the very fact that it was sent

---

⁴² Mikkonen, "To control," 246.
⁴³ Ien Ang, *Desperately Seeking the Audience* (London, 2006); Jérôme Bourdon, "Detextualizing: How to Write a History of Audiences," *European Journal of Communication* 30.1 (2015): 7–21.
⁴⁴ R. Eugene Parta, *Discovering the Hidden Listener: An Assessment of Radio Liberty and Western Broadcasting to the USSR during the Cold War* (Stanford, CA, 2007); Alban Webb, "A Leap of Imagination: BBC Audience Research over the Iron Curtain," *Participations* 8.1 (2011): 154–72; Webb, *London Calling*, 186–7.
⁴⁵ Graham Mytton, "Audiences for International Broadcasts," *European Journal of Communication* 3 (1988): 471–3.
⁴⁶ Roth-Ey, *Moscow Prime Time*, 268–71; Simon Huxtable, "In Search of the Soviet Reader: The Kosygin Reforms, Sociology, and Changing Concepts of Soviet Society, 1964–1970," *Cahiers du monde russe* 54.3–4 (2013): 623–42; Christine Evans, *Between Truth and Time: A History of Soviet Central Television* (New Haven, CT, 2016), 47–81.

to us can be considered as proof of the effectiveness of our broadcasts," declared Radio Moscow's in-house journal.[47] Like all Soviet media operations, international radio received a huge amount of mail (upwards of 100,000 letters a year in the 1960s and over 200,000 in 1975)[48] and devoted considerable resources to it; letters were translated into Russian, read, and categorized by theme, discussed and used in program planning; every letter earned a reply, at least in theory (practice evidently sometimes lagged), and many letters also triggered souvenir gifts. Editorial groups organized contests to stimulate correspondence, such as "What do you know about the USSR?," a quiz put on by the Latin American desk in 1956 and answered by 140 listeners, each of whom got a small prize, such as a set of postcards or a book.[49] In 1973 alone, Radio Moscow sent out 290,000 letters and packages.[50] Editorial groups were judged by the volume of their correspondence and, to a lesser extent, by how prompt was their response.

The great Radio Moscow worldwide survey program represented a singular mode of research: a hybrid of the Soviets' letter fixation and the sociological survey model. In scope and complexity, it was a remarkable operation. The first of the five worldwide surveys, in 1966–7, entailed distributing 73,000 questionnaire forms (one to two pages) printed in thirty-nine languages. Subsequent studies, in 1970, 1974, 1980, and 1982, were larger still: 89,000 questionnaires in forty languages for the 1974 study, an astonishing 137,000 in forty-six languages in 1980. Completed surveys were returned to Moscow to be tabulated, translated into Russian (the open-ended questions, typically two of fifteen), and analyzed. As in any survey research, distribution numbers dwarfed returns, but even at the overall rate for the 1974 survey, 23%, this still meant over 20,000 items to be processed. As of 1974 the records mention using a proto-computer (punch card) system located at the USSR Council of Ministers. But even this brave new world of automation still meant sifting through mountains of correspondence by hand.

Thinking about Radio Moscow's research program, we need to visualize those mountains of handwritten letters and survey forms and imagine the individuals with the linguistic abilities to process them—the rare Gujarati speakers of Moscow, the Swahili, the Japanese. How often would these people have had contact with native speakers or seen the native language penned? Piece by piece, they translated faraway voices into Russian, coded them for use on the proto-computer system, then counted them, sorted them, and studied them. The reports they produced bristled with impressive-looking statistics, with percentages calculated to the decimal point. (I have rounded them up here.) But the research process itself was intimate and laborious, and in fact, the hard work of knowing the audience had begun long before and fed into the research design.

Radio Moscow's distinctive research method was to survey only known or presumed listeners; it eschewed sampling and other techniques. The title of the first survey— "How Do You Listen to Radio Moscow?"—is indicative of its approach. Known listeners

---

[47] E. Ushakov, "K nam prishlo pis'mo," *Biulleten' inoveshchaniia*, in GARF f. 6903, op. 46, d. 6, l. 36.
[48] *Obzor pisem zarubezhnykh slushatelei Moskovskogo radio poluchennykh v 1973 godu* (Moscow, 1974); GARF f. 6903, op. 3, d. 140, l. 3.
[49] V. Andrianov, "Radioveshchanie na strany Latinskoi Ameriki," in GARF f. 6903, op. 3, d. 119a, l. 233.
[50] *Obzor pisem zarubezhnykh slushatelei*, 3.

were people who had corresponded with them in the past and were logged, by hand, in its extensive card catalog system; in theory, every single person who had ever written in—to ask a question, make a suggestion, participate in a quiz—would receive a survey form. Presumed listeners were members of friendship societies and other communist-party affiliated groups, local Friends of Radio Moscow clubs, and Russian-language students.

The approach was a pragmatic one, no doubt—a palliative for genuine headaches with survey distribution, particularly in the developing world. But much more than that, I think, it was also a principled stance, motivated by ideas of self and other. When Radio Moscow staff discussed research results in their in-house journal, for example, they consistently (and at least in print, unreflexively) substituted the set of the letter writers and survey respondents for the audience as a whole. The individuals in their address books were not seen as a self-selected group; they were their listeners. And the task at hand was not so much to respond to their opinions, but rather to know their opinions in order to assess to what extent they were "prepared for the reception of our programs."[51] In other words, although Radio Moscow was working through broadcasting's innate blindness no less than the BBC or any other international broadcaster, its research method obviated the problem and made the imagined listener real, tangible, and visible. My point is not that Moscow's broadcasters were wrong about their audience. (We do not know.) My point is that they did not see the problem of their own imaginations in their research; the audience they "got" is the one they went to find.

Who was that audience? Unsurprisingly, listeners appeared divided—first, by historical stage of development (socialist, capitalist, developing), and second, by language. Whereas production was organized geographically, survey results were always grouped in developmental terms for analysis: Colombian alongside Cameroonian, but not Cuban; Vietnamese with Polish and Hungarian, but not Indonesian. Within this framework, the socialist and capitalist worlds had the bigger presence. Listeners from the socialist bloc and the capitalist world dominated both the Radio Moscow mailbag and the survey returns: not only did a larger number of surveys get distributed in those areas, but they also had a higher rate of return. To give one example, of the 30,000 surveys returned for the 1980 study (from a total of 137,000), 14,000 came from the socialist world, 10,000 from the capitalist world, and 4,000 from the developing world.[52]

As viewed through the prism of the surveys and other correspondence, the three worlds' audiences were thought to differ in some basic respects. Capitalist world listeners were most likely to criticize programing and to express political opinions at odds with the Soviet line; developing world listeners were most likely to write about Soviet foreign policy and to express praise and gratitude for Soviet aid and for Radio Moscow itself.[53] Socialist bloc listeners distinguished themselves by addressing Radio Moscow as an

---

[51] Z. Petrova, "Chto daet nam anketnoi opros slushatelei," *Biulleten' inoveshchaniia* (1975): 31, in GARF f. 6903, op. 46, d. 28.
[52] GARF f. 6903, op. 46, d. 54, ll. 41–3.
[53] *Obzor pisem zarubezhnykh slushatelei*, 18.

institution with some familiarity. A good number wrote about themselves and asked for help of some kind—sorting out housing problems, for instance—and offered suggestions for improvement in programming based on their domestic radio services. But both socialist and developing world listeners often expressed themselves using stylized political language—the language of the propaganda pamphlet or, for that matter, the Radio Moscow broadcast. "Today all Somalis understand that they are the builders of their own country's future," read a letter from Somalia in 1975. "It is the Somali Revolution that gave them this power, bringing to their lands the ideas of Great October, of Marxism-Leninism."[54] A listener in Syria wrote to say that "a celebrated event in the life of the Soviet people will take place in the coming year: the 25th Party Congress of the Communist Party of the Soviet Union." He continued, "The peoples of the Arab countries delight in the achievements of the Soviet Union whose flag has been flying over the planet for fifty-eight years already, inspiring people in the struggle for justice."[55]

Although Radio Moscow considered developing-world listeners its most complimentary on the whole, its reports are also full of their suggestions for improvement, usually in response to an open-ended question in the survey. These ranged from general recommendations for things like changes to broadcasting schedules and programing ("More programs for the former Portuguese colonies. Your programs really help us build socialism," wrote a man from Guinea-Bissau;[56] and "unmask the reactionary essence of imperialism, Zionism, and Maoism more actively," suggested a Tanzanian)[57] to the very specific: "You should devote time every day, if only five to ten minutes, to the high principles of V.I. Lenin" (India);[58] "Broadcast more interviews with foreign guests in the USSR ... In part, I would like to hear Africans themselves comment on African events" (Nigeria);[59] or "Introduce a program 'Letter of the day' in which you would name the author of the most interesting letter" (Pakistan).[60]

Listeners often complained about announcers' archaic language and pronunciation; one sent a detailed list of specific sounds (in Bengali in this case) for them to work on; while another offered, "Try to be closer to conversational language. Take the BBC and VOA as an example."[61] Music was another frequent focus: in particular, requests to broadcast less Soviet music, and more music from the listeners' regions. A young man from Israel wrote to say he did not think Radio Moscow paid enough attention to "Arab and Eastern songs. But you are broadcasting for Arabs after all. Your broadcasts should give Arabs the chance to feel that only they are being broadcast to."[62] "Soviet music is probably very good," offered one listener, "but it's not popular in East Africa, so broadcast African music."[63]

---

[54] *Obzor pisem zarubezhnykh slushatelei*, 63.
[55] *Obzor pisem zarubezhnykh slushatelei*, 50.
[56] GARF f. 6903, op. 46, d. 58, l. 100.
[57] GARF f. 6903, op. 46, d. 58, l. 64.
[58] GARF f. 6903, op. 46, d. 58, l. 10.
[59] GARF f. 6903, op. 46, d. 58, l. 77.
[60] GARF f. 6903, op. 46, d. 58, l. 36.
[61] GARF f. 6903, op. 46, d. 58, l. 39; ll. 21–2.
[62] GARF f. 6903, op. 46, d. 58, l.114.
[63] GARF f. 6903, op. 46, d. 58, l. 67.

Towards an (not the) Audience

Radio Moscow's audience materials present a seductive combination of precise math ("47.6%") and first-person expression. But they are not scientific studies, and interpreting them presents challenges on multiple levels. To begin, we should be clear that what we have are not the surveys and letters themselves, which were not archived, but rather excerpts chosen by Radio Moscow staff: selected quotes from a self-selected group—a subset of a subset. We know that citizens of socialist countries, at least, did approach their domestic media in similar ways: to ask for advice and assistance and to signal political allegiances. But what are we to make of listeners from Asia, Africa, Latin America, and the Middle East writing to Moscow to praise Brezhnev, laud the heroism of the Soviet people in the fight against fascism, and ask for more of what was, after all, the very bread-and-butter of the broadcasting schedule (Lenin, Soviet foreign policy, etc.)?

One point to consider is the process that went into preparing the audience materials we have; it goes without saying that the selection of quotes from surveys and letters was tendentious, and we cannot be sure about what did not make the cut. Renata Lesnik, whose very first task as a new hire on the Hungarian desk was to prepare the program "We Respond to Our Listeners," recalled that when she wanted to answer a lengthy letter accusing the USSR of inflaming tensions in the Third World, a colleague told her it was clearly from one of their "crazy" correspondents (they kept a list) and she must ignore it. "We don't argue with crazy people." She was counseled told to look for letters from "our faithful friends, like Malych, from the Koposzvar [sic] Meat Factory" who "wrote about interesting topics and exactly as needed."[64]

In some cases, the comments from Third World respondents are so polished as to read like one of Radio Moscow's own broadcasts; in others, they read like a rehearsal for something, as if the person writing were practicing a language, flexing his muscles. Some correspondents did mention that they relied on Radio Moscow for their work in political agitation.[65] Lesnik noted, too, that many of the letters she saw had been written by students as a class assignment. It is also worth thinking about how actively Moscow encouraged people to write, distributing souvenirs and making it clear that everyone stood a chance of having their letters read on air; they also ran regular lotteries with prizes to stimulate survey returns. Some listener input shows a keen awareness of these incentives. "I think it is essential for you to improve your work with listener letters: your answers often arrive with great delay. I advise you to send listeners photos of RM staff and souvenirs, as do the BBC and Deutsche Welle, for example," wrote a Nigerian student.[66] Other correspondents bring in elements of playfulness and friendly flattery. "I get a great deal of pleasure from your broadcasts," wrote one Indian peasant listener. "You write that you will send listeners a present for participating in this survey. I think that we are the ones who should send you presents for your work."[67] There are notes of

---

[64] Lesnik, *Ici Moscou*, 143, 139.
[65] GARF f. 6903, op. 46, d. 58, l. 31.
[66] GARF f. 6903, op. 46, d. 58, l. 74.
[67] GARF f. 6903, op. 46, d. 58, l. 7.

formality and informality, of artificiality and of what comes across on the page at times as heady political exuberance.

Interpreting this global chorus of voices effectively would mean somehow getting to grips with what the basic act of writing and listening to Moscow—and listening to radio, full stop—meant in vastly different contexts. Anthropologist Debra Spitulnik dissects this point powerfully in her work on radio in Zambia:

> We need to remain aware that the individual interpretive moment of decoding a media message may not be the only—or, indeed, the most significant—aspect of what a particular media form "means" in a given sociocultural context ... the impact of a media technology changes with both its context and the activities [e.g. cooking, cleaning, driving, socializing] that accompany it. This forcefully suggests how media create social spaces but simultaneously merge with them.[68]

How Radio Moscow broadcasts merged with social spaces across the world depended on a wide range of factors, as identified by media scholars in other contexts: the nature of the technology used (portable or fixed radio sets); ownership practices and the status of radio listening in a given social context (who controlled the set?); the quality of the signal; and whether listening demanded close attention or allowed people to continue other activities, such as housework, at the same time (a key factor in the gendered use of media worldwide, researchers have found); the legality or illegality of listening—to name but a few. Spitulnik herself found that in Zambia at the time of her research, the late 1980s, the radio experience was shaped predominantly by the mobility of the technology in use (transistor) and the ways that radio listening interacted with local kinship patterns and status relations. The ownership of the radio space was not only a metaphorical question, but a literal one with real-life consequences for how people were able to listen and interact with the information broadcast.[69]

There are some hints in the surveys and letters about listening practices around the world. The issue was one that interested Radio Moscow, which held strong opinions about what constituted good listening. The ideal or "active listener" was one who listened in a group, rather than alone; who listened regularly (preferably daily and over a long period of time, not sporadically); who listened to specific programs, as opposed to tuning in haphazardly; and finally, one who was in contact with Moscow.[70] Surveys were in fact partly a "listener activation" technique (Radio Moscow's term), a method for getting people involved; several of the questions addressed these points directly (e.g. "How often do you listen to RM? Daily/2–3x per week/a few times per month/ once per month or less"), and so Radio Moscow had some data at its disposal to say that listeners in certain regions were more likely to tune in as groups than as individuals, or that people in one of the three "worlds" tuned in less frequently than another.

---

[68] Debra Spitulnik, "Documenting Radio Culture as Lived Experience: Reception Studies and the Mobile Machine in Zambia," in Richard Fardon and Graham Furniss (eds.), *African Broadcast Cultures: Radio in Transition* (Oxford, 2000), 145.
[69] Spitulnik, "Documenting Radio Culture," 157.
[70] GARF f. 6903, op. 46, d. 54, ll. 17–18.

Considering these hints, we need to keep in mind the specificity of the survey, its self-selectivity, along with the very selective nature of the data Radio Moscow generated about it. It makes no sense based on this data to speak of the "Third World audience" for Radio Moscow, or the African one, or even, say, the Ethiopian.

Yet even so, Radio Moscow research does tell us about something about someone, about an audience, if not the audience: the people Lesnik's colleague tagged as "faithful friends," the substantial group of people who took the time and expense to write. And from this group, a portrait emerges marked overwhelmingly by two characteristics: youth and male gender. The predominance of young men in the group is mostly consistent worldwide, but particularly striking for the Third World, where in some countries it reached well over 80% of listener-correspondents, a large proportion of them students. The space of Radio Moscow and institutional educational spaces very clearly overlapped, particularly with reference to Russian language teaching. References to studying Russian in the letters and surveys are very common. What is more, the general portrait of the listener as a young man can be shaded in with some details: he was someone interested in politics, above all, eager to learn, pro-Soviet, urban, and inclined to listen often with friends and family. A significant proportion of listeners in Radio Moscow's files were also repeat correspondents: they listened to Moscow and wrote letters to Moscow; they cultivated a relationship. Radio Moscow understood them as the future leaders of their countries, but also elided the distinction between them as a specific group (listeners on the rolls, so to speak), the "developing world audience," and the Third World as a whole.

Transnational radio broadcasting in the Cold War era generated new spaces—though not yet the "infinite vicarious universe" of Daniel Lerner's revelry—for many people across the globe, a genuine fissure in the familiar, unprecedented in scope, that exposed new worlds and opened new options. Political struggle drove radio's great expansion into the "Third World," and Radio Moscow was of course a political enterprise, as were the other great "national radios on an imperializing scale," and many Third World broadcasters, too. But as the Radio Moscow case shows, the airwaves were as important a social space as a political project, and possibly more effective as a social space than anything else.

Year after year, every carefully produced report on Radio Moscow's correspondence contained the same listener critiques: the programming was wooden and generic, "hard on the ears." Yet, paradoxically, people listened and people wrote. Soviet foreign broadcasting was very much a standard product. But a huge portion of its broadcasting practices—contests, gift-gifting and correspondence, reading listener letters on air, calling out listeners' names on air—was oriented toward generating a specific experience of community, a space in the airwaves that reflected an ideal of internationalist intimacy or, in the socialist idiom, "friendship." Think again of those huge stacks of letters and surveys waiting for translation in Moscow, and of the Soviet people who would have done that work. For most of them, their primary travel experience in the region of their expertise was in the lines of those letters. (For many of them, it would be their only experience.) And think of a young male listener writing his third letter to Moscow that year, congratulating the Vietnamese on their victory and Brezhnev on his recent speech, requesting more Lenin lessons or African music, suggesting programs about mechanization in agriculture, the Soviet way of life. Who was he? The written record offers a good deal more certainty about Radio Moscow's imagination than his. Like the broadcasting itself, the written record instrumentalizes the "Third World" subject as a vehicle for political aspiration and personal longing. Yet for all its subjectivity, it also suggests that tens of thousands of people around the globe did find in Radio Moscow a space for themselves: an internationalist intimacy, a social space of respect and belonging.

3

The Great Industrial Project: Concepts of Space—Aswan's Distinctive Production Culture

Elizabeth Bishop

At the time, the granting by Moscow of technical assistance to Egypt's Aswan High Dam construction project was understood to mark a new post-Stalinist turn toward the postcolonial world. Late in 1955, even though the proposal still lacked its final technical specifications, student-journalists at the University of Illinois—more than 8,000 kilometres from Moscow, and 10,000 from Aswan—chose to reprint in their *Daily Illini* an article by Drew Pearson, then the most widely syndicated columnist in the US. Pearson observed that "Premier Bulganin and party boss Khrushchev are being received with wild acclaim in the Middle East." This "wild acclaim" stemmed from the Soviet Union's "earlier offers to build the Aswan dam on the upper Nile for Egypt."[1]

This was a unique political moment best appreciated through a series of concepts serving to define "space." Egypt had just changed its government, while members of the Soviet political hierarchy were in the process of restructuring how the Soviet Union functioned after Stalin's death. At the same time, they were reordering the Union's economic, military, and cultural relationship with nations within what was coming to be referred to as the "Third World," Egypt among them. The Soviet offer of financial and technical assistance for a massive embankment dam across the Nile at Aswan transformed the Stalin-era "socialism in one country" doctrine as a strategy toward global postcolonialism. The name of Soviet Premier Nikita Khrushchev would soon become associated with a new foreign policy, which served to distinguish his authority from that of the Stalinist past, in turn giving rise to novel concepts of "space."

Soviet media announced that their state-led economic development program from before the war would serve as a model for those "new nations" (which was how Egypt—the last to join the League of Nations—was viewed in Moscow) emerging from the break-up of colonial empires. Eventually, foreign aid of this kind would serve to indicate the USSR's recognition and understanding of a country's aspirations. In short, Moscow was willing to help in the development of the capitals of the "new nations." This process unfolded over time, with years passing before Moscow tendered any formal offer. Let us continue where we began, with students at one of the US's largest

---

[1] *Daily Illini*, November 23, 1955.

universities showing their appreciation of the importance of global conflicts for local communities.

Aswan Between Moscow and Washington, DC

A number of recent historical studies shine light on the social and economic context of the High Dam proposal, showing how hydroelectric construction projects emerged as key spaces for Second–Third world relations and Cold War power politics.[2] During the events under discussion, even American student-journalists in Illinois would seem to have understood the politics of the Cold War in terms of space. In 1952, the Egyptian dancer Samia Gamal toured the United States, as featured in a *Life* magazine photo-essay. Some four years later, the *Daily Illini* newspaper again reprinted Drew Pearson, this time hinting to Congresswoman Gracie Pfost that she take inspiration from the tulle and sequins of the dancer's costume, "that she dresses up as an Egyptian and make a speech on the floor of Congress inviting Bulganin and Khrushchev to visit Moscow, Idaho." American students knew Aswan to be located between Moscow and Washington, DC; if the Representative were to don Samia Gamal's dress, the Eisenhower administration might offer Idaho as much money to build a dam in Idaho as Egypt hoped to invest in the High Dam at Aswan.[3]

A brief account of the High Dam project may prove helpful here. Egypt's new Prime Minister Gamal Abdel Nasser (previously a lieutenant-colonel in the army) was determined to modernize his nation's armed forces. Even as Nasser announced a major purchase of weapons from Czechoslovakia, on September 27, 1955, US Secretary of State John Foster Dulles sought to improve relations with Egypt, pledging tens of millions of dollars toward the construction of the High Dam. The following year, Nasser took the decision to seize the Suez Canal Company's assets in Egypt, nationalize them, and put them in the service of the High Dam proposal, prompting the US State Department to announce that financial assistance for the High Dam was "not feasible in present circumstances." The following year, the USSR offered Egypt the equivalent of $1.12 billion at 2% interest. An initial, substantial offer was announced in Arabic, on Radio Moscow's Near Eastern Service, amounting to 400 million roubles (£34.8 million, $220 million at that time) for the first phase of construction of the High Dam. Denominated in roubles, this could be pledged against labor and materials coming from the USSR, not for billable items coming from the US (denominated in dollars), or for items from Great Britain and the Commonwealth (denominated in sterling). In this way, the master plan for the Aswan High Dam was drawn up at the Gidroproekt research institute in Moscow.[4]

---

[2] Jennifer Derr, *The Lived Nile: Environment, Disease, and Material Colonial Economy in Egypt* (Palo Alto, CA, 2019); Thayer Scudder, *Aswan High Dam Resettlement of Egyptian Nubians* (Singapore, 2016); R. Pastor-Castro and J. Young (eds.), *The Paris Embassy: British Ambassadors and Anglo-French Relations 1944–79* (London, 2013).
[3] *Daily Illini*, January 5, 1956.
[4] *Elektrifikatsiia SSSR* (1967), 251.

The Soviet side took responsibility for the interpretation of design drawings, for ensuring timely equipment deliveries, and for the installation of machinery and equipment. Soviet export organizations would supply all construction machinery, permanent infrastructure, and the fir lumber required for concrete forms. Initially, the rock excavation, hauling, and placing were the responsibility of the Egyptian Ministry of the High Dam. Khrushchev would later claim that, during negotiations, the Egyptians suggested that the Soviets should take on the role of contractor, but that the Soviet side refused. "It would have led," Khrushchev reminisced into a tape recorder, "to an employer–employee relationship between us and the Egyptian people, and they would have begun to resent us as exploiters. In order to avoid conflict with local populations we made it a matter of policy never to be a contractor in countries to whom we gave credit loans." Instead, Soviet specialists worked within different departments of the High Dam Authority.[5]

The High Dam at Aswan emerged as the first of several large-scale Soviet development aid projects in the Third World, and in fact the one with the highest profile. Over the following decades, Soviet advisors would facilitate construction of a major steel plant at Bhilai in India and other large-scale industrial facilities in Cuba, Vietnam, Pakistan, and Syria. Political scientist Alvin Rubinstein defined "influence" as "a relationship transferring preference patterns from the source to a destination in such a way that the outcome pattern corresponds to the original preference pattern,"[6] and among Cold War-era commentators in the West, the High Dam served as a clear case where the Soviet Union purchased "influence" in the Third World by means of development interventions derived from Soviet models. Rubinstein's concept of "influence" echoes the Soviets' own statements of their goals at the Aswan High Dam construction site. Soviet designers thus referred to Aswan as a *stroika* [industrialization site] abroad," connecting Egypt with the territory of the USSR, in celebrated Stalin-era projects like Magnitogorsk and Dnieprostroi and, in the postwar, the Kuibyshev hydroelectric power station.

By offering assistance to Egypt, the Soviet Union was already understood to be further extending its concern for the welfare of "peoples of the colonial and dependent countries." The space of Egypt's nation-state might in this regard be compared with the Belgian Congo or French Equatorial Africa (neither of which had been members of the League of Nations). Moscow conceded, however, that control over the Nile was an integral part of colonial-era visions for Egypt. While at present the Nile's drainage basin includes eleven independent nation-states (Egypt and its neighbors, Burundi, the Democratic Republic of the Congo, Eritrea, Ethiopia, Kenya, Rwanda, South Sudan, Sudan, Tanzania, and Uganda), only two were sovereign when World War II ended. Egypt's neighbors relied on the Foreign Office in London for a "single Nile Valley authority," and proposals for any constructions on the Nile came from London.

During the colonial era, the space of technical authority was unbounded. At the end of World War I, British hydraulic engineers proposed a "century storage" plan for the Nile that would serve to eliminate differences between fluctuating high- and low-flood

---

[5] "Svet novogo Asuana," *Novoe vremīa* (1988): 27.
[6] Alvin Rubinstein, *Moscow's Third World Strategy* (Princeton, 1990).

levels over a hundred-year period.[7] Economic development, on the other hand, was severely restricted by tariff regimes that held back the development of manufacturing, ensuring that seven out of ten Egyptians sustained themselves by agriculture. Writing before the USSR committed to a High Dam proposal, A. Markin acknowledged this:

> [T]he [existing, 'low'] Aswan Dam on the Nile River was designed and built exclusively for irrigation purposes. The enormous potentialities for building a powerful hydroelectric station producing billions of kilowatts were not taken advantage of; this did not enter into the plan of British colonizers, who were not at all interested in the industrial development of Egypt but rather in holding it back economically.[8]

In the Soviet Union, engineering, like science, was integral to Soviet claims to be a distinctive society and intellectual world. The Soviet press acknowledged as much, with S. Kondrashov, in *Izvestiia*, quoting the Egyptian daily newspaper *Al Ahram*, asserting indirectly that "the projected Aswan High Dam on the Nile heads the list of important economic measures being undertaken by the United Arab Republic; apparently this is the reason that no economic delegation ever received such a reception here or been so popular as the Soviet experts who came here to negotiate the agreement on the nature and scale of Soviet participation in the building of the Aswan Dam."[9]

Aswan, an Extension of Soviet Space?

Soviet specialists advanced claims about the affiliation of the Aswan project with its prototypes in the USSR, such as Magnitogorsk, Dneprostroi, and Kuibyshev. Magnitogorsk was the city which, famously, appeared out of nowhere, to become the capital of the Stalin-era "socialism in one country" policy.[10] The Chief Soviet Expert responsible for the Aswan project worked on the construction of the Magnitogorsk Iron and Steel Works as a senior engineer during the period of socialist construction; other veterans from that same project worked at Aswan,[11] and Magnitogorsk was the origin for many of the Russian terms that specialists used on the High Dam construction project.[12] The blast furnaces of Magnitogorsk did in fact provide reinforcing bars for

---

[7] James Dougherty, "Aswan decision in perspective," *Political Science Quarterly* 74.1 (1959): 25, refers to *The Observer*, July 22, 1956; H. E. Hurst, *Nile and Egypt, Past and Future* (London, 1952); M. Philips Price, *Parliamentary Debates*, Commons (July 25, 1956), 96.
[8] A. Markin, "Istoriia khishchnichestva, moshennichestva i prestuplenii. Zametki o razvitii gidroenergetiki v kapitalisticheskikh stranakh," *Izvestiia*, September 13, 1950, *Current Digest of the Soviet Press* 2.37.
[9] S. Kondrashov, "Kraeugol'nyi kamen' Asuanskoy plotiny," *Izvestiia*, December 30, 1959, *Current Digest of the Russian Press* 52.10.
[10] Nick Shepley, *Stalin, the Five-Year Plans and the Gulags: Slavery and Terror 1929–1953* (Luton, 2015).
[11] B. P. Pavlov, *Za rabotu tovarishchi! delegaty XXII s"ezda KPSS rasskazyvaiut* (Moscow, 1962), 68; *Revoliutsionnyi derzhite shag!* (Moscow, 1972); *Slovo o Magnitke: sbornik* (Moscow, 1979), 61.
[12] B. V. Ivanov "Skarabei, Nilsakaia voda, i Abdel Fattakh," *Ogonek* 25 (1963): 14–16; Vladimir Voronov and Nikolai Kruzhkov, "U Gory Magnitnoi," *Ogonek* 25 (1963): 16–17.

the High Dam construction project.¹³ Soviet school children were taught that both the High Dam and Magnitogorsk were a hugely significant aspect of the world they knew.¹⁴

From the very beginning of the Aswan project, the popular press in the USSR associated it with Soviet space, with Dneprostroi— and not with Washington, DC, nor indeed with London.¹⁵ The deputy chair of the Soviet Council of Ministers, former USSR Minister of Electric Power and Electrification, I. T. Novikov, was a construction engineer who dynamited the Dneproges dam during 1941, then rebuilt it after World War II ended. For Aswan, "Dneprostroi was an excellent school of hydraulic engineering, training up numerous personnel,"¹⁶ and Egypt's postcolonial state granted medals acknowledging Dneprostroi veterans' technical achievements.¹⁷

Finally, labor and technical specifications connected Aswan with the Kuibyshev hydroelectric station. One Soviet informant recounted his plans to a journalist: "I'll probably go to Aswan. Our team has experience: we built on the Volga, from there we moved here to the Dnieper ... experience in blocking the great Volga near Kuibyshev, Gorky and Stalingrad, the Dnieper near Kakhovka."¹⁸ A laborer's "decisiveness and [refusal to] give up [in the face of] difficulties" developed on the construction site of the Kuibyshev hydroelectric station were present at Aswan.¹⁹

The sovereign space of the post-colony served to extend the territorial space of socialist construction in the USSR. Yet if in some ways, Aswan functioned as a Soviet space outside the Soviet Union, and if its production culture could be compared with other major Soviet construction projects, the fact remains that Aswan was an Egyptian space built in Egypt by Egyptians. The High Dam construction project was a postcolonial encounter to which Egyptian engineers brought their own expectations and skills. Their engagement over several generations with colonial authority during the time of the British Raj did inevitably feed into both their agreements and their disagreements with Soviet specialists. Egyptians modified the project to fit within their national borders, and nine out of ten of its builders were in fact Egyptians.

Aswan as an Anti-Colonial Project?

Soviet specialists sent out to for Aswan fully intended to recreate the production spaces and relations that characterized contemporary construction projects in their own country, and they emphasized this point in meetings with their potential Egyptian clients. But the government of Gamal Abdul Nasser prioritized the development intervention in Aswan in order to resolve imperialism's expansive spaces in favor of

---

¹³ L. E. Epshtein, *Nekotorye ekonomicheskie voprosy stroitel'stva kommunizma v SSSR: sbornik statei* (Cheliabinsk, 1965), 23.
¹⁴ *Geografiia v shkole* (1959): 109.
¹⁵ P.A. Kazanskii et al. (eds.), *Svet nad Rossiei: ocherki po istorii elektrifikatsii SSSR* (Moscow,1960).
¹⁶ P. S. Neporozhnyi et al. (eds.), *Sdelaem Rossiiu elektricheskoi: sb. vospominanii uchastnikov Komissii GOELRO i stroitelei pervykh elektrostantsii* (Moscow,1961).
¹⁷ *Gidrotekhnicheskoe stroitelstvo* (1964): 59.
¹⁸ *Sovremennyi vostok* (1960): 24.
¹⁹ V. Mayevskii,"V ob'ektive, Afrika: kolonializm na svalku," *Ogonek* 52 (1960): 7.

transformed national ones.[20] In Egypt, the construction site was under the administrative authority of a Ministry of the High Dam—an Egyptian ministry which never followed the colonial-era model of "Egyptian national minister—foreign national, deputy minister."

As James Penn and Larry Allen argue, "dams [such as Aswan] are not meant just to provide irrigation water, as large amounts of hydroelectric power contribute to the development of both agriculture and industry in the region."[21] Rodric Braithwaite shows how a major irrigation project (such as the one outside Jalalabad, in Afghanistan) could employ "about six thousand people, and consisted of six large state farms, specializing in the production of citrus fruit, vegetable oils, dairy products, and meat; it included a dam and a major canal, a hydroelectric station and a pumping station, a repair works, a wood processing plant, and a jam factory."[22] According to Konrad Kuhn, the construction of a hydroelectric complex on the Zambezi river during 1969 was equivalent to the Biafran war in its regional effects.[23]

The USSR State Committee for Foreign Economic Ties signed an agreement with Egypt in 1958 at a time when construction of the Kremenchuk Dam on the Dnieper river in Ukraine was half-completed, making it a model construction site for development interventions.[24] Egyptian executives responsible for the construction project, headed by Egyptian Minister of Public Works Musa Arafa, visited Kremenchuk during May 1959.[25] There, researchers from the Moscow institute Gidroproekt demonstrated the characteristics of water flow at the future dam.[26] The visiting Egyptian engineers possessed limited experience in managing large construction projects and sought Soviet assistance to bring the High Dam concept to reality, watching the work with unflagging interest, admiring the precision and efficiency with which workers carried out their jobs. For the Egyptians whom A. P. Nikitin invited to the USSR, a high point of their visit was the river closing at Kremenchuk.[27]

This provincial city was in the process of being turned into the Ukraine's energy capital; in addition to the hydroelectric plant, an oil refinery to process crude oil drilled in east Ukrainian fields went into production shortly before the High Dam's hydroelectric plant started to contribute to Egypt's power grid. Kremenchuk was also headquarters for a rocket division within the Soviet strategic defense forces. The river closing was a single day's arduous task in which dump truck drivers dumped ton after ton of hardcore and reinforced concrete blocks at the rapidly receding river's edge. The

---

[20] Derek Gregory, *The Colonial Present: Afghanistan, Palestine, Iraq* (Hoboken, NJ, 2004).
[21] James Penn, *Rivers of The World: A Social, Geographical and Environmental Sourcebook* (Santa Barbara, CA, 2001), 80.
[22] Rodric Braithwaite, *Afgantsy: The Russians in Afghanistan, 1979–1989* (London, 2011), 147.
[23] Konrad Kuhn, "Liberation Struggle and Humanitarian Aid," in Samantha Christiansen and Zachary A. Scarlett (eds.), *The Third World in the Global 1960s* (New York, 2013), 69.
[24] *Soglashenie*, January 29, 1958.
[25] "Egyptians Going to Soviet," *New York Times*, May 6, 1959.
[26] I. V. Komzin, *Svet Asuana* (Moscow, 1964), 122.
[27] A career diplomat, A. P. Nikitin represented the USSR as vice consul in Iranian Azerbaijan after the withdrawal of the Soviet Army (1948–51), then First Secretary of the USSR Embassy in Warsaw as Poland joined a Soviet-led military alliance. See Elizabeth Bishop, "Soviet Policy Towards Egypt: D. S. Solod in the State Archive of the Russian Federation," *Maghreb Review* 45.3 (2020): 536–55.

Kremenchuk river diversion took place under a light drizzle, as a long line of trucks approached the ramp leading down to the river and dropped their load of stone and concrete into the roaring foam. MSES staff claimed that it took exactly eight hours and twenty minutes for bulldozers and trucks to move sufficient earth and rock to fill the Dnieper's channel to water level and divert the river's downstream flow through the man-made canal.

The spectacle Egyptian guests saw was framed with a precision based on military-level standards of discipline and order, with reference to the recent military victory in World War II. At Kremenchuk, to judge by the account given by MSES staff, the young women waving small pennants to guide the truck drivers looked "just like the traffic girls on the road that led to Berlin during the last war."[28] The foreign visitors were especially awed by the structured activity: "[T]his is magnificent! Everything is done so precisely, as at a military parade!" enthused Cairo University's Professor Sabry.[29] Beyond that day's spectacle, Soviet specialists' authority extended beyond their enterprises, consisting of support networks in the surrounding community, capable of bringing volunteer and other unremunerated labor to fulfill enterprise goals (as necessary).

In addition to credits and heavy equipment, Soviet foreign trade agencies offered the Aswan project the expertise of Soviet specialists, who would travel to Egypt with the goal of recreating Soviet production culture abroad. But individuals within Soviet and within Egyptian production cultures possessed dramatically different experiences and expectations for technical interventions. Not only did Egyptian engineers' and Soviet specialists' education and employment in state organizations differ; so, too, did their understandings of their own roles as wielders of technology. For example, the dam was located on Egypt's new boundary with an independent Sudan, the construction site included a training institute, and construction processes included "hydromechanization" techniques widespread during the Khrushchev "thaw." As a result, the construction site of the Aswan High Dam became a space that bore characteristics stemming from both Egyptian political priorities as well as from Soviet training models and distribution methods.

The Egyptians' trip to Soviet Ukraine was significant because the impressions they gathered about the Soviet production authorities and what they perceived to be their successes served to frame their expectations as to what they might themselves accomplish at the Aswan High Dam. Furthermore, lessons learnt on that trip would shape their contributions to the developing technical culture of their country's new administration. The USSR Minister of Electrical Power and Electrification, P. Neporozhny, chose the construction area of the Kremenchuk hydroelectric complex for a test site, and on the basis of a topographical model the axis of the Aswan Dam was moved 600 meters upstream of the Nile.[30] At Gidroproekt's field station, personal observation of the model convinced the Egyptian delegation of the necessity to grout

---

[28] A. E. Bochkin, "Iz letopisi velikoi stroiki," in *Rossiia elektricheskaia: vospominaniia stareishikh energetikov* (Moscow, 1975).
[29] Komzin, *Svet Asuana*, 21.
[30] *Novyi mir* (1961), 185.

all the way down to Aswan's granite substrate.[31] Production of 14-ton trucks for Egypt was transferred to the Kremenchuk Automobile Plant.[32]

Egyptian Elites and Production Culture

Experiences like these in Soviet Ukraine exemplify how Soviet managers expected to transfer entire "technical networks" to the Egyptians. A progressivist tendency in the history of technology considers the goals and ends of technical training to be constant across jurisdictions. As engineering elites of varying cultural backgrounds are educated and develop authority over natural processes, they come to understand universal principles common to all technical elites. Through their reliance on a mathematical means of expression and means of evidence, abstracted from natural language, all engineers should understand each other regardless of their cultural background. The case of the Aswan High Dam suggests otherwise.

The paper-bound volume *Materials for Final Engineering Report of the High Aswan Dam Project, Bulletin 10, "Organization of Construction"* spreads organizational charts, tables of engineers' names, and their photographs across its pages. Who were these men, the Egyptian engineers who traveled to Kremenchuk, who developed specifications for the High Dam proposal, and directed its construction? Photographs from the Egyptians' visit to Ukraine show Hassan Zaki (Director of the High Dam Authority), Professor Abdallah Sabry of Cairo University, Dr. Samir Helmy, Colonel Muhammad Sidqi Sulayman, Dr. Azim, and others wrapped up in overcoats on the Kremenchuk construction site.[33] Clippings files at the *Al Ahram* newspaper suggest certain commonalities among them: effectively all the dam's engineers were born around 1900, educated in Egypt, and took advanced degrees outside Egypt before joining the Ministry of Public Works' prestigious Irrigation Department. While Hassan Zaki was born in 1892, Musa Arafa (Irrigation Minister during the construction of the High Dam), was ten years younger, having been born in January 1900. Similarly, Ibrahim Zaki Kinawi (the High Dam Authority's Assistant Director) was born in 1901. What experiences did these men, representing adjacent birth cohorts, share?

Between 1882 and the 1920s, Egyptian notables residing in rural areas were increasingly convinced that cotton cultivation was no longer profitable. Their sons might do better, they now thought, to train as engineers. While local civil servants in the early twentieth century earned meager salaries and enjoyed limited prospects for advancement, engineers on the public payroll benefited from Egypt's 1919 revolution. The Milner Commission's report, which led to Egypt joining the League of Nations, gave them, the cohort of Egyptian engineers born around 1900, a "lucky break." Their advancement to posts in which they held technical responsibility was now unimpeded.

---

[31] A. I. Adzhubei, *Vstrecha s Afriki* (Moscow, 1964), 264.
[32] *Institut zur Erforschung der UdSSR, Vestnik* (1960), 6.
[33] For Sidqi Sulayman, see Robert Tignor, *Capitalism and Nationalism at the End of Empire* (Princeton, 2015), 177; Imad Harb, "The Egyptian Military in Politics: Disengagement or Accommodation?," *Middle East Journal* 57.2 (2003): 269–85.

Prior to this date, Anglo-Indian colonialists effectively excluded Egyptian engineers from technical authority. But as of the 1920s, the Egyptian technical intelligentsia, the sons and grandsons of rural notables, was vested with the power to reconfigure public space in Egypt. Egyptian engineers' written texts, just as much as the concrete structures they designed, were in fact indebted to colonialist visions of the Nile. Hassan Zaki acknowledged that he himself perpetuated colonialist mentalities, reminiscing in his old age that "it has been more than half a century since I have been connected, as a hydraulic engineer, with the study of controlling the river Nile." The fact remains that in post-1952 Egypt, Egyptian engineers inherited tasks with which Anglo-Indian colonialists had been entrusted.

As Robert Vitalis points out, terms such as "aborted development," "growth without development," and "lopsided development" do not account for the pre-1952 heroes and villains.[34] While Sa'ad Zaghlul and the political party he founded in Egypt (the Wafd Party) enjoyed widespread support during the 1919 revolution, events in Europe during their three decades in power tested the party's leadership. Scientific research and, by extension, engineering was linked with national sovereignty, on the one hand, and with corruption, on the other.[35] In the public imagination, this generation of engineers was associated with the constitutional era's claims to national independence. The High Dam was the largest and the most important of the projects that proclaimed independent Egypt's recovery from the colonialist denial of its technical authority.

Soviet Production Culture

In the Soviet Union, as early as 1920, V. I. Lenin declared that "communism equals Soviet power plus the electrification of the whole country," creating a State Commission for the Electrification of Russia (GoElero) to plan national development. Soviet management style, institutional support networks, and worker–management relations were developed during the Stalin era and relied on distinctive principles. The first was *vydvizhenstvo*—a policy of promotion of industrial management from the production line (*so skameiki*, "from the bench") that placed ill-prepared, yet politically reliable, individuals in responsible positions. *Edinonachalie* was its complement, the one-person management principle which assigned responsibility for the operation and performance of economic units (managers' despotic power, in a "workers' state"). Both depended on "storming" (*shturmovshchina*), the rush to complete a plan at the end of a planning cycle. Soviet production culture's distinctive practices ran deep, too deep in fact to be uprooted by Stalin's successors.

Domestic hydroelectric construction projects were particularly important spaces for Soviet production culture on account of their high political and economic visibility. I. V.

---

[34] Robert Vitalis, "On the Theory and Practice of Compradors: The Role of Abbud *Pasha* in the Egyptian Political Economy," *International Journal of Middle East Studies* 22.3 (1990): 291–315 (291).
[35] Charles Smith identifies Fuad Sirag al-Din with the government of Nahas *pasha* and the publication of Makram Ebeid's *Black Book*, which implicated Nahas's wife, Zaynab al-Wakil, in abuse of access to state power. See Cynthia Nelson, *Doria Shafik: Egyptian Feminist: A Woman Apart* (Cairo, 1996), 108.

Komzin was chosen to be the construction boss for the High Dam project. Born in 1905, he served as executive director of construction for the Kuibyshev dam and hydroelectric plant.[36] A celebrity awarded the Order of the October Revolution, two Orders of the Patriotic War, and two Orders of Lenin, Komzin often granted interviews to journalists and published a youthful memoir.[37] His prominence in public life, along with his experience building major hydroelectric projects in the USSR, made him the ideal advisor for the Aswan High Dam project.[38] He claimed to have told Harvard University's professor of engineering Karl Terzagi that "Russian hydro-technicians have, without a doubt, a great deal of experience in building large dams," to justify the Aswan project.[39]

How did Soviet specialists at the High Dam understand the responsibilities possession of technical knowledge conferred upon them and the space of the construction site? Soviet engineers' expectations at Aswan regarding the authority vested in management were conditioned by events both public and private that had occurred in the course of their careers. All the Soviet specialists who in 1959 showed the Egyptian delegation around the "Great Construction Projects of Communism" came from the ranks of the workers, or graduated from engineering school, during the late 1930s. Kozmin's title, "Chief Soviet Expert," obscures the fact that the individual who occupied the office had a limited technical education: his illustrious career exemplified the *vydvizhenstvo* concept. Kozmin identified Aswan with the great construction projects of Soviet industrialization and his own position at Aswan with the notion of *edinonachalie*: the one-person management principle. Responsibility for the poor performance of the High Dam project during the first years of construction fell on him, Soviet production culture's ambassador in Egypt, the Chief Soviet Expert in Aswan. By conceding that technical assistance would be personified by a resident Chief Expert and his staff, the Egyptian High Dam Authority effectively bought into the concept of *edinonachalie*.

Soviet technicians claimed that their production processes and technology offered Egypt a dam that would be built better, faster, and cheaper than a dam designed by either Europeans or Americans. But the High Dam project was an international venture and thus would be different from anything in Soviet production culture. What distinguished the High Dam project from other *stroiki* (construction sites) was the fact that Soviet advisors were unable to recreate successfully in Egypt the extra-legal support mechanisms they depended on in the USSR to complete construction projects. Soviet production culture was characterized by the extent to which it integrated, and was incorporated into, all sectors of society. Successful Soviet *stroiki* managers cultivated support networks outside the ministerial hierarchy and connections with district and local Communist Party organizations, the Komsomol, the Ministry of the Interior's corrective labor camps, and the army. So high a profile both politically and

---

[36] I. V. Komzin and E. V. Luk'ianov, *Volzhskaia GES imeni V. I. Lenina* (Kuibyshev, 1960); I. V. Komzin, *Zapiski sovetskogo energetika* (Moscow, 1960); I. V. Komzin, *Eto i est' schast'e: ocherki o stroitel'stve Kuibyshevskogo gidrouzla* (Moscow, 1961).
[37] I. V. Komzin, *Na velikikh stroikakh kommunizma* (Moscow, 1952).
[38] V. G. Golosov, *Nravstvennost' i nravstvennoe vospitaniie: materialy nauchnoi konferentsii* (Novosibirsk, 1962); *Zametki pisatelia o sovremennom ocherke* (Moscow, 1962), 286; Komzin, *Eto i est' schast'e*, 70.
[39] Haykakan Khsh, Gitut'yunneri Akademia.

diplomatically did the High Dam project have that observers failed to differentiate between progress made in its early stages and that of similar construction projects in the Soviet Union. Had Egyptian engineers recognized the extent to which actual practice differed from books they had read, they might have grasped that most of the successes of Soviet production culture were not sufficiently resilient to flourish in a new environment. Many Soviet construction bosses welcomed the opportunity to work in the stable environment they thought Egypt promised. While managers may have understood that they would lose the support networks that local and regional party organizations in the USSR provided, they also anticipated a boost to their authority in the guise of a comparatively pliable, definitely non-party labor force.

The Soviet workforce after the war differed from what it had been before the outbreak of hostilities. While prewar construction sites depended on labor migrants from the countryside unfamiliar with labor discipline, postwar construction sites hired workers familiar with the production environment. Workers who were military or shop floor veterans expected the system to reward them with greater production authority: they aspired (at the very least) to take control of production tempos and (at the most) to be promoted to management. Many construction workers, for their part, assumed that the training they gained during the war, as well as their membership in the Communist Party, would serve to justify their *vydvizhentsy* or promotion to production authority.

In Egypt, neither local nor imported Soviet workers could use Communist Party organizations and social forms to mount a challenge to their production authority.[40] Egyptian laborers for their part promised to be the opposite of workers on postwar Soviet construction sites. Contemporary Russian-language sources described the Egyptian labor force as untrained and without class consciousness. These same sources made much of the skills that Egyptian workers purportedly learned from Soviet specialists. These latter revelled in stories that recounted Egyptian laborers' alleged innocence of construction processes. From a manager's point of view, working on the High Dam as a Soviet expert attached to one of these different departments was like going back in time. Aswan thus called to mind a distant past when managers enjoyed seigneurial authority over workers (as opposed to full responsibility for the successful completion of planned project goals).

Newly trained Egyptian workers were supposed to fill the gap. Soviet foreign trade ministry officials, writing in the Moscow press, described how Soviet technicians taught Egyptian workers new skills:

> Soviet engineer Svitnev, for instance, taught Arab drivers to handle the huge 25-ton Minsk trucks, never before used in Egypt. And when one of his trainees, Baram [sic] Abdu, first drove a truck through Aswan he was cheered by people in the streets. Many Arabs were taught to operate excavators by Hero of Socialist Labor Dmitri Slepukha. All in all, Soviet technicians have trained more than 600 Aswan workers.[41]

---

[40] Alia Mossallam, "We Were the Ones Who Made This Dam High," *Water History* 6 (2014).
[41] I. V. Beliaev, "Na stroitel'stve Asuanskoi plotiny," *Novoe vremia* 11 (1962): 26.

While Soviet specialists at home in Soviet space (at Kuibyshev) concealed their claims to exclusive production authority behind the myth of *vydvizhenstvo* necessary to attract skilled labor to the construction site, these same managers in Egypt asserted claims to expertise that local labor left unchallenged.

Territorialized Space of Egypt's New Borders

Both Soviet and Egyptian contemporary authors gave detailed descriptions of how the development project would transform Egypt's economic sovereignty.[42] While the foreign policy and "State committee" system was new, production relations characteristic of the Stalin period came to maturity during and after Khrushchev's ministerial reorganization. After the Soviet offer to fund the High Dam was tendered in 1959, and up until 1962, Aswan was planned and implemented as a Soviet construction project, a *stroika*, located outside the borders of the Soviet Union. As equipment and materials were offloaded in Alexandria and Port Said, Soviet journalists published descriptions of the project. Even while it was still under construction, Soviet travel writers, for example, described the architecture of the complex in terms that combined the ancient and the modern within the territorialized space of Egypt's new borders.

Descriptions of the hydroelectric construction site in Russian are surprisingly similar to the texts in Arabic, which encapsulated different historical periods within the nation's borders. As Kristina Centore points out, "the Sixties in Egypt were born, so to speak, under the sign of the Aswan Dam."[43] Some texts drew comparisons between the High Dam's architectural modernity and Egypt's Pharaonic heritage.[44] "The hydroelectric stations' gigantic buildings' ... series of concrete columns somehow or other remind me of the ancient Egyptian temple of Abu Simbel, above these same waters on a high Nile bank a thousand years ago."[45] In the collectively-authored work *Insan al-Sadd al-'Ali* (*Man of the High Dam*, 1966), Son'allah Ibrahim compares the High Dam to the Pyramids, and a minister responsible for it—Sidqi Sulayman—to a Pharaonic statue, while *Man of the High Dam* begins with an epigraph by poet 'Abd al Rahman al Abnudi: "I feel that the arm of the High Dam needs some of my blood."[46]

---

[42] I. V. Beliaev, "Semnadtsat piramid Kheopsa," *Sovremennyi vostok* 11 (1959): 42; V. Galaktionov, "Plotina Asuana," *Novyi mir* 2 (1961): 173, 176; Beliaev, "Na stroitel'stve," 26.
[43] Kristina Centore, "Future Tense: Hamed Owais and the Aswan High Dam," *Sequitur* (2020): 5.
[44] Ministerstvo Vneshnikh Ekonomicheskikh Sviazi (MVES SSSR), f. 365, op. 2, ed. khr. 2359, l. 3; G. Gerasimov, "Egypet i Nil," *Novoe vremia* 52 (1957): 25; I. T. Novikov, "Ukroshchenie Nila," *Novoe vremia* 6 (1960): 16; P. Beliaev, "Asuanskii god," *Novoe vremia* 4 (1961): 15; Galaktionov, "Plotina Asuana," 172; N. A. Dlin, "Nil i Asuanskaia plotina," *Priroda* 2 (1961): 76; I. V. Beliaev, "Reportazh iz Asuana," *Aziia i Afrika segodnia* 12 (1962): 41; P. Beliaev, "Asuan-simvol druzhby narodov," *Vneshniaia torgovlia* 11 (1962): 41; I. Komzin, "Bol'shaia plotina na Nile," *Druzhba narodov* 5 (1963): 231.
[45] Boris Ivanov, *40 vekov i 4 Goda* (Moscow, 1966), 102.
[46] For an alternative reading of al-Abdudi, see Lila Abu-Lughod, *Dramas of Nationhood: The Politics of Television in Egypt* (Chicago, 2005), 72. For an alternative reading of Ibrahim, see Margaret Litvin, "Tongue-Tied Internationalism: Adventures with a Soviet Setting, an Egyptian Novel, and an Indian Press" (Boston University, April 10, 2020); Céza Kassem-Draz, "Opaque and Transparent Discourse: A Contrastive Analysis of the *Star of August* and *The Man of the High Dam* by Son' Allah Ibrahim," *Alif* 2 (1982).

Individual Soviet engineers considered Egypt to be a space where they could transform themselves: their arms, too, they thought, needed some of the High Dam's blood. When Ivan Komzin arrived in Aswan to take up his new responsibilities on the project, he parlayed his desk job into some high style menswear. As Komzin later remembered from the beginning of the project, "the first Arabic word which we were able to remember quite well was *karaka*, which means a 'canal', 'foundation pit'. This word served as an ID or a password, opening all doors before us."[47]

For Komzin and other Soviet workers, affiliation with the project made them into VIPs. Soviet specialists posted to Aswan were paid in hard currency, the justification being that they would spend their foreign cash on their living expenses while in Egypt. Soviet specialists received princely salaries: for example, a senior engineer was paid the equivalent of 195 Egyptian pounds a month, while an engineer got 186 Egyptian pounds a month—this at a time when five to ten Egyptian pounds would buy an acre of irrigated agricultural land. Just as Soviet specialists at the High Dam site were paid in Soviet certificate roubles (*valiota SSSR*), specialists on High Dam assignments in the USSR were also paid in certificate roubles. For Komzin, the High Dam turned into an "open sesame" invitation—if not a cave filled with robbers' loot, then at least the door to the tailors. Later, the chief expert remembered:

> My driver Sabri Muhammad took us to get ourselves kitted out. At that time in Aswan there were two made-to-measure tailors' workshops, and a suit or something like it could be made up in two or three weeks. We went to one of these workshops. Right away, Sabry started a lively conversation with the owner. Out of this conversation we understood only one word, repeated with different intonations: *Karaka? Karaka! Karaka* ... This was not the only time it worked its magic. The workshop owner, his son and his cutter, chortled over *karaka*, running his measuring tape over all of us. Within three days we'd all received summer weight suits. And we were no fewer than twenty-nine men.[48]

The tailor and his assistants must have sewed day and night in order to dress these Soviet construction workers in the latest fashions. Affiliation with the Aswan project overseas enhanced these workers' status in their own society, even as they gained the outward trappings—suits—of their newly-acquired status as development specialists. This international development aid project gave Komzin and other foreigners the chance to dress for their part in the struggle against "imperialism" and "feudalism."

Soviet journalists published illustrated travel notes about the Aswan project. The lengthiest of these popular works were V. Keroteev's "Among Arab Friends"[49] and N. Galochkin's "Assuan High Dam."[50] Just as Moscow's recent 1957 International Youth

---

[47] I. V. Komzin, "Plotina zhizni; beseda s glav. ekspertam AVP v OAR," *Pravda vostoka*, July 16, 1959; Komzin, *Svet Asuana*, 70; *Sovetskaia Latvia*, July 18, 1959; *Sovetskaia Belarus*, July 17, 1959; *Sovetskaia Moldavia*, July 23, 1959; N. A. Malyshev, "Asuanskaia plotina," *Pravda*, August 2, 1959.
[48] Komzin, *Svet Asuana*, 70.
[49] V. Keroteev, "U Arabskikh druzhei (vpechatleniia ot poezdki v Egipet)," *Don* 1 (1959): 143–52.
[50] N. Galochkin, "Sadd El'-aali Asuan (o znachenii soorruzheniia vysotnoi Asuanskoi plotiny dlia ekonomiki Ob'edinoi Arabskoi Respubliki)," *Kul'tura i zhizn'* 6 (1959): 6, 7–13.

Festival emphasized person-to-person diplomacy, so too both of these accounts addressed Egypt's economic, political, and historical situation through human-interest stories. Galochkin referred generally to his conversations with "Egyptian friends," while Koroteev introduced his readers to individual Egyptians from all walks of life. Both journalists' contacts—significantly—were exclusively with men. Koroteev interviewed writers Abd el Rahman al Sharkawi and Abd el Rahman al Khamisi, cartoonist Hakim at the popular illustrated magazine *al Masaa'*, translator Rugdi, tourist guide Magdi, and septuagenarian night watchman Hamid. Koroteev did mention women, but he did not describe them as workers. Egyptian women were identified only in terms of their relationships to men—even those who were employed outside the home.

The Soviet coverage of the Aswan Dam project made no mention of autonomous women. Journalists used their reportage on the development project to reassure men about their entrenched social status, thereby confining women to legal family relationships. Daily accounts in the press told of Soviet husbands and wives working together at the High Dam, and wedding or birth announcements illustrated the "normalcy" of the Soviet labor environment overseas. Anna Karaseva married Anatoli Dunaev;[51] children "quickly acclimatized."[52] A local patron—Zakariya Mohiedin, Minister of the Interior—gave a piano and toys to specialists' children in a new four-class school.[53]

Aswan is a provincial city on the furthest southern border from Cairo, and in many respects, Soviet development specialists found their assignments there similar to previous jobs. For example, the responsibilities of the executives were similar to those they had had in provincial Soviet cities before World War II. Their living conditions also resembled those enjoyed by specialists in the postwar USSR. While in the USSR, Soviet women's technical skills contributed to the construction industry at every level,[54] personnel records in the Gidroproekt archives list only thirty-five women among the 318 citizens assigned to Moscow-based design tasks affiliated with the Aswan project.[55] Specialists sent out to Aswan were exclusively male, with two identified exceptions—V. I. Kalygina, probably an economist in the Chief Expert's Authority, and L. P. Karataeva, a senior engineer in both Moscow and Aswan.[56] Where housing was in short supply, consumer prices high, and poor distribution networks required extra labor in the home,[57] Soviet women were restricted to civic, domestic, and sexual roles while in Egypt, their presence justified only by their marriage to employed specialists.

---

[51] Komzin, "Bol'shaia plotina," 233.
[52] A. Agar'shev, "Granit Asuana, po sledam sovetskogo diplomata," *Komsomol'skaia pravda*, January 9, 1970.
[53] Komzin, "Bol'shaia plotina," 233.
[54] I. V. Komzin, "Novaia sud'ba drevnego Nila," *Sovremennyi vostok* 12 (1960): 24; Komzin, *Zapiski sovetskogo energetika*, 100–3; Galaktionov, "Plotina Asuana," 186, 188, 190; Komzin, "Bol'shaia plotina," 225.
[55] Sixteen or seventeen women worked as engineers, nine as senior engineers, five or six as senior technicians, and two or three as technicians. Women's labor was represented throughout Gidroproekt's technical hierarchy; with more than twenty male department heads, one department head was female.
[56] Kalygina: Tsentral'nyi gosudarstvennyĭ arkhiv narodnogo khozaistva Sovetskogo Soiuza (TsGANKh SSSR), f. 9572, op. 1, ed. khr. 1927, l. 27; Karataeva: TsGANKhD, f. R-109, op. 1-6, ed. khr. 493, l. 15.
[57] The annual report for 1961 records 122 specialists and ninety-five family members including twenty-nine children, TsGANKh, f. 9572, op. 1, ed. khr. 1588, l. 58. *Materials for Final Engineering Report on the High Aswan Dam Project* 10 (Aswan, 1970), 96, identifies the number of laborers at 12,000, with 175 engineers on the technical staff and 660 Soviet specialists (dependents not specified).

In allocating priority employment to men, development interventions, in turn, deskilled women and precluded their incorporation into global hierarchies of technical authority. In building the dam, installing the turbines, and wiring the control room, Soviet engineers expressed their visions of domination of the natural world in what they considered to be the wisdom of the Egyptian countryside. Soviet journalists adopted the High Dam construction project as a metaphor for marriage, bringing together male technical authority and the female Nile.[58] When foreign journalists reported that construction at Aswan was lagging behind expectations due to poor communication between the Egyptian High Dam Authority and the Soviet Ministry of Foreign Economic Ties, the Soviet daily press responded that such disruptions were similar to the minor disagreements normally encountered in the course of married life.[59] The Nile's flow and a nation's economic productivity were similar to women's fecundity; all three required external agency. One Soviet reporter quoted an Egyptian peasant as saying, "You may have a wonderful cow ... but if there's no bull, it won't breed. The same with our land. It only bears when fertilized with the Nile waters."[60] Because electric power and flood protection were presented as more significant than irrigation in the press, such narratives served to combine the political, economic, and reproductive orders,[61] offering a potent sexual image instead of technical accuracy.[62]

Crisis in Production

Even though Soviet specialists attempted to recreate their Soviet experiences abroad, the basis for performance evaluation was different. There was scant negotiation of plan targets in Egypt; "storming" was not possible under the circumstances, given insufficient qualified labor, materials, and electric power; and managers found that their extra-institutional support networks were unavailable in Egypt. The planned basis for the High Dam was not a within-ministry directive, open to bargaining between the enterprise manager and his superiors, as in the USSR. Once in positions of production authority as enterprise heads, Soviet specialists were expected to muster the enterprises' productive capabilities toward the goal of meeting production plans.

Soviet specialists promised that the High Dam would be built in just the same way as projects in the USSR. As specified by the initial Technopromexport contract 059, a six-person Soviet delegation arrived in Egypt during spring 1959, and the construction equipment and supplies of dynamite began to arrive at the site late that same year. Having officially acknowledged the Aswan offer, Egypt's Field Marshal Abdel Hakim

---

[58] Gerasimov, "Egypet i Nil," 28; Komzin, *Zapiski sovetskogo energetika*, 86, 91; Beliaev, "Reportazh iz Asuana," 38; Galaktionov, "Plotina Asuana," 182-3; Beliaev, "Na stroitel'stve," 26.
[59] Beliaev, "Na stroitel'stve," 40, 41.
[60] Gerasimov, "Egypet i Nil," 27.
[61] Anne McClintock, *Imperial Leather: Race, Gender, and Sexuality in the Colonial Context* (London, 1995), 1-4.
[62] Elizabeth Bishop, "Control Room: Visible and Concealed Spaces of the Aswan High Dam," in Panayiota Pyla (ed.), *Landscapes of Development: Modernization and the Physical Environment in the Eastern Mediterranean* (Cambridge, MA, 2013), 73-87.

Amer hosted the six, led by Komzin and the G.K.E.S.'s deputy director for economic affairs A. P. Nikitin.[63] Other members of the delegation, experts in the construction of coffers (watertight enclosures, pumped dry to permit construction work below sea level) arrived in Cairo, tasked with assessing the financial offer's technical aspects.[64]

Soviet advisors accepted transfer to the Aswan High Dam project in Egypt gratefully, as foreign assignments of this sort also represented an opportunity to evade the workers' challenges to their production authority that characterized their experiences in the Soviet Union. The first task at the High Dam construction site, blasting a diversion channel (60 meters wide and 40 meters deep), was scheduled to begin the following summer. It would require 7,000 tons of dynamite to remove 9 million cubic meters of rock (dumped from both sides of the Nile, for a coffer dam 200 meters long). Once the coffer dams were in place, and the Nile successfully diverted, construction of the main dam could begin.[65]

Unlike Soviet domestic plans, the High Dam plan set clear targets which, from a manager's perspective, would have to be met. On the basis of their study of long-term cycles in the level of Nile flood, Egyptian engineers calculated that the ideal opportunity for diverting the Nile would occur during the spring of 1964; consequently, the sole chance to remove the coffer dams in order to complete the canals to the required section was during the summer of 1962, when the level of the old Aswan Dam's reservoir was calculated to be at its lowest. During the first year of construction on the High Dam, it became clear that there were not enough skilled laborers (wrote construction bosses back to I. T. Novikov), and while the project required 250 mechanical workers, only ninety were on the job (Komzin told an Egyptian newspaper).

A year after work officially began, there were only ninety-six Soviet technicians and engineers on the construction site. Early work indicated that the goal would not be attained—a little over a quarter of the annual plan for earth removal was fulfilled during 1961. Finding that construction was way behind schedule, Soviet specialists urgently appealed for extra labor from the USSR and turned to Egyptian officials for access to unremunerated labor in order to complete the plan for earth-moving operations.

Soviet writers compared Egyptian workers at Aswan with Soviet workers of the 1930s. Until very recently they had been peasants, and they were newly introduced to wage labor, easily divided by differential rewards, and not prone to offering direct challenges to managers' production authority. The construction schedule required that 85% of rock and soil would have to be excavated by May 1964; almost half of the concrete and reinforced concrete work, 37% of the fills, and 18% of the steel structures would have to be in place. When the work that was done did not measure up to plans or meet targets, Soviet specialists blamed the Egyptians, claiming that supplies of machines and spare parts failed to arrive on time at the High Dam construction site because Egyptians lacked discipline and efficiency: construction on the High Dam fell behind schedule because Soviet ships were tied up in Egyptian ports, waiting to unload.[66]

---

[63] "Russians in Cairo," *New York Times*, November 15, 1958; "Kogda-to v Asuane, Istoriia stroitel'stva Asuanskoi plotiny," *Ekho planety* 612 (2000): 1.
[64] "USSR Cofferdam Experts," Cairo Radio, October 29, 1958.
[65] Dana Adams Schmidt, "Soviet May Build All of Aswan Dam," *New York Times*, November 2, 1959.
[66] N.S. Khrushchev, *Khrushchev Remembers; The Glasnost' Tapes* (Boston, 1990), 60.

The Great Industrial Project 75

Figure 3.1 Aswan High Dam workers at work site 5/13/1964.

Conclusion

Egyptian engineers' understandings of themselves as technologists, and of technology's role and function in society, were conditioned by their historical experiences. Local concepts of technology, and of the technical elite's responsibilities, derived from engineers' experiences in a cotton-cultivating environment under colonialism. These engineers developed particular means of expression, and a particular rhetoric, which were appropriate to their understanding of themselves as the wielders of important Nile-control ideas in the Nile lands. While Egyptian engineers rejected some of the Anglo-Indian colonialist statements about the Nile, they appropriated concepts of Nile control built upon a colonialist method of mathematical modeling.

In the case of the Soviet technical specialists, recent historical experiences conditioned their expectations as well. Soviet concepts of technical authority came to inform notions of the authority of managers within the enterprise and in the community at large. It was through Soviet industrial enterprise and a distinctive Soviet production culture that the Soviet technical intelligentsia found its voice. The means of expression which Soviet specialists considered appropriate to themselves as wielders of technical authority were melded with the means of expression considered appropriate to the managerial cadre. While their designation as "experts" described the nature of their participation in the High Dam project, Soviet managers played up cultural differences between themselves and Egyptian laborers to further enhance their authority.

The space of the Aswan High Dam was a complex intermingling of Soviet production culture, with its values, its norms, its notions of leadership and power, and the Egyptian production culture, or the culture of Egyptian elites. If we follow Rubinstein's definition of influence—"a relationship transferring preference patterns from the source to a destination, in such a way that the outcome pattern corresponds to the original preference pattern"—there was no such thing at Aswan.[67] Soviet specialists hoped that the Aswan High Dam project would be an opportunity for them to demonstrate Soviet production culture's achievements. Their attempt to develop Aswan as a space of Soviet production culture, however, was thwarted. When project goals were not met in a timely manner, Egyptian engineers redeveloped the Aswan project, transferring many of the functions of Soviet specialists to Egyptian nationals who then presented Gidroproekt plans and designs for the structure as their own.[68]

---

[67] Rubinstein, *Moscow's Third World Strategy*, 230.
[68] Mūsa Arafa, *Al-Sadd al-'Aaly* (Cairo, 1965) 41; Ibrahim Rashid, *Al-Sadd al-'Aaly: hadiruhu wa mustaqbaluhu* (Cairo, 1969); Yousef Abu Al-Hajjaj, *Al-Sadd al-'Aaly wa al-tanmiat al'iqtisadia* (Cairo, 1964).

4

The Exhibition: Exhibitions as Spaces of Cultural Encounter—Yugoslavia and Africa

Radina Vučetić

Yugoslav Socialist Modernism and Cultural Diplomacy in the Cold War

Yugoslavia's unique position between East and West meant that her cultural policy was also between two blocs.[1] In the deeply polarized Cold War world, where the role of culture was also a political one, Yugoslavia sought to promote Yugoslav art abroad, but also to introduce the cultures of other countries, especially those of her allies and political partners, into Yugoslavia, and through Yugoslavia, to the world. One governmental report on cooperation with Asia and Africa from the early 1960s stated that Yugoslavia was looking forward "to keeping pace with both the East and the West's cultural development" and that her aim was to confirm herself in Asia and Africa as "an integral part of the cultural universe of the East and West," because "the present world is nowadays a cultural battlefield."[2] Culture thus emerged as a globalizing force that helped forge connections across vast spaces and geopolitical contexts.[3] The aim of this chapter is to show how Yugoslavia created an alternative cultural space as part of the promotion of a Yugoslav foreign and non-aligned policy, but also with a view to showcasing African and Third World art on a global stage.

To understand Yugoslav cultural diplomacy it is important to understand Yugoslav art, particularly Yugoslav modernist art. After the split with the Soviet Union, modernism became politically and aesthetically attractive in Yugoslavia—an acceptable option for Yugoslav communists and artists alike. Predominantly concerned with the means of expression rather than any social mission, this art mirrored the appropriation

---

[1] See Radina Vučetić, *Coca-Cola Socialism: Americanization of Yugoslav Culture in the Sixties* (Budapest, 2018); Zoran Janjetović, *Od Internacionale do komercijale. Popularna kultura u Jugoslaviji 1945-1991* (Beograd, 2011); Predrag J. Marković, *Beograd između Istoka i Zapada 1948-1965* (Beograd, 1996).
[2] Arhiv Jugoslavije (Archives of Yugoslavia; hereinafter AJ), 559, Nesređeni materijal, Kulturna saradnja Jugoslavije sa zemljama Azije i Afrike, s.a.
[3] Paul Betts and Radina Vučetić, "Culture," in James Mark and Paul Betts (eds.), *Socialism Goes Global. The Soviet Union and Eastern Europe in the Age of Deconolonization* (Oxford, 2022), 148-60.

of high modernism in the West as a weapon of the cultural Cold War.[4] The term "socialist modernism" has recently gained currency, mainly in the field of the visual arts.[5] From the early 1950s, Yugoslav socialist modernism was given material form in monumental sculpture, brutalist architecture, art influenced by American abstract expressionism and the European avant-garde, and continuous experimentation.[6] Throughout the 1950s, shows on European and American architecture and art traveled across Yugoslavia, and Yugoslav architects and artists were invited to participate in Western biennials and fairs.

This alternative form of high modernism developed as a result of Yugoslavia's ambition to be socialist yet open to Western capitalism and its cultures. With her socialist modernism, Yugoslavia did not seek only to show support for international modernism, but also to reflect her own stance and unique, alternative path to socialism. Alternative art needed alternative spaces. The first big international promotion of Yugoslav socialist modernism and Yugoslavia's "own way to socialism" was at the 1958 World's Fair in Brussels.[7] Architect Vjenceslav Richter designed the Pavilion of Yugoslavia, which represented the avant-garde status of Yugoslavia and reformed, open and modern Yugoslav socialism, liberated from Stalinist oppression. Its overwhelmingly positive international reception was in itself a political message, and one that served to bolster existing interpretations of Yugoslav modern art as a symptom of the country's break from the Soviet orbit. According to many observers, the lack of any obvious ideological signs raised the question of whether Yugoslavia was still a socialist country at all.[8]

But it was not only the West and Western art that were openly accepted. In 1954, President Josip Broz Tito embarked on a series of international visits, touring Asia, Africa, Latin America, India, and the Middle East in the 1950s.[9] The 1955 Bandung Conference and the 1956 Brioni meeting of Tito, Nasser, and Nehru opened up spaces not only for a new politics, but for a new art as well. As Bojana Videkanić has argued, it is not a coincidence that in 1956, the same year that a MoMA exhibition of American Modern Art was organized in Yugoslavia, the country embarked on a crucial new geopolitical trajectory. The modernist art introduced in the 1950s carried the messages of universalism, tolerance, and mediation that would become the official Yugoslav

---

[4] Vladimir Kulić, "The Scope of Socialist Modernism: Architecture and State Representation in Postwar Yugoslavia," in Vladimir Kulić, Timothy Parker, and Monica Penick (eds.), *Sanctioning Modernism: Architecture and the Making of Postwar Identities* (Austin, 2014), 39.
[5] See the 2018–19 Museum of Modern Art exhibition in New York, well presented in Martino Stierli and Vladimir Kulić, *Toward a Concrete Utopia: Architecture in Yugoslavia, 1948–1980* (New York, 2018).
[6] On Yugoslav socialist modernism, see Ješa Denegri, *Teme srpske umetnosti 1945–1970. Od socijalističkog realizma do kinetičke umetnosti* (Beograd, 2009); Lidija Merenik, *Ideološki modeli: srpsko slikarstvo 1945–1968* (Beograd, 2001); Vladimir Kulić, Timothy Parker, and Monica Penick (eds.), *Sanctioning Modernism: Architecture and the Making of Postwar Identities* (Austin, 2014).
[7] Vladimir Kulić, "An Avant-Garde Architecture for an Avant-Garde Socialism: Yugoslavia at EXPO '58," *Journal of Contemporary History* 47.1 (2012): 161–84; Anna Kats, "Yugoslav Pavilion at EXPO 58, Brussels," in Martino Stierli and Vladimir Kulić (eds.), *Toward a Concrete Utopia: Architecture in Yugoslavia, 1948–1980* (New York, 2018), 132–5.
[8] Kulić, "An Avant-Garde Architecture for an Avant-Garde Socialism," 172, 179–80.
[9] Radina Vučetić, "Tito's Africa: Representation of Power during Tito's African Journeys," in Radina Vučetić, Paul Betts (eds.), *Tito in Africa: Picturing Solidarity* (Belgrade, 2017), 19.

policy.¹⁰ On a global scale, Yugoslav socialist modernism, in its encounters with the contemporary art of the Third World, constituted a new, non-aligned art. According to Videkanić, Yugoslav non-aligned modernism had strong anti-imperialist characteristics, although it is hard to specify just how Yugoslav non-aligned modernism differed from socialist modernism. The important point to note, however, is that Yugoslavia was searching for alternatives, and in the course of that search, museums and exhibitions halls became spaces for cultural encounters but also spaces for promoting international communication in the context of diplomatic initiatives.¹¹ Thus, Yugoslavia, as she took her distance from the Soviet Union and developed her non-aligned policy, began to promote both Yugoslav socialist modernism and, on a global scale, non-aligned modernism, in which Africa and its cultures had a special place.

Yugoslavia used new cultural ties with Africa to promote her own modern image as an aspect of Yugoslav policy towards the non-aligned world. This could be seen not only in her development initiatives or in technical assistance, but also in her cultural policy. Yugoslavia often used high culture in order to display Yugoslav values and modernity, and always expressed a positive attitude toward traditional African culture as a way of recognizing authentic African values and bringing them to Europe. In the cultural Cold War, Yugoslavia set out to change deeply rooted stereotypical views of African culture. Furthermore, Yugoslavia, as a country between East and West, or both Eastern and Western, was in her cultural diplomacy towards Africa a kind of bridge that connected Africa with both the Second and the First World and thereby rendered African postcolonial culture global.

Spaces of Encounter: Exhibiting "Otherness"

One of the most prominent tools in Cold War cultural diplomacy was the exhibition space. An upsurge in fairs and expositions started in the mid-nineteenth century with the "World's Fairs" featuring national pavilions, in which the newest accomplishments of individual states were touted, and ethnological displays of the non-European world served to justify the expansion of European colonial power.¹² A great deal of the imperial propaganda at exhibitions involved informing onlookers about life in "exotic" regions of the world, with a focus on the "backwardness" of African peoples.¹³ Exhibiting non-European art was an opportunity for certain nations "to trumpet their power and dominance including over subject peoples." A number of scholars have stressed the role of World's Fairs in justifying colonialism and encouraging racism.¹⁴

---

¹⁰ Bojana Videkanić, *Nonaligned Modernism: Socialist Postcolonial Aesthetics in Yugoslavia, 1945–1985*, 111, 115.
¹¹ Jan Marontate, "Museums and the Constitution of Culture," in Mark D. Jacobs and Nancy Weiss Hanrahan (eds.), *The Blackwell Companion to the Sociology of Culture* (Malden, MA, 2005), 287.
¹² Rorbert H. Haddow, *Pavilions of Plenty: Exhibiting American Culture Abroad in 1950s* (Washington, DC, and London, 1997), 3.
¹³ John E. Korasick, "Collecting Africa: African material culture displays and the American image of Africa, 1885–1930" (Ph.D. dissertation, Saint Louis University, 2005), 69–71.
¹⁴ Neal Rosendorf, "Expositions," in Akira Iriye and Pierre-Yves Saunier (eds.), *The Palgrave Dictionary of Transnational History: From the Mid-19th Century to the Present Day* (London, 2009), 371–3.

This way of presenting non-European art was also evident in museums. African material culture had been on display in European museums since the seventeenth century, at first in the form of "curiosity cabinets," which imposed an idea of something unknown and even bizarre. As Korasick notes, displays of African art in colonial museums made the Dark Continent even darker. Among the common representations of Africa were religious objects, masks, musical instruments, and sculptures that would transport visitors into the realms of the exotic. This process of "othering" became one of the central features of postcolonial discourse.[15]

Although the 1950s and 1960s brought major changes in the political life of newly independent African countries, representations of Africa in museums and exhibitions around the world failed to reflect them. Nevertheless, a shift in emphasis was sometimes perceptible. At the 1958 Brussels World's Fair, Congolese art was displayed as if a part of Belgian colonial possessions; at the1962 Seattle World's Fair, non-Western art was included in the same pavilion with Western art; the 1967 World's Fair in Montreal exhibited African, Pre-Columbian, Asian, and Western contemporary art—all together.[16] Nevertheless, the exhibits themselves were nearly the same as in the colonial era, and contemporary African art was usually absent.

While most previous analyses have concentrated on representations of non-European art at the World's Fairs and in Western museums, the focus of this chapter is art exhibitions and museum displays stemming from Yugoslav–African encounters. In the context of an almost uniform image of an exoticized Africa on the world stage, Yugoslavia attempted to play a different role, and to emphasize not only traditional but modern art as well, showing Yugoslav and African contemporary art together within a single alternative, non-aligned artistic space. Consequently, Yugoslavia always pointed out the richness of African culture, thus mounting a challenge both to Western cultural superiority and to the Soviet imposition of cultural values. While the peoples of Africa felt pressure to conform to Western approaches to art and fought for the promotion of their culture, Yugoslavia for its part acted as a mediator, seeking to emphasize not difference but rather the importance and value of African culture. Although some responses recorded in the Visitors' books at the Museum of African Art in Belgrade show that sometimes African art in Yugoslavia was experienced as the "other," that "other" was interpreted as neither opposite, nor negative, but positive, reflecting traditional African art and the continuity of art.

Yugoslavia and Africa: A Glimpse of the Cultural Encounters

In the African struggle against colonialism, the latter signified not only external political domination, but also cultural domination by the colonizers' value systems.[17] Independent African countries struggled to project a variety of images that would

---

[15] Korasick, "Collecting Africa," 32–5.
[16] Julie Nicoletta, "Art out of Place: International Art Exhibits at the New York's World's Fair of 1964–1965," *Journal of Social History* 44.2, "The Arts in Place" (Winter 2010): 502.
[17] *Arhiv Muzeja afričke umetnosti* (Archive of the Museum of African Art; hereinafter, AMAU), f. 48, Medunarodni kongres afrikanista 1967.

serve to counter preconceived European biases, by stressing the African contribution to world civilization, and the common African cultural heritage, as well as national specificities.[18] In April 1980, when "Days of African cultures" were organized in Belgrade, Novi Sad, and Ljubljana, in cooperation with L'Institut Culturel Africain from Dakar (Senegal), the role of the non-aligned countries was emphasized in the battle for decolonizing culture and introducing an African culture long "under the veil of [the] cultural colonization of the colonial conquerors."[19]

Yugoslav-African cultural encounters started in the mid-1950s with a series of exhibitions, concerts, folklore group visits, book translation programs, and artists' exchanges. Yugoslavia also served as a bridge connecting African culture with Europe. The first modern theater from Africa to have toured in Europe came to the Belgrade International Theater Festival (BITEF), alongside other African artists in other contexts. BITEF played a specific role in bringing modern Third World theater to Europe. This Yugoslav festival, which from 1967 onwards promoted the theatrical avant-garde, welcomed the world's most famous troupes including La MaMa from New York, the Soviet Taganka Theater, the Schaubühne from West Berlin and the Volksbühne from East Berlin, the Laboratory Theater from Wroclaw, and others. As the meeting point of the East, the West, and the Third World, this festival became a space of promotion for African modern theater as well by hosting Theater Limited from Kampala, Uganda (1972), l'Ensemble national du Sénégal (1973), le Théâtre permanente from Tunisia (1975), le Théâtre national "Mobutu Sese Seko" from Zaire (1980), and le Groupe Dramatique du Théâtre National from Mali (1984).[20] With such a repertoire, BITEF made African theater a part of the world avant-garde scene. According to one Yugoslav official, after their breakthrough in Yugoslavia, a number of African artists were invited to various European cultural events.[21] Yugoslavia was, in that regard, a springboard for African culture in Europe.

For African countries in postcolonial times, there was a big difference between the "civilizing mission," a notion invoked by colonizers to facilitate direct rule and military conquest, and the cultural diplomacy deployed by a number of different countries during the Cold War, Yugoslavia among them.[22] One of Yugoslav cultural diplomacy's most important goals was to alter Europeans' deeply rooted stereotypes of Africa and African culture. Aware that "[f]or centuries, Europe had a perception of African culture as the frenzied rhythm of ritual dances and folkloric masks," Yugoslavia tried to change these views which were, according to the Yugoslav press, "intentionally formed in a wrong way." Conversely, Yugoslavia insisted on the rich storehouse of African cultural

---

[18] Jessica C. E. Gienow-Hecht and Mark C. Donfried, "The Model of Cultural Diplomacy: Power, Distance, and the Promise of the Civil Society," in Jessica C. E. Gienow-Hecht and Mark C. Donfried (eds.), *Searching for a Cultural Diplomacy* (New York and Oxford, 2010), 19.
[19] AMAU, Hemeroteka, Isečci iz štampe, 1976–1980; M. Milivojević, "Dokazivanje identiteta," *Borba*, April 12, 1980, 26.
[20] Olga Latinčić, Branka Branković, and Svetlana Adžić (eds.), *BITEF: 40 godina novih pozorišnih tendencija* (Beograd, 2007).
[21] "Razgovor o mogućnostima kulturne saradnje," *Kultura* 51.52 (1980–1): 115–16.
[22] Jennifer Dueck, "International Rivalry and Culture in Syria and Lebanon under the French Mandate," in Jessica C. E. Gienow-Hecht and Mark C. Donfried (eds.), *Searching for a Cultural Diplomacy* (New York and Oxford, 2010), 140.

heritage, and on the battle not only for the decolonization of culture, but also for a "decolonization of mind."[23] From the mid-1950s, African culture was presented from a new and different perspective, because as a socialist and non-aligned but nonetheless European country, Yugoslavia was itself different from all the other countries competing for influence in Africa. It was no longer a question of the imperialist world's presentation of a "far-away culture," but a new, anti-imperialist world's presentation, one that rejected the habitual assertions of European domination and insisted, rather, from an entirely different perspective, on the value of displaying new cultures in Europe.[24] Yugoslavia, together with prominent African intellectuals and artists, sought to represent African cultures as part of global culture, on equal terms with other cultures.

Throughout the socialist period, Yugoslavia's closest cultural ties on the African continent were with Egypt, as were its closest political and economic relations. A cultural convention between the two countries was signed in 1958, but cultural exchanges had started even earlier, in 1954. In January of that year a folklore troupe visited and an art exhibition was staged, while a delegation of Egyptian professors visited Yugoslavia that summer.[25] As early as 1960 there were book translations, visits of Egyptian writers and filmmakers to Yugoslavia, and architect exchanges. One of the first activities in cultural exchange was the sending of folklore groups to Egypt, but it would appear to have been unsuccessful because, in the words of one Yugoslav official, "the Egyptian audience was satiated with this genre, and wanted something else."[26] In the cultural exchanges with Egypt and the Maghreb organized in subsequent years, Yugoslavia pursued a different course, promoting Yugoslav socialist modernism and high culture instead.[27] Through her cultural activities Yugoslavia thus sought to present herself as a modern state not only politically and technologically, but also culturally. Although not as economically developed as West European countries, Yugoslavia was more developed than most of Africa, and so in demonstrating the superiority of the Yugoslav system, she took pains to show respect towards Africa's cultures and Africa's wish to cast off its heavy colonial burden.

Yugoslav Art in African Spaces

In understanding what kind of culture Yugoslavia sent to Africa, it is necessary to analyze not only Yugoslav diplomacy, but also the cultural scene in Africa. Different speeches of African representatives during the 1980 "Days of African Cultures" betray

---

[23] AMAU, Hemeroteka, Isečci iz štampe, 1976–1980; Divljak Arok, "Afrika otkriva svoju kulturu," *Dnevnik*, March 30, 1980.
[24] Edward W. Said, *Culture and Imperialism* (New York, 1993), xii.
[25] *Diplomatski arhiv Ministarstva spoljnih poslova Republike Srbije* (Diplomatic Archive of the Ministry of Foreign Affairs of the Republic of Serbia; hereinafter DAMSPRS), PA, 1955, Egipat, f. 13, Pov. 15/55, Izveštaj o protekloj godini u Egiptu, Kairo, January 10, 1955.
[26] AJ, 559-3-5, Opšti poverljivi materijali IV, 1960, Komisiji za kulturne veze sa inostranstvom, pov. br. 450/1, DSIP; Beograd, May 18, 1960.
[27] AJ, 559, Kulturna saradnja sa UAR 1959–1971, Izveštaj o izvršenju programa kulturne saradnje za 1964/1965 godinu.

a tension, especially among young Africans, between a wish to preserve traditional culture and a concern to promote Westernized high culture. To judge by the comments of certain Yugoslav officials, Yugoslavia would seem to have successfully combined these divergent African preoccupations. By sending her high culture to Africa, Yugoslavia transferred "fraternal" high culture, and not the high culture of the former colonizers.[28]

From the very beginning, Yugoslavia sent outstanding artists. Two of the best known sculptors of the day, Antun Augustinčić and Frano Kršinić, made the Monument to the Victims of Fascism in Addis Ababa, Ethiopia, at Haile Selassie's request.[29] Tito's first visit to Egypt in 1955 was swiftly followed by an exhibition of contemporary Yugoslav art in Cairo.[30]

Sending Yugoslav high culture to Egypt became an integral part of Yugoslav cultural diplomacy, though there was a certain indecisiveness at the outset. Initially, Yugoslav officials would seem to have underestimated the African audience, even in Egypt. We have already observed that the early Yugoslav decision to send folklore groups was not welcomed by Egyptians, who expected high culture. Something similar occurred when Yugoslavia sent a delegation of writers to Egypt. According to the cable from the Yugoslav ambassador in Cairo, the Egyptians were so dissatisfied, even humiliated, by the poor quality of the Yugoslav delegation that they decided not to return the visit, because "Yugoslavs [had] underestimated Egyptian writers."[31] A comparable situation arose during Yugoslav Film Weeks in Cairo. It seems that Yugoslav film distributors tended to send second-class films, without taking into account the view of the Commission for International Cultural Relations, which insisted that only the very best Yugoslav films be sent to Egypt.[32] However, despite a few wrong moves, Yugoslavia decided to send high culture to North Africa, whenever possible, and "help Africa build [up] her cultural institutions." Generally, according to a Yugoslav observation dating from 1961, North Africa had a "higher level of audience," with high culture therefore the focus of the cultural exchanges, while for "other parts of Africa" folklore was suggested, as being more accessible.[33]

In the 1950s and 1960s, Eastern European cultural diplomacy often consisted of exporting high culture to the rest of the world, so Yugoslavia was no exception in this regard. International tours of the Bolshoi Ballet (including to Egypt in 1958 and 1961) were used to present a highbrow image of Soviet culture.[34] During Tito's visit to Cairo in 1959, a Yugoslav conductor conducted the Cairo Symphonic Orchestra. Special attention was likewise paid to Belgrade Opera performances in Cairo: in 1961 they

---

[28] "Afričke studije: Benin, Gabon, Obala Slonovače," *Kultura* 51/52 (1980–1): 179.
[29] AJ, 559, Nesređeni materijal, Jugoslavija-Etiopija 1955–1966.
[30] AJ, 837, I-2/5, Plan propagandnih aktivnosti povodom posete Predsednika Republike Egiptu i Etiopiji, 1955.
[31] AJ, 559, f. 5, Opšti materijali 1964, Kulturna saradnja Jugoslavije sa zemljama Afrike, Beograd, December 10, 1964.
[32] Radina Vučetić, "Uspostavljanje jugoslovenske filmske saradnje sa Egiptom," *Godišnjak za društvenu istoriju* 2 (2017): 63–4.
[33] AJ, 559, f. 4, Opšti materijali 1961, Izveštaj komisije za kulturne veze sa inostranstvom za 1961. godinu, Beograd, December 1961.
[34] Betts and Vučetić, "Culture," 152.

performed seventeen times. So successful was the tour that afterwards the Egyptian Ministry of Culture supposedly asked Yugoslavia, rather than Italy or West Germany, for help in "establishing and developing the Cairo Opera."[35]

One of the first big Yugoslav breakthroughs on the African cultural scene in Egypt was her participation in the Alexandria Biennale for Mediterranean Countries. This event was inaugurated in 1955 by the Egyptian President Gamal Abdel Nasser, and Yugoslavia participated from the very beginning. The First Biennale was organized to celebrate Revolution Day in Egypt, and the idea was to gather together the various Mediterranean countries and their art. In the period of Africa's awakening, however, the Biennale would seem to have acquired a much greater importance than anyone had anticipated. At first glance, an international exhibition organized in terms of the Mediterranean basin appears reminiscent of Egypt's *ancien régime* and its pre-revolutionary cultural politics. However, a closer look reveals how the event, shaped by Third Worldism, served to revive the Mediterranean as a much more global space.[36] At the First Biennale there were 400 exhibits on display, the majority from France and Italy.[37] However, Yugoslavia won the most prizes at the first two Biennales (1955 and 1957), having sent the best of Yugoslav modernism.

To judge by the Egyptian reaction to the Yugoslav exhibits (as relayed by the Yugoslav Cultural Center in Cairo), out of all the countries exhibiting, Yugoslavia showed the greatest "freedom of expression."[38] However, the situation changed in the coming years. The Third Biennale in 1959 was accorded less attention by Yugoslav artists; some of the most celebrated artists concluded that it was more important for them to take part at the Biennale in Venice, or at other exhibitions in the West.[39] Yugoslavia won less praise in 1959 because, as the Yugoslav reports conceded, the quality of the art sent did not match the high standards of previous years.[40]

Nevertheless, the policy of sending high culture and socialist modernism to the Third World continued into the 1960s. The year 1962 saw an exhibition of Yugoslav contemporary art in India, and in 1963 there was a big exhibition in India and Indonesia of Yugoslav socialist modernist painter Petar Lubarda, whose work signaled a complete break with Soviet-style socialist realism.[41] In Africa, the Exhibition of Yugoslav Contemporary Art was organized in Tunisia (1963) and Morocco and Egypt (1964).[42]

Comparing Yugoslavia's art diplomacy in the East and West highlights the particularities of its approach to the Third World. Although the best artists, representatives one and all of socialist modernism, exhibited in galleries and museums

---

[35] AJ, 559, f. 3, Poverljivo 1961–1962, Operativni izveštaj Informativnog centra za mjesec juni 1961.
[36] Dina A. Ramadan, "The Alexandria Biennale and Egypt's Shifting Mediterranean," in Adam J. Goldwyn and Renée M. Silverman (eds.), *Mediterranean Modernism: Intercultural Exchange and Aesthetic Development* (New York, 2016), 343–61.
[37] AJ, 559, Bijenale u Aleksandriji 1955–1966, pov. br. 948/55, Kairo, May 10, 1955.
[38] AJ, 559, Bijenale u Aleksandriji 1955–1966, pov. br. 948/55, Kairo , February 9, 1958.
[39] AJ, 559, Bijenale u Aleksandriji 1955–1966, pov. br. 948/55, Kairo , February 9, 1958.
[40] AJ, 559-3-5, Opšti poverljivi materijali IV, 1960, pov. br. 450/1, DSIP; Beograd , May 18, 1960.
[41] AJ, 559, Kulturne veze sa Azijom i Afrikom 1965, Kulturno-prosvetne veze i odnosi Jugoslavije sa zemljama Azije i Afrike, July 17, 1965.
[42] AJ, 559, f. 5, Izveštaj komisije za kulturne veze sa inostranstvom za 1963. godinu, Beograd, decembar 1963.

in the West, the situation in relation to the East was different. Instead of sending Yugoslav modern art, which the governments in the East would not have welcomed, the exhibition "Yugoslav painting from the national liberation struggle 1941–1945" went to Moscow, Minsk, and East Berlin, while the "Exhibition of Yugoslav tapestry and sculpture" went to Budapest.[43] In this sense, Yugoslavia treated North Africa more like the West and as an important battlefield in its cultural diplomacy. However, the Third World only got to see second-class works in the socialist modernist tradition. Moreover, the situation in sub-Saharan Africa was completely different. There were no big exhibitions of Yugoslav modern art held there. It is possible that from the government's point of view there was no point in sending high culture to sub-Saharan Africa, as even such museums as did exist were almost empty. In the case of Mali, for example, the Keita government had tended to favor the popular folk arts, to the exclusion of high art. It was not until the early 1980s that the National Museum was built in Bamako, and even then it was financed by France.[44] In exhibition exchanges with sub-Saharan Africa, Africa came to Yugoslavia with its art and not vice-versa.

African Art in Yugoslav Space

For a long time, the only image of Africa in Yugoslavia was an exotic one. In the first half of the twentieth century, the image was formed by colonial literature, comics, and advertisements (which almost all had racist connotations) and in the 1950s and 1960s mostly by American films, such as *The Snows of Kilimanjaro*. The dominant conception was of a wild Africa, which fascinated with its landscape, animals, safaris, and unknown people with exotic rituals. That faraway and exotic Africa became a Yugoslav ally, and Africans became "our brothers."

As Tobias Rupprecht has noted, the exoticism of the 1950s and 1960s was an integral part of the cultural internationalism of those times; but just as much, it was the culmination of a phenomenon with a long history that went back to the early days of European colonialism. Distant places, known only to travelers and adventurers, were associated with thrills and excitement, and the depiction of the Third World in postwar Europe was not free of a certain sense of superiority. Given Yugoslavia's strong political ties and friendship with Africa, we can plausibly argue that exhibiting African art was not a way of expressing cultural imperialism, or Yugoslav (European) superiority. As Rupprecht has observed with reference to the Soviet case, what is evident is a mingling of positive stereotypes of the "exotic" with naïve curiosity.[45] Throughout the socialist period, Yugoslavia promoted African art not as a curiosity, and not by deploying what was at the time a still dominant Western discourse, but as original and authentic fine art,

---

[43] AJ, 559, f. 7, Opšti materijali za 1966, Izveštaj za 1965.
[44] Mary Jo Arnoldi, "Youth Festivals and Museums: The Cultural Politics of Public Memory in Postcolonial Mali," *Africa Today* 52.4, "Memory and the Formation of Political Identities in West Africa" (Summer, 2006): 66.
[45] Tobias Rupprecht, *Soviet Internationalism after Stalin: Interaction and Exchange Between the USSR and Latin America During the Cold War* (Cambridge, 2015), 77–8.

whose aesthetic value deserved celebration.[46] From the early 1960s, Yugoslavia helped African culture emerge from its isolation and take an active role in the dialog of cultures.

Eastern European interest in traditional African art intensified in the 1950s and 1960s, with the Soviet Union, Yugoslavia, the GDR, and the Czechs leading the way. Dozens of exhibitions on traditional African art were curated, dedicated museums were founded, and journals launched to deepen the sense of international solidarity.[47] However, African art and culture in Yugoslavia should be perceived through the prisms of *négritude* and pan-Africanism, which played an extremely important role in the African decolonization of mind, and which were widely accepted by Yugoslavs. Petar Guberina, the founder of the Yugoslav Institute for Africa, was in close touch with Aimé Césaire from the 1930s on. He was one of the most committed advocates of *négritude* in Yugoslavia: in 1961 he was invited by Léopold Senghor to Senegal's Independence Day celebrations; both Césaire and Senghor were welcome guests in Yugoslavia, and they were widely translated and respected.[48] This attitude towards African art and *négritude* was a first, important step away from the dominant Western view, but also from the Eastern one. In contrast to the Yugoslav approach, Eastern bloc intellectuals were never keen supporters of *négritude*, which to them seemed too Western, racist, and bourgeois.[49] Although Senghor frequently spoke about the importance of socialism and the need to blend socialism with *négritude*, and he was an inspiration on the world stage so far as anti-imperialism was concerned, for Eastern European critics, his idea of *négritude* was much too ethnically based.[50]

The embrace of *négritude* was not new in socialist Yugoslavia, but rather something inherited from the interwar period, influenced in part by the Parisian *negrophilia* of the 1920s. The hybrid synthesis of the avant-garde, the *art nègre* cult, and black modernism, manifest in bohemian Paris, was also present in Serbian Zenithism and Dadaism, whose manifestos and poetry used the *nigger lingua* of the Zurich Dadaists, and in the Serbian surrealist movement, inspired by André Breton and Pablo Picasso.[51]

In the socialist period, Yugoslavia, singled out by her non-aligned policy, not only promoted African traditional art, but modern art as well. The Yugoslav stance helped with the global promotion of African modern art and made the country's museums and exhibition halls spaces for embracing African culture and transferring it to the wider world. This was not recognized as cultural policy from the very beginning. At first, Yugoslav officials insisted on African art that "reflected the spirit and character of the folk tradition," and argued that exhibiting "contemporary art, which was essentially an import from Western centres, should take second place."[52] But this attitude changed very quickly. The closest ties were, as in politics, with Egypt, and this was reflected in

---

[46] *Art of Oceania, Africa and the Americas from the Museum of Primitive Art: An Exhibition of the Metropolitan Museum of Art 1969, May 10–August 17, 1969* (New York, 1970).
[47] Betts and Vučetić, "Culture," 157–8.
[48] Rorbert Fraser, *West African Poetry—A Critical History* (Cambridge, 1986), 44.
[49] Janet G. Vaillant, "Dilemmas for Anti-Western Patriotism: Slavophilism and Négritude," *Journal of Modern African Studies* 12.3 (September 1974): 377–93.
[50] Betts and Vučetić, "Culture," 169–70.
[51] Dejan Sretenović, *Crno telo, bele maske* (Beograd, 2004), 13–15.
[52] AJ, 559, f. 5, Opšti materijali 1963, Izveštaj komisije za kulturne veze sa inostranstvom za 1962. godinu, Beograd, March 1963.

the fact that not only was Egypt the first African country to welcome Yugoslav modern art, but was also the first African country to send its own modern art to Yugoslavia.

Egyptian modern art had played a very important role in the formation of national identity in the 1920s and in the later affirmation of Egypt's status as an independent state. Yugoslavia for her part recognized the role of modern art not only in her own, but also in Egypt's cultural diplomacy.[53] Beginning in the 1960s, there were several exhibitions of Egyptian contemporary art in Belgrade. The first, in 1962, left a strong and a very positive impression on the audience, who encountered contemporary Egyptian art for the first time. One has to bear in mind that the Yugoslav audience had grown familiar with the latest trends in the world's contemporary art since the split with the Soviet Union.[54] The 1962 "Exhibition of Egyptian Contemporary Art" presented the works of renowned masters such as Salah Taher, Ramses Younan, Abdel Wahab Morsi, Salah Abdel-Kerim, Seif Wanly, and Taha Hussein.[55] Belgrade also hosted two further exhibitions of Egyptian applied art (in 1967 and 1979) and the "Exhibition of Ethiopian Paintings" in 1964, which was displayed in Belgrade, Zagreb, and Maribor.[56]

Among African modern art exhibitions, of special importance were the Tanzanian "Contemporary Sculpture of Makonde" (1979) and "Contemporary Art from Ghana" (1980), which challenged the idea of exotic and primitive African art by bringing contemporary and modern sub-Saharan art into Yugoslav space. The "Contemporary Sculpture of Makonde" exhibition featured sixty works of modern Tanzanian artists belonging to the Makonde people. However, it seems that the organizers wanted to combine modern art with the traditional and, to the audience, more familiar kind, since the exhibited works had traditional sculpture as their foundation, being "inspired by mythology, traditional motifs, but also [the] modern life of Tanzania."[57] A similar scenario played out with the exhibition of Ghanaian contemporary art, where twenty-one modern paintings by Ghanaian artists were complemented by fifty artifacts representing "folk, traditional art."[58]

From the Yugoslav report about the exhibition, it is evident that the organizers wanted to emphasize the artists—"the works of specific artists are exhibited, and not 'nameless' African art," and the fact that they had all been "educated at art schools and academies."[59] Most of the artists now considered to be the pioneers of Ghanaian contemporary art were featured in the Belgrade exhibition in 1980—Kofi Antubam, Amon Kotei, E. V. Asihene, A. O. Bartimeus, E. Owusu-Dartey, R. T Ackam, Dr. A. Glover, S. Amenuker, E. K. Tetteh, A. Bucknor, R. J. Amos, T. Enghagha, J. H. Frimpong Ansah, C. E. Phillips, E. K. Tetteh, S. K. Prah, and N.A.K. Aduku.[60] Even a

[53] Narcisa Knežević-Šijan, "Egyptian Art: Important Belgrade Exhibitions of Fine and Applied Arts in the Second Half of the 20th Century," in Emilija Epštajn (ed.), *Egypt Remembered by Serbia* (Beograd, 2013), 81.
[54] Vučetić, *Coca-Cola Socialism*, 151.
[55] Knežević-Šijan, "Egyptian Art," 83.
[56] AJ, 559, f. 6, Opšti materijali 1965, Izveštaj o radu komsije za kulturne veze sa inostranstvom u 1964. godini.
[57] AMAU, Izložbe 1979–1980, A platform for the exchange of experience between Yugoslav and African cultural workers, February 1980.
[58] AMAU, Izložbe 1979–1980, Izveštaj sa izložbe "Savremena umetnost Gane."
[59] AMAU, Izložbe 1979–1980, Izveštaj sa izložbe "Savremena umetnost Gane."
[60] Ablade Glover, *Pioneers of Contemporary Ghanaian Art Exhibition: Catalogue* (Accra, 2012).

2012 book about the pioneers of the Ghanaian art states that contemporary art in Ghana was still considered as something "[that] is not known about, [with] little attention [being] paid to [it]," while "traditional Ghanaian Art is well known and recognized as a valid art form practiced during a [long] period in our history."[61] So it was that by the early 1980s, Yugoslavia, through her promotion not only of traditional but also of contemporary African art, was playing an important role in changing the general perception of African art.

By incorporating exhibitions of African modern art into Yugoslav cultural life, Yugoslavia showed her awareness of the important influence African sculpture had exerted on modern art. As already mentioned, during the interwar period, especially in the 1930s, there had been close ties between Yugoslav surrealists and the European avant-garde, who deeply respected African art. In the light of that prewar experience, Yugoslavia continued to be open to modern sculpture during the Cold War, and in the mid- 1950s hosted major exhibitions.[62] The Yugoslav decision to exhibit African modern art marked a watershed: by dispensing with the notion of exhibiting only African "primitive art," Yugoslavia by the same token jettisoned the whole narrative connecting African art with backwardness and exoticism. Yugoslavia wanted to present herself as a modern state with modern art and took the same approach to the African states that were presented in Yugoslavia—the space of the art exhibition was one that made those countries look modern and progressive.

Yet, at the same time, exhibitions from sub-Saharan Africa should be regarded from a different perspective. Indeed, in the perception of sub-Saharan culture, much of the earlier exoticism prevailed (the focus on the tribal, the primitive, the ethnographic). This should be understood from the perspective of the Yugoslav attitude towards *négritude*: accepting and promoting African blackness was a way of accepting and promoting an African identity. One of the first big exhibitions from sub-Saharan Africa was held in Belgrade, Zagreb, and Ljubljana in 1965, and it came in the guise of Senegalese propaganda, intended to attract people and inform them about a forthcoming Festival of African Culture in Dakar in 1966. Masks and traditional art were the main exhibits and they drew large numbers, whereupon it was decided to send the exhibition to the Ethnographical Museum in Zagreb, and to Ljubljana too.[63]

The biggest exhibition (before the official institutionalization of African art in the shape of the Museum of African Art) was "The Art of West Africa," held in 1973 at the Ethnographic Museum in Belgrade and based on the private collection of Veda and Zdravko Pečar. At the opening, Belgrade's deputy mayor emphasized the exhibition's political role, since its goal was not only "introducing African culture, but also getting to know the people with whom Yugoslavs are working in the creation and realization of the non-aligned policy, and just in the non-aligned movement are our most important partners—around forty countries with almost 400 million people in the

---

[61] Glover, *Pioneers of Contemporary Ghanaian Art Exhibition*, 5.
[62] Vučetić, *Coca-Cola Socialism*, 151.
[63] AJ, 559, Nesređeni materijal, Informacija o kulturno-prosvetnoj saradnji i vezama između SFR Jugoslavije i Senegala, October 19, 1965.

African continent."⁶⁴ The exhibited collection numbered over 420 objects of "black art" (as it was called in the catalog): masks, figural sculptures, ancestral figures, ritual artifacts, textiles, and musical instruments from Mali, Guinea, Upper Volta, Ivory Coast, and Ghana.⁶⁵ The predominance in the collection of masks and anthropomorphic figures would seem to reflect the influence of Western colonial museums. However, for both Belgrade and Yugoslavia (the exhibition toured throughout the country and was exhibited in the ethnographic museums in Ljubljana and Zagreb, as well as in some smaller local museums) this was an outstanding cultural event, placing before the general public a large collection of African art in a part of Europe where this art was regrettably under-represented in museums.⁶⁶

Another exhibition, "South of Sahara," was also curated with a clear propaganda aim: to bring sub-Saharan Africa to a wider audience. "South of Sahara" came to Yugoslavia as "a gift from UNESCO and the International Fund for Cultural Development."⁶⁷ The first preparations for this exhibition were made during the UNESCO General conference in Belgrade (September 1980), when the Museum of African Art in Belgrade opened an exhibition of artistic documentary photos by Israeli photographer Marli Shamir. "South of Sahara" opened in the Cultural Center of Belgrade, and on display were seventy photographs showing the landscape, traditional life, deserts and savannas, architecture, and art of African people. The photographic exhibition was complemented by exhibits from the Museum of African Art (traditional art from Mali), which made it more appealing to the audience.⁶⁸ The exhibition toured Yugoslavia for two years and was on display in 1981 in the Belgrade National Theater to mark the twentieth anniversary of the First Belgrade Conference of the Non-Aligned Movement. Parts of the exhibition toured all over the country, even to factories, so "that workers from 'Galenika' factory ... could see in their *menza* [canteen] an artistic photo exhibition of the everyday life, folk customs and art of African people."⁶⁹ The exhibition had an official journey to a number of schools, pioneers' centers, houses of culture, sports organizations, Yugoslav People's Army barracks, and even to the party schools.⁷⁰ It is hard to say if these kinds of exhibition drew people closer to African culture. But the fact that the African way of life could be seen not only in American films but in different Yugoslav spaces testifies to the strong desire to bring Africa closer to Europe.

Based on these few examples covering less than two decades ("The Exhibition of African masks" in 1965, "The Art of West Africa" in 1973, and "South of Sahara" 1980–2), it seems that the exotic image of sub-Saharan Africa remained dominant. It is hard to judge how much ordinary people understood the ideas of *négritude* and pan-Africanism. Senghor, Césaire, and other representatives of *négritude* and pan-Africanism were present in Yugoslav intellectual circles, but it is hard to believe that a

---

[64] *Umetnost Zapadne Afrike. Zbirka Vede i dr Zdravka Pečara—poklon Beogradu* (Beograd, 1973), 3.
[65] *Umetnost Zapadne Afrike*, 34.
[66] *Umetnost Zapadne Afrike*, 33.
[67] AMAU, II, Isečci iz štampe 1982–1986, V. S., "Izložba Muzeja afričke umetnosti," June 16, 1982.
[68] AMAU, VIII, Gostujuće izložbe, Izveštaj sa izložbe "Južno od Sahare."
[69] AMAU, II, Isečci iz štampe 1982–1986, B. Š., "Južno od Sahare," *Politika*, April 19, 1981.
[70] AMAU, VIII, Gostujuće izložbe, Izveštaj sa izložbe "Južno od Sahare."

pupil at a school or a worker from the "Galenika" factory could grasp the importance of traditional African art in promoting blackness and a common African identity. Yet even if it remained something far away and exotic to most, Africa was now also virtually in front of their eyes, even in their own work spaces. Thus African art became if not familiar, then closer.

The Institutionalization of African Art in Yugoslavia

In one of his speeches discussing underdevelopment in Asian and African countries, Tito concluded that "we must help these people as much as possible."[71] Not only Tito, but many different institutions in Yugoslavia worked hard to include African people and culture not only in Yugoslav space, but also in the mental maps of Yugoslavs trying to reject stereotypes and prejudices. Besides sporadic exhibitions, in the late 1970s and early 1980s Yugoslavia established two important institutions as spaces for the promotion of African and non-aligned art, which help us to understand not only the policy of exhibiting African art in Yugoslavia, but Yugoslav foreign policy as well. These two institutions were the Museum of African Art and the "Josip Broz Tito" Art Gallery of the Non-Aligned Countries.

The first ethnographic museums around the world were spaces that translated other cultures to Europe and were instruments of domination and colonial power.[72] Since Yugoslavia always emphasized her lack of a colonial past, it is not surprising that the biggest African collection in Yugoslavia was established not as a part of some pre-existing ethnographic museum, but rather as an autonomous institutional space, a Museum of African Art. The Museum of African Art opened in 1977 to present the collection of West African art donated to Belgrade by Veda and Zdravko Pečar, part of which featured in the 1973 exhibition discussed above.[73] It was during this 1973 exhibition that they decided to donate their collection in its entirety to the City of Belgrade.

To understand what kind of people these collectors were, it is important to consider their biographies.[74] Both Pečars joined the party in the 1930s, and both fought as partisans in the national liberation struggle. As Veda Pečar recollected, "my husband and I were children of the Party, and Tito had a special role in our lives."[75] The Pečars were among the first socialist explorers of Africa. Veda was a strong party figure (among other posts held, a member of the Central Committee) and cultural attaché in Tunisia,

---

[71] Ana Sladojević, *Slike o Africi = Images of Africa* (Belgrade, 2015), 1.
[72] Marisa Gonzáles de Oleaga, "Museums," in Akira Iriye and Pierre-Yves Saunier (eds.), *The Palgrave Dictionary of Transnational History: From the mid-19th Century to the Present Day* (London, 2009), 731.
[73] The full name of the museum is The Museum of African Art. Veda and dr Zdravko Pečar Collection.
[74] Nemanja Radonjić, "Drums of Revolution: Veda Zagorac and Zdravko Pečar," in Ana Sladojević, Emilija Epštajn (eds.), *Nympakorndzidzi: One Man, No Chop. The (Re)conceptualization of the Museum of African Art—The Veda and Dr. Zdravko Pečar Collection* (Belgrade, 2017), 156–75.
[75] AMAU, I, Isečci iz štampe 1976–1980, Milan Golumbovski, "Zbirka od prijateljstva: Muzej afričke umetnosti—doprinos Titovoj misiji mira," *Večernje novosti*, May 13, 1980.

where she worked on propaganda in the context of the Algerian struggle for independence. Her husband Zdravko was a journalist, editor of the prominent daily newspaper *Politika* and the journal *International Politics*, and towards the end of his career the director of Radio Yugoslavia. While in Algeria, he fought on the FLN side, and played an important role in promoting the Algerian struggle not only in Yugoslavia but also in Europe. Both husband and wife were outspoken in their anti-colonial convictions; support for the liberation of African peoples was a prominent theme in all their work.[76] Beginning in 1967, Zdravko Pečar served as ambassador to eight African countries and as a diplomat, he and his wife began to collect the art which would later form the basis for the collection of the Museum of African Art. The collecting of African art was a typical colonial practice.[77] However, the Pečars were not wealthy colonizers but rather "socialist collectors," with remarkable wartime and communist pedigrees. Their modesty and socialist values could be seen in their desire not to attend the opening of the Museum of African Art which carried their name: in a letter to one party functionary, Pečar explained that their presence would have been incompatible with their idea that the whole venture should have "the quality of communist ethics that it is necessary to share everything with society, and not keep it greedily for yourself."[78]

The original collection had 1,200 pieces of African art from West Africa (Mali, Senegal, Guinea, Upper Volta, Ivory Coast, Ghana, Togo, Benin, Nigeria, and Cameroon) and from various different tribes (Bambara, Dogon, Marka, Malinke, Mosi, Bobo, Kisi, Baga, Dan, Gere, Senufo, Baule, Ashanti, Fon, Yourka, and others).[79] At first glance, it resembled a colonial museum that focused primarily on acquiring objects defined as acceptable in Western aesthetic terms, such as statues and masks. This kind of colonial museum mostly concentrated on collecting objects from specific ethnic groups, but we have to bear in mind that within the international arena of *négritude*, these groups were considered to be the region's most prolific "art-producing cultures."[80] Even with the deep respect that the Pečars had for African art and culture, it is obvious that the museum was shaped on the Western model—at the time, the only one available.

Yet the Western model was developed and transformed in the Yugoslav case thanks to the presence of non-aligned and anti-colonial rhetoric. As the President of the Belgrade Municipal Assembly remarked at the opening of the museum, it was the first museum in Yugoslavia devoted to the art of the African peoples. He also stressed that it had not only cultural but broader social and political significance:

This museum will stand as a symbol of the times when the movement of non-alignment generated a new spirit in political relations among people and a new attitude of appreciation towards the achievements of folk art. There is symbolism in a museum of their art being opened in Belgrade, a city whose artistic achievements were also plundered through history by a series of conquerors.

[76] Radonjić, "Drums of Revolution," 164.
[77] Ana Sladojević, *Muzej afričke umetnosti. Konteksti i reprezentacije* (Beograd, 2014), 61.
[78] AMAU, XVI, Razno, Pismo Zdravka Pečara Miljenku Zrelecu, Accra, April 22, 1977.
[79] *Museum of African Art: the Veda and Zdravko Pečar Collection* (Beograd, 1977), 59.
[80] Arnoldi, "Youth Festivals and Museums," 68.

He also added that, by contrast with other museums of African art, established in the countries of former colonizers and as a consequence of imperial conquest, the museum in Belgrade was the result of "friendship and sincere love for the people of this world, with enthusiasm for the strength of their artistic expression."[81] At the time it opened to the public, in 1977, the facility was promoted as Europe's only anti-colonial museum.[82]

From its very beginning, the museum was strongly committed to acting as a space for cooperation with African countries, museums, and experts, while also encouraging encounters with politicians. The political importance of the museum was confirmed by visits from many African heads of state and intellectuals.[83] At the international level, besides its cooperation with a number of African and European museums and institutes, the Museum of African Art enjoyed major support from UNESCO from its inception.[84] Its cooperation with reputable institutions from the West, together with its intrinsic artistic value, led to the museum being ranked among the leading institutions of its kind in Europe and in the world in general. Its importance was all the greater given how few museums at that date were exclusively dedicated to African art.

In a number of works on the Museum of African Art, Ana Sladojević contrasted a set of practices of collecting, studying, and displaying objects in the museum that could be described as adhering to Western (colonial) practices, with another set that can be seen as anti-colonial.[85] The Museum of African Art, she has concluded, is a specific space of representation that combines two opposed ideologies and two different narratives. On the one hand, it was established in the Western colonial style with an ethnographic narrative. On the other hand, it conveyed the Yugoslav state's non-aligned policy in a contrasting, anti-colonial narrative, although, according to Sladojević, it was not precisely and clearly defined.[86] However, in this "duality of the museum's discourse," Ana Sladojević recognizes a space where contemporary African artists and theoretical approaches (lectures, a range of different programs) to African art could be seen by visitors.[87]

Galleries and museums are, in Eilean Hooper-Greenhill's definition, spaces of cultural encounter, but also spaces in which people may come to know new things and where their perceptions may radically change.[88] Over the years, the Museum of African Art has become an indispensable center for the study of African tradition, history,

---

[81] *Museum of African Art*, 4.
[82] Sladojević and Epštajn, *Nympakor ndzidzi*, 24.
[83] Moussa Traoré, president of Mali; Daniel arap Moi, president of Kenya; Kenneth Kaunda, president of Zambia; Mathieu Kérékou, president of Benin; Mobutu Sese Seko, president of Zaire; Robert Mugabe, president of Zimbabwe; Lansana Conté, president of Guinea; Ibrahim Babangida, president of Nigeria, and likewise many prominent intellectuals (Chinua Achebe, Basile Kossou, Théophile Obenga, Roger Dorsinville), in Marija Ličina, "Muzej afričke umetnosti u Beogradu (nastanak, tazvoj, perspektive)" (M.A. dissertation, University of Belgrade, 2012), 59–60.
[84] It was also visited by directors of UNESCO and the Horniman Museum, the museum with the longest tradition of exhibiting African art.
[85] Sladojević, *Slike o Africi* = *Images of Africa*; Ana Sladojević, "Museum as the Image of the World, the Space of Representations of Identity and Ideology" (Ph.D. dissertation, University of Arts in Belgrade, 2011); Ana Sladojević, "Muzej afričke umetnosti i njegov antikolonijalni diskurs," *Kultura* 134 (2012): 92–103.
[86] Sladojević, "Muzej afričke umetnosti u Beogradu i njegov antikolonijalni diskurs," 92.
[87] Sladojević, *Muzej afričke umetnosti: konteksti i reprezentacije*, 65–6.
[88] Eilean Hooper-Greenhill, *Museums and the Shaping of Knowledge* (London and New York, 2003), 2.

civilization, art, and contemporary cultural trends. Thanks to its curating of exhibitions, and thanks to its hosting of lectures, literary and music evenings, and other educational programs, the museum has built up its own public, especially of young people. During its first ten years, the Museum of African Art had 50,000 visitors, while its exhibitions at other sites and in other towns and cities were attended by approximately one million people. In terms of sheer scale, the Museum of African Art was the largest space for Yugoslav encounters with Africa within Yugoslavia.

However, it is worth questioning the real result of this kind of presentation. Visitors' books reveal some of the reactions of the public, which were mostly marked by their discovery of African culture and exoticism: "after looking at the collection, one is much closer to this civilization"; "this exhibition helps that far and exotic world come closer"; "this beautiful museum is striking confirmation of African culture and civilization. How could anyone claim that Africa didn't have civilization and history?" In almost all their written reactions, people mentioned their fascination with masks.[89] It is striking that not a single reaction or impression was connected with anti-colonialism, anti-imperialism, or non-alignment, but carried only fascination with African civilization, with the focus on something exotic.

Besides the Museum of African Art, another institution played a crucial role in the promotion of Third World art in Yugoslavia and worldwide: the "Josip Broz Tito" Art Gallery of the Non-Aligned Countries, which opened on September 1, 1984, the twentieth anniversary of the Cairo Conference of the Non-Aligned movement. The fact that it had in its title both the term "non-aligned" and the name of the Yugoslav leader and one of the key figures of the non-aligned movement defined its role not only in Yugoslavia, but in the Third World as well. The gallery was the first organized space for the global promotion of non-aligned art. As stated in the gallery's catalog, "all nations have the sovereign right to develop their national culture and share in cultural exchange with other peoples, and help create, on an equal footing, the cultural treasures of mankind." The idea was to overcome artificial divisions into "major" and "minor" cultures, into "metropolitan" and "peripheral" cultures, and to avoid an arbitrarily established hierarchy of values "imposed by certain cultural models."[90] The introductory remarks in the catalog were written by Raif Dizdarević, then the Federal Secretary of Foreign Affairs. He stated that it was essential to ensure equal respect for the cultural identity of every nation and the development of every national culture. In a way, by aiding the development of Third World countries' cultures and incorporating them into a wider cultural space in the time of Cold War divisions and tensions, Yugoslavia was creating a global culture.

Although the Art Gallery of the Non-Aligned Countries was a Yugoslav-based institution, it was more than a Yugoslav project. At the Seventh Non-Aligned Conference in New Delhi in 1983, non-aligned countries were invited to collaborate in the creation of the Non-Aligned Gallery for the promotion of non-aligned art. The First Conferences of Ministers of Culture of the Non-Aligned and Developing Countries in Pyongyang (1983) and Luanda (1985) further elaborated the activities of

---

[89] AMAU, Visitors' books.
[90] *Galerija umjetnosti nesvrstanih zemalja "Josip Broz Tito"—Titograd—Yugoslavia* (Titograd), 2.

the gallery. After a number of meetings of the non-aligned leaders, a decision was taken in New Delhi in 1986 that the "Josip Broz Tito" Art Gallery of the Non-Aligned Countries should become a joint non-aligned institution.

In its first five years, the gallery mounted over 100 exhibitions, and its permanent collection grew to over 750 exhibits from fifty-five countries, from ancient art history to contemporary works created at the gallery's studios by artists from non-aligned and developing countries. African culture was presented at the exhibition "African Bronze," at "Mask and African Wooden Sculpture," at the exhibition of Malian painters, and in the context of the Days of Tanzania.[91] Moreover, the gallery succeeded in breaking through to an international audience by organizing exhibitions at the Eighth Non-Aligned Conference in Harare in 1986, which subsequently toured Lusaka, Dar es Salaam, New Delhi, and Cairo. The exhibition in Harare in 1986 was therefore the first presentation of non-aligned modern art outside of Yugoslavia.[92]

The recognition of the autochthonous cultural values of non-aligned and developing countries was one of the main goals of the non-aligned movement. Catalogs for the gallery often mentioned avoiding the dangers of cultural colonialism and "preserving national identity despite colonialism, occupation, foreign domination, despite racism, economic exploitation, removal of cultural treasures, etc."[93] The art of the non-aligned countries, which was marginalized on the global artistic scene, according to the directors of the gallery, was meant to serve "for the development of cultural pluralism in the world."[94]

Even as ambitious plans were being floated for a Triennial Art Exhibition of the non-aligned countries, Yugoslavia itself collapsed. In 1995 the gallery was incorporated into the Center of Contemporary Art in Podgorica. Josip Broz Tito, in that sense, lost not only the city (the capital city of Montenegro, Titograd, was renamed Podgorica) but also "his" non-aligned gallery. With the collapse of Yugoslavia, the idea of the non-aligned movement faded away, but Yugoslav–African encounters had nonetheless done much to bring African culture and art closer to the Yugoslav peoples.

Overall, it cannot be fully determined how far Yugoslavia and Africa succeeded in getting to know each other via art, what their mutual perceptions were, and whether they managed to transcend local and international encounters by making them global. It would also seem fair to ask whether Yugoslavia, with all her openness to African art and culture, succeeded in rejecting prejudices and stereotypes that had been present for centuries. Certainly, Yugoslavia did a great deal not only through her promotion of Yugoslav socialist modernism in Africa, and even more through the promotion of African art and culture in Yugoslavia, but on the global level as well. In this positioning of African and non-aligned art globally, Yugoslavia showed profound respect for "small countries" similar to herself, and for autochthonous cultures which were usually rendered invisible in global Cold War cultural diplomacy. The aim announced at the opening of the "Josip Broz Tito" Non-Aligned Art Gallery to overcome artificial

---

[91] Lj. Šukanović, "Otvara se Galerija nesvrstanih zemalja," *Politika Ekspres*, August 29, 1984.
[92] *Galerija umjetnosti nesvrstanih zemalja "Josip Broz Tito,"* 3.
[93] *Galerija umjetnosti nesvrstanih zemalja "Josip Broz Tito,"* 9.
[94] *Galerija umjetnosti nesvrstanih zemalja "Josip Broz Tito,"* 9.

divisions into "major" and "minor" cultures, and into "metropolitan" and "peripheral" cultures, became reality by the beginning of the 1980s.

There were three different spatial levels of Yugoslav-African cultural encounters— local (Yugoslav exhibitions in Africa and their African counterparts in Yugoslavia), regional (the Alexandria Biennale, which promoted Mediterranean art and culture) and global (the "Josip Broz Tito" Art Gallery, which promoted Third World art globally; the Museum of African Art, which collaborated with African and Western museums and cultural institutions). Thus, Yugoslavia made local cultures global by accepting pluralities in art and the richness of both Yugoslav and African cultures. Yugoslav non-aligned policy, solidarity, and a sincere wish to go beyond the usual East-West promotion of her cultural achievements did much to create an alternative cultural space.

Apart from these remarkable results in the institutionalization of African art and the promotion not only of traditional but of modern African art as well, we can ask again what the promotion of African culture in Yugoslavia really achieved. Many Yugoslav politicians, as well as intellectuals, especially people like Zdravko Pečar, had hoped to achieve more, so there was a kind of dissatisfaction in their aassessment of Yugoslav-African cultural encounters. Summing up, Pečar claimed:

> We have moved forward in our effort to learn about the culture of African peoples, however this is still insufficient ... What novelty have we from the sixties to this day brought to Africa? You see, I have a poor opinion on this matter. I do not think that we have done all that much ... What is there that is new that we socialists, from the socialist countries have brought to the African continent?[95]

The pessimistic view could be seen on the other side as well. During the "Days of African cultures" in 1980, as a response to Pečar's bitterness, Basile Kossou added that in postcolonial times a number of socialist countries had positioned themselves as (ideological) colonizers, though Yugoslavia, he insisted, was not among them. Where this new colonization was concerned, his harshest criticisms were directed at the Soviet Union, whose imposition of ideological orthodoxy threatened freedom and the principle of self-determination. Probably for this reason, it seems that the Yugoslav third way of non-alignment, entailing a whole-hearted respect for African peoples and cultures, was acceptable to both Yugoslavia and Africa, as Kossou himself concluded.[96]

Considering the exhibition space as a space of encounter, it is clear that African culture took on real importance in Yugoslavia, and that as time passed perceptions of it ceased to be confined to a traditional view of the exotic "other," based on colonial stereotypes, and came to represent African modernity and progress. On the other side, however, in Africa itself, it is very hard to assess the real impact of Yugoslav culture. What we do know is that, through the Yugoslav iniatives described above, the modern high culture of one socialist country came to Africa as early as the 1950s. Generally speaking, Yugoslavia succeeded in the positive transformation of the image of Africa

[95] "Afričke studije: Benin, Gabon, Obala Slonovače," 189.
[96] "Afričke studije: Benin, Gabon, Obala Slonovače," 193–5.

from being an unknown exotic world to a true socialist friend, as African culture thereby became familiar to Yugoslav audiences.

It seems, despite Pečar's bitterness that "we have not done much," that Yugoslavia actually did a great deal to promote African culture not only in Yugoslavia but on the global art scene as well. Not only did Yugoslavia institutionalize African art in Yugoslavia and operate as a bridge that connected it with the world, but she also respected African cultural needs. Both Yugoslavia and Africa—thanks to exhibitions in Yugoslavia and Africa, the Alexandria Biennale, the Museum of African Art in Belgrade, and the "Josip Broz Tito" Gallery of Art of the Non-Aligned Countries—became a part of the global community and the global cultural sphere, combining East, West, and the Third World under the non-aligned cultural umbrella.

Writing about Africa and African culture, Edward Said noted how rare it was for anyone to take seriously the alternatives to imperialism, and therefore the existence of other cultures and societies, mentioning in this regard the rare artists and intellectuals who had "crossed to the other side," Basil Davidson or Albert Memmi among them.[97] While those who had "crossed to the other side" were still rare in the West, Yugoslavia in her cultural space actively promoted that "other side." Accepting both traditional and modern African culture as a way of recognizing African values and bringing them to Europe has forever changed not only Africa's place in the world, but the whole idea of global modern art.

---

[97] Said, *Culture and Imperialism*, xi–xv.

5

The Epistolarium: Socialist Internationalism Writ Small—Friendship, Solidarity, and Support Between Women in the Soviet Union and in Decolonizing Countries, 1950s–1960s

Christine Varga-Harris

In February 1964, Mrs. K. Sanghi from Delhi sent the *Komitet Sovetskikh Zhenshchin* (Committee of Soviet Women; KSZh) good wishes for the new year. The brief correspondence she initiated with Liudmila Balakhovskaya, head of the International Department of the Committee, suggests that the two women had never met in person.[1] As the Indian woman declared, "I long to meet my sisters who are caring for me in such a distant land"; she even insisted that members of the KSZh should inform her if they planned to travel to Delhi so that she might host them.[2] In response, Balakhovskaya urged Sanghi to write again, and to provide information about her life, work, and public activities. She also thanked her for the invitation and reciprocated by assuring that Sanghi and her friends, too, were welcome to visit the Soviet Union and see how women there lived, worked, and raised children.[3] That these two strangers seemed to connect so naturally might be explained by what Sanghi referred to as a "universal" fondness among women and their ability to "understand and communicate that language of affection to each other beyond all other barriers."[4]

A state organization with a global presence, the KSZh was meant to establish and maintain contact with individual women and women's organizations around the world, exchange informational material and delegations, and offer solidarity in struggles for national liberation and gender equality taking place worldwide. Correspondence was one of its most important vehicles.[5] A 1958 issue of the *Information Bulletin of the KSZh* revealed that the committee was an intermediary for more than 500 Soviet

---

[1] The names of women who did not appear to be public figures will be indicated by whatever semi-anonymous short form they used in their letters, or by their initials.
[2] *Gosudarstvennyi arkhiv Rossiiskoi Federatsii* (hereinafter, GARF), f. R7928, op. 3, d. 1295, l. 88.
[3] GARF, f. R7928, op. 3, d. 1295, l. 90.
[4] GARF, f. R7928, op. 3, d. 1295, l. 88.
[5] See, for example, GARF, f. R7928, op. 3, d. 363, l. 172.

women writing to women in forty different countries.[6] Among these correspondents were workers, peasants, service personnel, students, teachers, and "housewives"— grassroots activists composing letters in collectives formed at factories, collective farms, schools and universities, and in *zhensovety* (women's soviets).[7] On average, from 1956 through 1964, the KSZh yearly received about 2,000 pieces of mail and sent out around 10,000, factoring in letters, greeting cards, and telegrams.[8] Although the committee had for years already been making contact with women in the decolonizing world, broadening ties with individual women and organizations in Africa, Asia, the Arab world, and Latin America continued to be cited as problematic for, or a goal of, the KSZh.[9]

Focusing on correspondence between Soviet women and women in sub-Saharan Africa and South Asia in the 1950s and 1960s, this chapter examines contacts in parts of the world where the KSZh (and in some cases, the Soviet leadership) as yet had weak links. This condenses the volume of mail from thousands to hundreds, as does the fact that the letters analyzed here were not written by Soviet grassroots activists, but rather overwhelmingly produced by just a dozen or so leading figures of the committee. As for their more numerous correspondents in decolonizing countries, though their background and political persuasion were not always clear, some were evidently well educated and somewhat affluent.[10] A few were prominent individuals. Many were sympathetic toward the Soviet Union, or, at the very least, receptive to the messages and activities of the KSZh; they were overwhelmingly enthusiastic about forming friendships with Soviet women.

While the range of countries and number of women with whom the committee established contact in the decolonizing world was eclipsed by those in capitalist and Soviet-bloc countries, the breadth of types of organizations with whose members it had come to correspond was impressive. These included international friendship societies (e.g., the National Nigerian Friendship Society with Foreign Countries), women's organizations (e.g., the Federation of Gambian Women, the All-Africa Women's League, and the Nepalese Women's Voluntary Service), affiliates of national liberation movements (e.g., the Pemba-Afro-Shirazi Youth League in Zanzibar), and civic bodies like educational institutions (e.g., the Sri Avinashilingam Home Science College for Women in India). In short, the global reach of the KSZh was wide. What of the nature of its correspondence?

Two motifs, peace and humanity, permeated the epistolarium of the committee or the corpus of letters that its members generated in corresponding with individuals and

---

[6] GARF, f. R7928, op. 3, d. 201, l. 40.
[7] GARF, f. R7928, op. 4, d. 101, l. 14; op. 4, d. 109, l. 16; and op. 3, d. 201, l. 40.
[8] GARF, f. R7928, op. 4, d. 101, ll. 12–14; op. 4, d. 109, ll. 15–16; op. 3, d. 1, l. 13; op. 4, d. 118, l. 25; op. 3, d. 207, l. 19; and op. 4, d. 152, ll. 28–9. This imprecise estimate reflects the sporadic character of the KSZh archive.
[9] See, for example, GARF, f. R7928, op. 3, d. 206, ll. 14–17 and 34–5.
[10] Educational and class backgrounds can sometimes be verified by brief biographies (*kharakteristiki*) compiled for visiting delegates, or by surveys (*ankety*) submitted by students applying to study in the USSR.

organizations abroad.¹¹ Peace had been the initial purpose of the KSZh. Founded in 1941 as the *Anti-Fashistskii Komitet Sovetskikh Zhenshchin* (Anti-Fascist Committee of Soviet Women; AFKSZh), it aimed to mobilize Soviet women for the war effort and to unite women around the world in the struggle against fascism. The AFKSZh was renamed the *Komitet Sovetskikh Zhenshchin* in 1956 amid the policy shifts of the emerging "Thaw," though globalization also appeared to be a significant factor. As committee chair Nina Popova explained to the Central Committee of the Communist Party of the Soviet Union (CPSU) in April that year, because the AFKSZh had come to represent Soviet women in the Women's International Democratic Federation (WIDF), and because it was broadening ties with foreign women's organizations "of different political and religious persuasions," to continue to call itself "Anti-Fascist" might undermine its efforts to develop these links and initiate new contacts.¹² Still, the KSZh continued to strive for world peace through the end of the Cold War.¹³

Dovetailing with peace was the "language of common humanity." In the Soviet context, humanist discourse had first emerged in the 1930s amid impending war. By the middle of the 1950s, according to Eleonory Gilburd, it had broadened to become associated with "the oneness of humanity," "the formation of one international community," and "world civilization"—that is, neither socialist nor capitalist, and therefore in line with the idea of "peaceful coexistence" promulgated by Nikita Khrushchev.¹⁴ In the wake of the 1957 Moscow World Festival of Youth and Students, the notion of a common humanity generated a new approach to diplomacy, one based on mass participation and personal engagement. Within this foreign relations framework, letters were invested with the power to "awaken sympathies" in their recipients.¹⁵ The belief that correspondence could appeal to hearts and minds infused the epistolarium of the KSZh, for it was implicit not only in the approach that Soviet women followed, but also in the letters they received.

Until fairly recently among scholars (as among contemporaries), Soviet messages about peace and humanity were rendered suspect due to their prominence in official rhetoric.¹⁶ However, Soviet revulsion against war was not just a propagandistic mantra; it also "sprang from real popular feeling."¹⁷ The same can be said of socialist

---

¹¹ The concept of an "epistolarium" is borrowed from Liz Stanley, Andrea Salter, and Helen Dampier, "The Epistolary Pact, Letterness, and the Schreiner Epistolarium," *a/b: Auto-Biography Studies* 27.2 (Winter 2012): 265.

¹² GARF, f. R7928, op. 4, d. 99, l. 2.

¹³ David Scott Foglesong, "When the Russians Really Were Coming: Citizen Diplomacy and the End of Cold War Enmity in America," *Cold War History* 20.4 (April 2020): 419–40.

¹⁴ Eleonory Gilburd, *To See Paris and Die: The Soviet Lives of Western Culture* (Cambridge, MA, 2018), 30–2.

¹⁵ Eleonory Gilburd, "The Revival of Soviet Internationalism in the Mid to Late 1950s," in Denis Kozlov and Eleonory Gilburd (eds.), *The Thaw: Soviet Society and Culture during the 1950s and 1960s* (Toronto, 2013), 374.

¹⁶ Peace activism could be equated with Communism even inside the socialist camp. See Melissa Feinberg, "Battling for Peace: The Transformation of the Women's Movement in Cold War Czechoslovakia and Eastern Europe," in Joanna Regulska and Bonnie G. Smith (eds.), *Women and Gender in Postwar Europe: From Cold War to European Union* (London and New York, 2012), 22, 25.

¹⁷ Catriona Kelly, "Defending Children's Rights, 'In Defense of Peace': Children and Soviet Cultural Diplomacy," *Kritika* 9.4 (Fall 2008): 728–9.

internationalism, which served as the backdrop for the KSZh's activities. Socialist internationalism entailed nurturing individual ties, amicability, mutual understanding, and cooperation.[18] Given its connection to Soviet foreign policy, however, the cultural outreach and material aid associated with it have often been viewed as manipulative or insignificant, and this has certainly been the case with the KSZh: Cold War pundits and post-Soviet Russian feminists alike have characterized the committee as Communist Party-conformist. It did not begin to occupy itself in earnest with the situation of women *within* the Soviet Union until the 1980s, and it certainly did not employ the term feminist, at least not in the 1950s and 1960s.[19]

Yet alongside promoting peace and humanity, the epistolarium of the KSZh embodies features of feminist epistolary culture, particularly ones similar to those discerned in the Anglo-American context in the 1970s and 1980s.[20] For one, the letters exchanged between committee members and women in Africa and Asia from the mid-1950s through the mid-1960s were undergirded by the kind of care and interest in mutual understanding that Mrs. K. Sanghi and Balakhovskaya expressed in the passages at the beginning of this chapter. In tone, they conveyed moral support, alongside an enthusiasm for becoming acquainted with women of diverse places and cultures.

This internationalist spirit and sense of sisterhood was already evident in the wartime activites of the AFKSZh, as well as in the postwar work of the KSZh in the WIDF, an organization that it had contributed to founding in November 1945, roughly a decade before Soviet foreign policy came to be governed by peaceful coexistence. While the leadership role of the committee had marked the WIDF as a communist front organization, the federation, too, had been born of war and, like the KSZh, drew a connection between, and vociferously condemned, fascism, racism, and colonialism.[21] Throughout the Cold War, the committee and the WIDF collaborated to advance the status of women, the rights of children, and world peace, and recognized the place of social and economic structures in generating inequalities.[22] Thus, what Suzy Kim has

---

[18] See, for example, Celia Donert, "From Communist Internationalism to Human Rights: Gender, Violence and International Law in the Women's International Democratic Federation Mission to North Korea, 1951," *Contemporary European History* 25.2 (May 2016): 314.

[19] Linda Racioppi and Katherine O'Sullivan, "Organizing Women Before and After the Fall: Women's Politics in the Soviet Union and Post-Soviet Russia," in Bonnie G. Smith (ed.), *Global Feminisms Since 1945* (London and New York, 2000), 215–16. On the relationship to feminism in socialist organizations, see Kristen Ghodsee, "State Feminism and the Woman Question," in *Second World, Second Sex: Socialist Women's Activism and Global Solidarity during the Cold War* (Durham, NC, 2018), 31–52.

[20] On feminist epistolary culture, see Stanley, Salter, and Dampier, "The Epistolary Pact," 282; Celia Hughes, "Left Activism, Succour and Selfhood: The Epistolary Friendship of Two Revolutionary Mothers in 1970s Britain," *Women's History Review* 23.6 (2014): 874–902; and Margaretta Jolly, "Confidantes, Co-workers and Correspondents: Feminist Discourses of Letter-writing from 1970 to the Present," *Journal of European Studies* 32.2–3 (2002): 267–82.

[21] Francisca de Haan, "Continuing Cold War Paradigms in Western Historiography of Transnational Women's Organizations," *Women's History Review* 19.4 (September 2010): 547–73.

[22] See, for example, Melanie Illic, "Soviet Women, Cultural Exchange and the Women's International Democratic Federation," in Sari Autio-Sarasmo and Katalin Miklóssy (eds.), *Reassessing Cold War Europe* (London and New York), 157–74. Nina Popova was also vice-chair of the WIDF and served several other international organizations, including the Union of Soviet Societies for Friendship and Cultural Relations with Foreign Countries, the Soviet Committee for Solidarity with Asian and African Countries, the Soviet Committee for the Defense of Peace, and the World Peace Council. Illic, "Soviet Women," 159–60.

succinctly stated about "the early ... inclusion of Third World women in the work of the WIDF" can be applied to the committee as well, namely that it "adopted an intersectional approach by integrating the analyses of gender, class and race long before the 1960s 'second-wave' feminists."[23]

In projecting a multidimensional vision of womanhood and in employing the language of peace and humanity, the KSZh was marshaling concepts of critical importance to activism that were in use throughout the postwar world. Indeed, concern for children and the prevention of nuclear annihilation were common themes in peace movements in communist and democratic countries alike, despite differences in the role of the state.[24] Thus, women in very different circumstances during the Cold War used international contacts to enter into dialog about gender equality, peace, and human rights, in order to effect change.[25]

A product of this era of burgeoning global cooperation, the epistolarium of the KSZh is suffused with the conviction that correspondence could strengthen bonds between individuals, organizations, and countries, and indicates shared beliefs on issues like decolonization and disarmament. This space of paper and ink reveals women in different circumstances relating to each other as "confidantes and coworkers" discussing the activities that defined them, while romanticizing sisterhood and what female activism might achieve in terms of social justice and world peace.[26] Exploring letters that the KSZh exchanged with women in decolonizing countries, this chapter thus offers new insights into the practice and reception of socialist internationalism through a female lens, a perspective that remains underdeveloped.[27]

Notes on Letters as a Medium

Correspondence between the KSZh and women abroad was established in a number of ways. In some cases, communication was initiated by the committee and reciprocated by women whose curiosity had been piqued either by receiving a letter from the KSZh or reading a copy of its magazine, *Soviet Woman*. This was the case with Mabel Dove, a writer and the first female Member of Parliament in Ghana. In early 1959, the politician began a lively correspondence with Olga Bondarenko in response to a letter she had received in late 1958 expressing a desire to establish "friendly

---

[23] Suzy Kim, "The Origins of Cold War Feminism During the Korean War," *Gender and History* 31.2 (July 2019): 460–79.
[24] See, for example, Margaret Peacock, *Innocent Weapons: The Soviet and American Politics of Childhood in the Cold War* (Chapel Hill, NC, 2014).
[25] For two very different contexts that are illustrative, see Wendy Pojmann, *Italian Women and International Cold War Politics, 1944-1968* (New York, 2013), and Naaborko Sackeyfio-Lenoch, "Women's International Alliances in an Emergent Ghana," *Journal of West African History* 4.1 (Spring 2018): 27–56.
[26] The idea of correspondence as an interdependent space for both validating the self and reinforcing an idealized sense of community is informed by Jolly, "Confidantes, Co-workers and Correspondents."
[27] Among those who have made fruitful inroads is Alena K. Almagir. See, for example, Almagir, "Recalcitrant Women: Internationalism and the Redefinition of Welfare Limits in the Czechoslovak-Vietnamese Labor Exchange Program," *Slavic Review* 73.1 (Spring 2014): 133–55.

correspondence," and then an issue of *Soviet Woman* and a copy of *Equality of Women in the USSR*.[28]

In other instances, exchanging letters was an extension of personal encounters that women (or their friends or family members) had experienced while abroad. An Indonesian woman identified as "Sunantaria" began writing committee member Nina Voronina in June 1963, about a year and a half after the two had met at a congress of Gerakan Wanita Indonesia (Gerwani), the "Indonesian Women's Movement."[29] A letter from Mrs. K. Sanghi in Delhi to Balakhovskaya, subsequent to the one noted at the beginning of this chapter, revealed that her husband had been in Tashkent when she first contacted the committee.[30]

Roughly five months passed between the first and second rounds of correspondence between Sanghi and Balakhovskaya in the epistolarium of the KSZh. It is possible that the two women had exchanged letters in the interim that had ended up being filed elsewhere—perhaps in connection with whatever had taken Sanghi's husband to the Soviet Union. But lengthy intervals were characteristic of communication in the 1950s and 1960s. Reliance on the post across vast geographic distances made sustaining correspondence a challenge and strengthened the personal value that individuals placed on the letters they *did* receive. Women who succeeded in writing to each other for years on end, despite interruptions, opened their letters with statements of joy or relief upon finally hearing from a distant friend.

In October 1961, Giri R.K.M sent the KSZh a greeting card on the occasion of the Nepalese holiday Vijaya Deshami, identifying herself as a member of her national delegation in attendance at the 1957 Youth Festival.[31] Bondarenko responded to her "Dear friend Giri" expressing delight at receiving her letter and stating that in the intervening years since they had met, she had thought of and written to her many times, but that her letters had been returned or been unanswered.[32] There is evidence that on at least one occasion before this exchange, in July 1960, another committee member, Lydia Petrova, had tried to contact Giri, noting then that it had been a long time since they had been in touch, and hoping that "nothing is amiss."[33] Responding to her letter that arrived in 1961, Bondarenko said on behalf of the entire committee that it "made us all happy." She also urged Giri to write again with updates on how she was doing, adding, "it is so pleasant to realize that our friends still remember us" and "our friendship formed four years ago has remained intact."[34]

The kind of caring and amity exhibited in this exchange between Giri R.K.M. and the Soviet women with whom she had become acquainted suggests a heartfelt

---

[28] GARF, f. R7928, op. 3, d. 266, ll. 2–3. On Dove, see Wilhelmina J. Donkoh, "Nkrumah and His 'Chicks': An Examination of Women and the Organizational Strategies of the CPP," in Charles Quist-Adade and Vincent Dodoo (eds.), *Africa's Many Divides and Africa's Future: Pursuing Nkrumah's Vision of Pan-Africanism in an Era of Globalization* (Newcastle upon Tyne, 2015), 99–121.
[29] GARF, f. R7928, op. 3, d. 1107, ll. 106.
[30] GARF, f. R7928, op. 3, d. 1295, ll. 299–300.
[31] GARF, f. R7928, op. 3, d. 715, ll. 27 and 30.
[32] GARF, f. R7928, op. 3, d. 524, ll. 6–7.
[33] GARF, f. R7928, op. 2, d. 524, l. 6.
[34] GARF, f. R7928, op. 3, d. 715, l. 29.

connection. Yet the global character of the correspondence that came to fill the epistolarium of the KSZh, a state organization, also rendered it a public space. Most obviously, letters originating from, and responses sent to, a foreign country needed to be translated—a process that further slowed down communication. In the case of the committee, those who wrote to women abroad relied on translators fluent in languages like English, French, Bengali, and Indonesian. Among the KSZh files, this is reflected in duplicate copies of what appear to be the same letters in different languages, varying names and initials on original and translated incoming and outgoing letters, and accounting records allocating funds for translating committee correspondence.[35] Moreover, since it was difficult at the time to identify individuals in faraway places, it was not uncommon for letters to be addressed to the office of an organization, an educational institution, a library, and so forth, rather than a specific person. Consequently, in addition to being read by multilingual interlocutors, letters were likely to have been handled by more than one staff member as they were processed. It is also possible that letters were shared with friends or fellow activists, making them both "a conversation between friends" and a social affair.[36]

Members of the KSZh likely had less sense of the outlooks of women in a rapidly changing postcolonial world than their correspondents did vis-à-vis the Soviet Union, and they often included requests for information in their letters to them. The positive associations with Soviet women, their society, and their leadership that women abroad expressed in *their* letters suggest that some were acquainted with or receptive to socialism, or at least were open to learning about the Soviet Union. The aforementioned Sunantaria, for example, who had met Voronina at a conference of the left-leaning Gerwani organization, addressed Voronina as "comrade" and explained that she did so because she knew that the Soviet Union was communist, adding with confidence that the people who lived there were "fully happy" and that she was well versed in the principles of communist society. After stating that poverty and degradation—especially of women—still existed in her own country, she claimed that her people aspired to precisely the kind of "just and prosperous" society that socialism offered, declaring that eventually "Indonesia will move toward communism."[37]

If, as budgetary justifications for translators suggested, correspondence was a valued means of establishing ties abroad and propagating the advantages of the Soviet socialist system, what of the fact that committee members were sometimes preaching to the converted, so to speak?[38] KSZh discussions of shortcomings in its correspondence cited a tendency toward "oversimplification" (*skhematichnost'*) and "triteness" (*shablonnost'*) in elucidating the challenges that the Soviet people had faced.[39] One committee report decried the "pretentious [*deklarativnyi*] character" of some letters, asserting that they were weak in depicting the life of the Soviet people, or else "crudely"

[35] GARF, f. R7928, op. 3, d. 1208, l. 22.
[36] On letters as both private and public in nature, see Rebecca Earle, "Introduction," in Rebecca Earle (ed.), *Epistolary Selves: Letters and Letter-Writers, 1600–1945* (Farnham, 1999), 5, 7.
[37] GARF, f. R7928, op. 3, d. 1107, ll. 106–7.
[38] See, for example, GARF, f. R7928, op. 3, d. 1208, l. 22.
[39] GARF, f. R7928, op. 4, d. 109, l. 19.

presented state policy. In turn, it recommended that correspondents offer more concrete examples to illustrate the advantages of communism over capitalism; demonstrate that only under socialism could the full equality of women and a bright future for children be secured; detail how current party resolutions and state policies would transform the lives of Soviet citizens, especially women; and delineate Soviet reality in such a way as to counter propaganda discrediting the Soviet Union. In practical terms, this meant providing communiqués for correspondents explaining the life of women and children, as well as the unique features of a given country to which letters were being sent. Yet this kind of advice, together with accusations of the "limited horizons" (*krugozor*) of some Soviet correspondents, indicates that this criticism was directed at grassroots activists.[40]

Written by leading figures in the KSZh, the letters accessed for this study did not engage in blatant counterpropaganda. Any provocative political language was eclipsed by simple appeals to become acquainted. This is evident in a letter from Zinaida Fëdorova to M.S.T. in Ceylon (Sri Lanka). Here the General Secretary of the committee pronounced that mothers would only be able to sleep soundly once industrial production was geared toward peace and not war, for example, building hospitals rather than armoured vehicles. Yet, Fëdorova devoted more space to other matters, including thanking her Ceylonese correspondent for telling her about the life of women in her country and asserting that such interaction is necessary for women of different countries to get to know each other better and to unite for the peace and happiness of all children.[41]

In the absence of letters from Soviet women "from below" that might serve for comparison, or substantive explanations "from above" for these differing approaches, it is possible to say only that prominent committee members may have been corresponding with different types of women abroad than their counterparts in Soviet localities and therefore employed an alternative line. Their recipients, meanwhile—especially if affiliated with some organization or institution—might already have been somewhat informed about the Soviet Union through subscriptions to Soviet periodicals like *Soviet Woman*.[42] Among the women named thus far, Mabel Dove was a writer and government official and Mrs. K. Sanghi appeared to be highly educated, in one letter noting that she had written books on Hindi literature, was working on her doctoral thesis, and was a member of the Women's Graduate Association in Delhi.[43] Sunantaria, in highlighting her work with Gerwani and addressing the economic crisis in Indonesia, as well as mentioning a brother studying in Czechoslovakia, intimated that she, too, was well educated and from a family with disposable income.[44]

Members of the KSZh typically interwove measured comments on major issues like national liberation and world peace with subjects of a quotidian or personal nature.

---

[40] GARF, f. R7928, op. 3, d. 206, ll. 14–17.
[41] GARF, f. R7928, op. 3, d. 571, l. 43.
[42] See Christine Varga-Harris, "Between National Tradition and Western Modernization: *Soviet Woman* and Representations of Socialist Gender Equality as a 'Third Way' for Developing Countries, 1956–1964," *Slavic Review* 78.3 (Fall 2019): 758–81.
[43] GARF, f. R7928, op. 3, d. 1295, ll. 299–300.
[44] GARF, f. R7928, op. 3, d. 1107, ll. 108.

In this regard, leading figures in the committee might have been taking their cue from women in Africa and South Asia in terms of approach and subject matter. One KSZh survey of letters noted that women in faraway places tended to write about their family, joys and sorrows, and the status of women in their country, as well as to share their opinions on world politics, their concerns about nuclear war, and the value they placed on corresponding with friends in the Soviet Union.[45] Indeed, women from decolonizing countries generally refrained from the kind of militancy voiced in one atypical unsigned letter from Indonesia decrying "the Yanks" for "gangsterism" and the North Atlantic Treaty Organization as "lying hooligans" among the imperialistic "enemies of the working class" operating in liberated areas of Africa and Asia.[46]

Overall, however standardized they may appear—following a certain rhythm from salutation to closing, as typical of correspondence—whether penned by Soviet women or women in foreign countries, the content of the KSZh epistolarium was multilayered. To be sure, these letters could be officious, yet they were also conversational in tone, incorporating "small talk" (e.g., about the weather) and personal news (e.g., deaths and births). In such ways committee correspondence resembled diplomatic exchanges, as prescribed by official Soviet guidelines.[47] Whether or not this was intentional, its authors certainly engaged in diplomacy.

Exemplifying the criss-crossing of diplomatic convention and personal interest are the exchanges between S.R.S. from Manjeshwar, India, and her "friends" at the KSZh between 1960 and 1964. As a director of the reading room for her local Indo-Soviet Cultural Society, S.R.S. presented herself as a self-appointed emissary for her country. She assured her interlocutor that her facility had "become very popular" and that its members exhibited "great interest" in Soviet life, and she voiced solidarity with the Soviet Union over disarmament. She sought support from the committee for her activities—for example, in the form of instructional texts for Russian-language classes—and showed gratitude for the materials she received. S.R.S. also delved into more personal subjects, for instance sharing news about the birth of each of her children—a girl Vera, whose name she selected after consulting committee members about Russian names, and a boy she named Gagarin in the hope that he would become a pilot. She even provided occasional photographs and updates about them (e.g., when Vera had started to walk). As if assuming the role of godmother, alongside specific, requested, practical materials (including books about Soviet progress), Bondarenko sent gifts for the children that included a book about Yuri Gagarin, a model airplane, toys, and a harmonica.[48]

For members of the KSZh, it is possible that the medium and the message were one and the same. In writing to women they had previously met to sustain their acquaintanceship, or else to those they had not yet met in person but with whom they held common interests, Soviet women effectively enacted vital components of socialist internationalism like nurturing friendship, camaraderie, and understanding in the

---

[45] GARF, f. R7928, op. 3, ed. khr. 201, l. 69.
[46] GARF, f. R7928, op. 3, d. 1297, l. 81.
[47] F. F. Molochkov, *Diplomaticheskii protocol i diplomaticheskaia praktika* (Moscow, 1977).
[48] GARF, f. R7928, op. 3, d. 681, l. 44, ll. 47–8 and ll. 137–8, and GARF, f. R7928, op. 3, d. 864, l. 167, l. 169, l. 210 and l. 212.

interest of shared goals. In this vein, the files that fill the epistolarium of the committee are labeled as correspondence "with women" or "organizations" of a given country "about the establishment or strengthening of friendly contacts and participation in the international women's movement" (and sometimes "the development of the women's movement" in a particular country), and "the exchange of publications" and sometimes "of delegations." Yet interwoven with the strands of feminist epistolary culture and internationalism outlined above, there was also excitement and gratification at learning about others around the globe.

Annotating Letters "Marked by and Sent to the World"[49]

Exchanging information was a specified pursuit of the KSZh, and given its position as a state organization, acquiring knowledge about unfamiliar places and situations can be associated with effectively propagating a convincing image of the Soviet Union, even if not explicitly stated as such.[50] Meanwhile, women in developing countries seemed to value sharing information as much as Soviet women, and in both cases, doing so was bolstered by sentiments of friendship and peace. Thus, in requesting materials on Soviet women and education for a public library, A. K. Chakraborty in Calcutta claimed that "the exchange of information, whether in words or through printed matter ... promotes the establishment of friendly contacts and mutual understanding between the peoples of the world."[51]

The value that women ascribed to sharing information is also elaborated in correspondence between the KSZh and Miss Soedjanti in Indonesia. After obtaining the address of its office from the Soviet embassy in Jakarta, Miss Soedjanti wrote the committee that a study club of female teachers learning about labor activities in the Soviet Union was interested in publications on this topic, as well as on the general development of the country under Khrushchev. She concluded, "Long live friendship among Soviet and Indonesian women, among our countries and peoples! May there be peace throughout the whole world!"[52] Fëdorova sent the requested materials, alongside some photographs of Soviet women and children. She also reciprocated interest in her country by asking that Miss Soedjanti, in return, send her Indonesian women's publications in the service of exchange and mutual understanding.[53]

Sentiments like friendship and peace naturally aligned with diplomacy, but they also intersected with professional pursuits and with personal gratification. This is

---

[49] This concept is borrowed from Mary Favret, *Romantic Correspondence: Women, Politics and the Fiction of Letters* (Cambridge, 1993), 56, cited in Amanda Gilroy and W. M. Verhoeven (eds.), *Epistolary Histories: Letters, Fiction, Culture* (Charlottesville, VA, 2000), 1.
[50] On the mandate of the KSZh to exchange informational material, see, for example, GARF, f. R7928, op. 4, d. 118, l. 26. For indications of how perceptions about women abroad shaped the content of *Soviet Woman*, see Alexis Peri, "New *Soviet Woman*: The Post-World War II Feminine Ideal at Home and Abroad," *Russian Review* 77.4 (October 2018): 621–44, and Varga-Harris, "Between National Tradition and Western Modernization."
[51] GARF, f. R7928, op. 3, d. 102, l. 59.
[52] GARF, f. R7928, op. 3, d. 1297, l. 73.
[53] GARF, f. R7928, op. 3, d. 1297, l. 75.

evident in correspondence between Mrs. D. Majoedin from Bandung, who had visited the Soviet Union in late 1956, and Bondarenko. After the Indonesian woman stated that she valued an issue of *Soviet Woman* that she had received, her Soviet counterpart replied that she was happy to learn that Indonesians were "interested in the life of the Soviet people" and that for their part, they were "also keenly interested in the life" of Indonesia. She therefore proposed an exchange of letters, magazines, and other materials as a way for their peoples to come to know each other better.[54] In response to this letter, Majoedin wrote her "Esteemed Friends" at the KSZh requesting for her husband, a physician, a book on Soviet achievements in surgery, and for herself, the Russian words to the song "Indoneziia" transcribed into Latin characters so that she could sing it at parties.[55] In a letter that accompanied the specified book and the requested lyrics, a different committee member, Petrova, wrote, "We hope that when you ... sing this beautiful song in Russian, you will think of your Soviet friends."[56]

Together with a basic interest in getting to know one another, as this last illustration suggests, visits to their respective countries had the effect of imparting a more intimate tone to letters that might otherwise have been unduly formal. For instance, amid a brief overview of an ambitious economic plan that her country had just embarked upon, Fatou Cissé (neé Aribot), a Guinean activist in the Union of Women of West Africa, fondly recalled for her "Dear Friends" at the committee time she had spent in Moscow, the tireless concern she was shown during her stay, and the words Petrova had uttered on the rainy day she left the Soviet Union: "Fatou, Moscow is crying over your departure."[57] Writing to her about a month later to thank her for some "marvelous slippers," Fëdorova remarked that this gift would prompt her to think about the crafts of the Guinean people, as well as "each day ... remind" her of Cissé.[58]

As such exchanges indicate, letters could serve as vehicles for sharing keepsakes as well as sentiments, bringing joy to their recipients and making ties across vast distances more tangible. Relatively easy to ship by post, most typical among the kinds of objects that women exchanged were photographs and picture postcards of unique places like the Kremlin or the Taj Mahal. Soviet women also frequently sent women abroad images of famous Soviet figures such as Valentina Tereshkova, stamps, collections of photographs of Soviet life (e.g., depicting the status of women or amenities for children like pioneer palaces), and *znachki* (commemorative pins), while women in Africa and South Asia sometimes treated Soviet women to local or national "specialities." These made correspondence "a site of cross-cultural exchange" while rousing in the recipients fond memories of places visited and people met, or, alternatively, substituting for actual personal encounters.[59] Assurances of the value that recipients placed on objects sent to them, on top of the customary words of thanks, furthered a sense of friendship.

---

[54] GARF, f. R7928, op. 2, d. 1935, l. 8 and l. 11.
[55] GARF, f. R7928, op. 2, d. 1935, l. 57.
[56] GARF, f. R7928, op. 2, d. 1935, l. 60.
[57] GARF, f. R7928, op. 3, d. 475, l. 24.
[58] GARF, f. R7928, op. 3, d. 475, l. 35.
[59] See Fiona Paisley, *Glamour in the Pacific: Cultural Internationalism and Race Politics in the Women's Pan-Pacific* (Honolulu, 2009), 161.

Pritpal Kaur Wasu, a member of the Punjab Legislative Assembly who appears to have visited the Soviet Union in 1958, thanked Petrova for a "kerchief" she had sent her, claiming that it "speaks of the love and affection that you and ... Soviet women have for me and ... Indian women."[60] In July 1960, Mabel Dove sent Bondarenko a piece of kente cloth, and in response, Bondarenko expressed her appreciation, telling Dove that she liked it "tremendously" and that it would "always" be for her "a symbol of our friendship."[61] When Voronina wrote to Kapila Khandvala, a leading figure in the National Federation of Indian Women, to thank her for some unspecified published materials and a crate of mangos, the Soviet woman described the former as "very interesting and valuable" (explaining that they had been translated into Russian), and added that the entire committee had enjoyed the fruit, finding it a "very tasty and aromatic pleasure."[62]

Alongside exchanging niceties in the form of sentimental or exotic objects, women in decolonizing countries, like their young governments, sometimes wrote their contacts in the Soviet Union to acquire items of practical value. Typical among them were publications, film projectors, tape recorders, tapes, and gramophone records. One recipient of such support, S. Devi from Model Town in Karnal, India, wrote Bondarenko in January 1958 to thank her for some literature she had already received, stating that "many women" were reading it, and to request "other valuable" materials, including *Soviet Woman*, for a pictorial exhibition on the life of the Soviet peoples aimed at rural and urban Indian women.[63]

The organization that Devi was active in was not specified here, but her letter reveals another purpose alongside fostering transnational friendship for the items that women in Africa and Asia requested from the KSZh: to further local or national aims. With such an end in mind, the General Secretary of the National Council of Ghana Women, Margaret Martei, asked the committee for "donations" for an annual fundraiser for her organization, which was involved in development work in the countryside. The KSZh obliged by arranging for the purchase of folk art from throughout the Soviet Union for the cause.[64]

In a similar vein, over the course of 1959 through 1961, the committee engaged in correspondence with, and sent various materials to, Mrs. Perera at the Withana Reading Club in Ceylon. Perara initially approached the KSZh presuming that it would be happy to support an organization like hers, which aimed to "construct a good generation for a better society." The committee furnished her initiative, aimed at poor women and children, with books, *znachki*, and toys, including wooden ones purportedly made by Soviet children "as a souvenir" of their "goodwill ... towards Ceylonese children." In the letters that accompanied these items, different members of the committee engaged in

---

[60] GARF, f. R7928, op. 3, d. 681, l. 111. On the visit, see l. 134.
[61] GARF, f. R7928, op. 3, d. 473, l. 42 and l. 45.
[62] GARF, f. R7928, op. 3, d. 1295, l. 199.
[63] GARF, f. R7928, op. 3, d. 102, l. 46.
[64] GARF, f. R7928, op. 3, d. 1278, ll. 35–6, and l. 31. On gifts, see Elizabeth Banks, "Sewing Machines for Socialism? Gifts of Development and Disagreement between the Soviet and Mozambican Women's Committees, 1963–1987," *Comparative Studies of South Asia, Africa and the Middle East* 41.1 (2021): 27–40.

measured propaganda, presenting the Soviet Union as a model for literacy—for example, citing the prevalence of libraries and reading rooms in both rural and urban areas. They also enquired about the operations of the Withana Reading Club, offered Mrs. Perera best wishes for its "noble activity," and asked about the life and problems of women in Ceylon.[65]

Such pleasantries indicate that the moral support communicated through exchanges of letters and gifts was another key facet of correspondence, and while women in Africa and Asia might have explicitly sought it out in their perhaps more difficult situation, they also habitually extended it. It was in and through these expressions of camaraderie and concern that the motifs of friendship, peace, and humanity, and convictions about the power of sisterhood, most clearly manifested themselves in the epistolarium of the KSZh. Encouragement was especially vivid in correspondence involving women in countries whose independence was yet to be secured, as evinced by the letters exchanged between the committee and national liberation activist Gertrude Omog over the course of 1958 and 1959. During this time, Omog, head of the Union Démocratique des Femmes Camerounaises (the Democratic Union of Cameroonian Women/UDEFEC), forwarded to the KSZh a number of appeals related to the independence struggle in her country and to the global peace movement.[66] Among these were the formal "Appel aux femmmes du monde entier," which detailed the crisis in Cameroon and recommended the withdrawal of foreign troops, amnesties for political activists, and a referendum on reunification and independence, as well as a general statement against the Cold War and atomic weapons.[67] In a request addressed to "Dear Friends" at the committee sent in January 1958, Omog stated, "We beg you to transmit to all women and your whole people our friendship and our confidence for its collaboration in our struggle, and tell them that, in spite of the blood which is flowing … the most powerful army cannot vanquish the desire of a people to be free in this period of history."[68]

About a month later, Petrova wrote Omog to affirm Soviet solidarity with the people of Cameroon in their fight for national independence and to condemn "arbitrary measures" being carried out against them by the French government.[69] Suggesting the kind of conventional foreign relations diplomacy at play in KSZh correspondence, this sort of support for liberation and peace shown by members of the committee was also writ large in formal and public ways, including pronouncements published in its information bulletins and in *Soviet Woman*. Yet communication between Omog and the committee had begun before official Soviet recognition of Cameroon in December 1959; it also extended beyond 1960, when Cameroon gained full independence.[70] As their relationship developed, the committee provided Omog with a stipend to study in

---

[65] GARF, f. R7928, op. 3, d. 345, ll. 4, 18–20, 26, 29, 39, and 53, and GARF, f. R7928, op. 3, d. 571, ll. 10, 13–14, 48, and 50.
[66] For more on Omog, see Meredith Terretta, "Cameroonian Nationalists Go Global: From Forest 'Maquis' to a Pan-African Accra," *Journal of African History* 51.2 (2010): 189–212.
[67] GARF, f. R7928, op. 3, d. 120, l. 14, 17 and 24.
[68] GARF, f. R7928, op. 3, d. 120, l. 3.
[69] GARF, f. R7928, op. 3, d. 120, l. 6.
[70] George Ginsburg and R. M. Slusser, *A Calendar of Soviet Treaties: 1958–1973* (Alphen aan den Rijn, The Netherlands, and Rockville, MD, 1981), 762.

Figure 5.1 Gertrude Omog with two Stalinabad schoolgirls, Makhbube and Miroi Zaripov, during a visit to the Soviet Union, *Sovetskaya Zhenshchina* / *Soviet Woman*.

the Soviet Union, and she enroled at the Kalinin (Tver) Medical Institute.[71] In a note of thanks sent from Kalinin in August 1962, Omog remarked with apparent delight on the friendliness with which she was greeted in Russia and though she wrote her letter in French, she addressed it in Russian, indicating that she had been practicing the language of her hosts.[72]

In addition to extending various forms of support, Soviet women regularly recognized the accomplishments of peoples abroad through congratulatory letters, as well as postcards and telegrams on the occasion of national holidays. For instance, in January 1961, Fëdorova wrote on behalf of the KSZh to the prominent African figure Grace Ayensu to congratulate her on her election to the Ghanaian Parliament the previous June; to proclaim solidarity in the immediate aftermath of the assassination of the Congolese independence leader Patrice Lumumba and extend condolences to his wife and the wives of all Congolese "heroes"; and to condemn the actions of colonizers and voice support for the struggle of the peoples of Africa against them.[73] Sometimes articulations of solidarity were reinforced by details of commemorations organized in the Soviet Union to honour special occasions. For example, Voronina included in an August 1964 letter to A.B. in Calcutta a paragraph outlining how Soviet citizens were celebrating Indian Independence Day with meetings at the Indo-Soviet Friendship Society, schools, factories, offices, and other places, and with accounts in the press, and on radio and television, of Indian successes since independence was achieved in 1947.[74]

Soviet women showed themselves to be sympathetic correspondents not only by acknowledging major milestones and supporting activities of national significance, but also by demonstrating interest in grassroots initiatives. In these ways, they validated the pursuits undertaken by their counterparts around the world, and by extension, their sense of purpose and self. As Celia Hughes has argued of feminist epistolary culture, sharing circumstances and experiences "rendered ... women more visible and secure in who and what they understood themselves to be" and nurtured relational female selves by recognizing others.[75] This dynamic was evident in the aforementioned exchange between S. Devi of Model Town and Bondarenko. In addition to sending materials for the exhibition that the Indian woman was organizing, Bondarenko extended wishes for success, good health, and happiness as if to further encourage Devi, and stated that members of a recent Soviet delegation to India had enjoyed their visit and were now "reporting of" it "at meetings, over the radio, on television and in the press."[76]

Correspondence between Petrova and a Nepalese activist, Kamal Shah, in contrast, repeatedly referenced a matter of national import to the latter: family legislation aimed at improving the status of women. After Shah informed her of one of several setbacks she had experienced, Petrova encouragingly replied, "I am quite certain that your efforts to make Parliament pass a new marriage law will undoubtedly succeed." The

[71] GARF, f. R7928, op. 3, d. 693, l. 22.
[72] GARF, f. R7928, op. 3, d. 879, l. 22.
[73] GARF, f. R7928, op. 3, d. 669, l. 8.
[74] GARF, f. R7928, op. 2, d. 1295, l. 244.
[75] Hughes, "Left Activism, Succour and Selfhood," 877, 879.
[76] GARF, f. R7928, op. 3, d. 102, l. 48.

Soviet woman also reassured Shah that she was not alone but among women in many countries struggling "for their lawful place both in the family and society."[77]

Expressions of support and solidarity may have held special meaning for those engaged in a struggle for national liberation or gender equality, but women in developing countries reciprocated by voicing esteem for their Soviet sisters, regardless of their comparatively stable and favorable circumstances. This was manifested in praise for features of Soviet society they had witnessed while traveling in the Soviet Union, as well as for the achievements of Soviet women and their government that they had seen or heard about. For example, E. Sumanagara wrote the KSZh that since returning to Bandung from a trip to the Soviet Union, she had not stopped talking about the good things she had witnessed, and that everyone at home "tirelessly" and "with pleasure" listened to her stories. As if affirming the interest of her compatriots, she added, "Everyone very much wants to see this for themselves."[78]

Similarly, besides expressing appreciation on behalf of women of her country for the solidarity that committee members had shown her and the people of Cameroon, Omog stated her support for Soviet policy. In a letter co-written with a fellow member of the UDEFEC in March 1958, she declared her disapproval of the Cold War and "admiration" for the commitment of the Soviet government toward peaceful coexistence.[79] Endorsing Soviet foreign relations in a lighter vein, one Indian woman wrote Khimach that the people of her country had been following the "brilliant, wise and witty speeches" of the "great" Soviet Premier throughout his 1959 visit to the United States; that they were "unanimously favorable" to Nina Khrushcheva; that "the hearts of millions" were rejoicing over their negative reaction "to the vulgarity of Hollywood and that filthy movie 'Can Can'"; and that overall, the trip was a great step toward the peace that people everywhere longed for.[80] The glowing praise heaped upon the Khrushchev family might be dismissed as hyperbolic flattery, but the moral assertion about Hollywood indicates a shared perspective.

The epistolarium of the KSZh exhibits particular exhilaration among women in developing countries over Soviet successes in the space race, and women's role in it. Among the many letters sent to the KSZh to congratulate Valentina Tereshkova on her 1963 space flight was one from Wanita Demokrat (a women's organization affiliated with the Indonesian Nationalist Party) conveying "hearty felicitations" to the "courageous" cosmonaut and citing her as an inspiration to women worldwide.[81] Another, sent from Elise Osende, an activist in the UDEFEC, enthusiastically cited Tereshkova as the Soviet woman who "opened a path for all women" and showed that they are not inferior to men, as well as "the superiority of the socialist regime in comparison to the capitalist regime."[82]

---

[77] GARF, f. R7928, op. 3, d. 715, l. 17.
[78] GARF, f. R7928, op. 2, d. 1935, l. 33.
[79] GARF, f. R7928, op. 3, d. 120, l. 13.
[80] GARF, f. R7928, op. 3, d. 279, l. 32. On this episode, see Peter Carlson, "*K Blows Top: A Cold War Comic Interlude, Starring Nikita Khrushchev, America's Most Unlikely Tourist* (New York, 2009), 149–52.
[81] GARF, f. R7928, op. 3, d. 1107, l. 88.
[82] GARF, f. R7928, op. 3, d. 1116, l. 60.

As these illustrations suggest, laudatory comments about Soviet women and society were sometimes imbued with wide-ranging significance, even universal import. Recognizing the current Seven-Year Plan as a point of pride, in 1960, a leading member of Gerwani, who identified herself as Mrs. Suharti, sent "Friends" at the KSZh good wishes for the success of Soviet policy in creating a better life, asserting that the accomplishments of the Soviet people "inspire the women of all countries in the struggle for full national independence, emancipation, democracy and peace."[83] By illuminating connections between Soviet feats and their own experiences and challenges, women in developing countries also forged a sense of camaraderie and lent their own activities credence. For example, a letter from the same Indonesian organization congratulating the entire Soviet people on the 1964 *Voskhod* spaceflight declared that this triumph "again demonstrates the superiority of socialism over capitalism"—and the very kind of "strength" essential to "the struggle against neocolonialism."[84]

Suharti appears to have been prompted to write by the upcoming anniversary of the Russian Revolution. Although October 1960 marked a jubilee of no special importance, that she nevertheless chose the occasion to reach out to the committee demonstrates that for women in developing countries, as for their Soviet counterparts, marking and celebrating national holidays were established modes of recognition and bonding. Going beyond mere etiquette, K. Vimla wrote Petrova in September 1958 about a week-long program that the Women's Section of the Indo-Soviet Cultural Society in Ghaziabad was undertaking to celebrate the 41st anniversary of the October Revolution; it was to include a film exhibition, a cultural evening and public meetings, as well as a separate agenda of "Two days for ladies." She revealed that the organization was also planning to publish a magazine called *Indo-Soviet Friendship*, with articles by Indian and Russian writers, in the hope that this would strengthen friendship and lead to closer contacts.[85]

A letter from the aforementioned Cissé struck a similar chord. She claimed to be striving to follow "the remarkable example of fairmindedness and devotion" Soviet women had shown her and looking toward the day when their two countries would be closely united in building socialism, ending on a note of hope for world peace.[86] That the Guinean woman identified the place of Soviet women in her life and work, and the enduring nature of their friendship—"born in days of hard labour, in fraternal contact and expressed in the general will toward the struggle for liberation"—shows how the correspondence conducted by the KSZh could serve socialist outreach. At the same time, though, the seemingly reflexive nature of her concluding sentiment connected the amity and solidarity in their epistolary relationship with a more universal aim: world peace.

Peace as a shared objective repeatedly surfaced in the epistolarium of the KSZh and on all sides. For example, the singer Effie Tjoa from Indonesia, who had visited the Soviet Union, wrote to the KSZh to thank Fëdorova for a letter and photos she had sent

---

[83] GARF, f. R7928, op. 3, d. 684, l. 11.
[84] GARF, f. R7928, op. 3, d. 1297, l. 125.
[85] GARF, f. R7928, op. 3, d. 102, l. 118.
[86] GARF, f. R7928, op. 3, d. 475, l. 24.

her, stating that she was "happy and honored" to receive her "kind letter," casting it as "encouragement and inspiration" to continue to "struggle for peace and unity."[87] As Tjoa implied, simple exchanges could bridge distance to nurture or sustain a relationship, provide support and comfort in an uncertain world, and ensure the realization of common aspirations.[88] In a letter from Bombay, Mrs. D. R. Piroja Wadia affectionately addressed Balakhovskaya as "Lyusia" and expressed appreciation for the hospitality shown her in the Soviet Union. Acknowledging that they might never meet again given the distance between them, she asserted that life is short, making it all the more important to fight for peace.[89]

Exhibiting faith in the potential of women to effect positive change or avert catastrophe, in writing to Sumitra Devi, a member of a Nepalese delegation to the Soviet Union, Petrova declared that life shows that "personal contacts and relations between women of different countries help to promote good friendship and wider understanding between the women and people of these countries." These she characterized as "a great contribution to the common cause of … Peace on earth," assuring Devi that Soviet women had long stood for such contacts.[90] Born of wartime struggle, the KSZh most certainly had.

* * *

The fabric of the epistolarium of the KSZh is patchy, and in the absence of sustained communication, it is impossible to declare its efforts a definitive success in persuading women who were not already predisposed toward it of the superiority of socialism. The pleasantries exchanged might have been perfunctory, and the depth of sincerity of the letters cannot be determined with certainty. Yet it does appear that correspondence fostered contacts and a degree of mutual understanding and friendship, whether in the service of socialism, national liberation, gender equality, world peace, or even, simply, curiosity about the world.

This is evident in an admittedly unique thread of correspondence conducted over the course of 1961 and 1962 between various members of the KSZh and D. G. Patel in India, an individual whose initial communication exhibited disdain toward the committee. Interestingly, central to these exchanges, at least initially, was not the correspondence itself, but the postage stamps that marked it. In what appeared to be her first letter, Patel engaged in a mild rant explaining that like others in India, she subscribed to Soviet magazines "for the Russian stamps also," but that in her estimation, the publications themselves were "all propaganda."[91] The response was diplomatic, even accommodating: Bondarenko claimed that she had never before heard anyone speak this way about *Soviet Woman*, but welcomed suggestions for the magazine. What is more, after voicing her disappointment that Patel appeared to "measure the sincerity of

---

[87] GARF, f. R7928, op. 3, d. 684, l. 62.
[88] This assertion is informed by Ann McElaney-Johnson, "Epistolary Friendship: 'La prise de parole' in Mariama Bâ's 'Une si longue lettre,'" *Research in African Literatures* 30.2 (Summer 1999): 114, 118.
[89] GARF, f. R7928, op. 2, d. 1762, l. 35.
[90] GARF, f. R7928, op. 2, d. 1959, l. 15.
[91] GARF, f. R7928, op. 3, d. 681, l. 121.

Soviet women and their friendship by the presence of postage stamps on ... envelopes," and stating that she would like to believe that most Indians subscribe for "other motives," she nevertheless promised to put her in touch with a colleague at the KSZh who was also a collector. For the time being, she enclosed a stamp series on the Soviet republics.[92]

Others might certainly have shared with Patel her ulterior motive for contacting the committee and for subscribing to its chief publication. What is interesting is that this particular woman seemed to grow sympathetic to Soviet women over time. In a letter to Bondarenko about a year after she first contacted the KSZh, Patel jovially began, "Much water has flown down the Volga and the Ganges since you went for [a] holiday and both Russia and India have ... issued a number of stamps." She was especially keen to obtain a Soviet stamp honoring the celebrated Bengali intellectual, artist, and Nobel Laureate, Rabindranath Tagore. Yet she also asked Bondarenko about her vacation and stated that she knew full well from *Soviet Woman* that Russian women were very busy. She therefore recommended that Bondarenko might enlist one of her children to send her stamps. It appears then that correspondence prompted by philatelic interest had engendered a curiosity about Soviet life, as well as a personal acquaintance with members of the KSZh. Patel concluded by asking Bondarenko to convey her "love" to *another* committee member with whom she had also come to correspond; meanwhile Bondarenko sent the requested stamps.[93]

Most of the women with whom the KSZh exchanged letters did appear to be sympathetic correspondents, some even affiliated with leftist organizations in their own country. Nevertheless, alongside the kind of suspicion of Soviet women that Patel exhibited, divergences of opinion about the system under which they lived did occasionally surface. This is apparent in a letter sent to Krichigina from Ruby Quartey-Papafio, an activist in the National Council of Ghana Women. Here the Ghanaian woman remarked that she wished she had seen more of the country during a visit to the Soviet Union—casting it as "marvelous" and praising its "achievements in science"—but also admitted, "Sometimes when I am thinking about it, I feel sad that all these achievements are without the acknowledgment of God who gave the brains with which these marvelous feats are accomplished." Bemoaning socialist atheism did not, however, diminish her interest in fostering an acquaintance with the KSZh; her letter also expressed appreciation for some literature that had been sent to her, and was signed with "love."[94] Others seemed to be unaware of or to simply dismiss the relevance of Soviet differences.[95] For example, many women abroad sent the KSZh greetings at Christmas and even religious blessings—as in the case of the aforementioned Sumitra

---

[92] GARF, f. R7928, op. 3, d. 681, l. 125.
[93] GARF, f. R7928, op. 3, d. 864, l. 127 and l. 129. Evidence of stamps excised from incoming mail suggest Soviet appreciation, too. See, for example, GARF, f. R7928, op. 3, d. 1295, l. 88.
[94] GARF, f. R7928, op. 3, d. 845, ll. 3–4.
[95] Finding common ground does not mean, of course, that the aims of women of the Second and Third Worlds were always fully aligned, or that women in state socialist organizations were entirely egalitarian in their approach to collaboration with women in developing countries. See, for example, Yulia Gradskova, "Women's International Democratic Federation, the 'Third World' and the Global Cold War from the Late-1950s to the Mid-1960s," *Women's History Review* 29.2 (2020): 270–88, and Celia Donert, "Femmes, Communisme et Internationalisme: La Fédération Démocratique Internationale des Femmes en Europe Centrale (1945–1979)," *Vingtième Siecle* 126 (April–June 2015): 119–31.

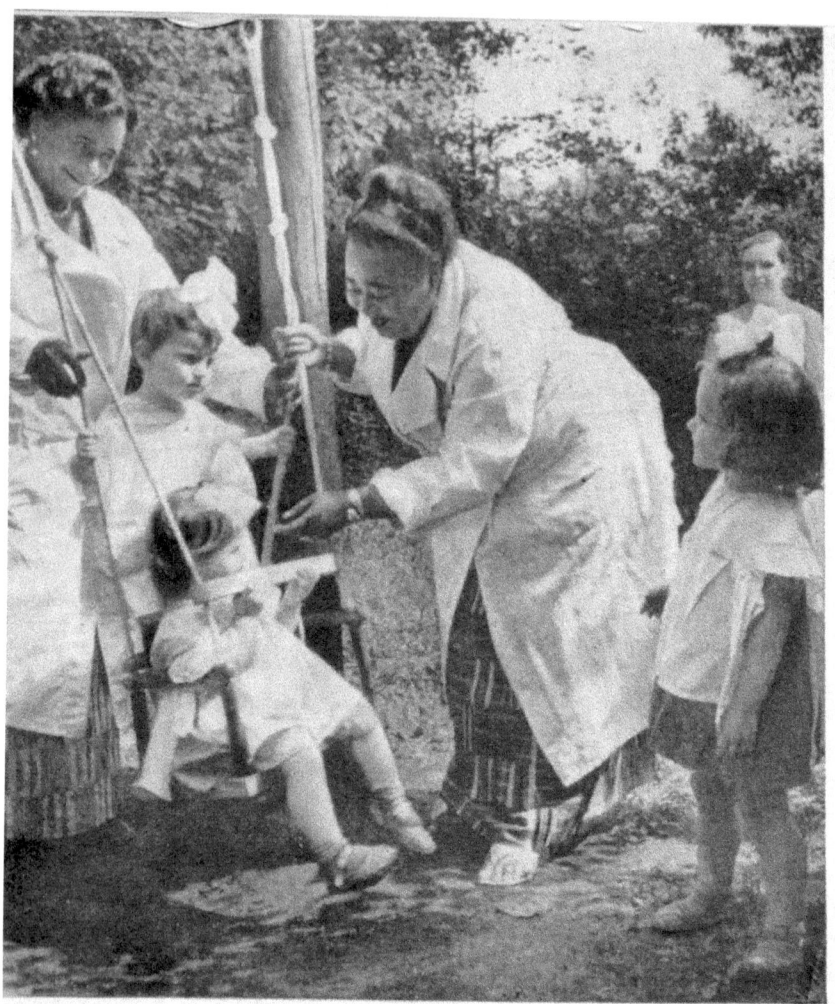

Meeting young Moscovites. Guests Ruby Quartey and Hannah Kudjoe, active in the women's movement in the Republic of Ghana, visit a creche

Figure 5.2 Guests from Ghana visiting a Moscow crèche: Hannah Kudjoe and Ruby Quartey, Papafio, *Sovetskaya Zhenshchina / Soviet Woman*.

Devi from Nepal who in a letter to the "President" of the committee prayed for the Hindi god Pashupati to "bestow his blessings" on her and her "other sisters of Russia."[96]

Overall, women in sub-Saharan Africa and South Asia seemed to counterbalance differences they discerned in their Soviet correspondents with mutual interest in common causes like justice and world peace. In this regard, the letters they exchanged were typical of feminist epistolary culture in that they concerned not only "the self and

[96] GARF, f. R7928, op. 2, d. 1959, l. 10.

the other" but also "other people, events, and circumstances in a world shared in common, even if not every aspect of the meaning of this" was agreed upon.[97] Meanwhile, expressions of friendship and encouragement, as well as humanist discourse, "spoke" to women in developing countries who may have been more preoccupied with national and female liberation than their Soviet counterparts. This is illustrated by a member of the All-Indian Women's Conference (AIWC) who wrote the KSZh to share her experiences at a conference she had recently attended in Indonesia. Touting its successes, she attributed them "to the fact that [attendees had] completely avoided discussing political questions," making "it … obvious … that women can accomplish more by way of understanding and international cooperation [and] by concentrating on constructive and humanitarian questions."[98]

Of course, issues like world peace were politicized during the Cold War, and to characterize interaction among women as purely apolitical, as did the AIWC member, was to romanticize sisterhood.[99] A letter from Dove to Bondarenko further illustrates this trait of the correspondence examined here. Writing in 1960, the Ghanaian woman commented that it was unfortunate that the recent American U-2 spy plane incident had undermined the subsequent summit between Khrushchev and President Dwight Eisenhower. Suggesting that women could do better, she added that leaders ought to laugh a bit and admit their mistakes, stating, "I think often that men have too much political power and women too little and one day the men will overreach themselves and bring disaster to mankind."[100] Expressing a similar conviction in a positive voice, one woman from Bombay wrote:

> There is a saying that "the hand that rocks the cradle rules the world." Is it not true? If we, the mothers, start in their own homes first to teach the children peaceful habits instead of giving them toy pistols and guns, most likely the world would be a better place for all.[101]

The KSZh might well have tapped into such idealized visions of female activism or shown sympathy and camaraderie in the interest of world peace, because these were deemed especially promising means of cultivating relationships with women abroad and spreading socialism. Yet the letters that the committee penned bore strong supra-ideological, humanistic overtones that held appeal for their recipients. Speaking to the ubiquity of the language of humanity at the time, one Indian doctor exclaimed in a 1963 letter, "May we all the children of this beautiful daughter of heaven, the earth, be united in one family unit, red or white, yellow or brown … we all are one in the term—Humanity."[102]

---

[97] Stanley, Salter and Dampier, "The Epistolary Pact," 280.
[98] GARF, f. R7928, op. 3, d. 102, l. 66. This letter was written in English, but the grammar has been adjusted for clarity.
[99] Jolly, "Confidantes, Co-workers and Correspondents," 279–80.
[100] GARF, f. R7928, op. 3, d. 473, ll. 23–4.
[101] GARF, f. R7928, op. 2, d. 1762, l. 24.
[102] GARF, f. R7928, op. 3, d. 1295, l. 156.

Discourse aside, writing to women in distant parts of the globe provided an entrée into discussions and activities on the international level as much for individuals and organizations in decolonizing countries in Africa and Asia as for women in the Soviet Union. Exchanging letters was a way to learn about others in faraway places during this era of postwar globalization; to garner moral support for serious pursuits like decolonization, gender equality, and world peace; and to foster cooperation across continents. In these ways, members of the KSZh may have served the cause of socialist internationalism, but through writing, they also enacted solidarity, validating the struggles or initiatives to which their fellow correspondents were devoting themselves and approaching those in very different circumstances as sisters. Just as significant, the epistolarium of the committee demonstrates that women in developing countries did the same for their Soviet counterparts when they put pen to paper.

6

The University: The Decolonization of Knowledge? The Making of the African University, the Power of the Imperial Legacy, and the Eastern European Influence

Małgorzata Mazurek

In May 1964, Kwame Nkrumah approached the University of Ghana's authorities with a request to eliminate the practice of maintaining separate high tables for faculty in all dining halls, and to introduce instead a self-service cafeteria system. The university had been established in 1948 in Legon Hills (near Accra) as a British colonial institution called the University College of the Gold Coast. In Nkrumah's conception, the university aimed to shape "the mind of Africa," creating a spiritual and intellectual force for African unity and decolonization.[1] The removal of the halls system was one of the first steps toward the goal of Africanization. Within this space, Ghanaians, the British, and other international powers that intervened in African decolonization negotiated who exactly would train Africa's elite. Education was an imperative for new, decolonizing nation-states. In the colonial era, as Nkrumah's confidant, the Ghanaian philosopher William Abraham, stated, "Education was devised not to serve African societies... It was devised to strengthen the service of Africa to Europe."[2] Ghana, being a hub for the African intellectual diaspora and for international experts and intellectuals, aspired to be a center of pan-African and global thought and education.[3] Historically, the process of remedying years of imperial neglect was not a simple metropole-colony affair because it relied in part on importing foreign nationals to newly established

---

[1] William E. Abraham, *The Mind of Africa* (Legon, 2005/1962); Gerardo Serra and Frank Gerits, "The Politics of Socialist Education in Ghana: The Kwame Nkrumah Ideological Institute, 1961–1966," *Journal of African History* 60.3 (November 2019), 407–28.
[2] Abraham, *The Mind of Africa*, 198.
[3] Francis Agbodeka, *A History of University of Ghana: Half a Century of Higher Education (1948–1998)* (Accra, 1998); Jean Allman, "Kwame Nkrumah, African Studies, and the Politics of Knowledge Production in the Black Star of Africa," *International Journal of African Historical Studies* 46.2 (2013): 181–203; Jeffrey Ahlman, *Living with Nkrumahism: Nation, State, and Pan-Africanism in Ghana* (Athens, OH, 2017).

African universities. Starting in the late 1950s, the University College of the Gold Coast (since 1961, the University of Ghana) or Legon, as it was known, witnessed an influx of European, Indian, American, and Israeli scholars, among them celebrities like Norbert Elias and rising stars of social science like Immanuel Wallerstein. There was also a small but influential group of Poles. Their task, officially formulated as "Africanization" or "Ghanaization," was to train Ghanaian elites and increase their numbers in leadership positions in public administration, education, and the local economy. This chapter traces how the Africanization of the University of Ghana happened not through an automatic replacement of colonial cadres by Ghanaians, but rather through the faculty's internationalization. Decolonization was thus not a bilateral story linking metropole and colony, but a more complex triangulation of post-imperial, international (including Soviet bloc), and Third World relations. I place particular emphasis here on the early and mid-1960s, when Legon's institutional dependence on London was gradually phased out as the recruitment of international faculty increased.[4]

In 1948, the University College of the Gold Coast was one of the biggest and costliest public institutions in late colonial West Africa, and the largest of a dozen or so overseas colleges that the British had established in Hong Kong, Africa, and the West Indies in the aftermath of World War II. African students at Legon received London degrees, thus a metropole-level education.[5] To harmonize degrees, exams, and curricula between the metropole and the colony, the British had fashioned an imperial institutional framework known as the "Special Relationship."[6] Like other institutions of mid-twentieth-century colonial development, Legon was originally set up to represent British interests, not undermine them.[7] By the time the Gold Coast had become independent Ghana, in 1957, the campus was known as "mini-Oxbridge," populated by a racial mix of white faculty and black students. This changed in 1961 when Nkrumah became both Ghana's president and the university's chancellor, and when Legon transformed from an overseas college into a national university. This institutional shift situated the university as a center of West African politics. Legon became a site of opposition to Nkrumah; the regime's press dubbed it the "Oxbridge ivory tower," a tenacious vestige of the metropole's symbolic power.

Eastern Europeans, who were an integral part of this postcolonial situation, formed a heterodox group on campus. In their ranks were to be found Nkrumah's Soviet advisors, who taught Marxism-Leninism; Czechs with scant knowledge of English and thus little impact; and finally Polish economists, who provided keen instruction on Keynesian theories and Anglo-American economics. In this chapter, I focus on two

---

[4] See Bruce Pattison, *Special Relations: The University of London and New Universities Overseas, 1947–1970* (London, 1984), 160; Eric Ashby, *African Universities and Western Tradition* (Cambridge, MA, 1964); Alexander Adum Kwapong, *A Life in Education: A Memoir* (Legon-Accra, 2016); Donald Harman Akenson, *Conor: A Biography of Conor Cruise O'Brien* (Ithaca, NY, 1994); Tamson Pietsch, *Empire of Scholars: Universities, Networks and the British Academic World, 1850–1939* (Manchester, 2013).
[5] Mary Dillard, "Testing Freedom: A History of the West African Examinations Council, 1952–1979," Ph.D. thesis, University of California, Los Angeles, 2001.
[6] Tim Livsey, *Nigeria's University Age: Reframing Decolonization and Development* (London, 2017).
[7] A. M. Carr-Saunders, *New Universities Overseas* (London, 1961), 254.

Polish economists, heads in turn of the Economics Department: Jan Drewnowski (who held the position from 1961 to 1964) and his former assistant from Warsaw, Zbigniew Sadowski (1965 -70). They were critical of Nkhrumah's self-aggrandizing rule but subscribed to his idea of the progressive nation-state; they had studied and worked in communist Poland but were integrated into Anglo-American scholarly networks. For nearly a decade, they supervised British and European colleagues and trained the new Ghanaian faculty in the time before African scholars and teachers were allowed to write their own curricula and hold faculty jobs.[8] The Poles survived every crisis on the campus, including Nkrumah's own fall.

Paradoxically, the presence of Poles in Legon demonstrated the importance of the British connection in the process of Africanization as internationalization. The story of Polish scholars at the University of Ghana illuminates a greatly underestimated factor in so-called "Second World–Third World" relations: the power of what Ann Stoler calls "imperial durability," but it also goes beyond that imperial framework. Stoler has defined imperial effects in a temporal way, as power relations that carried imperial practices and ideas into the postcolonial period.[9] This chapter, however, concentrates on specific historical actors and their actions rather than a diffused, Foucauldian microphysics of power. It focuses on the ways in which Polish scholars in Ghana operated as much as agents of Africanization as they did as transmitters of "the imperial effect" of an Oxbridge-style campus and Western-centric academic knowledge. I posit that the Oxbridge legacy was enacted and gradually transformed, rather than fully contested, due to the importing into Ghana of state socialist experts. Officially, the Poles had been hired as members of the progressive socialist world and experts in the national planning that Africa needed.

This story reveals, however, that the recruitment of foreign nationals—just like the spatial design of the campus and its ideological climate—was largely determined by the British administrators, and after the expiry of the Special Relationship between Legon and London, by their enduring symbolic power and personal connections. In the early and mid-1960s, any scholar from the "Second World" seeking appointment at the University of Ghana had to go through a vetting system controlled by the British. Tellingly, the recruitment office for foreign nationals applying for Ghanaian jobs was based in London. From the African perspective, this is far from being a straightforward story of continuing British dominance, however, because of the impact of Eastern Europeans in Legon as European-but-not-colonial agents of Africanization. We might imagine them to have been "red specialists," but that was not the case either. The most established Eastern Europeans in Legon—Polish economists—were plugged into the Western European, especially British, academy, and acted as intermediaries for cutting-edge Anglo-American economics (Keynesianism). They were formal representatives of

---

[8] See Gerardo Serra, "From Scattered Data to Ideological Education: Economics, Statistics and the State in Ghana, 1948–1966," Ph.D. thesis, London School of Economics, 2015; Robert Tignor, *Arthur Lewis and the Birth of Development Economics* (Princeton, 2006); Alden Young, *Transforming Sudan: Decolonization, Economic Development, and State Formation* (Cambridge, 2018).
[9] Ann Stoler, *Duress: Imperial Durabilities in Our Times* (Durham, 2015), 6–8.

the Soviet bloc without representing the party line. Neither of these roles fits squarely into binary narratives of neocolonialism and Cold War cultural diplomacy.[10]

Mini-Oxbridge: The Making of the Late Colonial Campus

The University College of the Gold Coast developed thanks to local pressure and financial commitment. Its striking grandeur had little to do with the politics of colonial development that characterized British rule in Africa after World War II. Following the creation of the first Western-style university in Africa, the Furah Bay College in today's Sierra Leone, after 1945, the British agreed to sponsor only one college for all of West Africa, in Ibadan. Ghanaians protested this decision and were promised their own college, but on condition that they paid for it. The relevant investment was financed through a tax on cocoa crops, collected through the Cocoa Marketing Board and with the Nkrumah government's support.[11] Cocoa trees planted in front of the Akufo Hall served as a reminder that African farmers had been the main donors. National pride, supported by local African resources, helped overcome years of imperial neglect.

As Tim Livsey has observed, post-1945 British colonial campuses reflected how it was that Africans, by embracing the comforts and institutions of European civilization, might acquire the cultural competences of those who had hitherto held power.[12] The University College of the Gold Coast became the key site for the Africanization of public service, based on acquiring standards of Western education and lifestyle. It was not designed as a nucleus of independent Ghanaian culture, but rather as a part of an overseas college network having its command center in the University of London. The campus was huge: it spread across five square miles of plains near Accra. It also resembled the oldest British universities in its structure: fully residential and based on the English system of quadrangles surrounded by lecture rooms, laboratories, and a library, with neatly manicured lawns. Both admirers and critics of the institution soon dubbed it a "mini-Oxbridge."[13]

The campus was designed with the idea of imperial durability in mind. Although residential halls were decorated with local Ghanaian timber, the campus's silhouette was dominated by an element of English urban landscape: a clock tower. The tower served to remind the students and university administration that Legon was under metropolitan control. The buildings were erected in the late 1940s and 1950s with an assumption that the British colonies would remain for a long time. Architecture and

---

[10] Małgorzata Mazurek, "Polish Economists in Nehru's India: Making Science for the Third World in an Era of De-Stalinization and Decolonization," *Slavic Review* 77.3 (2018): 588–610. This argument contrasts with seminal works on East–Central Europe's Cold War that center party-state politics: Elidor Mëhilli, *From Stalin to Mao: Albania and the Socialist World* (Ithaca, NY, 2017); Theodora Dragostinova, *The Cold War from the Margins: A Small Socialist State on the Global Cultural Scene* (Ithaca, NY, 2021).
[11] Kwapong, *A Life in Education*, 97.
[12] Livsey, *Nigeria's University Age*, 89–118; Francis Agbodeka, *Achimota in the National Setting: A Unique Educational Experiment in West Africa* (Accra, 1977), 81–2.
[13] Akenson, *Conor*, 224ff.

landscaping played a crucial role in establishing Legon as a site of elitist higher education. To transplant Oxbridge flair into a colonial setting, David Balme, the college's principal, hired Austen St. Barbe Harrison (a direct descendant of Jane Austen), who was known for his overseas architectural projects in Greece, the British Mediterranean, and in British Palestine during the mandate period.[14] Harrison's architecture represented a paternalistic and preservationist conception of colonial rule that made modest gestures towards the vernacular culture of dependent peoples. His architecture aimed to reconcile tradition and change, British rule with the cultural separateness of colonial subjects. Harrison deployed regional motifs to produce what art historians have called "stripped" or "abstract" Orientalism.[15] This aesthetic conveyed a message of forward-looking, reformist empire.

The open spaces of the Legon Hill offered a perfect site in which to implement a somewhat abstract idea of Oxford and the philosophy of an airy, splendid college.[16] Harrison tried, however, to reflect, at least symbolically, certain particularities of the local setting. He did not fix on the traditional round dwellings that many colonial officials found to be most representative of the "African tradition," but instead on the Orientalist architecture of the nearby prestigious Achimota School, out of which the University College of the Gold Coast had originally developed.[17] This private boarding school, created in 1927 by British colonial reformists, produced famous alumni, including Nkrumah and Kwapong, the future vice-chancellor of the University of Ghana. African intellectuals were proud of Achimota and admired its lavish, representational—even grandiose—character, which had been designed to impress the British. The politics of scale deployed at Achimota, beloved by the Africans and controversial among the British, became a model for the University College of the Gold Coast, later the University of Ghana.

The "Special Relationship" with London

Legon was designed, at least on paper, to deliver Africanization of public service while still operating within the imperial framework of the Special Relationship. It aimed to train Africans for self-rule, while the British for their part saw it as an extension of British academia overseas. This paradoxical situation favoured the British. In 1950, Africans occupied only 219 out of 1,700 senior governmental posts in the entire Gold Coast. When African nationalists began to share power with the British in the early 1950s, Nkrumah's government assigned generous funds to Legon to speed up the

---

[14] Samuel D. Albert, "Egypt and Mandatory Palestine and Iraq," in G. A. Bremner (ed.), *Architecture and Urbanism in the British Empire* (Oxford, 2016), 424–54; Ron Fuchs and Gilbert Herbert, "Representing Mandatory Palestine: Austen St Barbe Harrison and the Representational Buildings of the British Mandate in Palestine, 1922–1937," *Architectural History* 43 (2000): 281–333; Austen St. B. Harrison, R. Pearce, and S. Hubbard, *Valletta: A Report to Accompany the Outline Plan for the Region of Valletta and the Three Cities* (Valetta, 1945), 72–3; 104–5.
[15] Fuchs and Herbert, "Representing Mandatory Palestine," 305.
[16] Howard Colvin, *Unbuilt Oxford* (New Haven, CT, 1983), 166–74.
[17] Agbodeka, *Achimota in the National Setting*, 17.

Figure 6.1 University of Ghana aerial view, c. 1950. University of London Archive, UoL AC 11/3/4.

education of African elites. Yet so long as the campus remained under British control, this proved to be a slow process both countrywide and on the campus itself. Balme, who continued to promote British faculty, believed in the enduring nature of colonial relations between London and Accra.[18] In the 1950s, the British monopolized executive and curricular power on the campus. They supervised all staff recruitment or promotion and imposed European curricula with minimal African content. White men, especially Englishmen, dominated the faculty, although single white female academics and staff were not unusual. Britons were attracted to Africa by a sense of adventure and a high living standard for expatriates. Austerity and academic unemployment in postwar Britain made it even easier to employ British senior faculty in the colonies. The core faculty transferred to the University of the Gold Coast from Achimota, but many others arrived from British Isles universities and comparable Commonwealth establishments in Australia and Canada.

After 1957, when the colony became an independent state, Ghanaians began to perceive the modest progress of Legon's Africanization as a problem. African scholars on the campus became bolder in addressing British discrimination against African instructors and staff.[19] West Africa had long produced well-educated intellectuals and

[18] Pattison, *Special Relations*, chapter 11.
[19] Kwapong, *A Life in Education*, 120.

leaders. Many alumni of Achimota School and the University College of the Gold Coast continued their education in prestigious universities abroad. However, once back in Legon they were rarely promoted to posts commensurate with their achievements. One such scholar was Joseph Mensah, the future chief economist of Nkrumah's National Planning Commission. In a letter sent to the university's principal in 1958 after he had failed to get a lectureship in the Department of Economics, he accused the college administration of paying no more than lip service to Africanization. "I had watched with dismay the succession of proposals," he wrote to the British administrators, "that you had sponsored in the course of the year aimed at making the working conditions and status of Ghanaian recruits markedly inferior to those of the other members of your staff." "Presumably," Mensah continued, "you tolerated African instructors for two or three years before dismissing them only to show that you too have a programme of Africanization." The college administration rejected the argument by African nationalists that if there were two excellent and similarly qualified candidates, one British, the other Ghanaian, the Ghanaian should be hired.[20] In 1960, Legon employed thirty-four Ghanaian lecturers, the remaining majority—123 faculty members—were white expats from the UK and the rest of Commonwealth.

Legon's defensive staffing politics merely fueled Nkrumah's determination to end the Special Relationship with London. In 1961, after a few years of negotiations, University College officially separated from the metropole and became the University of Ghana. Nkrumah, who became Ghana's president in 1961, immediately declared himself the chancellor of the university. In this way Nkrumah's nationalist politics penetrated Legon's "ivory tower isolation," turning the campus into a political battlefield. Nkrumah was obsessed with the idea that the University of Ghana was a hotbed of political resistance to his rule and his Convention's People Party (CPP). That same summer, he suspended all job contracts under the pretext of formally establishing the University of Ghana. Although most faculty members were rehired, six professors (five white expats and one Ghanaian) had to leave. This caused an outcry among the expats as well as among some Ghanaians, who felt Legon's "academic freedom" to be seriously threatened by Nkrumah's political bravado.

Nkrumah's regime then went on to accelerate the Africanization of cadres.[21] Following British custom, he established an international commission to produce a White Paper on the Africanization of universities, while also staging an anti-Legon press campaign.[22] In June 1961 the governmental *Ghanaian Times* described the campus as "a stronghold of colonial mentality," and "a den of academic reaction." The language of Africanization reappeared now in a fiercer, more ideological guise: "Africa is in revolutionary ferment," the *Times* stated. They argued that "our institutions cannot stand still … Africa's New Man has to be fashioned in our institutions of higher education and the University of Accra and University of Science and Technology in

[20] Kwapong, *A Life in Education*, 121.
[21] Jean Allman, "Between the Present and History: African Nationalism and Decolonization," in John Parker and Richard Reid (eds.), *The Oxford Handbook of Modern African History* (New York, 2013).
[22] University of London Archive, AC 11/9/4, Organization of the University of Ghana. Chronological events.

Kumasi will soon prove their worth as within the vanguard of the world's institutions of higher learning."[23]

The Commission's conclusions, jointly coordinated by the Ghanaians and the British, suggested a gradual and somewhat paradoxical approach. If the decolonization and expansion of Ghana's higher education—that is, Africanization—was to be accelerated, it required even more overseas personnel to train Africans. Consequently, in that transitional period, African elites relied heavily on Ghana's international outreach to attract new instructors. The point was to attract high-quality academics while offering them only temporary appointments. According to new guidelines, new overseas professors would earn 20% more than Ghanaians, but their job contracts would last no more than three years.[24] At the same time, the Special Relationship with London would not cease immediately, but only in 1963. From an academic perspective, the two-year transition period of dispensing with colonial status had many advantages. Legon would, for example, maintain the educational standards that the London connection had so far guaranteed, which was crucial in recruiting qualified faculty and meeting the expectations of African students anxious to obtain the prestigious University of London degree.

The recruitment of new faculty was designed to balance the interests of African nationalists and the British by including scholars from other countries. "We shall diversify our lecturers. We shall welcome all those who may come from the socialist countries of the East, all those who may come from the capitalist countries of the West, and all those who may come from the uncommitted or neutralist nations prepared to give their best to our institutions of higher learning," announced the national press.[25] Ghana's government started recruiting Eastern Europeans, Israelis, Indian scholars, and, of course, progressive Ghanaians. Representing state socialist or socialist-oriented countries, these scholars seemed to promise dedication to nation-building and a more collectivist model of the academy. "No longer will lecturers and professors with 'safe' or 'conservative' views be recruited," announced the government press in 1961.[26] Yet as long as the Special Relationship with London guaranteed the University of Ghana's prestige, the British remained gatekeepers of the hiring process. Without London's approval, no representative of the Soviet bloc or the non-aligned movement could be selected to work at Legon.

Poles as Agents of Africanization

The appointment of Jan Drewnowski (1908–2000), a citizen of socialist Poland, as the first non-British chair of the Department of Economics, exemplifies a particular form of the "British connection" that developed in the context of the Cold War and

[23] Editorial, *Ghanaian Times*, June 6, 1961.
[24] National Archives of Ghana, Public Records and Archives Administration Department (PRAAD), GH/PRAAD/RG.11/296, Special Professorships, Statement by the Government on the Report of the Commission of University Education, Dec. 1960–Jan. 1961.
[25] Editorial, *Ghanaian Times*, June 6, 1961.
[26] Editorial, *Ghanaian Times*, June 6, 1961.

intensifying Second World–Third World relations. In early 1961, the Ghanaian government approached Poland, long known for its first-rate economists, in search of a candidate in economics. The search was conducted by an all-British committee and took place at the London School of Economics, a member of the University of London's consortium. Drewnowski met the basic criteria: he was a senior scholar steeped in the theory and practice of state-led planning, who, moreover, spoke excellent English. Most importantly, he was a citizen of the "East" (as the British called Soviet bloc countries) who was nevertheless perfectly familiar with the British academic system. His Anglo-Eastern European credentials rendered him a consensus candidate. By virtue of his Polish citizenship his appointment would fulfill the Ghanaians' wish to diversify Legon's faculty. The British, in turn, would get a trusted scholar without antagonizing Nkrumah. What seemed decisive were Drewnowski's personal connections with English and American scholars.[27] "Oddly enough," the University of Ghana's registrar commented, "I have discovered that we had mutual friends and everyone who knows him speaks very highly of him."[28]

Drewnowski's British contacts went back to a study year of 1934–5 spent at the London School of Economics. At the LSE, Drewnowski had attended the lectures of Friedrich Hayek and Lionel Robbins (who later oversaw the Special Relationship between Legon and London), and became acquainted with several Keynesian economists, Nicholas Kaldor (a future member of the search committee that found Drewnowski) among them. Paul Rosenstein-Rodan, a Cracow-born émigré lecturer in economics at University College London and the future founder of development economics, had been Drewnowski's academic mentor. Upon his return to Poland in 1935, Drewnowski had joined the faculty of the Warsaw School of Economics, where, as he wrote in his memoir, "it was literally impossible to become a lecturer without at least a one-year study in London."[29] Together with Michał Kalecki, Oskar Lange, Ludwik Landau, and a few other Warsaw-based scholars, Drewnowski introduced a Keynesian approach to Polish economic science.[30] The war, however, interrupted the Polish "Keynesian revolution." Drewnowski was on a research trip in London, working on a book about Keynes's theory and state interventionism, when he learned about the signing of the Ribbentrop–Molotov Pact. His decision to return to Poland just before the outbreak of hostilities cost him five years of imprisonment in a German Oflag as a prisoner of war.[31]

---

[27] University of Ghana Archives, 1/61, Interim Council of the University of Ghana. Recruitment of Academic Staff, August 4, 1961.
[28] University of Ghana Archives, UG 1/1/D24. Personal file of Jan Drewnowski, G. Sewell to C. Gbeho, July 18, 1961.
[29] Jan Drewnowski, "*Autobiografia naukowa*," Kwartalnik Historii Nauki i Techniki 35.4 (1990): 451–89
[30] Jan Toporowski, *Michał Kalecki: An Intellectual Biography*, vols. 1 and 2 (New York, 2013–17); Ricardo Bellofiore, Ewa Karwowski, and Jan Toporowski (eds.), *The Legacy of Rosa Luxemburg, Oskar Lange, and Michał Kalecki* (Basingstoke, 2014); Michele Alacevich, "Planning Peace: The European Roots of the Post-War Global Development Challenge," *Past and Present* 239.1 (2018): 219–64; Małgorzata Mazurek, "Measuring Development: An Intellectual and Political History of Ludwik Landau's Scale of World Inequality," *Contemporary European History* 28.2 (2019): 156–71.
[31] Jan Drewnowski, "Nauka w obozach jenieckich w Niemczech 1939–1945," in Bolesław Orłowski (ed.), *Nauka polska wobec totalitaryzmów* (Warsaw, 1994), 116–22.

In early postwar Poland, Drewnowski's Keynesianism and Anglophone education fitted well with the state-led politics of reconstruction, then dominated by Polish pro-Western socialists. During Stalinism, however, socialists were either purged or incorporated into the Communist Party. Drewnowski lost his governmental job in the Planning Commission and was appointed to a secondary post in the Warsaw School of Economics, which was nationalized and staffed with Stalinist cadres. His fortunes changed again with Poland's retreat from Stalinism, but not for long. Although in 1956, Drewnowski returned to the University of Warsaw to teach core seminars, he soon found himself sidelined by professors prepared to follow the party line. The invitation from Ghana came when his career prospects in communist Poland looked rather bleak.[32]

Drewnowski's appointment to run the Department of Economics in Legon gave the British a chance to make up for political mistakes that had weakened their cultural dominance on the campus.[33] With Legon's transition from overseas college to national university in 1961, London had failed to appoint a Ghanaian to the position of vice-chancellor. Nkrumah was furious. The search for a chair of the Department of Economics, an all-white British bastion, was one vehicle the Ghanaian regime used to push back against the Legon establishment. Just before Drewnowski's hiring, the *Ghanaian Times* attacked the university for not offering courses in statistics, even though Ghana was "wedded to socialist economic planning." African students "were taught nothing about Ghana's or Africa's economic history," the press pointed out, "nor was any guidance to be found about Ghana's or Africa's ... economic development."[34] Pure theory and what Marxists called capitalist political economy were not adequate subjects for a modern African university.

In an era of rising quantitative social science, the curriculum of the Department of Economics looked utterly anachronistic. It combined economic subjects with a liberal arts education in governance and political thought (theories of governance from Plato to John Stuart Mill and Karl Marx), but no planning, econometrics, or statistics. The point of reference was solely imperial (British), not regional (West African) or national (Ghanaian). With Ghana's independence, the University of London administrators felt obliged to introduce minor corrections to the program. For example, they replaced a class on "Ideas of Empire" with "Theories of Imperialism," which investigated such sensitive topics as military conquest or settler colonization.[35] Despite such gestures of critical self-examination, the British preferred to teach about empires rather than nation-states in the syllabi they dictated to postcolonial universities. In the realm of research, the department also stuck to old ways and avoided the national framework.[36] While the overarching political theory deployed was imperial, empirically-minded

---

[32] Drewnowski, *Nauka w obozach*, 116–22.
[33] University of London Archive, AC 11/9/1, Eustace to Robbins, July 15, 1961.
[34] Editorial, *Ghanaian Times*, June 6, 1961.
[35] University of London Archive, AC 8/17/4/9, Senate and Overseas Special Relations (1958–1960), Syllabus for Government (within BA in Economics) at the University College of Ghana; R. Eustace to L. Mair, December 1, 1958.
[36] University of Ghana Archives, UG 1/3/2/3/6, Organization and Establishment of Research Division of the Department of Economics, Application for financial assistance under the Colonial Development and Welfare Act for the establishment of an economic research unit, November 10, 1952.

practitioners produced local, urban, or village monographs. Financed by the British Colonial Development and Welfare Act and the Americans (sponsors of the Volta Valley Project), empirical work usually narrowed down to ethnography of specific geographical areas (the Volta Valley) or commercial centers (the Kumasi market). Ideologically, this politics of scale presupposed and tacitly affirmed the existing colonial economy and social order. In addition, the department welcomed corporate interests. In 1958, London thus approved a class, developed and co-sponsored by Mobil Oil, that promoted Business Administration studies in Ghana.[37]

Drewnowski's predecessor, Barbu Niculescu, who joined the department in 1949, had failed to reinvent the curriculum. On the one hand, he realized that Legon offered no courses specific to Ghana, like agricultural or development economics.[38] On the other hand, he acted like an old-fashioned British colonial expert. At first glance, Niculescu, a Romanian émigré and British citizen, had had a similar international trajectory to Drewnowski. He had also studied at the London School of Economics and collaborated with Paul Rosenstein-Rodan at Chatham House during the war. But while Drewnowski had taken Keynesian theories back to Poland before the war, Niculescu had stayed in Britain to work for Allied economic intelligence. The communist takeover in Romania "ruled out any thought of my return, my wartime activities branding me in the eyes of the Communists as a British-capitalist" spy, wrote Niculescu in his application letter to the University College of the Gold Coast.[39] The move to Legon in 1949 kept him isolated from the latest developments in economic science. Niculescu's overdue book on colonial planning from 1958 was devoid of any references to the booming field of development economics. Instead, it treated planning as an exclusively administrative issue and discussed how to improve colonial officials' rule over British overseas territories.[40]

Drewnowski had a strong mandate in 1961 to change the department's structure and align it with "Ghana's needs": a governmental plan to create a sovereign, rapidly developing nation-state economy. Between 1961 and 1964, he radically departed from Niculescu's colonial curriculum and dramatically expanded the departmental enrollment from 100 to 400 students. He also started training Ph.D. candidates, hired new professors, and regularly invited Ghanaian experts to give lectures. Drewnowski modernized the curriculum by introducing macroeconomics and forecasting in lieu of descriptive ethnographies of African social life. The dominance of quantitative methods and indicators, like the measurement of national income, aimed at constructing the object of an African national economy as a theoretical object. This approach emulated the development of national accounting in the West and in the socialist countries of the East, marking a clear departure from the liberal imperial framework that the British had imposed in the 1950s. Drewnowski had never been to

---

[37] University of London Archive, AC 8/17/4/9, R. H. Stoughton to R. Eustace, June 14, 1958.
[38] University of Ghana Archives, UG 1/3/2/3/53, Organization and Establishment of Department of Economics, B. M. Niculescu to the secretary of the Board of the Faculty of Social Sciences.
[39] University of Ghana Archives, UG 1/N 1, Personal files of Barbu Mihai Niculescu, Personal statement, December 27, 1950.
[40] Barbu Niculescu, *Colonial Planning: A Comparative Study* (London, 1958).

Africa before, but his task was precisely to connect theoretical and methodological innovations with the practical challenges Africa faced. During his tenure, students started taking classes on Ghana's economic life and history in the pan-African and developmental context. Here Drewnowski followed the agenda of the early United Nations and supported Keynesian and developmental economics, while rhetorically stressing the importance of the politics of growth coming from state socialist Europe. In reports to the Polish Embassy, he described his agenda as socialist, not communist or Soviet-style. The modernization of economics in Legon, as conceived and promoted by Drewnowski, was about embracing a kind of progressive economics that blurred Cold War distinctions, without pledging allegiance to one or other political camp.

Decolonization Through Internationalization

Drewnowski's mission to modernize the department did not lead to hiring more African faculty. This was a pattern that characterized other departments, too. Drewnowski explained in his defense that most Ghanaian economists already worked full-time for the government. He usually met them in the national Planning Commission, of which he was a member. His new faculty was nonetheless predominantly white. The department's early decolonization was thus attempted through the geographical diversity of white European faculty, rather than by replacing white professors with Ghanaians. Drewnowski also retained several previously hired lecturers, mostly women, who had thorough, first-hand knowledge of West Africa.[41]

The phenomenon of Africanization in the form of internationalization also reflected Ghana's dependence on international funding. The Legon campus was a space where the stakes and terms of Ghana's global position as a new nation-state played out. This included paying a political price for foreign aid, as Ghana did not want to alienate any of its potential international donors, especially the powerful United States. It was obvious enough to Ghanaians that if such donors offered overseas technical aid training, it was not really for free, but with the aim of exerting influence over decolonizing countries. Despite the official anti-imperialist rhetoric, Ghana could not afford and did not seek political and economic isolation. Ghanaian officials approached big power donors cautiously. The Minister of Higher Education advised "great tact [toward potential donors], lest we are ridiculed as being on the point of begging."[42] During the inauguration of the University of Ghana in October 1961, Nkrumah courted the British by sitting two former British principals at the high table and raising a special toast to the representative of the University of London.[43] Beginning in 1961,

---

[41] Annual Report by the vice-chancellor for 1961–62, University of Ghana: State Publishing Corporation, 1962; University of Ghana, Annual Report by the vice-chancellor for 1962–63 (section on Department of Economics, pp. 45–50); University of Ghana, Annual Report by the vice-chancellor for 1963–64.
[42] National Archives of Ghana, PRAAD, GH/PRAAD, RG.11/1/326, Overseas Financial and other Assistance to Higher Education in Ghana, 1962–1963.
[43] University of London Archive, AC 11/9/1-5, Report by Prof. Ingold from Birkbeck College on the visit to University of Ghana, Nov. 25, 1961, unpaginated.

the campus filled with equipment and visiting scholars from the United States (which put a great deal of pressure on Ghana to reject Soviet aid), Israel, West Germany, and United Nations agencies.[44] Even the British offered training in physics and geological laboratory techniques upon seeing that the Soviet Academy of Sciences had sponsored an entire magnetic recording station. China and US foundations poured money into the Institute of African Studies, a new laboratory of postcolonial African arts and humanities.[45]

With new foreign nationals came a different organization of work. Drewnowski, for instance, brought a rich pedagogical experience as a scout and ski instructor in interwar Poland. He unified teaching and research structures, stressing teamwork over individual projects. It is tempting to interpret these reforms as reflecting a socialist orientation. Historically, however, Drewnowski's style of running the department stemmed from a turn-of-the-twentieth-century collectivist culture of Central and Eastern Europe that had preceded Soviet and state socialist pedagogy. This work ethic contrasted with the leisurely, individualized lifestyle and work habits of the established British and Commonwealth faculty.

Socially, the outstanding leisure facilities were still monopolized by the white British expats who dominated Legon's faculty and administrative staff. All of them lived on campus, with little social contact with Accra, except for shopping. Until the early 1960s, professors received regular, sponsored first-class airline tickets to the United Kingdom because Balme believed that professors should remain in close professional contact with British academia. Generous salaries for the expat white faculty—much higher than those awarded the Ghanaians—allowed for a lavish social life, including dress-code dinner parties served by cook-stewards in white uniforms, amateur dramatics (mostly Shakespeare), and cricket. The faculty could also use a secluded university-owned beach hut at Labadi Beach, which had long been an exclusively white privilege. When in 1959, E. N. Omaboe, an African lecturer from the Department of Economics went there, he heard from a janitor that the beach hut was not open to any black man. In addition, Balme established a system of ceremonies and residential practices that were eagerly welcomed in late colonial Africa. The Africans refused a proposal from London that they wear distinctly African academic garb. They preferred the Latin grace, the tutorial system, and the academic gowns worn at lectures and dinners (each hall had its own colour).[46] Alex Kwapong, one of the few African professors on the campus, stressed that these "ancient traditions" would gradually be discontinued, but the attachment to the ceremonial was strong, especially among a tiny Ghanaian faculty group that had studied in Oxford or Cambridge. African Oxbridge alumni wanted to prove that they could outdo the colonizer and thus celebrated Oxbridge culture.[47] In their eyes, decolonization was a process of inventing a new, independent African

---

[44] Alessandro Iandolo, "The Rise and Fall of the 'Soviet Model of Development' in West Africa, 1958–1964," *Cold War History* 12.4 (2012): 683–704.
[45] National Archives of Ghana, PRAAD, GH/PRAAD, RG. 11/1/232, Statistics of existing technical assistance, University of Ghana, Dec. 10, 1963.
[46] Agbodeka, *A History of University*, 41, 79ff., 3.
[47] Kwapong, *A Life in Education*, 99.

leisure-class. If young educated African women and men were someday to replace the British, they would need to become real ladies and gentlemen.

The Failed Offensive of Nkrumahism, 1964–1966

Nkrumah combated the Oxbridge mentality, practices, and even the spatial order. He moved the cricket pitches to the peripheries and secured the empty terrain for new architecture. To break with what he now considered an anachronistic "imitation of the Oxbridge atmosphere," he invited Israeli architects Shulamit and Michael Nadler, who had designed Hebrew University's library and other public buildings in Israel, to design residential accommodation.[48] Their architectonic style represented the Bauhaus- and Le Corbusier-inspired international modernism of the 1950s.[49] The flat roofs, unornamented surfaces, and straight lines stood in explicit opposition to Harrison's imperial "abstract Orientalism." The Nadlers' work in Legon was limited in scope, however. The late colonial campus formed a unified structure that would have been hard to dismantle, and Nkrumah had no intention of removing any existing buildings.

When the Special Relationship with London lapsed in 1963, the Nkrumahist offensive intensified, focused primarily on staffing politics: Nkrumah was consulted on and approved every appointment at the senior faculty level.[50] As a consequence, several Soviet and Soviet bloc academics, known as "state professors," became Nkrumah's moles in Legon's strategic departments like Agriculture, Political Science, Law, and Philosophy, in addition to a group of Soviet advisors he kept in Accra.[51] Nkrumah's confidant when it came to hiring politics was William Abraham, one of the most talented philosophers of the postcolonial era and the first black professor in Oxford (at All Souls College). In 1964, he became the head of the Philosophy Department, and was promoted to pro-vice-chancellor.[52] Abraham introduced Marxism and Nkrumah's consciencism (a combination of pan-African, socialist, and anti-imperial thought) to the curriculum. He also made several trips to the Soviet bloc to recruit Eastern European faculty, especially mathematicians and physicists, an initiative reflecting Nkrumah's plan to privilege science-driven education over traditional liberal arts.[53]

Between 1962 and 1966, Legon witnessed an intensified influx of Eastern Europeans, which Legon's administration accepted reluctantly, often after forceful interventions from Nkrumah. Some reservations were reasonable. A group of Czechoslovak

---

[48] National Archives of Ghana, PRAAD, GH/PRAAD/RG/17/1/427, Nkrumah to O'Brien, May 2, 1964.
[49] Ayala Levin, "Exporting Zionism: Architectural Modernism in Israeli–African Technical Cooperation" (Ph.D. thesis, Columbia University, 2015); Judith Turner, *White City: International Style in Israel, a Portrait of an Era* (Tel-Aviv, 1964).
[50] University of Ghana, Annual Report by the vice-chancellor for 1964–1965, 89.
[51] National Archives of Ghana, PRAAD, GH/PRAAD/RG 11/1/44 Africanization of University Staff, 1962–1964; Archive of Modern Records [Poland], Komitet Współpracy Gospodarczej z Zagranicą, 16/28, O'Brien to E. Kulaga, the Ambassador of Poland in Ghana, January 15, 1963.
[52] University of Ghana Archives, UG/1/1/, A 1 [?], Personal file of William Abraham.
[53] National Archives of Ghana, PRAAD, GH/PRAAD/RG 11/1/112, Scientific and Technical Co-operation.

economists, who came to the Department of Economics after Drewnowski's departure to the UN Economic Council in New York, spoke little English and their impact on the department remained very limited.[54] Ghanaians, including Abraham, had no illusions, however, about Soviet bloc scholars: just like Westerners, Russians brought their own (mis)conceptions regarding Africa. In his seminal *The Mind of Africa*, written in Legon in 1962, Abraham advocated "radical solutions like socialism and speedy industrialization," while stressing that the Marxism from which these solutions derived conceived Africa "as an effect of Europe" rather than as a force on its own. Abraham observed that "the Soviets, starting with Lenin, projected their ideas onto Africa, rather than tried to learn from the continent," and they "have tended to see pan-Africanism romantically as being concerned more with the liquidation of the West than with African reconstruction."[55] Ghanaian elites realized that the Soviet—and the US—presence in Ghana was not a matter of brotherly solidarity or humanitarian aid. It was a consequence of Cold War competition. They also felt that unlike the Eastern Europeans—who were busy competing with one another for influence in the postcolonial world—the West had economic power to negotiate its position in Africa. The United States (in cooperation with the British) so arranged it that American aid to the university would be conditional on reducing the Soviet presence. In response to Nkrumahism's offensive on the campus, the Rockefeller, Ford, and other US foundations halted their funding. This situation temporarily set the University of Ghana on a different trajectory to that of Ibadan, Makerere, or Khartoum, which all transitioned to the American land-grant college model, or to that of Rhodesia and Nyasaland, which remained in the Special Relationship with London.[56] Nkrumah's tighter hold on the University of Ghana (including the deportation of six foreign professors on political grounds) reflected the ways in which his rule had degenerated into a dictatorship. The political crisis and devastating economic depression led to a large number of resignations among the white expatriates and even included some Ghanaian professors. Conor Cruise O'Brien, the vice-chancellor of the university in the mid-1960s, who had been in a love–hate relationship with Nkrumah, left for New York University. Perhaps his 1969 introduction to *Reflections on the Revolution in France*, Edmund Burke's paean to British political gradualism, was a coded response to his experience of the Nkrumahist bid for national revolution.[57]

In the midst of the Nkrumahist offensive, the British and the Ghanaian proxies still set the tone. One Polish professor of zoology in Legon reported to the Polish authorities that even though his department had become internationally diverse, many African students came from schools run by Anglophone Christian missionaries and were

---

[54] Archive of Modern Records [Poland], Komitet Współpracy Gospodarczej z Zagranicą, 16/28, O'Brien to E. Kulaga, the Ambassador of Poland in Ghana, January 15, 1963.
[55] Abraham, *The Mind of Africa*, 154–7, 166.
[56] National Archives of Ghana, PRAAD, GH/PRAAD, RG 11/1/326, Overseas financial and other assistance to higher education in Ghana 1962–3; RG 11/1/224, Technical Assistance form USSR; Agbodeka, *A History of University*, 150.
[57] Conor Cruise O'Brien, "Introduction," in Edmund Burke, *Reflections on the Revolution in France and on the Proceedings in Certain Societies in London Relative to That Event* (Baltimore, 1969).

shaped by a colonial mentality: "Britain remained for them the centre of the universe."[58] Another Polish scholar from the Institute of Statistics reported a sense of inertia and passive resistance that dominated the campus during the Nkrumahist offensive. "Nkrumah's brutal interventions" alienated many progressive foreign scholars from the Ghanaian regime. They chose a "wait and see" approach. The departments organized discussions about university reform, but no action plan emerged.[59]

The British connection also persisted thanks to foreign nationals like Drewnowski's successor, who, though supposed to cater to Nkrumah's preference for Soviet bloc representatives, in practice relied equally on Anglo-American scholarship. Zdzisław Sadowski, who became chair of the Department of Economics in 1965, sustained and further developed the existing curriculum. This might have come as a surprise to some British and Indian faculty, who apparently had come to see the Nkrumah's-era Soviet bloc "Easterners" as political opposition.[60] "Everybody saw me as a representative of a communist country and thought I would lecture on Marxist political economy," recalled Sadowski, "but I had no intention of doing that." Instead, he explained that he taught "what in English is called economics, a discipline that contained references to Marxism" but which could not be equated with any sort of Soviet-style socialist political economy.[61] Along these lines, he continued the Ghana-focused program of national planning.

Born in 1925 in Warsaw, Sadowski had been exposed to British culture from an early age. At six, he went to London, where his father was a trade advisor. He attended a primary school with Anglican, Jewish, and Hindu children—an experience in cultural diversity, but not one that inoculated him against eliminatory ethnonationalism. Just before the war, Sadowski adhered to the anti-Semitic, proto-fascist youth movement National Radical Camp, and during Stalinism was arrested on that account. In the 1950s, he reinvented himself as a socialist scholar, joining internationally-known Polish economists like Michał Kalecki and Oskar Lange. In the Warsaw School of Economics, Sadowski studied the economic problems of African, Asian, and Latin American countries with Kalecki, who had regularly received statistical data and literature from Legon-based Drewnowski. Sadowski wrote, "I attended Kalecki's lectures on so-called less developed countries like other people who wanted to take a break from problems of state socialist economy." He was eager to measure the statistical tables and economic models representing Ghana against Ghana's real experience.[62]

The 1965 recruitment effort for the chair of the Department of Economics showed that despite some changes in selection procedure, the search committee, still based in

---

[58] Archive of Modern Records, Komitet Współpracy Gospodarczej z Zagranicą, 16/28, Afryka- współpraca z uniwersytetami. Uniwersytet w Legon, Jerzy Prószyński do J. Schwakopfa, March 18, 1963.
[59] Archive of Modern Records, Komitet Współpracy Gospodarczej z Zagranicą, 16/28, J. Prószyński do J. Schwakopfa, February, 23, 1964.
[60] Archiwum Akt Nowych [AAN, Modern Records Archives], Komitet Współpracy Gospodarczej z Zagranicą, 16/28, Afryka- współpraca z uniwersytetami. Uniwersytet w Legon, J. Holzer to J. Schwakopf, Dec. 10, 1965.
[61] Z. Sadowski, *Przez ciekawe czasy* (n.p.p., n.d.), 195–6.
[62] Sadowski, *Przez ciekawe czasy*, 187.

London, ended up favoring a candidate whose profile defied both African nationalism and the British establishment. The British initially supported Kurt Martin (formerly Mandelbaum), who had worked at the Oxford Institute of Statistics and with W. Arthur Lewis in Manchester, but Nkrumah found the British candidate unacceptable. The search committee also considered the Ghanaian economist Joseph Mensah, the head of Ghana's National Planning Commission. The British eventually vetoed him. One of the reasons could have been a lukewarm letter from his competitor and external reviewer, W. Arthur Lewis, who wrote that he wished Mensah had showed "more evidence of intellectual rigour than his present job allows."[63] With Nkrumah (represented by Abraham) opposing Martin, and Mensah being sidelined for want of "academic excellence," vice-chancellor O'Brien decided to back Sadowski. Once again, a Pole turned out to be *the* consensus candidate, even though he had no publications in English. His reputation was entirely based on letters of recommendation and impressions he had made in the University of Ghana's London Office. Maurice Dobb, a search committee member, argued that "Sadowski had unusual intelligence and a most agreeable personality," but he admitted he could not assess his work. Dobb and other search members relied on the opinion of Drewnowski, who considered his former student "one of the best candidates, if not the best, the University of Ghana could get from Poland now," and Kalecki's laconic but enthusiastic letter.[64]

Once in Ghana, Sadowski quickly deciphered the fine social distinctions and petty animosities among foreign faculty that often ran along national lines. Alex Kwapong (later vice chancellor) described Sadowski "as broad-minded and pragmatic; getting along well with his colleagues of all races and nationalities."[65] Thanks to his wife, a doctor serving the African community who learned some of the Twi language, Sadowski was aware of the stark contrast between the leisurely and comfortable campus life and the tough, urban reality of Accra's shanty towns. He was also very self-conscious about his whiteness.

The Department of Economics that Sadowski had inherited from Drewnowski was basically all-white.[66] Most Africans he met were servants employed in his house and on campus. This wasn't a pleasant feeling: "I realized that Ghanaians did not like that the selected chair was a white guy. They respected the choice, but I sensed they would have preferred a local person." Sadowski, who had been an ardent nationalist in the past, was not resentful. He justified and, in a way, identified with what he called "the construction of Ghanaian nationalism from above." In Nkrumah's Ghana every film screening started with the national anthem. Each time Sadowski heard it, he was moved to tears, he recalled in his memoirs.[67] He questioned the colonial lifestyle in principle but embraced it in everyday life. "Our life in Legon was blissful," he recalled. After work, he would play tennis; he attended innumerable parties and went to the beach at weekends,

---

[63] University of Ghana Archives, UG 1/M 8, Personal file of Joseph Mensah.
[64] University of Ghana Archives, 4/64-65, Minutes of the Appointments Board held in London, August 19, 1964.
[65] University of Ghana Archives, UG 1/S 52, Personal file of Zdzisław Sadowski.
[66] Zdzisław Sadowski, *Przez ciekawe czasy: rozmowy z Pawłem Kozłowskim o życiu, ludziach, i zdarzeniach* (Warsaw, 2011), 195–6.
[67] Sadowski, *Przez ciekawe czasy*, 195–6.

almost always accompanied by other white expats. The bliss was sometimes marred by unvoiced tensions between white and black faculty. Upon Sadowski's departure in 1970, no Ghanaian colleague came to say goodbye.[68] Perhaps, he reckoned, this cold farewell reflected the ways in which Africans experienced and tacitly resisted the persistent white presence on the campus.

Conclusion

The British legacy that had shaped the University of Ghana was consolidated through Ghana's political changes of the mid-1960s. On February 24, 1966, a military coup supported by the CIA removed Nkrumah from power and launched numerous investigations into his and his followers' abuses of power. Kwapong, a liberal professor of classics and a graduate of the Achimota School and Cambridge University, was immediately appointed the new vice-chancellor. He was the first African scholar to be appointed to run an African university. His tenure promised a return to "academic freedom" and a more forceful Africanization of the faculty. But first, he settled scores with Nkrumah and Nkrumahist influences on the campus. The University of Ghana, he said to students in an inaugural address, "has been subjected to the most merciless and persistent attack by the regime of Kwame Nkrumah ... and appeared to be one of the few but most important bastions of freedom still left in the country." Kwapong sought to turn Nkrumahist anti-imperial discourse against itself: "If Nkrumah ridiculed academic freedom as a 'bourgeois concept' then his decisions to impose Soviet advisors and compulsory lectures in Marxist philosophy were acts of 'academic neo-colonialism'." Kwapong vilified Nkrumah as a fallen national leader, whose "dreams of grandeur outran the ability of the dreamer to make good his dreams." Nkrumah's "psychopathic greed for wealth" and monumental and sadistic indifference to the suffering and welfare of the people "set Ghana on a path of self-destruction."[69] Sadowski, who had himself once participated in governmental planning bodies, now joined the anti-Nkrumah chorus, and blamed the dictatorship's "over-optimistic" policies for Ghana's economic downfall. In a report to Polish officials, he described Nkrumah as a "declarative, inconsequential socialist" and argued that his removal could actually save African socialism.[70]

Kwapong used the concept of "academic freedom" to reinstate a more conservative social order on the campus. He condemned Nkrumah's loyalists for citing Marx and Lenin, but he himself cited an equally ideological figure, namely Benjamin Disraeli, fashioning a university in liberal-conservative terms as a tranquil, disengaged "place of light, liberty, and of learning."[71] This vision opposed the modern, socialist, and fiercely

---

[68] Sadowski, *Przez ciekawe czasy*, 217.
[69] Address of welcome on the occasion of the congregation of the university, March 26, 1966, by the vice-chancellor Alex Kwapong, *University of Ghana Annual Report by the vice-Chancellor for 1965-6* (Legon, 1966), 65
[70] Archive of Modern Records, Komitet Współpracy Gospodarczej z Zagranicą, 16/28, Afryka-współpraca z uniwersytetami. Uniwersytet w Legon, Z. Sadowski to J. Schwakopf, May 26, 1966.
[71] *University of Ghana Annual Report by the vice-Chancellor for 1965-6*, 64.

political pan-African project that Nkrumah had attempted but failed to deliver. The return to "academic freedom" partly reversed the process of Africanizing the university through the importing of academics with Soviet, socialist, or communist credentials. The post-Nkrumah regime used the rhetoric of "academic freedom" as a device to purge Nkrumah's loyalists from the campus, including Eastern Europeans, arguing that "academic freedom" had been dismantled "not only by external force, but also from within by international collaborators, both expatriates and Ghanaians." All Soviet advisors had to go, but Sadowski was spared, in large part because the university administration was more tolerant of Poles, Czechoslovaks, and Yugoslavs. It was decided that the purging of professors with "communist leanings" (with the exception of the Soviets) would be carried out on a case-by-case basis.[72] Kwapong respected Sadowski for his organizational skills and what the Pole described as "pragmatic socialism" (as opposed to Nkrumah's allegedly rhetorical and harmful socialism). Sadowski, who described the 1966 coup as the "most difficult time in his professional career," held on to the chair of the Department of Economics, on condition that he show due determination in Africanizing the faculty.

Thanks to Kwapong's determination, Legon remained unapologetically Oxbridge-like: it was the only African university that would preserve a Classics Department, and the High Tables were back. This conservative turn, or what the university administration called the "return to freedom," angered and politicized some students, who staged sit-ins in 1968. Kwapong used police squads to crush the protest, consulting administrators from the University of Columbia whom he had befriended about the best methods to use. This approach partly reflected Ghana's increasing contact with the United States.[73] It was only in 1987, after a decade of riots, workers' strikes, and economic depression, that students staged another protest to introduce "the pay as you eat system."[74] The slow change in the halls system demonstrated the capacity of the British university model in Africa to endure.

Paradoxically, after 1966, British decorum was matched by policies that sidelined foreign nationals. The Africanization through internationalization of faculty was over; now Africanization meant more jobs for local Ghanaians. The Legon campus eventually came to represent a hybrid institution featuring Oxbridge campus culture and a black faculty. Sadowski, who left only in 1970, witnessed through his own skin, so to speak, white faculty become less dominant after Nkrumah's coup, both culturally and statistically. While in 1966, 47% of the senior teaching staff was Ghanaian or African, at the end of the 1960s, the Africans constituted nearly 60% of the faculty.[75]

The case of the University College of the Gold Coast/University of Ghana offers a glimpse into two intertwined dimensions of imperial durability: the spatial politics and

---

[72] National Archives of Ghana, PRAAD, GH/PRAAD, RG 11/1/296, Special Professorship—University Staff with Communist Leanings, E. K. Minta, the secretary to the National Liberation Council to the Ministry of Science and Higher Education, March 17, 1966.
[73] National Archives of Ghana, PRAAD, GH/PRAAD/ RG 11/2/34, Students Disturbances; Kwapong, *A Life in Education*, chapter 4.
[74] Agbodeka, *A History of University*, 131.
[75] *University of Ghana Annual Report by the vice-Chancellor for 1965–6*, 102–3.

hiring politics of Africa's first university being shaped and negotiated by foreign powers and visiting faculty from around the world. It shows that the difference between imperial and sovereign African education was often blurred and confused as the university became a global hub for international organizations, governments, and scholars whose complex intellectual trajectories did not square with political divisions. The University of Ghana emerged as a space in which the entrenched practices of a colonial college effectively challenged, affected, or even sabotaged Nkrumah's bid to create a modern, socialist institution of higher learning: the High Tables remain in Legon to this day and are a constant reminder of the University of Ghana's colonial origins.

Paradoxically, foreign nationals, who had been asked to Africanize the curricula and staff, accommodated and largely sustained the "Oxbridge" model. Nkrumah saw Eastern Europeans as intermediaries of state socialism, but in fact relations between Ghana and the Soviet bloc were never bilateral. Histories of decolonization cannot be reduced to Cold War history or to the history of relations between an (ex)-colony and the metropole. They need to be narrated at the intersection of these histories if light is to be shed on the full experience of the Ghanaian bid for a global university. Legon served as a space of institutional and intellectual decolonization that nevertheless resisted change, and that relativized the transformative power of socialist nation-building that connected national elites in Africa with communist countries coming to their assistance. This may also remind us that the "metropolitan West," with its liberal ideology, needs to be included in histories of global communism and Second World–Third World encounters, and vice-versa.

7

The Expert Community: Expert Knowledge and Socialist Virtues—Czechoslovak Military Specialists in the Global South

Mikuláš Pešta

In the struggle for "hearts and minds" of newly decolonized countries, technological aid and its expert personnel became major strategic instruments.[1] Military and technical specialists not only helped modernize the partner country and contribute to the global exchange of knowledge, but also had the political function of promoting their homelands in the host country. Beginning in the mid-1950s, Czechoslovakia increasingly engaged in the global conflict as one of the most active countries in the socialist "Second World." A key aspect of Czechoslovakia's engagement was military in nature; the export of Czechoslovak weapons and technical knowledge helped construct many "Third World" armies in the postwar era. While most students from the Global South educated by Czechoslovak military experts trained at the Antonín Zápotocký Military Academy (Vojenská akademie Antonína Zápotockého, VAAZ) in Brno, which established a new Foreign Faculty for this purpose in 1960,[2] there were still numerous cases where the instructors taught in their partners' home countries, bringing their families with them and creating small communities overseas. In his classic study of expatriate communities in the postcolonial world, the sociologist Erik Cohen discussed the structure of such communities and relationships with the host countries, including local hostility toward the expatriates.[3] Odd Arne Westad observed that "the 'experts' that most often came with the aid were resented because they created a social sphere over which the recipient country had little control, even when they came from countries with which the regime had close relations, such as Soviets in Angola or Americans in Iran."[4] Thus, the study of

---

[1] David C. Engerman, "Learning from the East: Soviet Experts and India in the Era of Competitive Coexistence," *Comparative Studies in South Asia, Africa, and the Middle East* 33.2 (2013): 227–38.
[2] Václav Vondrášek, Sylvestr Chrastil, and Martin Markel, *Dějiny vojenské akademie v Brně* (Praha, 2001), 89; Daniela Richterová, Mikuláš Pešta, and Natalia Telepneva, "Banking on Military Assistance: Czechoslovakia's Struggle for Influence and Profit in the Third World, 1955–1968," *International History Review* 43.1 (2021): 90–108.
[3] Erik Cohen, "Expatriate Communities," *Current Sociology* 24.3 (1977): 5–90.
[4] Odd Arne Westad, *The Global Cold War: Third World Interventions and the Making of Our Times* (Cambridge, 2005), 96.

the expert missions has more dimensions than the military alone; expert communities can also be analysed as spaces, contact zones of foreign and hosting societies, of two different cultures, ideological backgrounds, educational systems, military–scientific systems, and mutual prejudices. We can examine the links between teachers and students, Czechoslovak and local colleagues, the interactions with the people outside the military and academic environment, and also the relationships within the community of Czechoslovak experts and their families.

One of the countries where this Cold War of the experts was most intense was Egypt (United Arab Republic).[5] Changes in the country's foreign policy, its non-aligned stance in the global Cold War, and the different interest groups involved made it a target destination for expert missions from both socialist and capitalist countries. After the Six Day War, the number of advisors from the Eastern bloc rose to several thousand; the Soviets represented the largest contingent, but there were Czechoslovaks and East Germans, too.[6] West German and French specialists also got their share of work.

The first Czechoslovak–Egyptian military contract was signed in 1955.[7] This contract marked not only the beginning of more than twenty years of military cooperation with the Arab republic, but was also a first step in Czechoslovakia's new foreign policy and involvement in the "Third World." In subsequent years, the cooperation included deliveries of arms and civilian technology, scholarships for Arab students in Czechoslovakia, pilot training courses in Egypt, and the presence of Czechoslovak experts at the Military Technical College in Cairo. The partnership developed even further after the Six Day War, and then faded away in the mid-1970s.[8]

The Military Technical College (MTC) for training future Egyptian army officers was the first and the most significant of the Czechoslovak experts' foreign missions. After two years of successful tuition at the University of Alexandria, the first thirty-six Czechoslovak experts, coming mostly from the VAAZ in Brno, arrived at the MTC in summer 1959. The number of experts then grew continuously until the mid-1960s, when it reached 200 in one academic year.[9] Following the model established at the MTC, Czechoslovakia helped create further military–scientific spaces in the "Third World." There were similar military training projects in Iraq, Syria, Libya, Afghanistan, Yemen, Guinea, and Indonesia, while smaller or one-off missions were sent to many more countries.

This chapter examines Czechoslovak military expert communities and, in particular, the one in Cairo. It explores the diverse spaces in which the specialists lived and

---

[5] For international competition in the largest project, see Elizabeth Bishop, "Talking Shop: Egyptian Engineers and Soviet Specialist at Aswan High Dam" (Ph.D. dissertation, 1997, University of Chicago), 12–57.
[6] Klaus Storkmann, *Geheime Solidarität. Militärbeziehungen und Militärhilfen der DDR in die "Dritte Welt"* (Berlin, 2012), 183–243.
[7] Guy Laron, "Cutting the Gordian Knot: The Post-WW2 Egyptian Quest for Arms and the 1955 Czechoslovak Arms Deal," in *CWHIP*, Working paper No. 55 (February 2017); Petr Zídek and Karel Sieber, *Československo a Blízký východ v letech 1948–1989* (Praha, 2009), 54–9.
[8] Petr Zídek, "Vývoz zbraní z Československa do zemí třetího světa v letech 1948–1962," *Historie a vojenství* 3 (2002): 523–67; Youssef H. Aboul-Enein (ed.), *Reconstructing a Shattered Egyptian Army: War Minister Mohamed Fawzi's Memoirs, 1967–1971* (Annapolis, 2014).
[9] "Protokol o metodickém zaměstnání k vyhodnocení akce MTC" (příloha), 30.4.1978, VSA, f. VAAZ, ka 418.

worked: first, the space of the military institution, a workplace, co-constructed with the local actors and requiring professional conduct and expert knowledge; second, the space of the community, formed by the expat experience of everyday life; third, the socialist space, circumscribed by a set of rules that bound all experts and their families as representatives of socialist Czechoslovakia. The chapter explores each of these spaces and the tensions to which they gave rise, including the crises they sometimes provoked, such as the "rebellion" in Cairo in 1968.

With a few exceptions, the sources for this chapter come from the "Second World," that is, from the Czechoslovak side. The archival records of the Ministry of Defense and the documentation of the VAAZ, including the activity of its teachers abroad, are stored in Czech military archives.[10] Given the nature of the sources, the narrative could be viewed as one-sided: the framing of the chapter is centered on the Czechoslovak experts' relations within the contact zone. Yet the sources, composed mostly of regular monthly reports, correspondence, memoirs, the minutes of meetings, and the college's own documentation, depict the outlined space from different angles. Even without direct evidence regarding the perspective of the Arab students and teachers, what emerges from the Czechoslovak archives is a sense of the space as one marked by rivalry and complementarity—indeed, as a space co-constructed by Egpytian and Czechoslovak actors.

Expert Knowledge as an Instrument of Business and Solidarity

Military cooperation between Czechoslovakia and "Third World" countries was based on certain common, anti-imperialist grounds, yet it was usually also seen by both sides as economically advantageous trade.[11] From this perspective, the specialists abroad might be viewed as products of Czechoslovak state socialism, meant to extract profit from a third, non-allied country. The experts were indeed treated as products in some ways; both Egypt and Czechoslovakia were at pains to stress their functional role at the MTC. The MTC asked for "deliveries" of experts and preferred experienced teachers, if possible only professors or associate professors ("docent"). To meet this request without having to actually send all of its most skilled teachers, the Ministry of Foreign Trade temporarily conferred a degree of "docent" upon many experts leaving for Cairo, or faked their papers, making them a few years older (and seemingly more experienced).[12]

Interestingly, it was the Ministry of Foreign Trade, via its so-called "foreign trade corporations" Omnipol and the Main Technical Administration (*Hlavní technická správa*), that drew up the contracts, both for incoming students at the VAAZ and for outgoing experts. Archival records show that the Ministry of Foreign Trade stressed the economic aspect of the cooperation; it called for more autonomy in negotiations and underlined the need to develop trade with non-socialist countries, which would

---

[10] Vojenský ústřední archiv: Vojenský historický archiv (VHA) and Vojenský správní archiv (VSA).
[11] See Richterová, Pešta, and Telepeneva, "Banking on Military Assistance."
[12] Milan Vyhlídal, *Činnost československých instruktorů v egyptských ozbrojených silách. Účast na egyptském vojenském školství v letech 1956–1977* (Praha, 2016), 53.

bring hard currency to Czechoslovakia. In 1968, the ministry defended its independence, asserting that more autonomy would lead to "more effective and flexible decision-making." It highlighted the advantages of arms export and expert missions, such as high rates of profit and the opportunity to rearm and modernize the Czechoslovak Army by selling off old unused weapons. It even planned to use the democratization process then under way in Czechoslovakia, which had captured imaginations worldwide, to connect with new countries in order to sell arms.[13]

However, while the Ministry of Foreign Trade negotiated the contracts, it was the Ministry of National Defense that ran the VAAZ and was responsible for delivering the experts, and it insisted time and again that the operation was not solely economic. Defense archival records highlight the importance of the political dimension for the Czechoslovak Army. Politically motivated expert missions to Yemen or Guinea were covered by loans that were not expected to be paid back.[14] After the Six Day War, Defense called for a broadening and prolonging of aid to Egypt, and this at the expense of Foreign Trade. The director of the Main Technical Administration refused to fund this gesture of solidarity. Implying that the struggle between the two ministries had been underway for some time, one high-ranking army officer wrote, "I would point out that this decision reflects the old conflict [between the two approaches]; the question is whether the build-up of the MTC in Cairo is a real help with long political reach, now emphasized by the latest events and by the situation in the UAR army, or if it is only a matter of the profitability of a simple transaction."[15]

The Ministry of Defense also stressed that their partners abroad found it confusing that contracts were negotiated by the Ministry of Foreign Trade, and that that this cast Czechoslovakia in a negative light, as a country that did not care about anti-imperialist struggle and put its own profit above political aims.[16] A report from the MTC from 1966 suggests, rather bitterly, that the Arabs did not understand why traders had to interfere in a discussion among soldiers. The commander of the MTC repeatedly said that he did not understand why the Ministry of Foreign Trade mediated the talks between the two military schools (MTC and VAAZ). He further added that they were "soldiers, open and friendly people" and should act as such, without caring too much about trade and finance. He also implied that this kind of negotiation resembled the behavior of the capitalist countries, which only cared about profit.[17]

Furthermore, representatives of Defense also complained that the deals closed by Foreign Trade harmed their material interests, as they were a burden upon its budget. While Defense incurred expenses in securing all the contractually agreed obligations,

---

[13] Václav Valeš—vláda ČSSR, 18.6.1968, "Zpráva k návrhu Zásad pro uskutečňování zahraničního obchodu se speciálním materiálem a pro pojednávání a schvalování obchodních jednání o jeho dodávkách," VHA, f. MNO 1970, ka 254.
[14] "Provádění základního leteckého výcviku v Jemenu," undated (June 1961), VHA, f. MNO 1961, ka 453; Petr Zídek and Karel Sieber, *Československo a subsaharská Afrika v letech 1948–1989* (Praha, 2007), 75–94.
[15] Josef Širůčka, "Informační zpráva o čs. odbornících v SAR," 20.7.1967, VHA, f. MNO 1967, ka 64.
[16] "Technická pomoc poskytovaná ČSSR ozbrojeným silám rozvojových zemí," undated, VHA, f. MNO 1966, ka 245.
[17] Jan Bělohoubek, "Zpráva č. 10/66," 29.6.1966, VHA, f. MNO 1966, ka 243.

the profit from the trade stayed at Foreign Trade, or went to the state budget.[18] In the case of the MTC operation, a 1968 agreement between the two ministries established the division of the profit as 50/50.[19]

Yet even the Ministry of Foreign Trade had to accept the fact that there were political reasons for cooperation, and it tried to win over the Egyptian Army by providing more favorable conditions. Under threat of an Egyptian deal with West Germany, Czechoslovakia agreed in 1964 to include rocket construction in the curriculum, with experts to teach it. The re-evaluation of the general contract on more economically advantageous terms for the Czechoslovaks had been postponed for over a decade for political reasons, and when the time came for renegotiation of the contract, it was stressed that the new version should not jeopardize relations with Egypt. With the widening gap between Sadat's cabinet and the socialist countries, Egypt expressed more openly its determination to choose trading partners on its own terms. In 1974, Egypt's debt to Czechoslovakia came to 4.2 billion Czechoslovak crowns,[20] and Sadat kept reducing exports, thus disturbing the mutual balance even more.[21] As it was still desirable for political reasons to maintain cooperation, Czechoslovakia had to adapt, and the economic merits of the case grew less important. The Main Technical Administration offered reduced fees for eighty Egyptian students at the VAAZ in Brno, after the Arabs threatened in 1977 to send the students to France instead.[22] Officially, the end of the Czechoslovak operation at the MTC was motivated by the economic disagreements about a new contract, but in reality, the reason was purely political, as Egypt steered towards the West.

Cooperation and Rivalry: Experts and the Co-construction of the School

After one year in temporary locations in a former royal palace in Cairo's Dokki quarter, the MTC found a new home in old British military buildings on the fringes of a suburban area, Heliopolis; the new, larger facility enabled the school to enroll more students and subsequently more Czechoslovak experts. At first, the MTC occupied a peripheral position within the Egyptian education system. The civilian universities, with the University of Cairo at their head, saw the MTC as unwelcome competition, and certain military circles from the Ministry of War preferred their cadets to be educated by Western instructors. Only after President Nasser's decree of 1962 did its position become more stable. Competition among foreign experts, however, was not eradicated. The West Germans were very active in Egypt in the 1960s, and there was a constant threat that their experts might become involved in MTC tuition; the French

---

[18] "Technická pomoc poskytovaná ČSSR."
[19] "Návrh na zrušení funkce představitele GŠ ČSLA v Káhiře," 16.2.1970, VHA, f. MNO 1969, ka 170.
[20] About US $700 million according to the official 1973 exchange rate.
[21] Zídek and Sieber, *Československo a Blízký Východ*, 84
[22] Jaromír Machač, "Zpráva o činnosti vedoucího čsl. odborníků na MTC," 30.5.1977, VSA, f. VAAZ, ka 418.

supplied the college with technology and also sought to bring in their specialists.[23] The Egyptians were further courted by the Chinese, who offered their own experts, who would, they promised, work for the same salary as Arabs.[24] Interestingly, the Czechoslovaks objected even to the presence of Soviet instructors, on the grounds that it would undermine Czechoslovakia's efforts in Egypt.[25] In his 1973 summary report, the departing head of the expert group wrote:

> Construction of the MTC is a common task. A main prerequisite of success is close cooperation based on the shared understanding of tasks. Requests to pursue a "hard-line" policy toward the command of the MTC are ill-advised and unreasonable. We must grasp that the Western countries are interested in this operation, and some of their efforts have already been averted by General Selim [Commander of the MTC from its foundation until 1971]. A rupture in our correct relations could have irreparable consequences.[26]

Czechoslovak teachers were always in the minority among the staff; the MTC in Cairo had the biggest share, amounting to around 40%. Collaboration with local colleagues and students was therefore not a choice, but rather a necessity. When assessing relations with the local staff, in most cases the experts agreed that both professors and assistants behaved respectfully and recognized their expertise—in particular the assistants who had been educated at the VAAZ. In some cases, the Czechoslovaks also had to collaborate with other experts—namely at the MTC in Baghdad with Egyptian, Indian, and Pakistani instructors and during the courses in Yemen, where several Egyptian and Soviet teachers were present.[27]

It was the local command of the military school that decided which subjects would be taught, and the experts, once the deal with the VAAZ and the Ministry of Foreign Trade had gone through, had no choice but to comply. However, the experts by and large agreed that the relations with the school command, aside from petty arguments, were marked by mutual respect. The Czechoslovaks also had ways to influence the curriculum. At the Cairo MTC, they held most of the professorial and head of department posts, wrote their own textbooks, and chose the reading lists. There is no record of any complaints from the Egyptian side regarding the content of the courses. The declared purpose of long-term Czechoslovak expert missions was to educate a new generation of local army officers in "modern warfare"[28]—and Czechoslovak

---

[23] For confrontation with German specialists, see for example Plk. Foršt, "Zajištění výuky nových specializací na Vojenské technické akademii v Káhiře," 20.9.1962, VHA, f. MNO 1964, ka 323. For the French, see Jaromír Machač, "Informace VEX pro Prahu," 19.12.1973, VSA, f. VAAZ, ka 421.
[24] Osvald Vašíček, "Zpráva o činnosti od 10. do 31. ledna 1964," 28.1.1964, VHA, f. MNO 1966, ka 324.
[25] Lomský to Malinovskij, "Zabezpečení výuky na VTA v Káhiře—žádost," undated, VHA, f. MNO 1964, ka 324.
[26] Josef Vosáhlo, "Zkušenosti z práce vedoucího čs. odborníků na MTC," 12.4.1973, VSA, f. VAAZ, ka 419.
[27] Svatopluk Slavíček, "Skupina čs. odborníků na MTC Bagdád," 22.11.1980, VSA, f. VAAZ, ka 427; Jaroslav Knébl, "Zpráva ze služební cesty do Jemenu," 27.3.1959, VHA, f. MNO 1959, ka 351.
[28] Jan Bělohoubek, "Výuka taktiky čs. experty" (příloha), 28.7.1967, VHA, f. MNO 1969, box 211.

experts concurred that every army that had the "ambition to defy imperialism had to be modern, systematic, and built on the basis of the scientific-technical revolution."[29] Thus, the students were taught not only tactics, ballistics, weapons construction, or tank and aerial engine construction, but also mathematics, physics, descriptive geometry, mechanics, metallurgy, electronics, aero-, thermo- and hydromechanics, or radiolocation.

Most experts teaching abroad agreed that the work was much harder than their job at the VAAZ had been. Teaching in English in a different military system, preparing for lectures and very often also covering for absent colleagues, sometimes far outside their specialism—all this pushed the experts to their limits. To catch up with their backlog, the experts complained, they often had to work through the night. In their feedback upon their return from Cairo, the specialists—in particular young assistants—were often critical of the command both in Czechoslovakia and in Cairo, and the exhausting working conditions were one of the reasons for the lengthy and unbridled expressions of discontent during the critical period in 1968.[30]

In the construction of a military school, Czechoslovak experts and local teachers could work not only together, but also against one another. Czechoslovak experts were not contracted to teach people how to use "socialist" military technology and strategy. The Arabs requested only their expertise, not socialist indoctrination; in this regard, the MTC reflected the complicated relations that the Nasser regime had with socialism.[31] Nasser wrote in a MTC memorial book in 1963 that he "was deeply impressed by the obvious socialist spirit in the work that is meant to overcome the gulf between the intellectual and the manual worker and that will lead us to the achievement of our socialist goal—creating a society, in which class differences will be eradicated."[32] Czechoslovak professors were not allowed to teach Marxism-Leninism, as they were accustomed in Brno. However, there were always other, more subtle ways to promote socialism under these circumstances.

One way was to incorporate Marxist interpretations into other subjects, and a perfect candidate for that was the course in Russian. A character assessment of the Czechoslovak teacher of Russian at the MTC in 1959 specifically emphasized that he was aware of the political aspect of his job and of his responsibilities, and that he was not influenced by the capitalist milieu in which he was teaching.[33] However, the MTC command excluded Russian from the curriculum as early as 1960 and replaced it with English courses. The readily comprehensible argument deployed was that English was much more useful for Arab officers and that students from Syria needed the courses to

---

[29] "Protokol o metodickém zaměstnání k vyhodnocení akce MTC" (Jaroslav Machač, "Zpráva vedoucího čs. odborníků na MTC o výsledcích akce MTC a poznatcích i zkušenostech z její realizace"), 30.4.1978, VSA, f. VAAZ, ka 418.
[30] For example, Josef Vosáhlo, "Současný stav rozvoje MTC a hlavní úkoly čs. pomoci při dokončování její výstavby," 19.4.1971, VSA, f. VAAZ, ka 419; J. Machač, "Informace VEX pro Prahu ..."
[31] Zeinab Abul-Magd, *Militarizing the Nation: The Army, Business and Revolution in Egypt* (New York, 2017), 35–77.
[32] "Naser navštěvuje kadety," VHA, f. MNO 1964, ka 323, transcript from *Egyptian Gazzette*, March 26, 1962.
[33] Group heads regularly sent character assessments of experts to the VAAZ command. Josef Zuska, "Služebně-politické hodnocení," 1.1.1959, VHA, f. MNO 1960, ka 462.

understand the lectures (given in English), but the Czechoslovak side suggested that the reason for this change was also political.³⁴

The opportunities for direct propagandizing were severely limited, but in an important way, the entire educational approach of the Czechoslovak visitors was, at least in theory, an extended lesson in the superiority of socialism. "There is a battlefront of two different types of education. Bourgeois education is unrestrained, immature, accidental, traditional in its technique, depraved in its aims," proclaimed the 1963 handbook for the experts, written by the head of the group and circulated to new teachers prior to their arrival.³⁵ In the socialist education system, he continued, students had to adopt both theory and practice. One of the great merits of socialist education was supposed to be the fact that students learned the meaning of hard work. In the final report on the 1957 mission at the University of Alexandria, its chief explained that the students from capitalist countries, among which he counted Egypt, had had to deal with a different kind of education. The students at the MTC often came from bourgeois officers' families and were not used to manual work. Some students had officers' manners, requesting that they be served coffee by servants during lectures, and the teachers had to bring them into line.³⁶

The manual for the experts further stressed that the work awaiting them would be very hard: because of the capitalist mode of education, the students had low levels of knowledge and were unable to organize self-study or to work systematically. According to the author of the manual, the lectures by Arab teachers were "formal thought-gymnastics," suppressing the intellectual activity of a student, exercising only mechanical memory and verbal understanding. The important intellectual characteristics were overlooked or even suppressed. By contrast, socialist education was supposed to promote rational thinking and both theoretical and practical skills.³⁷

In the Czechoslovak instructors' eyes, discipline formed a cornerstone of the socialist way of education. What teachers criticized most about their Arab students was that they had no work and study habits; students in the first year did not pay attention, dozed, or else disturbed other students. The perceived lack of discipline was thus conflated with "bourgeois education" and even with the remnants of Egypt's feudal political structure ("officers' manners"). As we will see, such feelings were also motivated by racial and cultural stereotypes.

One might argue that discipline would be considered important at any military school, but the Czechoslovak experts would seem not to have agreed. In the feedback after his return home, one expert compared Egyptian graduates from Czechoslovakia with those from similar schools in the USA, UK, Japan, and West Germany. He emphasized the leading and paternalistic role of the teacher, who was supposed to "care" about his students and lead them to discipline and through discipline to good results. As he said, this "care" was lacking in the West, where students had to study and

---

³⁴ Osvald Vašíček, "Pravidelné hlášení k 15. srpnu 1960," 12.8.1960, VHA, f. MNO 1960, ka 462.
³⁵ "Souhrn zkušeností a poznatků z působení na MTC v Káhiře," undated. VSA, f. VA AZ, ka 415.
³⁶ Vyhlídal, Činnost československých intruktorů, 30.
³⁷ "Souhrn zkušeností a poznatků."

work alone, without close cooperation with teachers, and tended to neglect their duties.[38] The above-mentioned manual explained, "We try to instill in the Arab students and colleagues especially a conscious attitude to work, that is, so that they know why they are working and implement this stance in their whole life."[39] In this sense, the teacher was supposed not only to give classes, but also be a role model. The expert continued:

> The main success of our activity in Egypt was that to thousands of students, we presented a new man—socialistically thinking man, and socialistically acting man. A man without personal interests, who seeks to provide all the information he can for the good of the country that hosts him. How different this was to the local teachers I had the opportunity to meet. For them, teaching itself came last.[40]

In order to create a socialist space at the MTC under these circumstances, Czechoslovak experts themselves had to behave accordingly. While they could not make the whole of MTC a socialist zone, it was of fundamental importance to preserve an untarnished image. Experts, it was stressed, must show understanding and tolerance for their Arab partners, and must behave openly and honestly. Everything they said in and out of class must be carefully considered. In 1973, the head of the group emphasized the representative aspects of the experts' task:

> An indivisible part of our mission is our attitude to problem-solving, personal example in work and seriousness in dealing with partners. We have to make socialism attractive to our partners, and remain down to earth about the pace of its implementation. Our words must match our deeds, in work and behavior we must show deliberation, principles, tact, industriousness, organization, planning, consistency, decisiveness, and a resolute and active stance toward socialism. Do not underestimate the partners and do not let it seem like you do. We do not only have expert tasks here.[41]

His statement corresponded with the defined role of a Czechoslovak expert: "An expert is not only a highly qualified specialist, but also a political representative of socialist Czechoslovakia abroad."[42]

---

[38] "Protokol o metodickém zaměstnání k vyhodnocení akce MTC" (Mojmír Cenek, "Vědecká příprava arabských asistentů, vědecko-výzkumná spolupráci s ostatními školami, ústavy a závody"), 30.4.1978, VSA, f. VAAZ, ka 418.
[39] "Souhrn zkušeností a poznatků."
[40] "Protokol o metodickém zaměstnání k vyhodnocení akce MTC" (Mojmír Cenek, "Vědecká příprava arabských asistentů, vědecko-výzkumná spolupráci s ostatními školami, ústavy a závody"), 30.4.1978, VSA, f. VAAZ, ka 418.
[41] J. Vosáhlo, "Zkušenosti z práce."
[42] Marta Edith Holečková, "Univerzita 17. listopadu (1961–1974) a její místo v československém vzdělávacím systému a společnosti" (Ph.D. dissertation, Faculty of Arts, Charles University, Prague, 2017), 65.

Racial and Cultural Stereotypes in the Contact Zone

The co-construction of a common workspace was complicated not only by disparate educational ideals, but also by mutual distrust caused by racial prejudices and cultural differences. Complaints about a lack of discipline among the Arabs are very frequent in the Czechoslovak records. The question is, however, to what extent this sense of grievance was justified, and to what extent this was a vision of "lazy" and "undisciplined" Arabs influenced by schematic "Orientalist" perceptions, which had a long tradition in the Czech lands.[43] The official 1971 summary of the MTC operation written by the head of the experts stated that most teachers had "cordial and honest relations" with their local colleagues, but that one factor complicating the work was that some experts did not have a positive attitude towards Arabs. It even emphasized that the experts should not have anti-Arab feelings and that this factor should be taken into account in choosing suitable experts in Czechoslovakia.[44]

In 1963, the head of the Czechoslovak group warned the incoming experts that the students were undisciplined and that it was necessary to insist upon strict obedience. Questions in class should be limited, as students used them to stall lectures. Crucial information was to be repeated several times and students were to be obliged to take notes.[45] The Czechoslovak staff at the MTC lamented not only the lack of discipline, but also the general intelligence and capability of the students. One expert stressed that lecturers should employ short, clear sentences, and that teachers should dictate definitions and conclusions and write everything on the blackboard, at any rate in the first two years. The students had underdeveloped imaginations and low-level technical thinking, the expert continued, and the use of illustrative aids was therefore recommended. Another difficulty was the poor level of English of many of the students, in particular those from Syria in the period of the federation—but to be fair, many Czechoslovak teachers themselves struggled with the language.[46] According to an analysis conducted in 1957 by the head of the first Czechoslovak expert group at the University of Alexandria, the Egyptians tended to thinking metaphysically and had difficulties understanding the graphic plans of weapon construction. The designs "contradicted their Eastern mentality, apt for mathematical and philosophic speculations rather than technical comprehension."[47] In the 1967 regular report home, the head of the group said harshly that when dealing with Arabs, one must bear in mind that they never admit they are wrong, only act in their own interests, do not honor their word and see a written contract as meaning nothing. Furthermore, he added, "their traditions and national pomposity prevent them from closing good deals."[48]

---

[43] Edward Said, *Orientalism* (New York, 1978). On Czech Orientalism, see Hana Navrátilová, "Krásný, báječný, nešťastný Egypt!" in Adéla Jůnová Macková et al. (eds.), *Případ českého orientalismu* (Praha, 2009), 512–69.
[44] Vosáhlo, "Současný stav rozvoje."
[45] "Souhrn zkušeností a poznatků."
[46] A frequent complaint. See, for example, Vosáhlo, "Současný stav rozvoje."
[47] Vyhlídal, *Činnost československých instruktorů*, 30.
[48] Jan Bělohoubek, "Zvláštní zpráva č. 2 o činnosti čs. odborníků na MTC Cairo do 25. června 1967," undated. VHA, f. MNO 1969, ka 211.

The Expert Community 149

However, not all statements were so dismissive. One Czechoslovak expert mentioned that his colleagues were overly sensitive about their Arab students' conduct and exaggerated their bad education. Another recalled in his memoirs that despite the differences in mentality, when all was said and done, Egyptian students worked just as hard as students in Czechoslovakia.[49] When returning from Cairo, many experts in their official feedback also expressed their surprise at the mathematical skills and logical thinking of Egyptians. As the experts testified, their Egyptian students readily understood theoretical problems that were complicated even for Czechoslovak students at the VAAZ.[50] This suggests that the harsh critiques were in all likelihood based to some extent on cultural or racial prejudice.

Another cultural difference which the Czechoslovak teachers had to address was the role of Islam in Egyptian society, including the educational system. Experts were forbidden to talk about religion with their Arab colleagues or students.[51] In 1959, the head of the group remarked that the UAR was fighting against communism and atheism and that it was better not to provoke Arab colleagues and students. The religiosity of the Arabs was sometimes seen neutrally (for example, in making necessary adjustments during Ramadan), but sometimes also projected in the form of cultural stereotypes: one teacher, for example, said that the students were "not able to apply techniques in science and fell back on memorizing, as they were used to it from studying the Quran."[52]

In April 1974 the teachers also witnessed a religious attack at the MTC. The incident, which was intended to be a first step in the overthrow of Anwar al-Sadat and to "lay the foundations of the Islamic state under the leadership of *Hizb al-Tahrir al-Islami* (the Islamic Liberation Party)," was organized by the Shabab Muhammad group (also known as the Military Technical Organization) and led by Palestinian doctor Salih Sariya.[53] Two students were killed and one officer seriously injured, as their names were on the attackers' list of MTC's "bad Muslims"—those who smoked, did not pray, or possessed pictures of naked women. Almost a hundred people were arrested in connection with the incident, and the commander of the college, General Selim, blamed the MTC's mosque. Some staff later indirectly accused the Czechoslovak experts of being partly responsible for the attack, on the grounds that they had not paid sufficiently close attention to the students' activities and had not checked on their regular attendance. The arrested men also testified that they had counted on the Czechoslovak teachers' benevolence.[54]

---

[49] Lubomír Popelínský, *Můj život mezi zbraněmi* (Praha, 2016), 47.
[50] Bedřich Chrastil, "Informace od expertů na MTC v Káhiře," 10.11.1965, VHA, f. MNO 1965, ka 231.
[51] "Protokol o metodickém zaměstnání k vyhodnocení akce MTC" (J. Machač, "Zpráva vedoucího čs. odborníků").
[52] "Protokol o metodickém zaměstnání k vyhodnocení akce MTC" (Josef Pávek, "Nezbytnost vědecké práce a budování odpovídající MTZ pro ní na katedrách zabezpečování výuky taktiky a její organizační začlenění na katedry"), 30.4.1978, VSA, f. VAAZ, ka 418.
[53] Ellen Lust-Okar, *Structuring Conflict in the Arab World: Incumbents, Opponents, and Institutions* (Cambridge, 2005), 116; Adnan Musallam, *From Secularism to Jihad: Sayyid Qutb and the Foundations of Radical Islamism* (Westport, CT, 2006), 183.
[54] The Egyptian press also suggested the involvement of Muammar Gaddafi. Jaromír Machač, "Zpráva o činnosti čs. odborníků na MTC," 11.5.1974, VSA, f. VAAZ, ka 421.

Czechoslovak experts were advised to be wary of local people and not to provoke them, as many distrusted white people because of colonial rule.[55] And with the shift in Egyptian foreign policy and the rise of nationalism in the 1970s, the reports of hostility only increased. As the Czechoslovak teachers recalled, students were being educated by their Egyptian instructors in a nationalist, sometimes almost racist, way: they were urged not to forget that they were Egyptians, Arabs, and Muslims. Some Czechoslovak staff reported that they were criticized and mocked for accepting Soviet supremacy. After the cancellation of the friendship agreement with the USSR, a Czechoslovak expert was approached by his Egyptian assistant who dared him to do the same, as a symbolic restitution for the 1968 invasion.[56]

Fears of Arab nationalism were also reflected in how the teachers were chosen for the MTC, in particular in the context of the Six Day War. Despite previous criticism of experts who had proved to be overly fond of the Egyptian capitalist system, it was now desirable, said a 1967 report, to "require strict discipline and choose the experts for the mission more carefully" and to send people who are "politically and morally mature."[57] Experts chosen for the MTC should not be indifferent to the Arab cause and should be actively fighting for proletarian internationalism. In order to avoid controversy, Czechoslovaks of Jewish origin should be ruled out, as well as experts whose primary motive was material advantage; the same rules should be applied to an expert's own family.[58] The experts teaching the piloting courses in Aleppo, Syria, were likewise more than a little wary in their descriptions of their Arab colleagues using strong words: "They behave correctly, but they let us know that we are paid for our work. They are pathologically proud of their Arab past. They hate Israel and the Jews, and the SS-men are their ideal because of their mass murders of the Jews." According to the 1964 final report, the Syrian officers were fanatical Muslims and did not like the Soviet Union on account of its suppression of Uzbek Islam; they only asked the socialist countries for help, or so they said, because the West supported Israel.[59]

The Expert Community: Social Status and the Expat Experience

The life of those belonging to the expert community extended beyond the walls of the workspace and into the everday spaces of home, school, market, and beyond. When writing their memoirs, some experts described their time abroad almost as if it had been a holiday. Many had had financial motives for accepting a post abroad: the salaries were higher than at home. Nonetheless, many experts did not want to go to Egypt and,

---

[55] Vosáhlo, "Zkušenosti z práce."
[56] Jaromír Machač, "Zpráva o činnosti skupiny čs. odborníků na M.T.C.," 26.3.1975, VSA, f. VAAZ, ka 415.
[57] "Závěry z chování občanů ČSSR v SAR," undated, VHA, f. MNO 1967, ka 64. For "previous criticism," see, for example, Vasil Valo, "Poznatky ze skupiny čs. vojenských expertů v SAR—oznámení," 8.2.1960, VHA, MNO 1960, ka 462.
[58] "Závěry z chování občanů ČSSR v SAR," undated, VHA, f. MNO 1967, ka 64.
[59] František Kaválek, "Závěrečné hlášení o ukončení kursu číslo 644 v Aleppu, SyAR," 11.2.1965, VHA, f. MNO 1965, ka 231.

as a result, the VAAZ had to search for suitable specialists in the civilian universities, and did in fact depend on them.⁶⁰ Archival documentation suggests working and living conditions were often difficult, and relations with the local population and within the Czechoslovak community were often fraught: the expat experience was by no means idyllic.

As at work, so too in their free time, experts had to be careful about their behavior and to strive to create an idealized picture of life in socialist Czechoslovakia. One important aspect of this picture was the ideal of a modern socialist family. To foster this image, and also to prevent experts from having too much unnecessary contact with local people, it was recommended that they bring their wives and children with them (according to the documentation, the military experts were all male). The experts' family life was observed closely, and regular character assessments sent to Czechoslovakia emphasized whether they lived in proper matrimony; any distortion of this idealized image was punished forthwith. When one MTC expert had an affair with a Czechoslovak female interpreter, who moreover had a husband and a child in Cairo, they were both recalled from Egypt. The same measures were taken when two experts were caught flirting with prostitutes in an Egyptian nightclub.⁶¹

The behavior of wives and children was also supposed to reflect well on their homeland. Advice given to the spouses of incoming MTC experts in 1963 mentioned that the "work that all women in Czechoslovakia consider common is seen as humiliating in the UAR, as every family has several servants here. Even though we try to stick to our way of life, women should not do any rough work that would contradict the social perspectives or that could prove detrimental to our image (floor or window cleaning)." In these situations, it was deemed appropriate to hire a servant.⁶² In her published memoirs, the wife of a Czechoslovak civilian expert in India said that wives had to let the servants do the work if they wanted the local people to respect their husbands, and if they did not like what the servants had done, they had to correct it in secret.⁶³ It was also recommended that wives not go shopping themselves and have basic food delivered in order to avoid spending time in potentially risky queues. Czechoslovak wives were advised not to go out alone and while being kind to local people, keep their distance from them.⁶⁴ Other forms of behavior deemed inappropriate included wives "getting drunk and acting shamefully, bringing discord in the community" (as observed in Jakarta), flirting with foreigners, and making racist comments (Cairo).⁶⁵

Even though being a housewife was not a prestigious occupation in socialist society, wives of experts were not encouraged to have their own paid employment—mostly for

---

⁶⁰ "Protokol o metodickém zaměstnání k vyhodnocení akce MTC" (J. Machač, "Zpráva vedoucího čs. odborníků").
⁶¹ Vasil Valo, "Poznatky ze skupiny čs. vojenských expertů v SAR—oznámení," 8.2.1960, VHA, MNO 1960, ka 462.
⁶² "Souhrn zkušeností a poznatků."
⁶³ Blanka Strašíková, *Indický kaleidoskop. Z historie jedné stavby v Ránčí* (Plzeň, 1982), 24.
⁶⁴ "Souhrn zkušeností a poznatků."
⁶⁵ "Zápis o pohovoru se s. Horákovou dne 16. 3. 1962 po návratu z Indonésie," 16.3.1962, VHA, f. MNO 1961, ka. 453; "Zpráva o činnosti skupiny čs. odborníků na MTC v Káhiře—20. červen až 20. červenec 1964," undated, VHA, f. MNO 1964, ka 324.

security reasons and in order to keep the community isolated. In India, if a wife wanted a job, her only options were to become a nurse, an accountant, or a teacher.[66] Most women only ran the household, which led to boredom, in particular in the small communities resident in Baghdad or the mission in Poll-i-Charkhi in Afghanistan.[67] In Guinea, the wives were altogether estranged from their husbands' work: the experts decided not to speak about work in front of them to avoid gossip and envy.[68]

Czechoslovak children were likewise expected to convey a positive image of socialist Czechoslovakia. Playing in the street was considered "undignified." Parents were supposed to ensure that their children did not say anything derogatory about local people, greeted people in the street, behaved well during excursions, and did not damage the host country's cultural heritage. It was also suggested that parents should have their children help at home as part of their socialist upbringing.[69]

Such positive representations of Czechoslovakia and the maintenance of a "socialist space" required as homogeneous and impermeable a community as possible. If possible, the whole community lived in one place. Contact with local people was to be limited to workplace and professional communication, or to controlled cultural exchange. The experts did not visit their colleagues, and if they somehow happened to enter their houses, the visit would be highly formal in nature. Experts were also not allowed to read newspapers in public, as it could provoke someone to strike up a political conversation.[70] The aim of the isolation was the creation of an autonomous "Czechoslovak socialist space," whose connection with the outer world would be as controlled as possible.[71]

The only way to send and receive letters from Czechoslovakia was via the embassy, so that they could be checked by censors. Any other way, for example entrusting missives to experts returning or going on holiday to Czechoslovakia, was prohibited; violators faced disciplinary consequences.[72] Photography, a popular hobby, was restricted. "Taking pictures is literally the sickness of most Czechoslovaks," said the head of the group after one expert had been arrested and expatriated from Egypt for this offence.[73] In their role as representatives of an ideal Czechoslovakia, the experts in Cairo were specifically told which clothes to wear, which houses to rent, and which means of transportation to use. Experts were supposed to read *Rudé právo*, the official press of the KSČ, and should any expert be found reading local newspapers in English, it immediately appeared in his character profile in the reports.[74]

[66] Strašíková, *Indický kaleidoskop*, 25.
[67] Jiří Mladějovský, "Závěrečná zpráva," 1.12.1965, VHA, f. MNO 1966, ka 246; Svatopluk Slavíček, "Skupina čs. odborníků na MTC Baghdad," 19.3.1979, VSA, f. VAAZ, ka 427.
[68] "Souhrnná zpráva o poskytování technické pomoci letecké společnosti Air Guinée," undated, VHA, f. MNO 1963, ka 360.
[69] "Několik informací a rad pro soudruhy nastupující na akci MTC a jejich rodiny," undated, VSA, f. VAAZ, ka 420.
[70] Osvald Vašíček, "Pravidelné hlášení č. 2," 15.4.1959, VHA, f. MNO 1959, ka 351.
[71] For a different view, see the memoirs of one expert who, working as a teacher in Ghana in 1964–6, recalls an open, socially mixed space. Evžen Menert, *Na západ od Londýna* (Praha, 1967).
[72] Vojtěch Srovnal, "Nelegální odesílání dopisů do ČSSR," 5.3.1970, VSA, f. VAAZ, ka 420.
[73] "Orientační příručka pro čs. odborníky na MTC," undated. VSA, f. VAAZ, ka 420.
[74] Vasil Valo, "Poznatky ze skupiny čs. vojenských expertů v SAR—oznámení," 8.2.1960, VHA, MNO 1960, ka 462.

One reason experts were so carefully observed was the fear of defection. As articulated by the Central Committee of the Communist Party of Czechoslovakia, people "whose close relatives had betrayed Czechoslovakia by escaping to a capitalist country must not be sent on a mission." Following the crackdown in 1968 and the subsequent wave of exiles, this was far from being a negligible group. Also undesirable were people whose relatives had been sentenced for "counter-state activity," and those who had betrayed the trust of their superiors on previous missions abroad.[75] Already in 1960, the military and air attaché in Cairo demanded that experts be chosen primarily in terms of their political profile and only then according to their actual expertise. The rigorous selection process and the strict rules in place were in all likelihood the reason why there was only one recorded escape in the operation's history. In July 1969, an expert fled to West Germany from Belgrade on his way from Prague to Cairo by train. As a consequence of this case, travel by car and train to Cairo was prohibited. All experts also had to hand over their personal passports to the Military Academy and closer attention was paid to their lives and dealings in Cairo from that point on.[76]

Despite the fact that the experts participated in the embassy's cultural life and that, according to the head of the MTC group in 1973, relations with the embassy were good, there was an underlying bitterness.[77] Although children were supposed to be placed in Czechoslovak community schools, usually run by the embassy or consulate, in reality, placements were not so simple because schools were often full. Furthermore, experts at the MTC complained that the school treated their children as inferior to the children of diplomats; when the classes did not have any spare room and a diplomat's child needed to enroll, the school would let an MTC expert's child go. As the experts pointed out, this approach needlessly created a gulf between the children from the embassy and those from the MTC.[78] The experts protested passionately against their apparent second-tier status and, after the Six Day War, they criticized the embassy ferociously for not having prepared a viable evacuation plan. An investigation of the experts' behavior during the war referred to the alleged "disinterest of the party and of the government in the Czechoslovak citizens in the UAR."[79] A similar experience was reported by experts in Indonesia, who complained that the embassy staff in Jakarta was arrogant and "made it clear that they were not welcome."[80]

In a foreign environment, cultural life was naturally very important. Czechoslovaks were instructed to avoid the cultural scene in Cairo: there were movies and performances hostile to socialist countries. The expectation was that expats would play an active part in the Czechoslovak community in Cairo. The experts and their families were all members of a club, which organized a cultural program (singing, poetry, puppet shows,

---

[75] "Zásady předsednictva ÚV KSČ pro výběr odborníků pro dlouhodobou expertizu v zahraničí," undated, VHA, f. MNO 1970, ka 254.
[76] Jaroslav Dočkal, "Ing. Jaroslav Plíhal, VAAZ—3F– Hlášení," 1.8.1969, VHA, f. MNO 1969, ka 211.
[77] Josef Vosáhlo and Jaromír Machač, "Zápis o předání a převzetí funkce vedoucího čs. odborníků na MTC- Káhira," 28.5.1973, VSA, f. VAAZ, ka 419.
[78] Josef Zuska, "Měsíční hlášení k 15.11.1961," 16.11.1961, VHA, f. MNO 1961, ka 451.
[79] Josef Širůčka, "Informační zpráva o čs. odbornících v SAR," 20.7.1967, VHA, f. MNO 1967, ka 64
[80] Pplk. Hanák, "Vyhodnocení činnosti v Indonesii od 15. září 1960 do 15. května 1962," VHA, f. MNO 1962, ka 373.

sport, parties, excursions, film evenings). Organized cultural tourism was permitted, especially before the Six Day War. Cultural trips were organized to the pyramids, Luxor, and Aswan, and holidays were spent at a beach near Alexandria. The experts also recalled going on holiday to "third" countries, like Cyprus, Libya, or Italy, and shopping trips in Syria, Lebanon, and Gaza.[81] The rules governing travel became stricter, however, after the war in 1967 and Israeli occupation of Sinai. Expert communities in other countries were more isolated: in Yemen, there was no access at all to newspapers, television, or correspondence, and only to a handful of films and books, which were anyway "politically unsuitable."[82] Experts in Indonesia complained about "having no cultural life" and in Guinea about having seen the few available films more than ten times during their regular Saturday movie nights.[83]

The most frequent complaints were directed at the living conditions and the food. Experts teaching in Indonesia in 1965 did not try to hide their disgust with their hotel rooms: according to their report, the unhygienic environment endangered their health.[84] The quality of accommodation also caused bad blood in the Czechoslovak community in Baghdad and was a constant problem even in Cairo, where the expert flats were relatively good; there specialists repeatedly pointed out that the accommodation did not correspond to their contract and complained about the rising rents. The living conditions were also often made more difficult by the weather, so unfamiliar to Central Europeans: the experts found it challenging, particularly in Yemen, Indonesia, and Guinea. In Uganda, military instructors were hospitalized with hepatitis.[85] Even in Egypt they were sick twice as often as they had been in the ČSSR.[86] This was probably also a consequence of the inadequate healthcare and lack of medicines, about which there were repeated complaints.[87] The community struggled with dysentery and one expert even died of elephantiasis.[88]

Even though the command of the college and of the Czechoslovak group strove to limit contact, experts in a foreign city naturally sometimes interacted with local people. In addition to shopkeepers, merchants, and tour guides, there were servants. One of the Czechoslovak instructors remembered that he was a little uncomfortable about being served, as he was not used to it, so he only made his servant "sweep the floor, make the bed and bring a Coke."[89] Another frequent space of contact was a taxi; officially, experts were supposed to use only special buses for commuting to work, but as they were highly

---

[81] "Pplk. Ing. Jaroslav Plíhal—nezákonné opuštění ČSSR," undated (September 1969), VHA, f. MNO 1969, ka 211. See also Vyhlídal, *Činnost československých intruktorů*, 56–7.
[82] Ladislav Košík, "Dílčí zpráva o pobytu v JAR," 15.10.1964, VHA, f. MNO 1964, ka 326.
[83] Jaroslav Hlaďo, "První zpráva o činnosti skupiny intruktorů pro letoun L-29 v Indonesii od odletu do 31.10.1965," 2.11.1965, VHA, f. MNO 1965, ka 234; "Souhrnná zpráva o poskytování technické pomoci letecké společnosti Air Guinée," undated, VHA, f. MNO 1963, ka 360.
[84] Hlaďo, "První zpráva o činnosti skupiny"; Pplk. Hanák, "Vyhodnocení činnosti."
[85] František Hroník, "Zpráva č. 2/69 o činnosti čs. odborníků v Ugandě za dobu od 25.5. 31.7.69," 31.7.1969, VHA, f. MNO 1969, ka 211.
[86] Vosáhlo and Machač, "Zápis o předání."
[87] J. Machač, "Informace VEX pro Prahu. . . ."
[88] Jaroslav Rajlich, unpublished memoirs, 63–4.
[89] Míťa Milota, *Létal jsem patnáctku. Vzpomínky na krásný letoun, jeho pilotáž, kamarády a věci okolo* (Cheb, 2010), 146–69.

unreliable, the Czechoslovaks started to use taxis. The only foreigners with whom the Czechoslovaks could make more or less unrestricted contact were the citizens of other socialist countries. As the experts recalled, relations with the Soviet and East German advisors were friendly—even more so at the MTC in Baghdad, where they played sports and organized common cultural programs. The Soviets even shared their library with the MTC experts. In Afghanistan, Czechoslovak specialists maintained good relations with Soviet embassy staff and attended Soviet cultural events.[90]

As if the living and working conditions were not already hard enough, the Czechoslovak community in Cairo was also tested by two wars with Israel, in 1967 and 1973. Even though the head of the group reported that the experts managed extremely well during the emergency—even the Arabs appreciated the fact that the experts did not flee Cairo and were ready to do their duty—the conditions were still extraordinary. As the group behavorial assessment stated, some of the experts were nervous or selfish, wanted to return to Czechoslovakia as soon as possible, or blamed the Czechoslovak government and embassy for not doing enough for them and for not having prepared a viable evacuation plan.[91] Teaching in a war zone was also experienced by the experts at the MTC in Baghdad, who described the effects on their morale during the war with Iran in the 1980s.[92] In Indonesia, in 1965, the difficult living conditions were exacerbated by martial law, which prevented the experts from moving around freely.[93]

The Prague Spring in Cairo

The greatest challenge for the socialist space in Cairo came in 1968 with the reform movement in Czechoslovakia and subsequent Warsaw Pact invasion. The reform movement, however, did not only have political contours at the MTC; dissatisfaction with the strict rules, arduous living conditions, and the war, as well as grievances over their second-tier status, erupted in an unprecedented rebellion with a social subtext. In March 1968, a group of experts sent an outspoken letter to the powerful director of the Main Technical Administration, František Langer, asking him to reconsider their inadequate salaries and unsatisfactory working conditions. "We deem the continuation of the current state of affairs unjustifiable," they wrote.[94] The content of the letter was not the only issue; the fact that it had been sent outside the official communication channels directly to Langer was also problematic. According to a retrospective analysis ordered by the General Staff, the majority of experts supported the Prague Spring reform, including the head of the group. As the analysis states critically, during 1968 the experts had started to read the foreign press and listen to foreign radio.[95]

[90] Cyril Sirotný, "Zpráva stranickej skupiny z priezkumovej skupiny akcie 101," 18.4.1961, VHA, f. MNO 1961, ka 453.
[91] Josef Širůčka, "Informační zpráva o čs. odbornících v SAR," 20.7.1967, VHA, f. MNO 1967, ka 64.
[92] Svatopluk Slavíček, "Skupina čs. odborníků na MTC Bagdád," 22.11.1980, VSA, f. VAAZ, ka 427.
[93] Hlaďo, "První zpráva o činnosti skupiny."
[94] Professors—Experts MTC to František Langer, 31.3.1968, VSA, f. VAAZ, ka 421.
[95] "Služebně-politická analysa vývoje situace na MTC od ledna 1968 do konce června 1970," undated, VSA, f. VAAZ, ka 420.

With the liberalization at home, attempts to alter working conditions also appeared in Egypt—or, as the report puts it, the "atmosphere of hysteria" produced "anarchist tendencies and unrealistic requests." At a meeting of the group, one expert called work at the MTC a form of "modern slavery" and questioned the competence of the Czechoslovak Army, as in his view it had failed to arrange good working conditions for them. Another expert said that the option of a strike should be considered, and two others refused to run courses in Alexandria until they had received expense allowances. Others demanded unrestricted travel and other arrangements that would improve their position. "Especially dangerous were the requests that called into doubt basic valid documents, in particular the contract with the MTC. Among the issues discussed was the forty-hour working week, evening stints, on Fridays and holidays too, accommodation standards, healthcare etc." A member of the group's Working Committee, a lawyer, demanded that Czechoslovak laws be obeyed, insisting that they were above the contract with the UAR. The analysis also stated—perhaps to shed a bad light on the rebelling experts—that these demands were in some cases accompanied by anti-Arab sentiments.[96]

All these expressions of disobedience naturally have to be viewed in the perspective of the Prague Spring and the reform atmosphere that swept Czechoslovak society. The experts undoubtedly reflected the abolition of censorship and sharpening political critique in their homeland, and used the opportunity to voice their own grievances. Indeed, the words about "modern slavery" may have been exaggerated, but as a part of the series of complaints vocalized in 1968, they evince a deeper frustration. The problems themselves should not be seen as something new, as the discontent had been covertly present the whole time.

The invasion of Czechoslovakia was a shocking turn of events. As one expert recalled in 2008, the "Arab colleagues welcomed us with compassionate looks and expressions of sympathy."[97] A group of experts wrote a protest letter and sent it to the five invading countries' embassies in Egypt and to the embassies of Romania and Yugoslavia. In the letter, the experts spoke about betrayal, demanded the immediate withdrawal of the armies, and emphasized that they were the true proponents of socialism:

> To whom or what can this international intervention be helpful? Certainly not socialism in Czechoslovakia or in the world. Nor the reputation of the Soviet Union and its allies. Building world peace even less. Against whom was it aimed, then? Against a few extremists, who came up with anti-socialist slogans? We ourselves would have dealt with them democratically. The only possible explanation is the fear of the leaders of the intervening countries that the successful Czechoslovak experiment could mean their loss, as it would show to the people of their countries the true nature of socialism.[98]

---

[96] "Služebně-politická analysa vývoje situace na MTC od ledna 1968 do konce června 1970."
[97] Ivo Kameníček, "Vzpomínky na srpen 1968 z Káhiry," *Listy Univerzity obrany* 1 (2008): 17–18.
[98] "Opis dopisu, který byl předán ZÚ SSSR, NDR, Polska, Maďarska, Bulharska, Rumunska a Jugoslávie," undated (original 21.8.1968). VSA, f. VAAZ, ka 420.

According to the 1970 analysis of the MTC, the atmosphere at the college was very nationalist, anti-Soviet, and depressed. Most experts backed the demands for withdrawal of the armies and for fresh negotiations. People just arriving from Czechoslovakia for the new academic year or returning from their holidays also exacerbated the negative mood, as they brought back their own personal experiences and impressions of the event.[99] In 1968, the experts sent a protest letter to Gustáv Husák. They fully supported the extraordinary congress of the KSČ and demanded the resignation of those who had forfeited the trust of the people—namely Husák, Vasil Biłak, Lubomír Štrougal, Alois Indra, Miloš Jakeš, and others.[100] The experts took part in a political demonstration related to the victory of the Czechoslovak ice hockey team over the Soviets at the world championships, and some of them approved the self-immolation of Jan Palach in January 1969. The party committee of the experts at the MTC unanimously refused to join in with the congratulations sent to the USSR on the anniversary of October Revolution and, in March 1969, the group declined to re-establish friendly relations with Soviet advisors in Cairo, which had been ruptured after the invasion.[101]

Although most of the experts backed down in 1969, the situation at the MTC was not fully under control until the spring of 1970, when the political pressure for "normalization" strengthened, and the remaining rebellious experts either repented or were withdrawn. In the following years, political life within the expert community was strictly regimented. All experts were required to perform self-criticism and attend obligatory courses in Marxism-Leninism, where they studied how to be proud of their socialist homeland, how to stay immune from bourgeois propaganda, and how to influence their Arab colleagues and students. Participation was not pro forma: everyone had to do the requisite reading and contribute to class discussions; the activity and preparation of each participant was observed and reported on. Relations with Soviet advisors were re-established; under the leadership of Soviet generals Samokhodskii and Sutormin, the Soviets took part in the "normalization" of the situation at the MTC.

Conclusion

The role of specialists was not only to be an extension of the Czechoslovak military education system abroad. Different actors would attribute different functions to them. The foreign trade corporations exported expert services in a manner identical to that used in relation to arms or technology. For the Defense and the Military Academy, they represented a welcome opportunity to promote the Czechoslovak Army and its socialist modernity. For the secret services, expert communities could serve to extend

---

[99] "Služebně-politická analysa vývoje situace na MTC od ledna 1968 do konce června 1970," undated, VSA, f. VAAZ, ka 420.
[100] Biłak, Štrougal, and Indra were the members of the Central Committee of the KSČ who sent the "invitation letter" to Leonid Brezhnev, asking for help against "counter-revolution," thus giving a pretext for the invasion. Husák and Jakeš became the figureheads of the subsequent "normalization" regime.
[101] "Služebně-politická analysa vývoje situace na MTC od ledna 1968 do konce června 1970," undated, VSA, f. VAAZ, ka 420.

intelligence operations abroad. For the experts themselves, the experience might be a career opportunity, or something of an an adventure, or else a period of one's life spent in a small, insular community under strict rules.

The spaces that the Czechoslovaks constructed—that is, the workspace, the community space, and the socialist space—functioned as contact zones and channeled the operative influences in both directions. Together, Czechoslovaks and their colleagues, students, and other locals exchanged knowledge and, despite the authorities' efforts to build homogeneous expat communities, also culture. But the spaces also involved conflict, expressions of nationalism, and racism, in defiance of the ideals of proletarian internationalism. In the eyes of their colleagues in Czechoslovakia, the experts in the Global South might have seemed to be highly favored, given their salaries and the opportunities they had to travel. However, the sources suggest that their experience was more complicated and, in some cases, far from enviable. The experts had to learn how to cope with the specific challenges and expectations of the new and unfamiliar working environment in teaching, language, and professional development, while being viewed as commodities, and not getting the working arrangements promised. Within the expatriate community, they had to maintain relations and cope with the challenges of everyday life, all under difficult climatic conditions. The socialist space required them and their families to behave in a particular way and to represent all the time their own country and its socialist values—at work and outside of work and even inside the Czechoslovak community itself. Some were able to derive benefit from their travels and to remain focused on what was to them a positive experience; for others, an already difficult situation culminated in an outburst, a breakdown, or a divorce. The situation at the MTC in 1968, when the experts used the democratization process in Czechoslovakia to discuss their own terms of work, proved that there was great discontent underlying the bureaucratic language of the official reports. From this perspective, the unprecedented display of insubordination could be viewed as a protest against their instrumentalization and a refusal to be treated as merely products. The events following the Soviet invasion only reflected the developments in Czechoslovak society at home, which learnt to hide its problems and vent its discontent in other ways.

In the case of Cairo, the original aim had been to train a new generation of Egyptian teachers and hand the college over to them within several years, while also influencing the students and local teachers politically. However, economic and educational problems, as well as the complications brought about by the dissolution of the federation with Syria and by the wars with Israel, prolonged the Czechoslovak presence substantially. In time, many Egyptian graduates, having received their Ph.D.s either at the MTC or at the VAAZ, were ready to take over the school, but the end of the cooperation was due more than anything else to changed political circumstances. As Anwar Sadat's policy gradually turned against the Soviet Union, so too did Egypt's formerly friendly relations with its socialist allies in Europe become cooler or even hostile. In 1977, five years after the withdrawal of the Soviet advisors, it was time for the last Czechoslovak experts to return home.

8

The Military Training Camp: Co-Constructed Spaces—Experiences of PAIGC Guerrillas in Soviet Training Camps, 1961–1974

Natalia Telepneva

The late 1950s was a period of dramatic change in Africa, with thirteen countries scheduled to achieve independence in 1960 alone. In Portuguese colonies—Angola, Mozambique, and Portuguese Guinea and Cape Verde—a struggle against white power emerged in the 1960s, as it became clear that Portugal's prime minister António de Oliveira Salazar was not prepared to surrender control. In Guinea-Bissau, the Portuguese Army fought against a guerrilla movement, the Party for Independence of Guinea and Cape Verde (Partido Africano da Independência da Guiné e Cabo Verde, PAIGC). The PAIGC was led by Amílcar Lopes da Costa Cabral (hereafter Amílcar Cabral), a Cape Verdean agronomist educated in Lisbon who would become a famous theoretician of African revolution. The guerrilla war in Guinea-Bissau started in January 1963 and would last until the coup of April 25, 1974 overthrew the Portuguese dictatorship and led to domestic reforms, paving the way for the independence of Guinea-Bissau and the other Portuguese colonies in 1974–5.[1]

The Soviet Union was a crucial ally of the PAIGC. Between 1963 and 1974, the USSR supplied 21.7 million roubles in military, and 4.4 million roubles in humanitarian aid to the PAIGC. The USSR also provided the bulk of training in various training facilities across the Eastern Bloc. Before the Portuguese coup in 1974, they trained 2,000 PAIGC recruits, the majority of them at Perevalnoe, a large facility in Soviet Ukraine.[2] This chapter uses oral history and memoirs to compare the experiences of PAIGC guerrillas who underwent military training at Perevalnoe and Skhodnia, a smaller facility near Moscow. The chapter argues that Soviet training camps were in large measure "co-constructed" spaces, operating around a set of modernizing goals shared by African elites and their Soviet interlocutors.

---

[1] Patrick Chabal, *Amilcar Cabral: Revolutionary Leadership and People's War* (Cambridge, 1983); Julião Soares Sousa, *Amilcar Cabral (1924–1973), Vida E Morta de Um Revolutionario Africano* (Coimbra, 2016).
[2] Kulikov to CC CPSU, July 18, 1973, Russian State Archive of Contemporary History (hereafter RGANI), f. 5, op. 66, d. 190, l. 133.

Training and education were fundamental to Cabral's modernizing project in Guinea-Bissau. Having worked as an agronomist across the Portuguese empire, Cabral accepted a Marxist-Leninist framework for the analysis of Portuguese colonialism. He believed that capitalism and imperialism were closely intertwined, and that socialism was the only way to achieve true liberation. Armed struggle was an essential part of such liberation, and armed men were to be the agents of modernity in the countryside. Cabral thus famously paid a great deal of attention to the education of recruits, teaching not only practical skills but also guiding revolutionaries to achieve the level of "political consciousness" necessary for genuine emancipation.

These goals fitted well with Soviet objectives for the military training program. At least some Soviet instructors saw the training camps as sites for turning Africans into modern subjects. These modern soldiers would be able, they hoped, to adhere to Soviet standards of *kul'turnost'* (culturedness), which entailed a basic set of skills and habits, but also political consciousness—the ability to interpret their local struggles in terms of the Marxist-Leninist theory of imperialism. As a result, the "space" of the training camp was co-constructed by the Soviets and by the African elites, who held similar modernizing objectives. In a practical sense, the military training followed the demands of guerrilla struggle in Guinea-Bissau. In a metaphysical sense, the content and meanings of the political instruction were shaped by Cabral's ideological agenda. Overall, educated and thus higher-status soldiers tended to possess a greater sense of agency over their immediate environment and served as "translators" and "retranslators" of meaning for their less educated colleagues.

Thousands of soldiers from the Global South went for military training in the USSR after 1945. In recent years, scholars have started to examine the daily lives at the military training camps, with many underlining the transnational or "un-national" nature of these spaces, and thus of the "national liberation" movements in Southern Africa overall.[3] However, we know very little about the content, structure, and intended outcomes of these programs. To date, there is not a single study of the Soviet military training program for the PAIGC, despite the scale of the support offered between 1961 and 1974. We also know little about the experiences of African guerrillas who were trained across the Soviet bloc; the little we do know comes almost exclusively from memoirs of select soldiers who underwent specialized training at facilities in Moscow.[4]

This chapter is based on archival evidence, memoirs, and selected interviews with former trainees in Soviet training camps. Some of those interviewed—Osvaldo Lopes da Silva, Júlio Carvalho, Olívio Pires, Silvino da Luz, António Leite, and Pedro Pires—underwent training at Skhodnia in 1967. Others, including João Pereira da Silva, Fode Cassama, Brandão Bull da Matta, Arafan Mane, and Afonso Manga Badganny, were

---

[3] Miles Larmer and Luise White, "Introduction: Mobile Soldiers and the Un-National Liberation of Southern Africa," *Journal of Southern African Studies* 40.6 (2014): 1271–4.
[4] Some examples include Barry Gilder, *Songs and Secrets: South Africa from Liberation to Governance* (London, 2012); Hugh Macmillan, *Chris Hani—a Jacana Pocket Biography* (Auckland Park, 2014), 27–9. For a rare scholarly account, see Jocelyn Alexander and JoAnn McGregor, "African Soldiers in the USSR: Oral Histories of Zapu Intelligence Cadres' Soviet Training, 1964–1979," *Journal of African History* 43.1 (2017): 49–66.

trained at Perevalnoe at different points in time. Differences arose on account of the diverse backgrounds of the interviewees. Almost all interviewees who studied at Skhodnia in 1967 were born and interviewed in Cape Verde. Many among the group became prominent wartime figures and occupied positions of power after Guinea-Bissau became independent in 1974. Most notably, Pedro Pires became President of Cape Verde in the 1990s. Osvaldo Lopes da Silva, Júlio Carvalho, João Pereira da Silva, and Silvino da Luz would also later occupy governmental posts at ministerial level. Those who studied in Perevalnoe (with the exception of João Pereira da Silva) were born in Guinea-Bissau. Although the men in that group came to hold less senior posts, their entire professional careers remained connected with the armed forces. The specificity of the interview evidence means that the narrative presented here inadvertently tends to prioritize elite experiences, often of those men whose lives were firmly connected to the PAIGC and Cabral's modernizing project.

"A Golden Prison": Secrecy, Hierarchy, and Control in the Training Camps

The Soviet tradition of training revolutionaries from abroad grew out of the Comintern. The Soviet military advised the Chinese nationalists in the 1920s and, in the late 1930s, a substantial contingent supported the Republicans during the Spanish Civil War. In the 1950s, the Soviets launched a massive program to build up and rearm the People's Liberation Army (PLA) in China.[5] The Cold War and decolonization lent new impetus to providing training and advisory support to clients in the Global South. Soviet military advisors became active in Egypt under Gamal Abdel Nasser, in Ethiopia in the 1970s and 1980s, and in the People's Democratic Republic of Yemen.[6] In the wake of Patrice Lumumba's murder in 1961 in the Congo, the Soviets negotiated to train the Ghanaian Army as part of Kwame Nkrumah's ambitious plan to create an all-African army.[7]

A series of military coups that swept across Africa in the mid-1960s exacerbated the trend towards the militarization of Soviet engagement with the continent. The Soviets believed they had overlooked the importance of the military and security actors in postcolonial Africa and sought to correct their mistake by strengthening their links with, and providing support for, these forces.[8] By the 1980s, the training of soldiers from the Global South had become a massive logistical enterprise, employing hundreds of military instructors, interpreters, and support staff in multiple training facilities across the Soviet bloc.

Perevalnoe was the largest training facility in the USSR for soldiers from the Global South. Constructed in 1965, it contained all the necessary facilities: headquarters, a

---

[5] Sergei Goncharenko, "Sino-Soviet Military Cooperation," in Odd Arne Westad, (ed.), *Brothers in Arms: The Rise and Fall of the Sino-Soviet Alliance, 1945–1963* (Washington, DC, 1998), 141–64.
[6] Artemy M. Kalinovsky et. al., *Missionaries of Modernity: Advisory Missions and the Struggle for Hegemony in Afghanistan and Beyond* (London, 2016).
[7] Nikolai Debriukha, "Iz Dnevnika Marshala I.V. Kulikova," *Ogonek* 26 (2001): 8.
[8] See Natalia Telepneva, "Saving Ghana's Revolution: The Demise of Kwame Nkrumah and the Evolution of Soviet Policy in Africa, 1966–1972," *Journal of Cold War Studies* 20.4 (2018): 4–25.

cultural club, a Russian sauna, two-storied houses for officers, a canteen for officers and one for trainees, a library, a two-storied medical center; a four-storied building for housing trainees, and a five-storied house with flats for officers and their families with a nursery and a shop. Nearby there was also a building for driving lessons, an obstacle course, and a shooting range. By the late 1960s, the facility had been extended to allow for the education of 500 trainees at the same time. The majority came from Angola, Mozambique, and Guinea-Bissau.

Most trainees at Perevalnoe were rank-and-file soldiers, often with limited levels of education. Many could not speak Portuguese or Creole (the local, Portuguese-derived dialect). That meant there were often many layers of translation, with Soviet instruction often translated into Portuguese, then Creole and then African languages, such as Mandinka and Balante. To assess the educational level of the trainees, Soviet instructors at Perevalnoe administered basic numeracy and literacy tests.

Arafan Mane arrived for training at Perevalnoe in 1968. Born in 1950 in a Balante village in southern Guinea-Bissau, Mane was the son of a fisherman who was also a musician and made musical instruments. His father sent him to school, but many of his peers were illiterate.[9] Brandão Bull da Matta and Afonso Manga Badganny arrived at Perevalnoe in 1971. Brandão's father had managed to enroll him in a Portuguese school, but once the war started, in 1963, his family had had to move.[10] For his part, Afonso had had no schooling before the guerrillas took over his village in 1965. The main occupations were fishing and cattle-herding.[11]

Secrecy was a fundamental feature of Perevalnoe. The small village of Perevalnoe is located off the main highway that connects the capital of Crimea, Simferopol, and Alushta, a famous holiday destination on the Black Sea. It was protected from view on all sides by picturesque mountains. The men were flown to Perevalnoe with several transit stops. They often arrived at night and were driven to the school in a special bus with drawn curtains. They were also not allowed to venture off the premises unless in organized tours. There was a concern to keep trainees well away from the prying eyes of Western intelligence services, but evidently not with complete success. In fact, the Portuguese secret police, the PIDE, knew about the location of Perevalnoe and regularly compiled lists of men who underwent training at the center. Still, the Soviets tried to protect the identity of the trainees. Arafan Mane recalled that they were advised never to identify themselves as guerrillas from Guinea-Bissau outside of the training grounds.[12]

The daily lives of the trainees and their instructors were governed by strict rules of military discipline and hierarchy. This entailed waking up and going to bed at a certain time, marching to the canteen in military formation, and observing rank.[13] Soldiers lived and ate in separate quarters to Soviet instructors. Vladimir Sukhorukhov worked

---

[9] Arafan Mane, conversation with the author, April 1, 2019, Bissau (hereafter "Mane, 2019")
[10] Brandão Bull da Matta, interview with the author, March 25, 2019, Bissau (hereafter "da Matta, 2019").
[11] Afonso Manga Badganny, conversation with the author, March 24, 2019, Bissau (hereafter "Badganny, 2019")
[12] Mane, 2019.
[13] João Pereira da Silva, conversation with the author, January 6, 2017, Praia, Cape Verde (hereafter "João Pereira da Silva, 2017").

as an interpreter at Perevalnoe in the early 1970s. He recalled in a 2012 interview that among the PAIGC soldiers, there were many educated, older men from relatively well-off families who had received higher education in Portugal, France, and England. There were also very young men, only seventeen or eighteen years old, with little education.[14] Military hierarchy at Perevalnoe applied to all Soviet personnel and foreign cadets and was respected. Iurii Gorbunov, who arrived in 1966 to work as translator, recalled it was not easy for him to adjust to the strict military regime after attending a "civilian university" and the less controlled life he had become used to abroad, as he had to wear a military uniform, salute to the senior in rank, and carry out regular military exercises day and night.[15]

João Pereira Silva was twenty-five years old when he arrived at Perevalnoe in March 1971. Originally from Boa Vista, Cape Verde, he had studied at the only high school in the archipelago. In 1963, he left for Portugal on a scholarship to study agronomy at the University of Lisbon, where he became involved with the PAIGC. After spending some time as a teacher at a party school in Conakry, he was dispatched to Perevalnoe where he was put in charge of a group of PAIGC soldiers in training. He also recalled that trainees' life at Perevalnoe was strictly regimented, but believed the discipline was important for building group solidarity among the trainees. After one year of training, the group had integrated as a single military unit, bridging regional divides.[16]

Perevalnoe's isolation was underlined by the high fence that surrounded the training site and the Soviet soldiers who guarded it. Although the trainees sometimes saw these soldiers, they were permitted no contact with them.[17] The fence was supposed to protect the trainees from inquisitive civilians and also to serve as a physical means of control. The commandant Vladilen Kinchevskii remembered that the strict discipline and isolation caused some problems: "It used to happen that one [trainee] would help the other over the fence," said Kinchevskii, "and one could see black heads above the fence. Civilians, those who did not know, would take fright. So, I had to [pull] their trousers like some kind of teenagers: 'Come down!'"[18]

It is difficult to ascertain whether the trainees objected to such a restricted lifestyle. A few would scale the fence, go to the shops nearby, buy alcohol, and come back. One could be punished with disciplinary measures if caught in the act.[19] Yet some men emphasized that the lack of physical autonomy was not a problem. As Arafan Mane recalled, they were "revolutionaries," and as such they grasped that the training would help them liberate their own country, especially since the Soviets treated them well and provided all the support staff, such as cooks, cleaners, doctors, nurses—all inside the camp.[20]

[14] Larisa Kucherova, "Nad Yemenov-bezoblachnoye nebo," *Armiya* 1 (January–February 2012): 24–31.
[15] Iurii Gorbunov, "Partizany dlia Afriki," 16 December 2013, *Voennoye Obozrenie*, http://Topwar. Ru/37349-Krym-Partizany-Dlya-Afriki-Chast-1.Htmlmilitari.
[16] João Pereira da Silva, 2017.
[17] João Pereira da Silva, 2017.
[18] "Shkola terroristov s marksistskim uklonom," *Segodnya*, April 22, 2005, https://www.segodnya.ua/oldarchive/c2256713004f33f5c2256fea00516140.html.
[19] Da Matta, 2018.
[20] Mane, 2019.

The Soviet Union was dotted with similar "secret spaces." These were mainly research laboratories and military installations, but there were also dozens of towns, the "closed cities," where one could only gain access with a special permit. Information about these towns was closed to the general public, too: "closed cities" were absent from maps and media coverage. Akin to these Soviet spaces, the training camps for African soldiers were usually secluded sites, where an individual's power depended on his place in set hierarchies.

To João Pereira da Silva, these Soviet hierarchies were obvious. That ultimate authority lay with the military leadership in Moscow was not in doubt. He recalled an episode in their artillery training when his cohort went out to the fields to learn how to identify distances topographically. It was winter so the fields were covered in meters of snow, making the exercise quite pointless. On a different occasion, they were taught to use churches and power lines to identify distance, which was of limited use since the interior of Guinea-Bissau had few of either. When da Silva raised objections, the instructors admitted the shortcomings, but told him that it would be easier to cut the page out of the textbook than to argue with Moscow about changing it.[21]

Another obvious hierarchy concerned the position of the "political representative," most likely a KGB officer, stationed at the camp. Silva remembered him as a "nice young man from Moscow" who liked sports and boxing. Yet at the same time, he was also clearly the most powerful man at Perevalnoe, who was entitled to take one for a "nice walk outside, invite one to a restaurant in the town or for a late night drink in his quarters." He argued that the experience opened his eyes to the reality of Soviet hierarchies. The military hierarchy that he observed was obvious even in the fabric of the Soviet uniforms, and it was quite different to the sense of equality he had read about in books.[22]

However, the strict regimen at Perevalnoe could be adjusted in line with the requirements of the PAIGC leadership and the status of the incoming group. Fode Cassama's contingent arrived in November 1972 as part of a group of twenty-four men hand-picked to learn how to operate Strela-2, a new Soviet shoulder-fired air-defense system that would, it was hoped, break the military stalemate in Guinea-Bissau. Cabral argued that time was of the essence, and the Soviets had agreed that a group of select recruits could come for a three-month crash course. Cassama recalled that the special importance of their mission meant that they were treated like officers rather than regular trainees. They did not have to line up at regular intervals, only in the evening to check attendance, and they regularly went to the city after class, accompanied by Soviet officers.[23] Although groups like Cassama's had a special status, Perevalnoe was designed mainly for the training of rank-and-file soldiers.

Skhodnia, by contrast, was a site suitable for the training of small groups for special missions. In 1968, Skhodnia hosted a cohort of thirty members of the PAIGC. The majority had arrived from Havana, Cuba, where the group had been undergoing training for a mission to launch the armed struggle in the Cape Verde archipelago.

[21] João Pereira da Silva, 2017.
[22] João Pereira da Silva, 2017.
[23] Fode Cassama, conversation with the author, March 22, 2019, Bissau (hereafter "Cassama, 2019").

The Military Training Camp

Although the war in Guinea-Bissau started in 1963, the PAIGC attracted many Cape Verdeans, including in leadership positions. In 1963, the Cuban revolutionary Che Guevara met Cabral, and the two discussed the prospects for a guerrilla struggle in Cape Verde. Guevara believed that the conditions in Cape Verde were similar to the Sierra Maestra mountains, and offered Cuban training. By 1967, however, it became clear that the mission would prove too risky, and the group of thirty-one Cape Verdean trainees in Cuba was flown from Havana to Moscow for an artillery training course at Skhodnia.

The Cape Verdeans who arrived at Skhodnia in 1968 thus had considerable military experience and a high level of education. The leader of the Cape Verdean group was Pedro Pires. A thirty-four-year-old from Fogo, Cape Verde, in 1956 Pires went to study engineering at the University of Lisbon where he became involved in the underground anti-Salazarist movement. After a major anti-colonial uprising in Angola in 1961, Pires, like many African student activists in Portugal, feared conscription into the colonial army and fled the country in the same year. He officially joined the PAIGC and was dispatched to Dakar, Senegal, where he recruited volunteers to join the movement. Another member of the group was Osvaldo Lopes da Silva, another student who had fled Portugal in 1961. Da Silva went on to receive a scholarship place at the prestigious Plekhanov Institute of the National Economy in Moscow and, thanks to the language skills he aquired there, he doubled as a translator at Skhodnia. The twenty-seven-year-old Silvino da Luz had for his part taken an officers' training course in Portugal in 1960 and was among the first recruits to undertake military training in China after fleeing the Portuguese Army and joining the PAIGC. Júlio Carvalho studied engineering at the University of Lisbon before joining the PAIGC and going for military training to Cuba.

Like Perevalnoe, Skhodnia was a secret space, and the life of trainees there was strictly controlled. Trainees would have their classes as a group and would go outside to practice, but they were never unaccompanied and were not allowed contact with anyone. "It was almost like a golden prison," Olívio Pires jokingly recalled.[24] However, it seems that the isolation was to a great extent imposed by the trainees themselves because of the top-secret nature of the mission. Júlio Carvalho remarked, "We lived in a self-regulatory regime, therefore, we imposed total control upon ourselves. Let us just say that during this period, perhaps not everyone, but the vast majority did not have any contact with their families. No letters, no news. We were totally cut-off."[25] Silvino da Luz, however, believed that their group was controlled by their Soviet hosts. There were "invisible eyes," watching over them; the Soviets certainly monitored the internal dynamics of their group. As the Minister of Defense and Security for Cape Verde many years later, da Luz tried to apply the same principle of surveillance to foreigners.[26]

The special status of the 1968 group was reflected in their daily lives. At Skhodnia, the trainees lived in a spacious villa outside Moscow, with two per room.[27] Meals and

---

[24] Olívio Pires, conversation with the author, January 13, 2017, Mindelo, Cape Verde (hereafter "Olívio Pires, 2017").
[25] Júlio Carvalho, conversation with the author, February 13, 2018, Sal, Cape Verde (hereafter "Carvalho, 2018").
[26] Silvino da Luz, conversation with the author, January 14, 2017, Mindelo (hereafter "Da Luz, 2017").
[27] António Leite, conversation with the author, January 13, 2017, Mindelo (hereafter "Leite, 2017").

housekeeping were provided by the Soviet staff. Júlio Carvalho recalled that living arrangements at Skhodnia contrasted sharply with those in Cuba, where their group had to prepare their own meals and do their own cleaning. In the Soviet Union, their only role was to study. Their relations with their Soviet instructors were also less hierarchical than was the case for regular trainees at Perevalnoe: they were "treated as equals."[28] The course at Skhodnia was very brief. They spent only a couple of months learning artillery before moving on to Baku, the capital of Soviet Azerbaijan on the Caspian Sea. There they spent a few more months, learning the basics of navigating a boat—a crucial means of transportation in Guinea-Bissau.[29]

The spaces of Perevalnoe and Skhodnia differed according to function. Perevalnoe most of all resembled a "regular" Soviet training establishment, which was run on the basis of military hierarchy and other unspoken rules, where one's power depended on role and status. While the soldiers' daily lives were strictly regulated, these Soviet hierarchies were visible to some of the former trainees. In contrast, the trainees who underwent training at Skhodnia had far less direct access to Soviet realities, their physical environment being much more easily managed by their hosts. Nonetheless, the testimony of soldiers in Perevalnoe and Skhodnia suggests that they saw themselves as having some control over their environments and, in this sense, as co-constructors of the space of the training camp.

"The Greatest Contribution": Soviet Military Technology and African Liberation

The nature of the armed struggle in Guinea-Bissau evolved in the course of the 1960s. While the early stages of the guerrilla warfare mainly involved brief hit-and-run raids against Portuguese contingents, by 1967 the PAIGC had started to launch attacks against heavily fortified Portuguese installations such as at Madina do Boe in the east of the country. These required access to new types of heavy weaponry, which would be supplied by the Soviets. In a 1968 interview with the *Tricontinental* magazine, Cabral emphasized the importance of "modern weapons" and training to armed struggle: "But today we must wage a modern war. A guerrilla war, but a modern one, with modern tactics."[30]

The PAIGC leadership supervised most parts of the course, selected trainees for particular specializations, and oversaw the final exams.[31] Each trainee also received grades for exams and personal reports, which would be communicated to the PAIGC leadership. João Pereira da Silva remembered that these would be sent on to headquarters in Conakry. Their content was not made available to the trainees.[32]

---

[28] Osvaldo Lopes da Silva, conversation with the author, January 9, 2017 (hereafter "Osvaldo Lopes da Silva, 2017"); Leite, 2017.
[29] Carvalho, 2018; Leite, 2017.
[30] Amílcar Cabral, "Practical Problems and Tactics," in *Selected Texts by Amílcar Cabral: Revolution in Guinea. An African People's Struggle*, trans. Richard Handyside (London, 1969), 108–22, https://www.marxists.org/subject/africa/cabral/1968/ppt.htm.
[31] Mane, 2019.
[32] João Pereira da Silva, 2017.

The military training program at Perevalnoe evolved to reflect the shifting tactics of anti-colonial war in Guinea-Bissau. In Perevalnoe's first year, recruits were taught to handle Soviet weapons, mainly light artillery, and learnt how to blow up railway tracks, bridges, and buildings—all fundamental to guerrilla warfare. Much emphasis was placed on the rapid arming and disarming of weapons. The Soviet instructors would take trainees to the polygon, and teach them how to disarm mortars and cannons quickly—an important skill in mobile warfare. In terms of guerrilla tactics, the Soviets would cite examples from Cuba, the Soviet Union during World War II, and Vietnam.[33]

However, as the war progressed, the Soviets adjusted their training accordingly. By the 1970s, Perevalnoe operated three main specializations: artillery; mines and explosives; and anti-aircraft defense. Those who specialized in artillery were taught how to operate mortars, while those in anti-aircraft defense would learn how to handle heavy machine guns, such as the DShK 1938. By 1970, the Soviets had started to supply more advanced weapons, such as the Grad-P, a lightweight version of the multiple rocket launcher BM-21, which was developed in the 1960s for the North Vietnamese.

The content of the program at Skhodnia in 1968 reflected the PAIGC's decision to switch from mainly hit-and-run guerrilla tactics to certain aspects of conventional warfare. In fact, artillery training was the main focus for the Skhodnia group, who were taught how to operate cannons and 120mm heavy mortars that could be used to destroy fortified buildings. This type of training, recalled Júlio Carvalho, differed significantly from that received in Cuba, where the emphasis had been on navigation, disembarkation in Cape Verde and classic guerrilla training which prioritized the handling of light weapons, thus allowing the guerrillas to adapt to the terrain.[34] Olívio Pires confirms that "Cuba gave us basic training in guerrilla warfare. At the basic level. It was our first training. The Soviet training was complementary. And they gave us, let's say, training to a more advanced level."[35]

The mastery of advanced Soviet military technology was thus the main focus of the training programs. Silvino da Luz recalled that they had become trained artillery commanders by the end of the course at Skhodnia, able to shoot heavy weapons, which could be deployed anywhere in the world with only a little knowledge of trigonometry.[36] According to Pedro Pires, who was in charge of the PAIGC training program for a while, technology was the main Soviet contribution to the struggle: "Every guerrilla, from South America to Africa, passing through Asia, used this weapon. The great weapon of the guerrillas was the automatic machine gun AK of the Kalashnikov [AK-47]. That is the great contribution of the Soviet Union to the national liberation struggles."[37]

The importance of Soviet military technology for liberation was embodied in the Soviet anti-aircraft system Strela-2, developed specifically for guerrilla warfare in Vietnam. Cabral held high hopes that it would serve to end the war with minimum bloodshed and in 1972 brokered a deal with the Soviets to train a small group of

---

[33] Badganny, 2019; da Matta, 2019.
[34] Carvalho, 2018.
[35] Olívio Pires, 2017.
[36] Da Luz, 2017.
[37] Pedro Pires, 2017.

guerrillas to operate the Strela-2 complex at Perevalnoe. On January 20, 1973, Cabral was murdered in Conakry in the course of a failed coup d'état. This crisis notwithstanding, the war continued. In 1973, Fode Cassama's group started hitting Portuguese airplanes with the Strela-2, putting significant pressure on the armed forces. After the PAIGC shot down the Fiat G-91 belonging to Almeida Brito, the chief of the Portuguese Air Force, the Portuguese suspended all aerial operations.[38] According to Pires, the Strela-2 was the "fatal weapon" that liquidated Portuguese air superiority, thus effectively ending the war.[39]

To the trainees, Soviet weapons were a means and a symbol of liberation. Although the African revolutionaries were inspired by a number of revolutionary examples and practices—the Cuban, the Vietnamese, the Chinese— it was the Soviets' military technology that had the capacity to drastically change the outcome of the war. Overall, the trainees derived their own meanings from the training program; and their choice was often determined by a number of factors, including pre-existing political beliefs and experiences. Many of the soldiers who came to train in the USSR were attracted to the Soviet system because they saw socialism as something that equaled liberation from the colonial past and promised rapid modernization. However, as we shall see, it was the individual soldiers who shaped the ways in which they interacted with the "political training," often using their previous experiences as a benchmark.

"Who Shoots Whom": Politics and Culture in the Training Camps

Cabral believed that the campaign in Guinea-Bissau required not only a guerrilla war to achieve independence, but a political struggle for true national liberation. Like the ideologue of the Algerian Revolution, Frantz Fanon, Cabral was concerned that capitalist countries had vested interests in maintaining exploitative relationships with African countries after independence. The series of military coups that ousted some of the first post-independence leaders lent further credence to Cabral's theory about the lingering influence of colonial powers. Speaking at the funeral of Ghana's first president, Kwame Nkrumah, deposed in a coup d'état in 1966, Cabral wondered how much the army's betrayal was linked to questions of class struggle and social structure. Nkrumah had discovered these too late, Cabral believed, and it was thus crucial for the anti-colonial movements to educate their members that only with the instruments of Marxism-Leninism could one build truly independent, internationalist and economically viable states.[40]

Cabral therefore paid close attention to the political preparation of the military cadres. The majority of young people, having mobilized to join the guerrillas, would

---

[38] Interview with Manuel dos Santos in João Paulo Guerra, *Descolonização Portuguesa—O Regresso das Caravelas* (Alfragide, 2009), loc. 778, Kindle.
[39] Pedro Pires, 2017.
[40] Odd Arne Westad, *The Global Cold War: Third World Interventions and the Making of Our Times* (Cambridge, 2005), 108.

receive the basics of political instruction. Such education often started in the bush, and then continued at bases such as Madina do Boe, where young men would be trained by Guinean and Cuban instructors. Cabral himself would often explain the reasons for the struggle to young recruits. The volunteers had to abandon their "tribal" affiliations and prejudices and embrace Cabral's vision of a bi-national future, a unity of Cape Verde and Guinea-Bissau, based on ideas of social justice and equality. The subordination of the military commanders to the "political leadership" in Conakry would nonetheless prove to be a problem. By 1964, reports started to come in that some guerrilla commanders had behaved like "warlords" in areas under their control and were harassing the civilian population. At the Cassaca Congress in February 1964, those military commanders who refused to submit were arrested and put in prison. Some were executed.[41]

To Cabral, the development of soldiers' political consciousness remained a crucial aspect of the liberation struggle. As he told an interviewer in 1966, "We are political people, and our Party, a political organization, leads the struggle in the civilian, political, administrative, technical, and therefore also military spheres. Our fighters are defined as armed activists."[42] By sending volunteers for military training to the Soviet Union, Cabral wanted his men to come back with some theoretical and practical knowledge so that they could act as agents of modernity in the countryside.

The military training program cannot be understood without reference to *kul'turnost'*, a Soviet concept referring to a set of unspoken rules and norms about proper modes of dress, hygiene, public behavior, and the use of free time, originating in nineteenth-century ideas about European modernity. The Soviets did not speak about "modernization" or creating "modern subjects," but the whole notion of *kul'turnost'* was a modernizing one, meant to turn peasants into good urban citizens, which, importantly, also meant politically conscious socialists. By the 1960s, these notions of *kul'turnost'* had long become fundamental to Soviet identity. *Kul'turnost'* was central to the Bolsheviks' development projects domestically, in Soviet Central Asia, as well as in the Global South.[43] African trainees were to become "cultured" agents of change in their country by learning the ropes of modernity.

There were several ways that the Soviet training camps sought to achieve these transformations. One was through classes in political theory. At Perevalnoe, so-called "political classes" were held three times a week and covered the basics of historical materialism, the Leninist theory of imperialism, and its application to Africa. There were also classes on the anti-colonial movement in Africa, including in the Portuguese colonies. The head of political training, Aleksandr Antipov, justified the need for his subject with a joke he would repeat very often to his colleagues: "First we should teach whom to shoot, and then how to shoot."[44] After spending several years at Perevalnoe as

---

[41] On the Cassaca Congress, see Mustafah Dhada, *Warriors at Work: How Guinea Was Really Set Free* (Niwot, CO, 1993), 18–20; Chabal, *Amilcar Cabral*, 81–2.
[42] Cabral, "Practical Problems and Tactics."
[43] Artemy Kalinovsky, *Laboratory of Socialist Development: Cold War Politics and Decolonization in Soviet Tajikistan* (Ithaca, NY, and London, 2018), introduction.
[44] "Shkola terroristov."

a translator, Iurii Gorbunov became a lecturer in "political disciplines." He writes that their main goal was to explain to Africans that their enemies were not the "whites," but the whole system of "colonialism and neocolonialism." He wrote, "We explained to the trainees that besides colonial slavery there is also socio-class slavery, when the white and black bourgeoisie exploit the labor of workers of any skin color."[45]

Political theory classes were supplemented with "cultural events" (*kul'turnye meropriyatiya*), such as guided tours. Trainees at Perevalnoe visited Soviet factories, schools, and sports centers. Fode Cassama even remembered them attending a football match.[46] Another popular destination was the Livadiya Palace, the summer residence of the Russian Tsars and the location of the 1945 Yalta Conference in the Crimea. Brandão Bull da Matta recalled being very struck by the beauty of Livadiya.[47] The trainees were also usually taken to visit a *kolkhoz* (collective farm), which many trainees remember being impressed by. Guinea-Bissau was then, as now, predominantly an agricultural country, heavily reliant on the cultivation of peanuts, a cash crop introduced by the Portuguese. The Soviet system of collective farming seemed attractive and, as many former trainees recalled, applicable to Guinea-Bissau and the rapid modernization of the agricultural sector.[48] The trainees from Perevalnoe were also taken to Moscow to visit the main sights, usually during holidays. In Skhodnia, cultural events included outings to the Bolshoi Ballet, the circus, and art exhibitions in Moscow.[49]

A particularly important category in the cultural program of Soviet training camps was film screenings. Films were fairly regularly shown at Perevalnoe and other sites and were often the main mode of entertainment, especially where trainees could not exit the camp. These included films about Soviet achievements in agriculture and industry. Another important theme included films about the Vietnam War and the role of Soviet military technology, including of anti-aircraft weapons, in the war against the US. Some films revolved around Lenin, the Russian Revolution of 1917, and the Civil War. The film screenings would often be matched with material that was covered during political classes the preceeding week and paired with real-life visits to agricultural and industrial sites.[50]

Fode Cassama remembered watching *Chapaev* (1934), a famous and hugely popular Stalinist classic about the Russian Civil War, which revolved around the relationship between a brave but hot-headed commander (Chapaev) and a sober and experienced political commissar (Furmanov). Cassama argued that *Chapaev* showed the importance of political commissars to ensure appropriate civilian–military conduct (i.e. in the film, Furmanov helps Chapaev by making sure that Red Army soldiers who stole from the peasants were punished). The political commissars were crucially important in installing patriotism in the minds of the soldiers, believed Cassama, leading to the adoption of that structure in Guinea-Bissau after independence.[51]

---

[45] Gorbunov, "Partizany dlia Afriki."
[46] Cassama, 2019.
[47] Da Matta, 2019.
[48] Da Matta, 2019; Cassama, 2019; Saia na Breia, conversation with the author, 22 March 2019, Bissau.
[49] Carvalho, 2018.
[50] Da Matta, 2019; João Pereira da Silva, 2017.
[51] Cassama, 2019.

The vast majority of screenings were of Soviet World War II films. In Perevalnoe, Arafan Mane still clearly remembered watching *Private Alexander Matrosov* (1947), a famous Stalin-era film about a Soviet soldier who sacrificed his life in battle for the common cause. The film stayed with him, continued Mane, because Matrosov was a *commandante* (commander), and the basic realities and choices that faced Matrosov were very similar to those of the anti-colonial struggle.[52] João Pereira da Silva enjoyed the films about the war, as they corrected the Western narrative, which, as he believed, often neglected the Soviet role in the victory against the Third Reich.[53]

Screenings of World War II films were also a regular feature of life in Skhodnia. Júlio Carvalho especially recalled a film about a Soviet pilot whose plane was shot down; crawling through deep snow, he managed to survive, but lost both feet due to frostbite. Nonetheless, he recovered through sheer willpower and returned to the air force (most likely, the 1948 drama *The Story of a Real Man*, another Stalin-era classic). The story of sacrifice and heroism made a deep impression upon Carvalho.[54] Film screenings were often paired with visits to locations of World War II battles and were followed by discussions of the Soviet experience and sacrifice on the Eastern front.[55] Many of the Soviet instructors at Perevalnoe and Skhodnia were World War II veterans; some even took part in the partisan movement.[56] This fact was well known to the trainees, who not only appreciated the sacrifice of the Soviet soldiers on screen, but also learnt from the very same people who participated in the war.[57]

Taken together, the "cultural events" and the "political classes" were meant to serve a number of purposes. First, they were meant to convince the cadets about the practical benefits of socialism, especially of collectivized agriculture. Second, political education was also meant to depict the Soviet Union as the leading actor in the fight against colonialism, imperialism, and fascism. The role of the Soviet Union in defeating Nazi Germany, which represented the apex of racist and imperialist thinking, was a particularly important part of the classes. By watching Soviet movies and attending memorial sites, the trainees were meant to be inspired by the sacrifice and heroism of soldiers on the Eastern front. As Jocelyn Alexander and JoAnn McGregor have argued, based on interviews with intelligence cadres of the Zimbabwe People's Liberation Union (ZAPU), the engagement with Soviet history was a key part of the Soviet training program; it served as a "lesson in the necessity of sacrifice and political commitment in war."[58] The same conclusion can be applied to the interviewed PAIGC recruits, who seemed to internalize some of the key messages about the major role of the Soviet Union as a champion of the anti-colonial and anti-fascist cause.

In their reports to their party superiors, Soviet instructors continuously proclaimed the success of the political training program. Reporting on the first group of PAIGC

[52] Mane, 2019.
[53] João Pereira da Silva, 2017.
[54] Carvalho, 2018.
[55] Badganny, 2019.
[56] Vladimir Shubin, "Unsung Heroes: The Soviet Military and the Liberation of Southern Africa," in Sue Onslow, (ed.), *Cold War in Southern Africa: White Power, Black Liberation* (London, 2009), 156.
[57] Badganny, 2019;
[58] Alexander and McGregor, "African Soldiers in the USSR," 60.

militants who arrived at Perevalnoe in 1965, General Aleksei Yepishev concluded that the introduction to "Soviet realities"—trips to factories, collective farms, and museums, along with meetings with former members of the partisan movement in Crimea—heightened the cadets' sympathies for the Soviet Union: "The majority of trainees declared they would build socialism in their countries after independence."[59] While some of these evaluations may have been formulaic, there certainly were former instructors like Gorbunov who believed that the program had been transformational for the African soldiers:

> As a teacher, I saw how in a very short time the cadets—those shy and illiterate people—acquired a feeling of human dignity and were spiritually transformed. There arose in them a sense of equality and justice. They gradually became convinced of the righteousness of their struggle for the freedom and independence of their people or ethnicity. They got used to the fact that the Soviet people with white skin—officers, servants, soldiers, civilian workers in the center, collective farmers, city dwellers whom they would meet during trips around Crimea—did not have racial prejudices and treated them as equals.[60]

Gorbunov's account is typical of several memoirs written by Soviet employees at Perevalnoe. These emphasize the instructors' dedication in educating their students, whom they describe as dedicated and effective soldiers. The memoirs are also full of recollections of humorous stories, such as the trainees' refusal to "sleep in proper beds" or eat the Russian staple buckwheat (trainees believed it was rotten rice).[61] These recollections do in fact suggest that many Soviet instructors often saw common soldiers in paternalistic ways. They did not satisfy the Soviet criteria of *kul'turnost'*. Soviet instructors believed it was their duty to help non-European people—what has been referred to as the "Red Man's Burden."[62]

It is difficult to evaluate the impact of such programs on the trainees and to separate Soviet from other influences. The majority of trainees who came to Perevalnoe had already received some form of political instruction. The recruits were taught first by senior peers who had often themselves received instruction in China, Czechoslovakia, or the Soviet Union. After 1967, many received political instruction from Cuban instructors in Guinea-Bissau. In fact, political instruction was a key element in the mobilization of young people, mainly young boys, who first received training at the so-called Center for Political and Military Instruction (Centro de Instrucao Politico Militar, CIPM). To the majority of guerrillas, the "political classes" served as a continuation of their studies, rather than a revelation.

Arafan Mane was only sixteen when he joined the PAIGC in 1966. He spent his first year training at Boke, a PAIGC military base in Guinea. It was there, he recalled, that

---

[59] A. Yepishev to CC CPSU, April 12, 1966, RGANI, f. 5, op. 47, d. 496, ll. 108–9.
[60] Gorbunov, "Partizany dlia Afriki."
[61] "Shkola terroristov."
[62] Botakoz Kassymbelova and Christian Teichmann, "The Red Man's Burden: Soviet European Officials in Central Asia in the 1920s and 1930s," in Maurus Reinkowski and Gregor Thum (eds.), *Helpless Imperialists Imperial Failure, Fear and Radicalization* (Freiburg, 2012), 163–87.

he received his initial political instruction from older peers and then from Cuban instructors. It was the Cubans who first explained to him the importance of the Russian Revolution for Cuba and of World War II for Africa. It was the Cubans who taught him that the PAIGC had to seize the moment and wage revolutionary struggle on the continent.[63] Before arriving at Perevalnoe in 1971, Brandão Bull da Matta received instruction at the CIPM in Madina do Boe. He recalled that besides the Cuban and PAIGC instructors, Cabral himself would come to the base, where he would teach young recruits about the reasons for the war, and also talk about the countries that supported the struggle: the Soviet Union, China, Russia, and East Germany. His was a common experience.[64] Thus, most trainees arrived at Perevalnoe with a basic understanding of "friends and enemies" of their liberation struggle, even if many had limited formal schooling.

Moreover, the topics discussed during "political training" classes in Perevalnoe mainly focused on the program of the PAIGC. As Afonso Manga Badganny recalled, the political training was "aligned" with Cabral's own ideas. The main emphasis was on teaching "nationalism," that is, the overcoming of ethnic division through the building of a nation-state. The training center itself had a library, which contained many books, including works by Lusophone African leaders. In fact, the Soviets were not the only— and probably not the key—instructors at Perevalnoe. Each group that arrived at Perevalnoe had its own leader who was often an educated and relatively senior PAIGC commander. The leaders also instructed the trainees in political matters, focusing mainly on Cabral's ideas. Although some Soviet political instructors knew Portuguese, and a few could even speak African languages, most content had to be translated by one of the trainees.[65] The very act of "translation" and retranslation" thus limited the ability of the Soviets to control meaning.

Such a sense of control was even more true of the Cape Verdeans who arrived at Skhodnia in 1968. These were people with high levels of education and wide-ranging experiences in Portugal, China, Cuba, and the Soviet Union. Pedro Pires recalled that when he went to the Soviet Union, he had already well-formed ideas about social justice, independence, and the need for the liquidation of colonialism.[66] Meanwhile, Silvino da Luz had gone for training to China, where he was inspired by the Chinese revolution and its model of peasant-based rebellion.[67] Júlio Carvalho was impressed by the Cuban revolution he was able to observe "in action" during his time there.

> On one hand, we lived nearly every episode of the hard fight in Cuba, even the tensest moments with the United States; on the other, the Cuban Revolution itself: in the fields of education, health, production and in the areas of security organization, military training, homeland defence, etc. For us, that was like an open compendium.[68]

[63] Mane, 2019.
[64] Da Matta, 2019; Badganny, 2019.
[65] Badganny, 2019.
[66] Pedro Pires, 2017.
[67] Da Luz, 2017.
[68] Carvalho, 2018.

Once at Skhodnia, they continued studying politics, but opted out of compulsory political classes.[69] The Cape Verdeans thus already had a great sense of intellectual autonomy; and it is not clear how much their time in the USSR shaped their opinions.

Overall, the aims of the Soviet training program coincided with the modernizing ethos of the PAIGC leadership. By participating in the daily rituals of European modernity and military hierarchy, young recruits had no choice but to start thinking in terms of a nation-state. They thus had to be "civilized" in order to abandon the colonial mindset and embrace new realities. The first preliminary discussion of trainees' experiences in Perevalnoe shows that many were indeed impressed with the socialist experiment and drew parallels between their own struggle and that of the Soviets in World War II. However, the unique Soviet influence is difficult to decipher in this case. In fact, most trainees arrived at the camp with their own experiences of colonialism, as well as ideas about the benefits of socialism, as propagated by Cabral. Once in the camp, their "political education" continued to be shaped by the agenda of the PAIGC, with senior commanders often acting as "translators" and "interpreters" of meaning. Nonetheless, it does seem that the "cultural events"—such as the film screenings, the experiences of "lived socialism" through sightseeing tours, and the informal discussions with Soviet instructors—solidified for many notions of the USSR as a champion of the anti-colonial and anti-imperialist cause, that the PAIGC had first encouraged via instruction given to young recruits in the bush.

Conclusion

The space of the "training camp" at Perevalnoe and Skhodnia was a co-constructed space in both a practical and a metaphysical sense. Although the training camp was constructed according to the rules of the Soviet military hierarchy, the program itself was shaped by the aims of Cabral's modernizing project. Like the Soviets, Cabral saw himself as training modern men who would not only learn practical skills but also attain the requisite level of political consciousness in relation to his revolutionary project. Far removed from the everyday realities of war and survival in Guinea-Bissau, training in the USSR was supposed to provide recruits with an ideal educational experience, where soldiers could grow and develop. The spaces were also co-constructed because both the military and the political training program were shaped by the needs of the war in Guinea-Bissau, with senior PAIGC figures acting as "retranslators" of Soviet terms and concepts. In fact, many trainees who came to the camps were not the "empty vessels" that some Soviet instructors imagined them to be. They were often young men with their own ideas and experiences, including some political instruction they had received from senior peers in the bush or in other socialist countries.

What united most of the men who went for training in the USSR was their appreciation of Soviet military technology and its contribution to liberation. The Vietnam War was crucial to the ways these men saw the Soviet Union. These young

---

[69] Da Luz, 2017.

men of high status within the PAIGC definitely saw themselves as the active subjects of their own liberation. The more highly educated, and thus higher status, trainees saw themselves as autonomous subjects with the capacity to shape the content of the political discussions and wield a degree of control over their physical environment. In fact, they believed they were co-creators of their own spaces, picking what served best from the menu of Soviet military experience. The desire to emphasize one's own agency comes through in many interviews with former trainees. Pedro Pires summarizes such feelings thus:

> The Soviets were our allies in this struggle, given that they provided us with the means and trained our people, but the fundamental objective was ours, it wasn't the Soviets'. We weren't Soviet agents, as the story goes. We were actors of our independence and we were going to get the means wherever they were, because those who were against us and ruled our country were going to take them wherever they pleased as well.[70]

The voices of these elite soldiers often exercise control over the historical record, and they do dominate the narrative in this chapter. However, the comparative study of training sites in Perevalnoe and Skhodnia starts to reveal how these programs differed from each other, and the power disparities that came with them. While the high-status soldiers who went to Skhodnia for artillery training may have shared in the values of the training program, we lack the perspective of thousands of "common" soldiers, many of them from Guinea-Bissau, who filled up the barracks at Perevalnoe each year from 1965 until 1974. As we know, Perevalnoe was the one training site where Soviet hierarchies were visible for some to see. We have yet to find out if they were able to co-construct the spaces of the training camp to the same extent as their higher-status comrades had done. We also have yet to find out whether they shared the modernizing imperative to the same degree, or in the same way, as their hosts. Given the history of long-standing tensions among men with origins in Cape Verde and Guinea-Bissau, we are yet to discover how much (if at all) the military training camps became sites of conflict and dissent among African soldiers. A further examination of the training camps could lead to fruitful new insights not only into the ways the Soviets interacted with Global South subjects, but also into the dynamics of anti-colonial movements, whose politics and culture often developed in "un-national" spaces such as the training camp.

---

[70] Pedro Pires, 2017.

9

The Hospital: Uncomfortable Proximities—Romania's "One Nation Hospital" in Gharyan, 1974–1985

Bogdan C. Iacob

In early 1974, fresh from a tour of Libya, Lebanon, Syria, and Iraq, Nicolae Ceaușescu, the general secretary of the Romanian Communist Party, informed his ministers that "relations with developing countries were vital for Romania."[1] Ceaușescu assigned multiple functions to the expansion of relations with the so-called Third World: enabling Romania to assert independence from the great powers (especially the United States and the USSR, but also China, Great Britain, and sometimes France); bolstering the Romanian leader's credentials as proponent of cooperation among small and medium-size states founded on political equality, mutual benefit, and anti-imperialism; and providing access to the natural resources and economic benefits made available by decolonization.[2] Countries in the Middle East and North Africa were particularly appealing to Romania because of the "petrodollars" made available through the first oil shock of 1973. At the time, these countries implemented ambitious infrastructure programs and were willing to pay for them in either hard currency or valuable raw materials (e.g., oil) or, sometimes, both.[3] Ceaușescu emphasized that Romania's

---

I would like to acknowledge the generous support of the Hungarian National Research, Development and Innovation Office (Grant no. NN 115711, 2015–2018) as well as Dora Vargha's and Jill Massino's insightful comments during the various stages of writing the chapter.

[1] "Stenograma ședinței Comitetului Executiv al CC al PCR," February 22, 1974 (Arhivele Naționale Istorice Centrale), CC (Comitetul Central) al PCR (Partidului Comunist Român), Cancelarie 13/1974 (Romania), 43. Until the late 1960s, Romania ranked second to last among countries in the socialist camp, after Bulgaria, in terms of the numbers of specialists in decolonized states or experts at international organizations. Bogdan C. Iacob, "From Africa to the World: Romania's Global Turn in the 1970s," *Studii și materiale de istorie contemporană* 19 (2019): 149–62.

[2] Cezar Stanciu, "Romania and the Third World during the Heyday of the Détente," *Third World Quarterly* 39.10 (2018): 1883–98; Elena Dragomir, "The Perceived Threat of Hegemonism in Romania during the Second Détente," *Cold War History* 12.1 (2012): 111–34; Roham Alvandi and Eliza Gheorghe, "The Shah's Petro-Diplomacy with Ceaușescu: Iran and Romania in the era of Détente," *Cold War International History Project Working Paper Series* 47 (2014): 1–11; Colin Lawson, "National Independence and Reciprocal Advantages: The Political Economy of Romanian–South Relations," *Soviet Studies* 35.3 (1983): 362–75.

[3] Thomas Barnett, *Romanian and East German Policies in the Third World: Comparing Strategies of Ceaușescu and Honecker* (London, 1992), 36.

newfound commitment in the region would be defined by a spirit of solidarity and equality between partners. In Libya, Syria, and Iraq, he warned officials back home, local populations were apprehensive of foreigners because of their past exploitation by Europeans. Romanians had "to break that wall," as he put it, and gain the trust of their prospective hosts by engaging in mutually beneficial endeavors.[4] Despite exacerbated cost-benefit concerns since the mid-1960s, Romania, along with other socialist states, dressed up assistance to the Global South in tropes of local empowerment. This model of partnership was strikingly similar to what during the 1980s became known among aid agencies and international organizations as "participatory development." Socialist officials stressed "the correctness" of such endeavors and "the importance of shared responsibility."[5] The Romanian–Libyan encounter was to be an example of the mutually beneficial effects of collaborating with the shared goal of avoiding dependency on either the great powers or Western financial interests.

The Romanian idea of bilateralism as the consolidation of the two partners' political and economic independence was well received by Arab states, Libya in particular. During the first high-profile visit to Bucharest of a delegation of the new revolutionary government in Tripoli, Abdel Salam Jalloud, the Libyan Minister of the Economy, praised the Romanian socialist regime for its "policy of independence," which, he argued, brought the two countries together in global politics.[6] In 1974, the same year as Ceaușescu's first trip to Tripoli, Libya's director of public health laboratories visited Romania and confided to his counterpart in Bucharest that he preferred cooperation with "small states that pursue negotiations on the basis of equality." For him, exchanges "with great powers are disadvantageous because they are always undercut by political pressure [and are] followed by unwanted political and economic engagements."[7]

One way to "break the wall" between Romanians and Libyans was for Bucharest to provide healthcare assistance. Libya's capacity to pay for that assistance in hard currency made it an attractive partner to all socialist states. It also helped that Libya's ruler, Colonel Muammar al-Gaddafi, was then one of the most prominent and radical voices on the global anti-imperial front. This combination of economic and political interests transformed Libya into an epicenter of socialist trade, in general, and of Eastern European medical transfers to the Global South in particular. In Libya, thousands of healthcare workers from the East mingled with Western and postcolonial personnel (from Egypt, Iraq, India, Pakistan, and the Philippines) in a complex space of competing claims of supporting the modernization of healthcare.[8] The everyday proximity of large numbers of Romanians to Libyans delivered a cultural shock that fundamentally

---

[4] "Stenograma ședinței," Cancelarie 13/1974, 44.
[5] Eva Spies, "Dilemmas of Participation: Developers and the Problem of Doing the Right Thing," in Johannes Paulmann (ed.), *Dilemmas of Humanitarian Aid in the Twentieth Century* (Oxford, 2016), 417–35.
[6] "Stenograma întâlnirii dintre Nicolae Ceaușescu și Abdel Salam Jalloud," March 8, 1972, ANIC, CC al PCR, Relații Externe, 14/1972, 3.
[7] "Vizita dr. Mahomed Mabrouk El-Hageh," November 8–12, 1974, MS (Ministerul Sănătății)-DCCPI (Direcția Coordonare, Control Personal și Învățământ)-Libia 41/1974 (Romania), 5.
[8] Telegrama no. 068876, Ambasada României în Tripoli, December 4, 1983, MAE (Ministerul Afacerilor Externe)-Libia 1200/1983 (Romania), 1.

altered the nature of this East–South encounter. Officially, Libya and Romania were brought together by anti-imperialist solidarity and the common goal of defending their independence. However, the dynamics of this bilateralism chipped away at the image of a relationship premised on equality and mutual respect.

The One Nation Hospital

Socialist states had been founding and staffing hospitals in postcolonial contexts since the late 1940s and, in most cases, locals would comprise the majority of the staff or else the personnel was multinational.[9] Beginning in the 1970s, in Libya, Ethiopia,[10] or Nicaragua,[11] a new type of organization came about, just as the numbers of professionals from Eastern Europe in the Global South increased exponentially: the "one nation hospital." A consultant with the World Health Organization (WHO) defined this institution as a medical space where "the professional staff all come from the same country, can communicate freely with each other and, having been trained in the same country, can more readily fit into an agreed pattern of work." He went on to note that "this system eliminates many difficulties which affect the efficiency and morale of the hospital."[12]

One example was a brand-new, very modern hospital in Gharyan in the northwest part of Libya. Built by Bulgarians and opened on April 11, 1975, the institution was under Romanian medical administration until 1985. This chapter uses a diverse range of sources to explore this case: staff reports to the Romanian Ministry of Health, telegrams from Romania's embassy in Tripoli, Libyan–Romanian official correspondence, minutes of the Romanian Communist Party's (RCP) Central Committee, documents from the Romanian secret police archive, as well as World Health Organization (WHO) collections. Unfortunately, the author did not have acess to documents from the Libyan side.

The chapter analyzes the hospital in Gharyan as a living organism[13] that tested the limits of Romanian–Libyan bilateralism as well as the Romanians' claim to be bringing socialist modernity to a postcolonial context. It zooms into this local site and focuses on the individuals populating it. It connects this micro-history to macro-processes such as Romania's engagement with the Global South, the debt crisis, the WHO's policies in the developing world, and the problems of late socialism. The chapter therefore proposes a

---

[9] Young-Sun Hong, *Cold War Germany, the Third World, and the Global Humanitarian Regime* (New York, 2015), 129.
[10] Iris Borowy, "Medical Aid, Repression, and International Relations: The East German Hospital at Metema," *Journal of the History of Medicine and Allied Sciences* 71.1 (2015): 64–92.
[11] Iris Borowy, "East German Medical Aid to Nicaragua: The Politics of Solidarity between Biomedicine and Primary Health Care," *História, Ciências, Saúde-Manguinhos* 24.2 (2017): 411–28.
[12] Alexander Hutchinson, "Assignment Report: The Organization of the Health Services in the Libyan Arab Republic, 13 April to 17 November 1975," LIY-SHS-001, WHO (World Health Organization) 22.0338 (Geneva), 8.
[13] Laurinda Abreu and Sally Sheard, "Introduction," in Laurinda Abreu and Sally Sheard (eds.), *Hospital Life: Theory and Practice from the Medieval to the Modern* (Frankfurt am Main, 2013), 1.

social history in transnational perspective.¹⁴ It analyzes multiple spatial levels rooted in the hospital's overlapping and contrasting meanings for medical workers, Romanian and Libyan officials, WHO experts, and, in mediated fashion, for the local population.

Politics, medical or everyday life practices, and cultural norms were intertwined and entangled at the hospital in Gharyan. It was a space co-constructed by Romanian and Libyan actors (along with nationals of other states). The importance of this "one nation hospital" grew since the success or failure of the institution affected more lucrative infrastructural contracts, which mattered greatly to the government in Bucharest, always searching for hard currency and oil imports. Hospitals such as the one in Gharyan were central to Muammar Gaddafi's social contract, which was based on universal access to healthcare, a comprehensive network of medical institutions, and the creation of specialized national cadres.¹⁵ Gharyan was a space where the legitimacy of Romania's healthcare system and Libya's modernization came under scrutiny. The hospital was not a "gift," as had been the case with other socialist health transfers to the Global South,¹⁶ but the result of a contractual relationship, and its fate mirrored Bucharest's engagement with the decolonized world. The hospital opened in 1975, the year that Romania began a two-year term as non-permanent member of the UN Security Council; it expanded until 1979 just as the communist regime pushed to consolidate and diversify relations with the Global South. By the beginning of the 1980s, the hospital's tribulations reflected Romania's growing domestic problems, exacerbated by its debt crisis and its negative trade balance with the developing world.¹⁷ By 1985, the Romanian presence in Gharyan had become nearly irrelevant just as Romania's image as beacon for "the militant alliance of all those who fight for independence"¹⁸ against the great powers and international finance was fading.

Because of the large number of Romanians who worked there, the hospital was also a socialist microcosm in Libya defined by the rules and practices of the regime at home. Gharyan was a lived space where the abstractions of Romanian–Libyan cooperation became concrete, where socialist life-worlds clashed with postcolonial ones, and where multiple hierarchies of power became entangled. Hundreds of Romanian healthcare professionals were immersed in a political, social, and economic milieu that constantly stretched the limits of individual and collective self-representations as well as those of the postcolonial "other." Gender and labor relations, conceptualizations of tradition, visions of medical modernity, patterns of consumption, or the management of space and intersubjectivity subverted tropes of solidarity as well as Romania's claims to civilizational superiority.

---

[14] Bernhard Struck, Kate Ferris, and Jacques Revel, "Introduction: Space and Scale in Transnational History," *International History Review* 33.4 (2011): 573–84.
[15] Saskia Van Genugten, *Libya in Western Foreign Policies, 1911–2011* (London, 2016), 110.
[16] Ruth Prince, "From Russia with Love: Medical Modernities, Development Dreams, and Cold War Legacies in Kenya, 1969 and 2015," *Africa: The Journal of the International African Institute* 90.1 (2020): 51–76; Dora Vargha, "Technical Assistance and Socialist International Health: Hungary, the WHO and the Korean War," *History and Technology* 36.3–4 (2020): 400–17.
[17] Robert Weiner, *Romanian Foreign Policy and the United Nations* (New York, 1984), 120; Barnett, *Romanian*, 76–7.
[18] Ceaușescu during his meeting in Lusaka with Zambian president Kenneth David Kaunda on March 23, 1972. See ANIC, Fond CC al PCR, Relații Externe, 23/1972, 22.

The Hospital 181

Contradictions of Bilateral Space

According to Romanian officials in 1976, the hospital in Gharyan was "well equipped with the latest medical technology, a cafeteria and modern sanitary installations ... it is well stocked with medicines from the most important Western brands and from Bulgaria, Yugoslavia, or Hungary." "Comfortable and affordable" housing for the staff stood close to the institution. Working and living conditions were considered excellent "if one takes into account that the salaries are very good, food and appliances are of high quality ... at affordable prices."[19] The first group of Romanians to work in the new hospital in Gharyan praised its facilities, comparing it with the old one in the town, which they deemed inappropriate for medical practice. It symbolized a new medical beginning for the region brought about by socialist expertise, a departure from its colonial past and contrasting starkly with the antiquated hospital the Italian occupation authorities had built in the course of the 1920s.[20] Libya was also a site of medical modernity because of the influx of petrodollars. One Romanian expert wrote in 1979 that the country had "the best medicine in the world, for all diseases."[21] Sometimes the personnel sent back home medicines hard to find in Romania.

The location of the institution was, however, a challenge. In 1973, the region in which it was situated only had four old, badly equipped, small hospitals. It had the fifth lowest number of hospital beds among Libya's ten provinces, yet was also the third largest in terms of territory.[22] When the "one nation hospital" opened in Gharyan two years later, with a stationary treatment unit of 250 beds (in the 1980s it grew to 300), it reflected the central government's ambitious modernization plans; its success or failure would affect the legitimacy of Gaddafi's regime. Romanians opted for Gharyan because it was only 100 kilometres from Tripoli, which ensured that the group was not too far from the embassy (easier to control) and that it was not isolated in the desert. Generally speaking, socialist governments preferred to send medical teams to cities and towns that were close to either Tripoli or Libya's littoral—that is, to comparatively accessible, better-off regions. This reflected a growing focus in Eastern European healthcare during the 1970s on urban spaces at the expense of rural areas both at home and in relations with the Global South.[23]

Romanian–Libyan bilateralism in Gharyan underscored the tension between the official script of mutually advantageous relations and perceptions on the ground rooted in the interactions between the nationals of the two countries. Gharyan may have been better off and more accessible than other possible locations, but it did nonetheless elicit derogatory civilizational comparisons among Romanian observers. One surgeon

---

[19] "Raport privind activitatea delegației Ministerului Sănătății care a vizitat Libia," February 19 to March 1, 1976, MS-DCCPI-Relații Externe 2/1984, 11–12.
[20] "Informare," February 13, 1976, MS-Libia dosar personal no. 27/D.V, 1–2.
[21] "Jurnalul tatălui," http://www.terteci.ro/?p=7310.
[22] Amin Haddad, "Assignment Report: Pharmacy Education in Libya, 25 March–2 April 1973," LIY-HMD-004, WHO 22.0335, Annex I, 1.
[23] Michael Kaser, *Health Care in the Soviet Union and Eastern Europe* (London, 1976); Randall Packard, *A History of Global Health: Interventions into the Lives of Other Peoples* (Baltimore, 2016), 232.

Figure 9.1 A dirt road between newly-built apartment buildings in the town of Gharyan, 1979. Courtesy of Getty Images.

described the town in 1978 as "a dirty township, scattered across the hills with narrow, winding streets littered with numerous traders' shacks that displayed foodstuffs hanging at the entrance covered in dust and flies ... There is a main road, with asphalt here and there, where only now a few apartment buildings are built."[24] In his view, Gharyan could best be compared with a poor town from Romania's pre-socialist past—an inference of the superiority of contemporary Romania over the postcolonial locale.

Once the Romanian group had begun its activities in Gharyan, the negotiations with the Libyan Ministry of Health broadened: Libyan authorities proposed other locations for medical take-over only for the government in Bucharest to prove incapable of expanding its footprint in the country. The central hospital in Zliten (180 km from Tripoli) was targeted, but by 1977 the Romanian side failed to recruit enough personnel; Polish doctors and nurses took over the institution. Other locations were offered over the years, but ultimately, the Romanians limited themselves to Gharyan. The Romanian presence remained scarce in other places (e.g., a polyclinic in Tripoli).

Another means of expanding healthcare bilateralism in Gharyan involved training local personnel in Romania. Initially, Libyan medical workers sent to Romania for specialization came from Gharyan. This policy improved the skills of Libyan auxiliary personnel aiding the Romanians and gave them the opportunity to learn Romanian. By November 1979, the program brought to Romania twenty-two auxiliary cadres

---

[24] E.A., "Informare," September 10, 1978, ACNSAS (Arhiva Consiliul Național pentru Studierea Arhivelor Securității), D11273/5 (Romania), 56.

(medical technicians or laboratory workers from all over Libya) who attended courses for two years with all expenses paid by the Libyan state.[25] It reinforced the teacher-pupil hierarchy that represented one facet of the Romanian–Libyan encounter. That same year, during a meeting in Bucharest of the Communist Party's Central Committee, an economic expert described Romania's mission in the developing world as a "commitment to helping [the locals] understand what they have to do and what to begin with."[26] This idea of teaching less developed peoples how to modernize was a long-standing feature of socialist (and for that matter Global North) medical exports to postcolonial spaces.

According to the original contract, the Romanian group in Gharyan was supposed to comprise 108 medical workers (in 1974); the target figure grew to 150 (1976), then to 325 (1981).[27] The drive to increase personnel originated with the hospital's first director, who by winter 1974 had convinced Libyan authorities to request forty-two additional cadres from Bucharest. In a harshly phrased letter to the ambassador in Tripoli, the Romanian Minister of Health complained about constantly ballooning personnel requests. He reminded the diplomat that according to Romanian legislation for "a hospital such as the one in Gharyan, the functioning standards [in Romania] require fourteen doctors and forty-eight mid-level sanitary workers"[28]—far lower numbers than those requested by the Libyan government. The minister considered that a "developing country" should not have more personnel per hospital than in an "modern" socialist society. What he overlooked was that the Libyan authorities perceived the hospital in Gharyan to be a healthcare hub for the entire region: Romanian personnel also served the population beyond the town limits, being expected to travel to surrounding rural areas, so as to substitute for the weak local medical infrastructure.

In fact, Gharyan was a space that reflected the dynamics of expertise shortage in Romania itself. During the entire period when Romanians alone operated the hospital, the government in Bucharest was not able to cover even two-thirds of the personnel chart. In 1978, one Romanian official had a panic attack during negotiations with his Libyan peers, as he desperately tried to find a balance between Tripoli's requests and what was needed at home.[29] The reaction signaled the conflict between the RCP's commitment to obtaining maximum profit from Libya and the Romanian side's difficulties in meeting personnel quotas set by the two governments. This state of permanent personnel scarcity affected the prestige and the morale of the Romanian medical workers. In 1982, a telegram sent by the embassy of Romania in Tripoli described the staff of the hospital in Gharyan as "exhausted, ill and depressed."[30]

---

[25] "Referat," November 4, 1979, MS-DCCPI Relații Externe 35/1980, 6.
[26] "Protocol nr. 8 al ședinței Comitetului Politic Executiv," April 27, 1979, ANIC, CC al PCR, Cancelarie 32/1979, 25.
[27] Though impressive, these numbers pale in comparison with the Polish (1986, 1,400 people) or Yugoslav (1981, 800 people, but in 1977 the figure had been much higher) presence in Libya.
[28] "Radu Păun, ministrul sănătății către ambasadorul României în Tripoli," June 4, 1976, MS-Relații Internaționale 7/1977, 5.
[29] Sursa "Gariana," "Notă informativă," August 21, 1978, ACNSAS, D11273/5, 61verso.
[30] Telegrama no. 068559, Ambasada României în Tripoli, February 2, 1982, MAE-Libia 1506/1982, 7.

The Romanian authorities were unable to control the terms and dynamics of medical assistance to Libya. The story of this relationship is mostly one of frustration on both sides, but frustration that never quite boiled over into a total withdrawal of the Romanian team. The authorities in Bucharest became desperate for hard currency and Tripoli faced the gargantuan task of staffing its sprawling network of medical facilities under circumstances of scant numbers of local personnel. In May 1981, bilateral negotiations set a quota of 106 doctors in the hospital, but only forty-eight actually worked in Gharyan. There were supposed to be 217 mid-level practitioners, of whom only 166 were actually present.[31] The situation looked increasingly dire when entire cohorts completed their two-year contracts. If they were to leave before the Romanian government sent replacements, the functioning of entire sections of the hospital would break down. The Libyan authorities decided in mid-1976 not to allow the departure of those whose contracts expired until they had been replaced by similarly qualified experts. The tensions and operational difficulties caused by the dwindling personnel got so bad that in March 1982 the interim director of the hospital suffered a heart attack. At the time he was also serving as director of the polyclinic and the laboratory of the institution.[32] That same year, Libyan officials' refusal to release the incumbent Romanian medical team upon the completion of their contracts was labeled by the authorities in Bucharest as "sequestering" its citizens, an infringement of their constitutional rights and a breach of international law.[33]

The insufficient personnel in Gharyan was also ill-prepared for life in Libya. Romanian doctors were trained for two weeks at the Ștefan Gheorghiu Party School, an institution in Bucharest responsible for the ideological education of leading cadres of the Romanian party-state. Nurses were given only one day of pre-orientation, a reflection of the in-built inequalities of the system between white- and blue-collar work. Medical workers volunteered for jobs overseas, which were coveted because of the opportunity to travel and earn significantly more money than at home, and they were thoroughly vetted at county, party, and governmental levels. However, the ministry did not inform the teams that, though on paper accommodation was provided by Libyan regional authorities, the latter's offer was limited, and the Romanians would need to find their own housing. No fewer than thirty medical staff lived on the hospital premises in 1981, while in other locations three or four families shared a kitchen and a bathroom. Libyan officials' inability to make good on their accommodation promises was invoked by the authorities in Bucharest to justify the non-fulfillment of the contract's personnel quota.[34] Poor housing along with difficult weather, culture shock, and a demanding work schedule sometimes led medical workers to request a return to Romania only a few months into their two-year contracts.[35] Others refused to return to

---

[31] "Notă deplasare în Libia a unei delegații pentru negocierea creșterii retribuției personalului medical român și prelungirea contractului colectiv," May 26, 1981, MS-DCCPI Relații Externe 2/1984, 1.
[32] Telegrama no. 068599, Ambasada României în Tripoli, March 9, 1982, MAE-Libia 1506/1982, 9.
[33] "Romconsult către Ambasada României în Tripoli," May 22, 1982, MAE-Libia 1506/1982, 16.
[34] "Ministerul Sănătății către Ambasada României în Tripoli," December 30, 1980, MAE-Libia 1228/1981, 1.
[35] "Notă a ministrului-adjunct al sănătății," April 21, 1975, MS-DCCPI Relații Externe 1977/13, 1.

Gharyan after their paid holidays had ended. A WHO report noted in 1975 the "rapid turnover among the expatriate health personnel."³⁶ The problems that plagued Gharyan reflected a more general failure to adapt on the part of socialist health workers in Libya.

Another source of conflict was the fact that though the personnel was assigned certain wages in the collective contract of the "national team," upon reaching Gharyan, they received, sometimes after lengthy delays, individual contracts with terms and conditions different from their initial appointments, which meant lower salaries paid late. Throughout the existence of the "one nation hospital," Romanian officials failed to curb this practice, which produced payment backlogs on the Libyan side. Local authorities penalized individuals for early or sudden terminations of contract by refusing to remunerate them for the time they had worked in the hospital or, if a position had been filled more than twice in four years, by cutting bonuses of the entire group. From 1979, paid holidays were granted only upon the completion of the contract and after replacements had arrived.³⁷

Imbalances in the Romanian healthcare system had repercussions in Gharyan too. Among socialist countries, Romania had the lowest ratio of physicians to auxiliary personnel. Moreover, nurses and medical assistants lacked experience in the specializations and sections to which they were assigned. By 1982, Libyan authorities started to complain that the hospital was lacking "the majority of specialized physicians" it needed, which hampered the functioning of entire wards. That same year, of the fifty-two files submitted by Romania's Ministry of Health to Tripoli, only five featured specialized physicians;³⁸ there were no experts in infectious diseases, orthopaedics, ophthalmology, and gynaecology.³⁹ Three years later, Libyan officials bitterly remarked that in Gharyan, from the standpoint of doctors' contributions to the hospital, the Romanian activity "is close to zero."⁴⁰

The government in Tripoli compensated for the shortages in Romanian personnel by hiring professionals of other nationalities. In 1982, there were thirteen non-Romanian physicians (from Egypt, Iraq, Pakistan, the Philippines, or Palestinians).⁴¹ Reactions to the presence of foreigners in a medical institution supposedly run exclusively by Romanians varied. Some employee reports tell of fruitful cooperation; others complain about an alleged lack of professionalism. In 1980 the Ministry of Health unambiguously stated that "the employment of medical cadres of other nationalities in leadership positions ... without consulting the Romanian side ... causes moral damage to Romanian personnel. [Because of this] one can even notice the tendency among some cadres to interrupt their contracts and return home."⁴² The presence of foreign personnel among the Romanian staff called into question the very ability of the Romanians to implement their modernizing mission.

³⁶ Hutchinson, "Assignment," 2.
³⁷ "Aide-Mémoire," July 22, 1980, MS-DCCPI Relații Externe 2/1982, 1-2.
³⁸ Telegrama no. 068523, Ambasada României în Tripoli, January 11, 1982, MAE-Libia 1506/1982, 2.
³⁹ Telegrama no. 068709, Ambasada României în Tripoli, June 17, 1982, MAE-Libia 1506/1982, 20-1.
⁴⁰ Telegrama no. 069027, Ambasada României în Tripoli, January 27, 1985, MAE-Libia 895/1985, 3.
⁴¹ "Notă de convorbire: întalnire cu delegația Secretariatului Sănătății din Libia," July 14, 1983, MS-DCCPI Relații Externe 2/1984, 4.
⁴² "Aide-Mémoire," July 22, 1980, MS-DCCPI Relații Externe 2/1982, 1-2.

In 1985, there were only 180 Romanian medical workers in Gharyan out of the 310 stipulated by the contract. Among them was a meagre seventeen doctors, mostly generalists.[43] There are three explanations for this outcome. First, there was not much enthusiasm at the local level in Romania for assigning medical personnel to Libya. The Ministry of Health complained that the county health departments and hospitals were guilty of negligence in failing to provide Bucharest with a constant flow of candidates. Second, the difficult living conditions in Gharyan combined with delays in payment of wages tempered initial enthusiasm among medical professionals. Furthermore, Romanian workers abroad had a large chunk of their salaries appropriated by the state. In the case of the staff in Gharyan, 60% of their wages was paid in convertible currency directly to a government account at the Commercial Bank in Bucharest, while a fluctuating quota of the rest was deposited at the embassy in Libyan dinars. The embassy used this money to pay for its expenses and upon their return home the medical workers never recovered these sums in full. As Romania's debt crisis worsened, control over the inflow of hard currency became stricter. While the approach of the government in Bucharest was harsher than the practice of other socialist countries, it was by no means atypical: the government in Havana did not disclose to its experts in Angola that half of their wages were paid in dollars by the local government.[44]

The third reason for the staffing problems was that control over personnel grew increasingly draconian as the Romanian regime's domestic security fears intensified. In 1983, the embassy in Tripoli was instructed by the Ministry of Foreign Affairs to withhold the passports of the Romanian doctors and nurses during their stay in Libya.[45] There were indeed defections in Libya, but fewer than in Algeria or Morocco, where it was easier to flee to France or Spain.[46] Furthermore, by the late 1970s there was a dramatic drop in the number of graduates (in ratio to the overall rise in population) from Romanian medical schools—another sign of the economic crisis affecting the country as investment in higher education was curtailed.[47] The last straw perhaps was the gradual worsening of relations between Romania and Libya: as Tripoli suffered an economic downturn from 1981 onwards, Romania failed to fulfill its contracts in multiple fields, losing out to competition from the socialist camp, the postcolonial world, or the West.[48]

---

[43] Telegrama no. 069236, Ambasada României in Tripoli, June 26, 1985, MAE-Libia 895/1985.
[44] Christine Hatzky, "Cubans in Angola: Internationalist Solidarity, Transfers and Interactions in the Global South 1975–91," in Sandra Bott et al. (eds.), *Neutrality and Neutralism in the Global Cold War. Between or Within the Blocs?* (London, 2016), 205.
[45] "Ministerul Sănătății către Ambasada României în Tripoli," December 21, 1983, MAE-Libia 1200/1983, 24.
[46] "Extras din nota U.M.0195 nr. 00571250/30.03.1979 referitoare la 'acțiuni întreprinse în străinătate împotriva constructorilor și cooperanților români,'" Ministerul de Interne, Departamentul Securității Statului, Direcția I, no. 154/VG/0075952, April 5, 1979, ACNSAS, D11273/5, 2.
[47] Valentin Maier, "Foreign Students Enrolled in the Medicine and Pharmacy Higher Education in Romania (1975–1989)," *Clujul Medical* 89.2 (2016): 307–12.
[48] Aurel Turbăceanu, *Întâlnire cu trecutul. Din amintirile unui ambasador în Golful Arab* (București, 2006), 200.

Socialist Microcosm

The hospital in Gharyan was a site of socialist everyday life—a space where ethical and political codes imposed by the regime in Bucharest were adapted and acted upon by Romanian citizens in Libya. Their distancing from norms at home was limited, a sign of the degree to which Romanian socialism as a lived system structured the lives of its representatives overseas. Daily interactions were constantly evaluated from the standpoint of preserving and enhancing the group's prestige and morale. Breaches of professional and interpersonal conduct were labeled subversions of the very mission entrusted by Bucharest to its medical ambassadors in Libya. Officials at the Ministry of Health and the hospital's leadership desperately sought to ensure a "healthy atmosphere" that highlighted socialist superiority and preserved the efficiency of medical bilateralism.

In 1976, there were 127 Romanians at the hospital, of whom thirty-four had higher education (thirty doctors, three pharmacists, and one biologist) and ninety-three were mid-level (i.e., medical assistants, nurses, technicians) and maintenance workers. The gender distribution was fifty men (physicians and auxiliary personnel) and seventy-seven women, mostly nurses.[49] Despite the growing presence of women in the medical profession in Romania, the majority of doctors in Gharyan were male.[50] Since the 1970s, the government in Bucharest had channeled women into jobs deemed by the state to be compatible with "feminine qualities"—in the case of healthcare, the capacity for caregiving. However, this "re-gendering from above"[51] also applied to the decision-making hierarchies of the profession: women had lower-ranking and lower-paid positions, working as pediatricians, general practitioners, and dermatologists rather than as surgeons.[52] Indeed, in the hospital in Gharyan none of the surgeons were women, and the few female doctors worked in the three above-mentioned fields. Another explanation for the gender imbalance among physicians in Libya was the Romanian officials' belief that management responsibilities in (sub)tropical countries were too demanding for women's health—a conclusion reached as early as 1966, when a group of five physicians (one woman among them) was sent to Conakry, Guinea.[53]

Reflecting the situation at home, the Romanian medical team in Gharyan was officially enrolled in politics in some form or another (seventy-eight were party members, forty-six were either members of the Communist Youth Union or trade unionists), and this meant coupling professional with ideological accountability. There were twenty-five families—couples who worked in the hospital or personnel that had brought their spouses and/or children with them. The remaining eighty-six individuals in Libya were either without their families or were single. Both Romania and Libya

---

[49] "Raport privind activitatea," 12.
[50] Luciana Jinga, *Gen și reprezentare în România comunistă: femeile în cadrul Partidului Comunist Român 1944–1989* (Iași, 2015).
[51] Wendy Goldman, *Women at the Gates: Gender and Industry in Stalin's Russia* (Cambridge, 2009), 155.
[52] Jill Massino, *Ambiguous Transitions: Gender, the State, and Everyday Life in Socialist and Postsocialist Romania* (Oxford, 2019), 151, 178.
[53] "Informare grup specialiști români," February 21, 1966, MAE-Guineea 201/1966, 1–2.

encouraged the employment of married personnel. For the Libyan authorities, employing married staff meant speedier recruitment and less troublesome interpersonal dynamics. For Romanian officials it was a way of ensuring the transfer of socialist family values and, by the same token, a source of additional income, since bonuses for families applied. Moreover, Bucharest was reluctant to approve the appointment of single women for medical missions abroad for fear that the harsh realities overseas might nurture "immoral behavior" that infringed on the Code of Socialist Ethics adopted at the Eleventh Congress of the RCP in 1974, a document outlining the expected conduct of the Romanian citizen.[54] Concerns about immorality seldom applied to men. This traditionalist framing of sexuality reflected the radicalization of the communist regime's paternalism: starting in 1966, the government in Bucharest implemented increasingly draconian legislation that effectively banned abortion and labeled divorce "antisocial."[55]

Gharyan was a heavily gendered space that mirrored the politics and everyday mores of socialism in Romania: misogynistic and disciplinary attitudes among male workers at the institution and officials in Bucharest; and, conservative views about sexuality that contradicted the formal difference between women's socialist emancipation in Romania and their subordination based on religion in Libya. Reports by male (and sometimes female) personnel to either the Ministry of Health or the secret police revealed an obsession with the negative effects of living in Gharyan according to the Romanians' official morality. A gynaecologist was lambasted for her "libertine manifestations" and for "publicly offending her husband"; corrupted, it was said, by assignments abroad, the only solution was for her to return to the national and socialist fold where "with the help of the collective at her old job, she will correct her attitude."[56] In 1975, only four months after Romanians had taken over the hospital, a male surgery assistant complained that female colleagues who had sex with locals "have debased the collective, lowering the prestige that we did our utmost to maintain at the highest level of humaneness, honor and earnestness."[57] A physician suggested to the authorities in Bucharest in June 1977 that "these elements should be recalled immediately ... their behavior drags into the mud the reputation of all Romanian women."[58]

The specter haunting the Romanian presence in Libya was the possibility of "the destruction of [socialist] families."[59] Spouses played a central role in the dynamics of the hospital in Gharyan. They could request that their partners return home if the stay abroad was felt by them to endanger family dynamics. Accusations of prostitution were common, as any form of female non-marital sexual activity, especially if the partner was a foreigner, could be labeled as such. Such prejudice turned into socialist ethics had

---

[54] Massino, *Ambiguous*, 121.
[55] Corina Doboş et al., *Politica pronatalistă a regimului Ceauşescu: Instituţii şi practici* (Iaşi, 2011); Massino, *Ambiguous*, 206–7.
[56] "Adresa Ambasada Romîniei în Tripoli către ministrul sănătăţii," December 16, 1977, MS-DCCPI Relaţii Externe 1975–53, 1.
[57] "Referat," July 29, 1975, MS-Libia, Dosar personal no. 6/G.A., 3.
[58] "Raport," June 8, 1977, MS-Libia Dosar personal no. 4/S.T.S., 4.
[59] E.A., "Informare," September 10, 1978, ACNSAS, 11273/5, 56 verso.

a racial component, as the term "foreigner" referred to Arab men. Back in Romania, a similar language was deployed to reproach women who had relationships with Arab and African students at local universities.[60] The stigma of "immorality" forced two Romania nurses from Gharyan accused of prostitution to defect in 1976 rather than return home.[61] The criminalization of sexuality was an expression of the social and political construction of women's bodies as the property of the state because of their reproductive and care-giving duties. It also echoed the state decree issued in 1970 against "social parasitism" which penalized a broad range of behaviors, styles of dress, and leisure activities deemed by the regime to contradict socialist ethics.[62] The racialization of sexuality reflected the growing suspicion in Bucharest about postcolonial citizens—non-white others threatening the miscegenation of the socialist nation.

The hyper-regulated, punitive environment that framed the Romanian medical staff's presence in Libya fueled mutual distrust and constant denunciation within the group. It was another symptom of late socialist Romania: draconian legislation concerning social life blended with the intensification of surveillance by the secret police through informers among the personnel. This situation fostered a culture of fear and suspicion. Nevertheless, Romanian citizens abroad proved highly adept at deploying the ideological and bureaucratic codes of the regime to negotiate with the party-state. In November 1975, orthopaedist I.D. pleaded with the authorities in Bucharest that his wife, an engineer, be allowed to come to Gharyan. The reasons invoked were personal and contractual: she had obtained the necessary documentation and approvals (but the Ministry of Internal Affairs had not issued her passport); and, I.D.'s two-year contract contained a clause that entitled him to bring dependents to Libya. The spouses' separation was described as anti-socialist because it kept the family apart, thereby creating the possibility of immoral behavior.[63] The wife, C.R.D., considered the non-issuing of her passport an abuse that cast aspersions on her morality and socialist identity: "being a communist ... I know that our daily life must be founded on the Codes of Socialist Ethics. They contain a clause about the role of the family in the healthy development of our socialist society." C.R.D. added that her not being allowed to work in Libya, combined with her husband's inevitable return home, would lead to loss of hard currency for the Romanian state.[64] This skillful appeal to the norms of the regime was successful: in early 1976, I.D. reunited with his wife in Gharyan.

Socialist morality was meant to function in non-professional dealings too. A recurring problem was medical workers' indebtedness to Libyan businessmen. Romanian personnel indulged in a level of consumption that was not possible at home, purchasing electronic appliances, furniture, gold, and other goods that were scarce in

---

[60] Mihai Dinu Gheorghiu et al., "Étudiants d'Afrique en Roumanie et en RDA. Les cadres sociaux et politiques de leurs expériences," in Monique de Saint Martin et al. (eds), *Étudier à l'Est. Expériences de diplômés africains* (Paris, 2015), 106.
[61] "Notă a ministrului-adjunct al sănătății," February 26, 1976, MS-DCCPI Relații Externe 13/1977, 1–2.
[62] Massino, *Ambiguous*, 335.
[63] "I.D. către ministrul sănătății," November 8, 1975, MS-DCCPI Relații Externe, 54/1977, 1.
[64] "R.C.D. către ministrul sănătății," August 26, 1975, MS-DCCPI Relații Externe, 54/1977, 3 and 5–6.

Romania. Buying consumer goods was also a way to invest the money earned in Libya because the socialist regime severely regulated the possession and circulation of hard currency. Indebtedness among the Romanian staff was so widespread that, according to a report of the director in 1979, when large numbers of employees completed their contracts, the police notified the town's traders by megaphone to collect unpaid debts.[65]

Although consumption of this sort was not officially proscribed, it fueled anxiety among officials in Bucharest who feared for the moral fibre of their citizens exposed to a capitalism-tainted society. In 1976, a delegation from the Ministry of Health sent to assess the situation in Gharyan concluded that "a flexible work style" was required in Libya. Personnel had to show "comradely grace, strictly necessary in a world in which the power of money can lead to de-humanization and a person's alienation" from the socialist collective.[66] Officials in Bucharest instructed Romanians to avoid all contact with the local populace outside of work. Most activity reports insist on the absence of interaction with Libyans; Romanian–Libyan relations appear only as departures from "socialist ethics," thereby contradicting the official narrative of friendship based on mutually advantageous cooperation.

The unsocialist features of the postcolonial space perplexed officials in Bucharest, while Romanians in Libya counterbalanced their inability to adapt to this locale by entrenching civilizational hierarchies in the accounts they gave. They were thus able to reassure themselves that professional failures and mismanagement in Gharyan did not interfere with Romanians' self-representation as modernizers of a "developing" people. The local space was often described as being "at a backward stage in culture and civilization"; a leitmotif of various reports was the description of Libyans as only "recently removed [by the state] from their caves."[67] This discourse of superiority sometimes invoked racist tropes. For one surgeon, a Libyan official had "mongoloid eyes," another "had a mug like a Jew, extremely cunning," while the local gold trader "looked like a fox, very slippery."[68]

The medical staff argued that postcolonial conditions were profoundly destabilizing, while local people were lumped into an amorphous group of backward germ carriers with unclean social habits—an environment extremely dangerous for the socialist personnel's morality and health. These Romanian perceptions of Gharyan amounted to a quasi-colonial mindset sustaining European, socialist whites struggling to fulfill their civilizing mission in a region afflicted by widespread clinical and cultural pathologies. Undoubtedly, working conditions were challenging due to the shortage of personnel. However, medical workers' reports are full of descriptions of malaise caused by what they saw as the trauma of isolation from "civilization." Accounts stated that "symptoms of neurosis" set in after only a few months in the staff's contracts.[69]

---

[65] "Scrisoare director P.B. către ministrul sănătății," [undated] MS, Spitalul Garian, 2/1979, 2.
[66] "Raport privind activitatea," 14.
[67] Sursa "Enescu," "Informare," July 21, 1978, Ministerul de Interne, Departamentul Securității Statului, U.M. 0625/C.P., ACNSAS, 11273/5, 67 verso.
[68] E.A., "Informare," September 10, 1978, ACNSAS, 11273/5, 58 verso.
[69] "Raport," March 3, 1976, MS-Libia Dosar Personal/SF, 3; "Scrisoare de la spitalul Garian" [unintelligible signature], February 1, 1977, MS-Libia, IX/C1/78, 1.

Unsocialist behavior was blamed on the perverting effects of Gharyan, which was characterized, according to members of the group, by capitalism, unculturedness, obscurantism, difficult living conditions, and moral turpitude. Depression, ennui, and immorality were the side effects of the stress-based disorders affecting socialist consciousness. Accounts went as far as to mention neurasthenia,[70] a pseudo-illness drawn from the vocabulary of European colonialism designed to explain away "aberrant behaviors and regrettable incidents between natives and Europeans."[71] Such self-diagnosis also reflected the status of neurasthenia as a condition of Eastern European scope. In its socialist meaning, the illness was supposed to reflect the mental stress rooted in the persistence of "bourgeois mentality" within societies engaged in the construction of socialism. In Romania, by the 1970s, the disorder was the most frequently invoked condition for medical leave or work absence.[72] Bringing together the socialist and colonial usages of neurasthenia, I argue that its use in postcolonial contexts signaled that socialist men and women sought to distinguish their Europeanness and self-worth in locales that challenged their representations about "civilization."

Malfunctioning Care

Mistrust between patients and medical staff loomed large at the hospital in Gharyan. Professional failures called into question the very rationale of medical assistance in the service of friendship between the two peoples as well as the Romanians' sense of superiority. Romanian personnel considered Libya "a foreign country with people who are not always welcoming and unable to understand certain facts properly."[73] Chronic understaffing increased the likelihood of malpractice. In April 1975, a surgeon reported that he was the only physician in a ward of seventy beds, a situation, he thought, to "sabotage the country's prestige" made by incompetent officials in Bucharest. He continued, "In my section there are only three mid-level practitioners ... we will fill the empty positions with local personnel, which is of low quality, and it will only hinder us."[74] Some reports mentioned instances of "inadmissible negligence,"[75] "superficiality and lack of care,"[76] which "seriously dented the prestige of the group."[77]

Perhaps the most serious dysfunctionalities at the hospital were in the obstetrics–gynaecology section, which had only two doctors between 1975 and 1977, half of the contractually required number. One physician was fired by the Libyan authorities in June 1976 because a patient died after he failed to track post-surgery symptoms; he

---

[70] L.I., "Informare," ACNSAS, D011723/10, 417.
[71] Anna Greenwood, "The Strange History of Tropical Neurasthenia," *The Psychologist* 24.3 (2011): 227.
[72] Corina Doboș, "Psychiatry and Ideology: The Emergence of 'Asthenic Neurosis' in Communist Romania," in Sarah Marks and Mat Savelli (eds.), *Psychiatry in Communist Europe* (New York, 2015), 93, 103, 107.
[73] "Notă informativă," November 26, 1975, MS-Libia, Dosar personal no. 9/A.D., 2.
[74] "Scrisoare P.P.," April 2, 1975, MS-DCCPI-Libia 27/1974, 1.
[75] "Raport privind activitatea," MS-DCCPI Relații Externe 2/1984, 14.
[76] "Scrisoare către ministrul sănătății," January 25, 1977, MS-Dosare personal Libia no. 4/E.A., 3.
[77] "Raport director I.S.," October 27, 1975, MS-Relații Externe 60/1976, 3.

defected, fearing imprisonment at home. There were three other investigations of suspicious deaths during childbirth that year.[78] Meanwhile, the other Romanian gynecologist, whom the Libyans deemed unsatisfactory and sought to replace, continued at the hospital until March 1978. An acute shortage of specialized nurses prompted the Libyan authorites to bring in Pakistani and Syrian staff to ensure the continuation of medical services.

The reality of the state of Romanian medicine at home had a profound impact on its "one nation hospital" in Libya. In Romania, the field of obstetrics–gynaecology was overstretched and over-politicized because of the regime's ever more draconian anti-abortion policies. The strict control over these professionals reduced the pool of individuals from which the Ministry of Health in Bucharest could select and who might pass the vetting process of the Ministry of Internal Affairs or the RCP's Central Committee. In 1975 and 1976, there were instances when replacements for Gharyan were found but rejected: the reasons remained undisclosed, but a likely explanation was alleged involvement in illegal abortions.

Abortion was a recurrent topic in the reports about the hospital's activity. Though illegal in Libya, the procedure was probably not as policed among expats as among locals. In late 1975, a nurse claimed that the director "imposes on the obstetrics–gynaecology department to perform abortions and he profits from them."[79] In March 1977, the deputy minister of industrial construction requested that the Ministry of Health recall a nurse who, in collaboration with an Iraqi doctor and a Romanian physician, had issued medical certificates for abortions among the wives of the Romanian specialists in Libya (who totaled over 9,000 employed in various infrastructure projects by the end of the decade).[80] At the time, it was extremely difficult to procure an abortion in Romania, so Libya was apparently an overseas alternative, facilitated by the direct flights from Bucharest to Tripoli between 1975 and 1982. The fact that Romanian women went abroad to undergo abortions confirms historian Maria Bucur's argument that pregnancy interruptions were acts of resistance against a state that legislated violence against women in the name of life.[81]

Mirroring the tumultuous situation of the medical field in Romania, the turmoil at the hospital in Gharyan generated a high turnover in its leadership. As we have seen, one director died while employed there. Its first director, I.S., was accused of fostering a noxious atmosphere among the personnel and of showing "a servile" attitude toward the Libyan authorities. The last accusation should not be taken lightly. As Ceaușescu and his cronies intensified nationalism at home, servility to foreigners became a grievous fault for a socialist citizen. I.S. was recalled (probably arrested, though it is unclear from the documents). His replacement, F.D., asked to be relieved of his duties

---

[78] "Scrisoare," January 25, 1977, 3.
[79] I.E., "Informare," February 20, 1975, MS 1976, Plecari Libia 1974–1978, Adeverințe, vol. 58, litera I, 6.
[80] "I.T. către Ministerul Sănătății," March 25, 1977, MS-Relații Externe 24/1977, 1.
[81] Maria Bucur, "Gendering Dissent: Of Bodies and Minds, Survival and Opposition under Communism," in Angela Brintlinger and Natasha Kolchevska (eds.), *Beyond Little Vera: Women's Bodies, Women's Welfare in Russia and Central/Eastern Europe*, Ohio Slavic Papers 7 (Columbus, OH, 2008), 9–26.

The Hospital 193

which, he said, were so burdensome that they were undermining his health. The fourth, I.H., was accused of not dealing with his subordinates from the standpoint of "socialist fairness," unsettling the necessary hierarchies within the hospital's sections.[82] In September 1979, I.H. and his wife left Libya without returning to Romania. The contract of the fifth, P.B., was terminated a year into his tenure; officials in Bucharest complained that he had ignored the requirements of "collective leadership" for "he claimed to be endowed with "absolute" power" and "abusively interpreted directives from home."[83] Only the sixth director, V.M., held his position for a full contract. The leadership of the hospital in Gharyan buckled under the weight of having to showcase Romanian healthcare, while also meeting Libyan requirements and expectations.

Romanians experienced blowback from their Libyan partners, who challenged the hierarchies implicit in the very project of exporting socialist modernity through healthcare bilateralism. Socialist medicine had to adapt to local customs—for example, the presence of family representatives during hospitalization or surgeries performed on women—and professional failures were often framed by Romanians as cases of backwardness that could not be overcome. In 1976, the hospital's first director argued in a report to his superiors in Bucharest that the institution was geographically isolated, with few possibilities of communication, and it had to treat "a semi-savage population" while the town did not have central sewage.[84] Another Romanian doctor stated that auxiliary local personnel as well as hospital visitors "did not obey the sanitary norms, visiting hours, or medical therapeutic instructions."[85]

Romanian officials understood the provision of medical assistance in Gharyan to be an awkward compromise between "local conditions and the requirements imposed by civilization," in the words of one 1976 report.[86] One solution was reached in 1977, when the locals were allowed to visit patients only three times a week instead of once or even twice a day, as had previously been the practice. Conflict over visitation rights was endemic in the Libyan system dominated by expatriates. A WHO report reminded expat personnel in the country that "hospital visitation of patients is not a favor given by the hospital but a right of the patient."[87] This contentious issue reflected a deeper conflict: Romanian physicians, along with those from other socialist countries, rejected the traditional Arab custom of families helping in the nursing of their relatives—such practice was deemed inappropriate for a modern hospital.

One factor Romanians invoked to explain the difficulties in the obstetrics-gynaecology division was "local mentalities," by which they meant the lack of prenatal monitoring, delays in bringing women to hospital for childbirth, and reluctance in giving family consent for emergency interventions. There were multiple reports recounting how surgical interventions had been rejected by locals, with Romanians

---

[82] S.V., "Informare," April 5, 1978, MS-DCCPI Relații Externe, 59/1976-1978, 1-2.
[83] Eugen Proca, "Informare unele aspecte ale cooperării cu Libia," October 17, 1980, MS-DCCPI Relații Externe 2/1984, 1.
[84] "Stimate tov. Ozun," Garian, July 12, 1976, MS-Libia, Referate, Note de convorbire, no. 104, 2.
[85] I.A., "Informare," December 23, 1975, MS-Libia, Referate, Note de convorbire, no. 104, 1-2.
[86] D.F., "Memoriu," June 7, 1976, MS-Relații Externe 60/1976, 1-2.
[87] Hutchinson, "Assignment," 8.

placing the blame on "religious beliefs."[88] Opposition to autopsies on religious grounds made it difficult for physicians to verify diagnoses, check errors, or investigate unusual pathologies. More generally, Romanian personnel blamed the wider population in Gharyan for "a lack of culture, especially of hygienic education."[89] The whole district was described by the hospital's second director as "one of the most backward in Libya from a natural and civilizational point of view." [90]

The Libyan authorities used bilateralism with other socialist countries as leverage in their negotiations over, and evaluation of, the Romanian group. Pressure from the local population was an important framework of accountability for Romanian claims to represent medical modernity. In 1983, a Libyan official declared that "the Libyan population has grown to see the level of Romanian doctors as only average, not on a par with Bulgarians and Indians."[91] The Minister of Health in Bucharest was conscious that Libya could opt for another partner in Gharyan. In October 1980, arguing that Romania had never been able to fulfill its contractual obligations, he warned his superiors that "Libya maintains relations with as many countries as possible, so that its healthcare system will not depend on one state or another." In an attempt to revitalize the mission in Gharyan, he insisted that while officials in Bucharest wavered, Czechoslovakia and Poland were renewing their contracts relating to their medical exports to Libya.[92]

Gharyan was a space where both sides struggled over control in terms of authority and income. The symbol of this clash was, during the 1980s, the very nature of the contractual agreement. Romanians wanted to continue with a collective contract for the hospital, but the Libyans wished to switch to individual ones that allowed them to make use of the medical personnel as they deemed fit and gave them more leverage in setting salaries. In parallel, the wage quotas requested by the Romanian party-state for various developing countries increased, thus widening the gap between the financial expectations of the two partners.[93]

Such wrangling was not exclusive to the bilateral relationship with the Romanians. Libya attempted to impose similar conditions on all foreign medical teams. At the time, the government in Tripoli faced growing economic difficulties occasioned by the US boycott of its oil exports and collapsing oil prices. It tried to compensate for such hardship by imposing lower rates of pay on skilled expatriate labor, much of which came from Eastern Europe.[94] The spike in personnel from Yugoslavia, Bulgaria, and Poland in the early 1980s indicates that a middle ground was found between collective and individual agreements in Libya. In December 1983, Libyan and Romanian officials reached an agreement to switch for the most part to individual contracts. Bucharest

---

[88] "Raport," June 20, 1978, MS-Libia Dosar Personal no. 2/G.T., 1; N.C., "Raport de activitate," July 12, 1978, MS-Dosare Personal Garian 1974–1979, Litera C, 2.
[89] "Raport," January 23, 1978, MS-DCCPI Relații Externe, 59/1976–1978, 1 [unintelligible signature].
[90] Jaroslav Helcl, "Assignment Report: Epidemiological Services, Libyan Arab Republic, 5 September 1971 to 30 September 1974" and "Project of Epidemiology Services: Libya, Annual Review Report 1973," January 12, 1974. LIY-ESD-001, WHO 22.0333.
[91] "Notă de convorbire," MS-DCCPI Relații Externe 2/1984, 2.
[92] Eugeniu Proca, "Informare," October 17, 1980, MS-DCCPI Relații Externe 2/1984, 3.
[93] F.B., "Nota," November 4, 1983, MS-DCCPI Relații Externe 2/1984, 1.
[94] Vandewalle, *A History*, 115–16.

committed to provide Tripoli with no fewer than 1,400 medical cadres, of whom 444 were specialized physicians—a contract that was to incur a net income for the Romanian government of 9.7 million dollars per year. This agreement was concluded at a time when Bucharest was sending to Gharyan only a little over half of the agreed personnel.[95] In fact the hospital turned into a crucible of this grand plan of health bilateralism—meeting the contractual staff quotas became a precondition for its continuation. The replenishing of the personnel in Gharyan failed and the same happened to the Romanian plan of expanding its healthcare exports in Libya.[96]

Conclusion

In January 1977, a surgeon in Gharyan wrote to his superiors in Bucharest, "I never left the hospital, and I believe that I was the only one who bravely 'guarded' its walls."[97] While the physician manipulated the regime's definition of citizenship as unrelenting toil, his phrasing also invoked the imagery of a socialist microcosm under siege. The walls that Ceaușescu sought to break down through mutually beneficial cooperation with Libya were symbolically consolidated in the "one nation hospital."

Romanian–Libyan healthcare bilateralism was unstable despite official narratives of friendship and counter-hegemonic collaboration. On the surface, the resilience of the Romanian medical presence in Libya seems to confirm that the government in Bucharest successfully showcased its socialist modernity. However, the long-term presence of Romanians in Gharyan tells us more about the Gaddafi regime's dependence on foreign expertise than Bucharest's ability to live up to its commitments. The willingness of the communist regime to persevere with this hospital should be connected to its symbolic and economic importance: it was a source of hard currency; and it legitimized Romania's support for mutually advantageous development, which opened the door to oil imports and to infrastructural and agricultural contracts.

The "one nation hospital" reflected the entanglement of two societies: a micro-Romanian world immersed in the broader Libyan environment. The socialist everyday was transferred and adapted in terms of moral codes, gender relations, consumption, and techniques of surveillance. Medical shortages and dysfunctionalities endemic to late socialism in Romania defined the very existence of the institution in Libya. The fate of the hospital mirrored the descending trajectory of socialist healthcare, particularly in Romania. Since the second half of the 1970s, the regime in Bucharest had become more concerned with policing the medical profession than with providing funding for the modernization of the existing infrastructure.[98] Though Romania was an extreme case because of Ceaușescu's austerity policies, across the socialist camp healthcare had been labeled an "unproductive" sector of the economy and therefore

[95] Telegrama no. 069116, Ambasada României în Tripoli, March 29, 1984, MAE-Libia 1106/1984, 12.
[96] Telegrama no. 069330, Ambasada României în Tripoli, October 10, 1984, MAE-Libia 1106/1984, 25.
[97] "Raport," January 25, 1977, MS-Dosare Libia nr.4/E.A., 2.
[98] Corina Doboș and Florin Soare, "Cei din lume fără nume: Politica pronatalistă a regimului Ceaușescu," http://politicapronatalista.iiccmer.ro/.

experienced severe budgetary cuts.[99] The shortages and tribulations of the hospital in Gharyan signaled Romania's faltering socialist modernity.

Gharyan offered an opportunity to bring together two peoples situated in separate geographies. While physical proximity was achieved, the distance between Romanians and Libyans lingered because of the insularity and malaise of the Romanian medical staff. In the face of contestation, officials in Bucharest and specialists at the hospital reverted to Eurocentric civilizational motifs that produced quasi-colonial characterizations of the local space and its people, including racist tropes. Romanian personnel were unable to overcome the unease they felt at being accountable to and in the employ of a people they perceived to be at a lower developmental and civilizational stage, and who were distinctive "others"—non-European, brown, and Muslim. Yet, the monetized nature of Romanian–Libyan bilateralism subverted the power relationship inherent in the idea of medical assistance: the postcolonial recipients could control the terms and impose their authority upon the donor. Undeniably, at Gharyan, Libyans and Romanians engaged in fulfilling a higher purpose: bringing healthcare to a population in dire need of it. Nevertheless, Romania's involvement in Libya, as part of the country's global turn, shows that postcolonial locales pushed socialist self-representations into crisis: the regime was confronted with its own failings, proving incapable of making good on its overseas ambitions. In their turn, Romanian medical staff were in thrall to Eurocentrism and late socialist mores, unable to relate to the people they were supposed to heal.

---

[99] George R. Urban (ed.), *Social and Economic Rights in the Soviet Bloc* (Oxford, 1988).

10

The Trade Union: Kindred by Choice—Trade Unions as Interface Between East Africa and East Germany[1]

Eric Burton

In the late 1950s, trade unions became a significant interface of East–South interactions and concrete social experiences, operative across the whole world as multi-sited spaces spanning administrative headquarters, waterfronts, factory floors, training institutions, and conference venues. Trade union functionaries, for their part, were caught between governments' interests and workers' demands. This was also the case in the East African countries of Tanganyika and Zanzibar, which became independent in 1961 and 1963, respectively, and merged in 1964 to form the United Republic of Tanzania. This chapter explores the agency of trade union functionaries in their different Tanzanian and East German incarnations. For many East German and East African functionaries, trade union contacts enabled them to imagine a shared struggle against imperialism; yet at the same time, what the union was, or should be, was highly contested. Due to the variety of actors and alliances involved, trade unionism was "an incubator where different visions of decolonized futures vied for ascendancy."[2] These futures were not imagined in isolation, but in the context of increasing transregional connectivity.

In the case of the German Democratic Republic (GDR), the forging of international labor networks primarily fulfilled a proto-diplomatic function. East Germany's ruling Politburo called for a foreign policy offensive towards the Global South in 1960, the United Nations' "Year of Africa," and this call also incited mass organizations such as the East German Confederation of Free German Trade Unions (Freier Deutscher Gewerkschaftsbund, FDGB) to quickly diversify their international connections. Trade union cadres were to combat West Germany's Hallstein Doctrine, which had threatened newly independent countries with punitive measures and the withholding

---

[1] Thanks to Kristin Roth-Ey and Immanuel Harisch for their helpful comments on previous versions of this chapter.
[2] Gerard McCann, "Possibility and Peril: Trade Unionism, African Cold War, and the Global Strands of Kenyan Decolonization," *Journal of Social History* 53.2 (2019): 348. See also the ongoing Ph.D. dissertation project of Immanuel Harisch, "African Trade Unions and the International Labor Movement. Institutions, Networks and Mobility during the 'Golden Age,' c. 1957–1968."

of aid, should they grant the GDR diplomatic recognition. Although the FDGB's initial emphasis was on progressive independent West African countries, it also sought to establish links with East Africa, where no country had yet attained independence. The region's labor unions, embroiled in ongoing struggles for decolonization, reached out into the Cold War world to win allies, gain access to resources, and enhance their domestic and international standing. Trade union exchanges opened up an arena of contested meanings, "working misunderstandings," and elective affinities at both national and transnational levels.[3] Those who believed that they were kindred by choice and invested in transregional ties between the trade unions—including East German functionaries and, to a more limited extent, East African leftists—were obliged in the end to concede that their hopes of cooperation along the lines of anti-imperialist proletarian internationalism would be overpowered by larger forces in play. Eventually, their perception of shared interests was difficult to uphold in the midst of the shifting sands of decolonization, demonstrations of national sovereignty, and government efforts to regain control over labor.

Engaging with African unions, the FDGB became involved in several interrelated struggles at once: the global confrontation between Western- and Soviet-dominated trade union federations that was played out on the African continent; the competition between class- and race-based strategies; and the growing tensions between governments and trade unions at a national level. The early and mid-1960s witnessed a turn to state-led nationalism and a heightened emphasis on workers' duties rather than rights across many postcolonial African states. This "productionist turn"[4] led to Tanganyika's and Zanzibar's trade unions being incorporated into a state-led, developmentalist regime committed to the disciplining of workers. As a result, trade union connections morphed from a zone of cosmopolitan, transnational, and anti-imperialist encounters, in which African trade unions fiercely competed among themselves for international recognition and resources, to a space of increasingly constrained bilateral exchanges where trade union representatives from both East Germany and Tanzania negotiated an uneasy relationship with postcolonial governments.

In tackling these questions, this chapter builds on a heterogeneous and asymmetrical set of sources. Whereas post-socialist Europe (the GDR in particular) has been an archival gold mine for historians, the records of postcolonial Africa are frequently, though by no means always, "dispersed, destroyed, fragmented, and accidental."[5] This is why many scholars of Africa's contemporary history have turned to what Jean Allman has called the transnational "shadow archive": official and non-official repositories beyond national and imperial borders.[6] With regard to several African labor unions, the FDGB's records are particularly worthy of that title. The materials collected reflect

---

[3] "Working misunderstanding" is borrowed from Toni Weis, "The Politics Machine: On the Concept of 'Solidarity' in East German Support for SWAPO," *Journal of Southern African Studies* 37.2 (2011).
[4] William H. Friedland, "Basic Social Trends," in William H. Friedland and Carl G. Rosberg (eds.), *African Socialism* (Stanford, CA, 1964), 19.
[5] Jean Allman, "Phantoms of the Archive: Kwame Nkrumah, a Nazi Pilot named Hanna, and the Contingencies of Postcolonial History-Writing," *American Historical Review* 118.1 (2013): 129.
[6] Allman, "Phantoms of the Archive," 121.

the shifting nature of international relations. Prior to independence, citizens of communist countries were usually barred from entering British-ruled territories, and East Berlin relied on information gathered from East African unionists during their visits to the GDR, or from conversations at trade union conferences in anti-colonial hubs such as Cairo.

The FDGB's ideological commitment to supporting Africa's liberation movements and workers assumed a practical guise only in connection with more pragmatic foreign policy considerations: its department for international relations was directly controlled by the ruling party's Central Committee. Not least because of their proto-diplomatic role, FDGB functionaries collected a wide variety of materials regarding the unions they maintained relations with, including not only direct correspondence, but also memoranda, news bulletins, and conference reports written for African or international audiences rather than the GDR alone. In the case of rival unions, as in Zanzibar, accusations, counter-accusations, and competing interpretations of trade union activism found their way into the archival record. Only after independence—1961 in Tanganyika, 1963 in Zanzibar—could East German unionists travel to these East African countries themselves, if invited. To some extent, this means an epistemological break in the sources, in that the lion's share of materials available to us was created or collected by East German advisors and delegations rather than authored, selected, and sent by East Africans. The reports filed by East Germans in East Africa lay claim to an insider perspective, sometimes asserting the importance of GDR initiatives, but they also reveal a sense of their own marginality vis-à-vis the overarching dynamics of decolonization, African trade unions' other transnational ties, and postcolonial politics in the region. Recent memoirs by Tanzanians involved in these exchanges[7] as well as scholarly accounts from the 1960s to the late 1980s also convey the impression that the FDGB's influence was marginal.[8] In these sources, the voices and interests of unionized workers appear only in heavily filtered and generalized terms; this contribution therefore highlights the unions' transnational connections by focusing on the better-documented agency of functionaries, advisors and "propagandists," and trade union students. It was these actors who would prove crucial in turning trade union activism into a contact zone and a space of transnational exchange between East and South.

Productionist Turns in Context: African Decolonization and Eastern European State Socialism

In both Eastern European and many African national histories, labor unions were subjugated to the imperatives of nationalist and productionist politics. The paths leading towards this outcome were, however, quite distinct. In most of Africa, trade unions developed under colonial conditions and often in cooperation with their

---

[7] Adam Shafi, *Mbali na Nyumbani* (Nairobi, 2013); G. Thomas Burgess, *Race, Revolution, and the Struggle for Human Rights in Zanzibar: The Memoirs of Ali Sultan Issa and Seif Sharif Hamad* (Athens, 2009).
[8] These accounts are cited below.

counterparts from the metropole or other parts of the relevant empire. Although labor organizations represented but a tiny fraction of the population—mostly civil servants and a portion of waged workers—they were crucial in a colonial economy dependent on the transportation of cash crops and raw materials from production sites to the metropole. The engagement with anti-colonial struggles in the late 1940s and 1950s changed the character of African trade unions by drawing them into the orbit of nationalist politics and radical activism.[9] Trade unions were a key force in this struggle as they had the capacity to channel workers' social and economic grievances into political campaigns. A workers' strike at the central nodes and arteries of the export-oriented economy such as plantations, railways, and harbours exposed the economic feet of clay of colonial rule.

In East Africa's British-ruled territories of Uganda, Kenya, Tanganyika, and Zanzibar, the spectacular growth and proliferation of unions in the mid- to late 1950s resulted from a mixture of colonial appeasement, nationalist politicking, and trade union cooperation within and beyond the region—particularly towards the West. For the sake of stabilizing revenues, both governments and employers became more interested in creating a comparatively well-paid and permanent labor force, considering "responsible" union officials as producers of a "reliable" and "respectable" working class.[10] This led to the formal recognition of trade unions—so long as they fitted colonial expectations of responsible labor action and shied away from politics.[11] Labour radicalism from below, however, was suppressed.

Trade unionism was revived by educated Africans seeking to create a "labour movement from above, on a territorial scale" through regional and transcontinental cooperation.[12] The Tanganyika Federation of Labour (TFL) quickly became the most important ally of the dominant nationalist movement in the country, the Tanganyika African National Union (TANU).[13] In 1957, the TFL set aside the ideal of non-political trade unionism promoted by colonial labor officers, and embraced TANU's declaredly nationalist objectives. Between 1954 and 1960, the number of strikes in Tanganyika quadrupled and made the TFL "the force most immediately threatening the government."[14] Membership skyrocketed from 2,700 in 1955 to 200,000 in 1961, with a spectacular 42% of all workers unionized.[15] This was the year that Tanganyika attained independence, the first East African country to do so.

Across the continent, trade unions were regarded as a potentially destabilizing force by transition and post-independence governments, many of which eventually co-opted and suppressed organized labor. This stance went along with a productionist

---

[9] McCann, "Possibility and Peril."
[10] Andrew Coulson, *Tanzania: A Political Economy* (New York, 1982), 107; Frederick Cooper, *On the African Waterfront: Urban Disorder and the Transformation of Work in Colonial Mombasa* (New Haven, CT, 1987).
[11] For Zanzibar, see Jonathon Glassman, *War of Words, War of Stones: Racial Thought and Violence in Colonial Zanzibar* (Bloomington, IN, 2011), 119.
[12] John Iliffe, *A Modern History of Tanganyika* (Cambridge and New York, 1979), 537.
[13] Tiyambe Zeleza, "Pan-African Trade Unionism: Unity and Discord," *Transafrican Journal of History* 15 (1986): 169.
[14] Coulson, *Tanzania*, 137.
[15] Iliffe, *Modern History*, 539.

turn in the rhetoric of nationalist politicians who had promised "development" and improved living conditions in the run-up to independence. Yet once anti-colonial leaders (and many trade unionists) had turned into governing politicians, championing workers' rights became subordinated to emphasizing workers' duties. The colonial refrain of "responsible" trade unions lingered on, but was reframed in terms of a nationalist and developmentalist rhetoric. As Ghana's president Kwame Nkrumah told trade unionists, their "former role of struggling against capitalists" was "obsolete"; their main task now was to "inculcate in our working people the love for labour and increased productivity."[16] In 1962, East Africa's ministers of labor convened after a wave of strikes to devise strategies to deal with widespread discontent and unemployment, agreeing that "East African governments are in a hurry to develop, and the countries' interests cannot be jeopardised by irresponsible actions or attitudes on the part of trade unions."[17] Neither in rhetoric nor in declared objectives was there anything specifically socialist in these efforts to instill new, state-related subjectivities into workers.

In the case of Eastern European trade unions, the productionist turn was rooted in the early Leninist view that a union's primary task was to elevate workers' struggles from the self-centered "economic" level—an attitude that Lenin dismissed as "trade-unionism"—to the "political" level. Workers were supposed to fight for the revolution, not just bargain for better wages or more convenient hours. In Lenin's conception of a guiding communist vanguard party and a guided working class, the trade union served—in a powerful and unidirectional metaphor—as the party's "transmission belt" to approach and educate workers *in situ*.

The FDGB, established as an autonomous trade union federation in 1945, ended up adhering closely to the Leninist line and became an arm of the party to increase output for postwar reconstruction. The GDR's June 1953 uprising, however, taught the political elite that an overly productionist attitude could backfire: it was dangerous to neglect workers' consumer interests.[18] In the following decades, the FDGB retained its formal autonomy and won a number of socio-political concessions, but effectively remained a mass organization obliged to mold workers' interests in line with party orthodoxy. An integral part of the FDGB's work on the "home front" was to connect this understanding of its tradition with the formation of solidarity-imbued subjectivities.[19] East German workers were thus drawn into consciousness-raising solidarity campaigns relating to the conflicts in Korea, Algeria, and Vietnam. They were mobilized (and sometimes set out themselves) to donate, work overtime "solidarity shifts," and participate in fundraising events connected to these struggles. In material terms, these campaigns were highly successful. The donations of FDGB members made up the largest

---

[16] Frederick Cooper, *Africa since 1940: The Past of the Present* (Cambridge, 2002), 162.
[17] Minutes of the meeting of ministers responsible for labor in Kenya, Uganda, and Tanganyika held at Kampala, August 20, 1962, SAPMO-BArch, DY 34/3380; M. A. Bienefeld, "Trade Unions, the Labour Process, and the Tanzanian State," *Journal of Modern African Studies* 17.4 (1979): 565.
[18] Detlev Brunner, *Sozialdemokraten im FDGB: Von der Gewerkschaft zur Massenorganisation, 1945 bis in die frühen 1950er Jahre* (Essen, 2000); Stefan Paul Werum, *Gewerkschaftlicher Niedergang im sozialistischen Aufbau: Der Freie Deutsche Gewerkschaftsbund (FDGB) 1945 bis 1953* (Göttingen, 2005).
[19] Péter Apor, "Homefront," in James Mark and Paul Betts (co-ords.), *Socialism Goes Global. The Soviet Union and Eastern Europe in the Age of Decolonization* (Oxford, 2022).

contribution to the coffers of the East German Solidarity Fund which paid, for instance, for the scholarships of students from the postcolonial world and material and military support for liberation movements.[20]

Anti-imperialist Bridges and Competing Vistas of Socialist Development

For both pragmatic and theoretical reasons, African trade unions were seen as more approachable than the nationalist parties. During the early 1960s, East Berlin, Moscow, and Prague were suspicious of the "bourgeois" nationalist movements which led the transition to independence in Tanganyika and, in a less clear-cut fashion, in Zanzibar, where independence was quickly followed by a revolution in January 1964.[21] No communist parties existed in East Africa, but given the crucial role of African trade unions in destabilizing colonial rule in the 1950s, the assumption that there was a small but powerful and progressive working class seemed sound. When East German unionists began to enter into relations with Zanzibar's unions, they sought both to support and influence the workers' movement in the whole of East Africa. Zanzibar was the best entry point in a region whose labor movement was perceived as "trade-unionist" in the Leninist sense—that is, apolitical and reactionary. This reading was informed by affiliations between national trade union federations and larger trade union federations of global reach aligned to the Soviet-aligned World Federation of Trade Unions (WFTU) and the Western-dominated International Confederation of Free Trade Unions (ICFTU). By the late 1950s, the ICFTU was active in all of East Africa's British possessions where political independence was still pending, offering financial and educational support to those who conformed with the ICFTU's anti-communist stand, even if only for strategic reasons.

Barred from entering British-ruled territories in East Africa, FDGB functionaries relied on travel in the growing anti-imperialist world to forge new connections. Conferences and trade union gatherings in Accra, Cairo, and Casablanca in the late 1950s meant opportunities to meet East African representatives, some of whom were themselves keen to establish new contacts with the communist world. In 1960, Zanzibar's sole trade union federation, the Zanzibar and Pemba Trade Unions (ZPFL), sent a delegation to Beijing, led by Ali Sultan Issa, a cosmopolitan Marxist who had become involved in communist circles in 1950s London and at the 1957 World Youth Festival in Moscow. In Beijing, Issa met representatives of the East German FDGB and gladly accepted their scholarship offers for Zanzibari unionists. When Issa returned to Zanzibar, the trade union split along political lines.[22] It was the beginning of a three-

---

[20] Ilona Schleicher, "Elemente entwicklungspolitischer Zusammenarbeit in der Tätigkeit von FDGB und FDJ," in Hans-Jörg Bücking (ed.), *Entwicklungspolitische Zusammenarbeit in der Bundesrepublik Deutschland und der DDR* (Berlin, 1998).

[21] Helen-Louise Hunter, *Zanzibar: The Hundred Days Revolution* (Santa Barbara, CA, 2010), 25.

[22] George Hadjivayanis and Ed Ferguson, "The Development of a Colonial Working Class," in Abdul Sheriff and Ed Ferguson (eds.), *Zanzibar under Colonial Rule* (London, 1991), 208–9.

year feud. Functionaries of both Zanzibari federations asked for similar kinds of support which would help them to gain the upper hand in internal struggles and bolster their standing as legitimate representatives of Zanzibari workers: scholarships, technical equipment for propagandistic work, symbolic paraphernalia of bureaucratic and trade unionist authority such as badges, membership cars, and office equipment, and funds to attend communist, Afro-Asian, and pan-Africanist union congresses.

The FDGB relied on information from the Zanzibaris themselves to make sense of the country's fractured political landscape. As Ali Sultan Issa told the FDGB, the split had occurred because General Secretary Hassan Nassor Moyo had expelled a number of progressive members. Moyo, Issa told his East German interlocutors in November 1960, was a "capable agitator," but young, inexperienced, and poorly educated; he was prone to fall for reactionary arguments because he did "not understand that our struggle is a class struggle and not a struggle between races." Issa claimed that the newly established federation he himself was part of—the Federation of Progressive Trade Unions (FPTU)—was led by experienced cadres who held a Marxist, non-racialist worldview and followed the guiding light of proletarian internationalism. This new union would politicize workers in the correct way; the FDGB should thus "support what is evolving, even though it seems weak."[23]

Issa's main rival Moyo had already introduced himself to the FDGB four months earlier with a letter written directly after the split. Having heard about the scholarships the FDGB had promised to Ali Sultan Issa in Beijing, he likewise requested bursaries for trade union courses.[24] Moyo also visited Budapest and Belgrade in 1960 and was successful in soliciting the support of the Soviet Union, which provided scholarships for twenty-five Zanzibaris selected by the ZPFL (or the political party it backed) to study at Moscow's newly established Friendship University.[25] In conversations with East Germans, Moyo claimed that his trade union saw "educating workers to become socialists" as key to its agenda; he lacked, however, the grasp of Marxist-Leninist theory that Ali Sultan and his "comrades" displayed not only in conversation, but also in their publications, such as their news bulletins. FDGB functionaries also noted that Moyo liked to bring up questions about life after death and the existence of God—a clear indication that his socialist views were not based on historical materialism.[26] From Moyo's letters, it becomes clear why Ali Sultan took pains to distance himself from a racialized reading of Zanzibar's political struggles: Moyo painted the FPTU as an organization of the well-to-do Arab minority, mentioning that Zanzibar's population was composed of 250,000 Africans against 25,000 Indians and 25,000 Arabs, with the minorities enjoying many privileges denied to Africans. In communicating with the FDGB and other communist trade unions, the competing Zanzibari unions blended anti-colonial, anti-racist, and anti-capitalist arguments, accusing each other of being

---

[23] Ali Sultan Issa, Bericht über die Gewerkschaftsbewegung in Sansibar und die Beziehungen, die der FDGB zu dieser unterhalten sollte, November 24, 1960, SAPMO-BArch, DY 34/3380.
[24] H. N. Moyo to Deubner, July 31, 1960, SAPMO-BArch, DY 34/2509.
[25] Memo on conversation with Dire Hassan (ZPFL), February 16, 1962, SAPMO-BArch, DY 34/2509.
[26] Bellmann, Report about Moyo's stay from September 14 to 24, 1960, September 29, 1960, SAPMO-BArch, DY 34/2509.

capitalist, delaying independence, and inciting racial hatred between "Africans" and "Arabs." Moyo and his allies claimed all anti-colonial credentials for themselves and demanded that the FPTU, "a blood sucking vampire" issuing "false propaganda to suit their capitalist leaders," not be recognized.[27] In contrast, Ali Sultan Issa's FPTU tried to discredit Moyo as one of the "nefarious leaders" and "stooges of Imperialism ... whose policy was based on the one plank of delaying Independence and work [sic] against the Nationalist movement."[28] A Soviet article from 1960, also circulated in the GDR, denounced the party close to Moyo's ZPFL, the Afro-Shirazi Party (ASP), as a party of plantation owners who advocated independence solely to pursue their semi-feudal interests.[29] ASP politicians, in turn, occasionally denounced their political opponents as communists.[30]

The bitter rivalry between Zanzibar's unions posed a dilemma for the FDGB and GDR foreign affairs officials. Should the FDGB support the federation with committed Marxist leaders but relatively few members (roughly one-third of the ZPFL) and a reputation for perpetuating Arab supremacy? Or conversely should it support the federation that played on its numerical superiority and "Africanness" but obviously used socialist and pro-communist rhetoric strategically rather than consistently? Until early 1962—and, notably, unlike the Soviet Union—the FDGB followed Ali Sultan's recommendation. It kept its channels open with both federations, leaning towards the FPTU while avoiding a formal cooperation agreement with the ZPFL.[31] Both federations continued to receive scholarships, but the FPTU also received additional material support. For the GDR, offering scholarships to both sides seemed like the best strategy because individuals from opposing factions were thereby exposed to the same ideology. Instead of a convergence, however, the conflicts were also played out in Bernau.

Transregional Mobility and Trade Union Education

As in the case of other Eastern bloc unions, training remained the FDGB's main channel of support and influence. Requests for scholarships and training from brokers such as Ali Sultan Issa spurred the institutionalization of trade union education for unionists from the decolonizing world in the bloc. Courses or specific institutes for trade unionists from Asia, Africa, and (at a later date) Latin America were established in the Soviet Union, Czechoslovakia, Bulgaria, and East Germany.[32] Contacts with West

---

[27] ZPFL, Press release, no date [February 1962], SAPMO-BArch, DY 34/2509; Moyo to WFTU, "Statement by the ZPFL on the struggle of trade unions to end colonialism, 29 October 1960," SAPMO-BArch, DY 34/2509.

[28] Mohamed Ali Masoud to I. Zakaria (WFTU), August 6, 1960, SAPMO-BArch, DY 334/2505. Copies of the letter went to trade union headquarters in Moscow, Beijing, and Berlin.

[29] Ludger Wimmelbücker, "Zur Entwicklung der Beziehungen zwischen der DDR und Sansibar in den 1960er Jahren," in Ulrich van der Heyden and Franziska Benger (eds.), *Kalter Krieg in Ostafrika: Die Beziehungen der DDR zu Sansibar und Tansania* (Berlin, 2009), 192.

[30] Anthony Clayton, *The Zanzibar Revolution and its Aftermath* (London, 1981), 44.

[31] Aktennotiz nach Gespräch mit Vertreter des Zanzibar Office in Kairo, Ali Sultan Issa, Berlin, April 17, 1961, SAPMO-BArch, DY 34/2505.

[32] Transcript of speech by WFTU secretary Edvín Chleboun, Bernau, April 17–18, 1963, SAPMO-BArch, DY 34/3291.

African countries also intensified, and the FDGB sent advisors and instructors to Ghana, Guinea, and Mali. East Africa, however, remained off-limits. Even Marxist-Leninist literature requested by Zanzibari contacts was intercepted and confiscated by the colonial authorities.[33]

In 1959, the East German FDGB opened its first special course for Afro-Asian trade unionists and then, in 1960, a special institute for foreigners at the FDGB's trade union college in Bernau, a small town outside Berlin. The goal was to produce class-conscious trade union leaders sympathetic to the GDR and the wider socialist camp.[34] The course was packed with topics that linked workers' movements, state socialism, and, to a lesser extent, decolonization. Adam Shafi, a former Zanzibari student at the college, recalled the college's director welcoming participants with "heavy politics," praising the GDR's support for anti-colonial liberation struggles and promising to eliminate all the "colonial brainwashing [kasumba] that had filled our minds."[35] Albeit clearly Marxist-Leninist, the program was not geared towards the production of revolutionaries. In fact, those with a more radical outlook were misleadingly branded "Maoists" in the East Germans' internal reports, designating a heretical strand of ideology that came to have a distinctly negative ring in the early 1960s.[36]

Several unionists trained in East Germany or the Soviet Union were (or went on to be) important figures in the labor movement, took up key posts in state administration and politics, and sometimes remained key contacts for East Germans. Between 1961 and 1976, ninety-seven Tanzanians (including both Zanzibaris and Tanganyikans) attended trade union courses in the GDR, including twenty-two who participated in the long-term course.[37] Given that there was no rigid mode of selection, it is not surprising that course participants were a mixed bag. Almost exclusively male, there were motivated high- and mid-ranking trade union functionaries with experience of strike action, but also career-minded youths with neither experience nor interest in labor struggles who were frustrated to find themselves at a trade union college rather than a university that would pave their way towards upward social mobility. In general, however, many of the course participants were sympathetic to socialism and willing to engage with Marxism-Leninism, though some expressed regret that the lessons were not suitable as guidelines for the concrete problems of trade union affairs or liberation struggles.[38]

---

[33] Moyo to Meier (FDGB), November 23, 1962, SAPMO-BArch, DY 34/7296.
[34] Immanuel Harisch, "'Mit gewerkschaftlichem Gruß!' Afrikanische GewerkschafterInnen an der FDGB-Gewerkschaftshochschule Fritz Heckert in der DDR," Stichproben. Wiener Zeitschrift für kritische Afrikastudien 17.34 (2018); Eric Angermann, "Agency and Its Limits: African Unionists as Africa's 'Vanguard' at the FDGB College in Bernau," in Eric Burton et al. (eds.), Navigating Socialist Encounters: Moorings and (Dis)Entanglements between Africa and East Germany During the Cold War (Berlin and Boston, MA, 2021).
[35] Shafi, Mbali na Nyumbani, 472.
[36] George Bodie, "Where do Correct Ideas Come From? The FDGB Institute for Foreign Students and the Coming of the Sino–Soviet Split," paper presented at conference "Socialist Educational Cooperation with the Global South," Gießen, May 12, 2018.
[37] In total, the FDGB financed university or vocational education for over 1,000 trade union members from sixty-one countries. See Schleicher, "Elemente," 118.
[38] Harisch, "'Mit gewerkschaftlichem Gruß!'" 89–92; Angerman, "'Ihr gehört auch zur Avantgarde,'" 80–1.

The East African labor movement remained an enigma to Eastern European trade union functionaries, who lamented to each other as late as 1963 that they knew almost nothing about local realities, rivalries, and ideological orientations.[39] Inviting delegations and unionists to study in the GDR also served the purpose of gathering precious information on Africa's labor movement, devising strategies to penetrate this space effectively and finding apt ways to offer support. Faculty members within the foreigners' institute at the FDGB college specialized in regional affairs and made efforts to gradually adapt the course to its participants' expectations. The authorities' tolerance for such a flexible understanding of theories and strategies was limited, however. In the 1970s the institute for foreigners was shut down in a bid to reassert the iron grip of theoretical rigidity and abstract Marxist-Leninist views on trade unionism.[40]

One graduate of the institute in Bernau, the Zanzibari Marxist Ahmed Badawi Quallatein, belonged to the group of activists who entered the GDR as seasoned and politically committed organizers. Born in 1930, he had worked as a customs officer for the government before becoming a full-time employee at the trade union's department of international relations. Beginning in the late 1950s, he recruited seamen and workers into the movement.[41] Quallatein and other activists turned the trade union into an important vehicle to mobilize followers and accumulate funds for the affiliated Zanzibar Nationalist Party.[42] Attending the FDGB's second course for foreigners, he stayed in Bernau from August 1960 until spring 1961 and left the GDR two months' early when his union called him back to put his contacts and organizational skills to good use. Together with a few other cosmopolitan Zanzibari Marxists, Quallatein maintained and extended the connections with the socialist world after his return.

Quallatein repeatedly expressed sympathy for the GDR in conversations and publications. However, like other Zanzibari leftists, he preferred to draw inspiration for political strategies from Cuban and Chinese radicalism. Another trade union leader from Zanzibar likewise recalled that his "one-month visit to China in 1960 had far greater impact than the ten months he had spent the previous year in East Germany, studying political economy."[43] Similarly, Ali Sultan Issa remembered that his visit to the 1957 World Youth Festival was superseded by his experiences in China: "I had not been as impressed by the greatness of the Russians as I was with the Chinese ... [T]his was the ideological line to follow."[44] But the Sinophile Zanzibaris, some of whom were on the Chinese payroll, withheld their Maoist sentiments in conversations with the FDGB. Letters by Quallatein, himself an admirer of Maoist China, ostentatiously addressed concerns like the "West Berlin question" that were central to East Germans, as he had learned in Bernau. The union's news bulletin, for which Quallatein was responsible,

---

[39] Transcript of speech by Botvinov (Deputy Director of the Soviet Trade Union College) during WFTU experience exchange, Bernau, April 17–18, 1963, SAPMO-BArch, DY 34/3291.
[40] Schleicher, "Elemente entwicklungspolitischer Zusammenarbeit," 118.
[41] Amrit Wilson, *The Threat of Liberation: Imperialism and Revolution in Zanzibar* (London, 2013), 24.
[42] Michael F. Lofchie, *Zanzibar: Background to Revolution* (Princeton, 1965), 187.
[43] G. Thomas Burgess, "Mao in Zanzibar: Nationalism, Discipline, and the (De)Construction of Afro-Asian Solidarities," in Christopher J. Lee (ed.), *Making a World after Empire: The Bandung Moment and Its Political Afterlives* (Athens, 2010), 208.
[44] Ali Sultan Issa cited in Burgess, *Race*, 61.

even contained occasional pieces supporting the GDR in intra-German rivalries that were irrelevant to most African nationalists.

While many African unionists conceived of the FDGB as a potential source of resources, they differed in the way they imagined these ties and the space shared with the socialist camp. Communicating with East Germans, Quallatein sought to give the impression that they were operating in one and the same socialist space, a rhetoric that resonated with his FDGB contacts. He reported to East Germans that he and other Marxists had converted leaders of affiliated trade unions to socialism and begun weekly sessions of workers' education, including lessons about class struggle, imperialism, and the development of human society which drew on lessons in Bernau.[45] His letters' closing formula was a multilingual rendering of the rallying cry of the Cuban revolution—"Venceremos—Tutafuzu—We will win."[46] Quallatein frequently made references to the achievements of the Soviet camp which linked Zanzibari class politics and anti-imperialism with socialism: "The workers and the people of Zanzibar are jubilant about the USSR's achievement in sending a man into space. This is yet another proof of the superiority of socialism over capitalism. The achievements of socialist countries are an inspiration to our struggle and weaken imperialism."[47]

To leading unionists from Tanganyika, these achievements were less obvious and hardly inspiring. In September 1962, the first delegation of the Tanganyika Federation of Labour (TFL) toured the GDR. Due to the TFL's established ties with Western union federations, some of its functionaries had already attended trade union seminars organized by affiliates of the Western-dominated ICFTU in Great Britain, the United States, and Israel (an Afro-Asian trade union school funded by US sources) as well as the ICFTU African Labor College in Uganda and the ICFTU headquarters in Belgium. During such seminars and visits, TFL functionaries familiarized themselves with concepts of socialism and trade unionism hostile to the Marxist-Leninist line.[48] The TFL delegation heading to the GDR in 1962 drew on experiences and models derived from these connections. They puzzled their East German interlocutors by heaping praise on Israel as a "completely socialist state" and declaring that workers' shareholding in their own companies was the appropriate path to socialism in Tanzania.[49] In contrast to Quallatein's waxing lyrical about the Soviet victory in the space race, TFL functionaries also deemed sending people into space a regrettable waste of resources which could be put to much better use in building Tanganyika's economy.

Yet even as delegation visits might sharpen a sense of disagreement, they also sometimes highlighted a trans-systemic ideological overlap concerning "expectations of modernity."[50] Most trade unionists, who saw Africa as being in the initial stages of proletarianization and requiring disciplined workers to enter the industrial age, had serious questions about how discipline was to be achieved. The TFL delegation

---

[45] Quallatein, "Vertraulich," no date [c. October 1961], SAPMO-BArch, DY 34/3380.
[46] Quallatein to FDGB, August 9, 1962, SAPMO-BArch, DY 34/2505.
[47] Quallatein to FDGB, April 15, 1961, SAPMO-BArch, DY 34/2505.
[48] Paschal B. Mihyo, *Industrial Conflict and Change in Tanzania* (Dar es Salaam, 1983), 75.
[49] Abschlußbericht zur Delegation der TFL, September 26, 1962, SAPMO-BArch, DY 34/2504.
[50] James Ferguson, *Expectations of Modernity: Myths and Meanings of Urban Life on the Zambian Copperbelt* (Berkeley, CA, 1999).

marveled at the degree of organization evident in FDGB-run tours through factories, agricultural enterprises, and cultural sites. The Tanganyikan functionaries admitted that they had expected police standing behind the workers' backs to ensure productivity—a view perhaps resulting from anti-communist propaganda. Instead, they were shown a disciplined and even cheerful working force without obvious enforcers.[51] The FDGB also routinely included displays of gender equality in its tours, introducing the all-male delegations to female trade union functionaries and leading workers or arranging visits to textile factories crowded with female workers. Emancipation in terms of labor relations—partial and contradictory in the eyes of many scholars today, but impressive for contemporary delegations from African labor unions—was presented as the hallmark of socialist modernity. The presence of women on factory floors and in trade union roles was generally accepted as a yardstick of modernity by both sides, but this did not lead to any in-depth discussions about the gendered character of labor relations. Women's welfare was usually considered an issue for the compartmentalized women's organizations attached to the ruling party.

The GDR's workscape did not, however, provide models for tackling other inequalities bequeathed by colonialism. In Tanganyika, trade unions and government leaders clashed over racially charged questions of socioeconomic uplift and citizenship for non-Africans. Calls for "Africanization" (i.e., the replacement of Asian and European officers with Africans) led to a crisis during the transitional period of self-government in preparation for independence as leaders of the trade union federation called in late 1960 for the nationalization of major enterprises and a race-based citizenship law.[52] The same tried-and-tested practices of non-violent resistance and strikes that had troubled the British now provoked first the transition and then the post-independence government's fears of the trade union movement's "destructive capabilities."[53] The National Assembly passed a bill that granted citizenship on non-racial criteria, but the issue remained a bone of contention. In 1962, the postcolonial government responded heavy-handedly to TFL-organized strikes (in favor of speeding up the Africanization of positions in the economically vital sisal industry) by curtailing trade union rights.

GDR officials became increasingly aware that tensions over emancipatory strategies and their racial content in East Africa was a delicate question. Kenyan and Zanzibari delegates at the FDGB's trade union school, for instance, had also voiced their protest against a piece in the FDGB's mouthpiece *Tribüne* that lauded the "Arab" faction and discredited the "African" faction in Zanzibar.[54] While East Germans sought to teach foreign trade unionists to see world history in terms of class struggles, activists from East Africa tried to educate East Germans about the central significance of historically entrenched racial inequalities. The wrong choice in Zanzibar could have serious

---

[51] Abschlussbericht zur Delegation der TFL, September 26, 1962, SAPMO-BArch, DY 34/2504.
[52] Andreas Eckert, *Herrschen und Verwalten: Afrikanische Bürokraten, staatliche Ordnung und Politik in Tanzania, 1920–1970* (Munich, 2007), 209.
[53] Cranford Pratt, *The Critical Phase in Tanzania, 1945–1968: Nyerere and the Emergence of a Socialist Strategy* (Cambridge, 1976), 189.
[54] Mwakanjuki and Oyoo to the editors of Tribüne, Bernau, January 21, 1961, SAPMO-BArch, DY 34/2509.

repercussions in sub-Saharan Africa as a whole. In 1962, the GDR Ministry of Foreign Affairs warned that continued one-sided support in Zanzibar threatened "to estrange us from Black Africa's trade union and liberation movement."⁵⁵ These considerations about racial relations led the FDGB to recalibrate its relations with Zanzibari trade unions. Henceforth it officially took an agnostic stand on the matter by describing the rivalry as internal conflict but in fact shifted its support to the ZPFL. The change had come at just the right moment. In August 1963, the FPTU leadership informed the FDGB that it had ceased to support the ZNP and was now backing the newly founded Umma, a "party of a new type" which aimed to transcend the racial divisions.⁵⁶ Together with the "Africanist" forces of the ZPFL and ASP, Umma's leftist cadres (including Ali Sultan Issa and Quallatein) took up central positions in Zanzibar's revolutionary government and administration.

The Itinerant Trade Union School

Zanzibar's independence from Great Britain in December 1963 was followed by a revolution. In January 1964, a group mainly made up of members of the ASP Youth League originating from the African mainland overthrew the Omani Sultanate and the elected ZNP government, discredited as "Arab" by its political opponents, which the British had left in power. The more experienced politicians and trade union cadres quickly wrested power from the insurgents and implemented a number of radical policies both in the domestic sphere and in foreign relations. Zanzibari Marxists from the new Umma Party occupied important posts in the regime and drew on their resources and networks to reorient the islands' economic relations from the British metropole towards the Eastern bloc and China. Mid-1964 marked the high tide of optimism in the GDR that socialism was conquering new spaces in East Africa and offering possibilities for a diplomatic breakthrough. These hopes led to an unprecedented commitment on the part of the GDR in aid and detachments of experts. In this context, trade union cooperation was seen as an apt means of supporting the build-up of socialism and friendly relations in the region, though the urgent drive towards diplomatic recognition was paramount. This explains why material aid for trade unions in post-revolutionary Zanzibar was framed among leading cadres of the FDGB as being "not about supporting a certain party or trade union organization, but about enhancing the reputation of the GDR in Zanzibar."⁵⁷

A key component of the FDGB's understanding of a trade union's tasks was that it should reach unionists and the workforce in all corners of the country through the spread of propaganda, a view that was anchored in German's pre-war history of labor activism. Itinerant teachers (*Wanderlehrer*) had exposed tens of thousands to Marxism

---

⁵⁵ Africa Department of the Ministry of Foreign Affairs to Deubner, Berlin, January 9, 1962, SAPMO-BArch, DY 34/2509.
⁵⁶ FPTU General Secretary to FDGB Director of International Department, Zanzibar, August 18, 1963, SAPMO-BArch, DY 34/2505.
⁵⁷ Dönitz to Beyreuther, Berlin, February 15, 1964, SAPMO-BArch, DY 34/3283.

in early twentieth-century Germany and played a key role in the spreading of Marxist thought on the factory floor. FDGB grandees like Hermann Duncker, himself a pioneering itinerant preacher of socialism in previous decades, embodied this tradition and passed it on to the new generation of GDR unionists who often had no personal experience of grassroots work, let alone industrial conflict.[58] Drawing on the experience of communist itinerant lecturers in the German Reich and the Weimar Republic, a *Wanderschule* ("itinerant school") project was devised for Zanzibar. This was the first experiment of its kind for the FDGB, which so far had only sent some advisors for short-term stays in West African countries.

Expectations ran high: the GDR's standing in Zanzibar was such that Zanzibari unionists welcomed East German proposals to engage in work on the ground, an option that was not yet available elsewhere in East Africa. Courses would be attended not only by Zanzibaris, but also by unionists from Tanganyika, Northern Rhodesia (Zambia), Kenya, and Uganda.[59] In this way, the itinerant school would represent both the GDR's gateway to East Africa and an appropriate riposte to the Western-affiliated ICFTU trade union school in the Ugandan capital of Kampala, established in 1958, which trained educators and organizers and had already begun sending out itinerant teachers to other countries on the continent. The FDGB expected the Zanzibari experience to raise the GDR's prestige in all of East Africa and provide lessons for the future; perhaps also to facilitate the opening of satellites of Bernau's trade union college. These plans capture the enthusiastic drive for expansion that took hold of the FDGB in the first half of the 1960s. The FDGB dispatched a truck, mobile technical equipment as well as tents and motorbikes to enable trade union cadres to reach places beyond the union's buildings and traditional centers of labor mobilization, such as the docks and branch offices.

More than any other instance of cooperation, the failure of the itinerant school to operate effectively revealed the limits of cooperation and the lack of mutual understanding. Filipowski and Fröhlich, two young lecturers from the FDGB's Institute for Foreign Students sent to implement the project, soon realized that Zanzibar's postcolonial-cum-socialist setting offered minimal room for manoeuvre both for them and the newly established trade union federation, the Federation of Revolutionary Trade Unions. The East German propagandists quickly rallied behind the government's productionist position on limiting workers' demands for participation and material improvements. According to an October 1964 report from the GDR embassy, workers expected the revolution's promises for African advancement to be translated into rising wages. East Germans found that Zanzibar was at a stage of material development that rendered such demands illegitimate. After some hesitation, the leadership of Zanzibar's newly unified trade union tried to convince its members that economic demands could not be satisfied.[60] The reversal of the union's role, barely a year after independence and the revolution, had profound implications for the welcome given to the FDGB's

---

[58] On Duncker, see Mario Keßler and Heinz Deutschland, *Hermann Duncker: Sozialdemokratischer "Wanderprediger", Spartakist, Gewerkschaftslehrer* (Hamburg, 2001).
[59] Beschluss Nr. S 512/64 des FDGB Sekretariats, September 5, 1964, SAPMO-BArch, DY 34/24842.
[60] [Illegible] to Warnke, October 29, 1964, SAPMO-BArch, DY 34/3283.

itinerant propagandists Filipowski and Fröhlich. Reputedly, Zanzibar's political leader Abeid Amani Karume estimated that their presence might fuel workers' discontent.[61] The revolutionary regime made no attempt to keep up appearances of trade union autonomy. Indeed, in September 1965, all unions were abolished and their remnants integrated into the ruling party's "Department of Worker's Organisation."[62] Whenever the department's functionaries dared to bring forward suggestions for improvements, they were cut short by the party leadership and reminded that their primary task was to enforce the party line. In a telling reversal of roles, they were told to be "political commissars."[63] In internal correspondence, East Germans distanced themselves from this quasi-Stalinist conception of worker representation but for diplomatic reasons opted not to openly voice that opinion when engaging with the Zanzibari authorities. In the view of the FDGB, this incorporation deprived workers of their "autonomous class organization" and showed that the working class had not yet been recognized as the "driving force" of history. The department's efforts to advocate the government's policies and increase productivity were seen as inadequate given that they lacked a system of Marxist training for functionaries.[64] By 1966, the ruling party had discarded any thoughts of introducing regular political courses because most workers used their leisure time to work their plots of land in order to supplement their meagre wages.[65] In 1968, the department was shut down altogether, closing a chapter of two decades of vibrant trade union activity in Zanzibar. By then, the FDGB had already shifted its attention to the Tanzanian mainland.

Anti-imperialism Redux: Invisible Advice

Having become useless in Zanzibar, the equipment for the itinerant school was shipped across the small strip of the Indian Ocean to Dar es Salaam, the Tanzanian capital on the mainland coast. It was picked up by Max Lamprecht, a trained legal practitioner and trade union functionary who was the first FDGB adviser in Africa to stay for several years. His main task was to put the itinerant school to good use and to assist in drawing up a national plan for workers' education that would combine literacy training and political education.[66] When Lamprecht arrived in Tanzania in October 1965, the TFL had ceased to exist as an autonomous trade union federation. Mid-ranking African army officers had mutinied in January 1964 over frustration at the painfully slow rates of Africanization in the military. When evidence of a plot to overthrow the

---

[61] [Illegible] to Warnke, October 29, 1964.
[62] Circular of Umoja wa Wafanyakazi to all trade unions, Zanzibar, September 17, 1965, SAPMO-BArch, DY 34/4174; Clayton, *Zanzibar Revolution*, 120.
[63] Delegationsbericht Tansania, August 1966, SAPMO-BArch, DY 30/98132.
[64] Information über FDGB-Delegation in Sansibar, Zanzibar, March 10, 1968, SAPMO-BArch, DY 30/98133.
[65] Konieczny to Franke, Zanzibar, February 19, 1966, SAPMO-BArch, DY 34/4174.
[66] Beschluss Nr. S 352/67 des FDGB Sekretariats, July 17, 1967, SAPMO-BArch, DY 34/24842; Berger, Arbeitsrichtlinie für den Kollegen Max Lamprecht, Berlin, October 23, 1965, SAPMO-BArch, DY 34/7296.

government was discovered and linked to radical labor leaders, hundreds of unionists were imprisoned. The TFL was disbanded and its remains were lumped together under a party-controlled body, the National Union of Tanganyika Workers (NUTA).[67] Despite being controlled by the one-party state, NUTA—in contrast to its Zanzibari counterpart organization—"continued with the old tradition of demanding higher wages and better terms of service for its members."[68] Tanzanian party stalwarts repeatedly complained that NUTA did not fulfill its supposed function as a top-down transmission belt: workers remained at a distance to the party and were reluctant to obtain membership cards.[69] Still, although briefly popular after the government gave in to demands for higher wages in 1964, NUTA gradually lost the workers' trust.[70]

NUTA did, however, also have a dimension beyond domestic labor relations. For East Germans, it was a window into pan-African labor affairs and policies at large. Following the overthrow of Kwame Nkrumah in Ghana in 1966, Dar es Salaam became the seat of the All-African Trade Union Federation (AATUF).[71] Lamprecht, consequently, had to address both domestic and international issues. His superiors at FDGB headquarters emphasized that NUTA's priority should be to ensure the public sector's productivity, a call for action that mirrored the contemporary emphasis on increasing efficiency in the GDR's state sector as well as the theoretical view that public enterprises (rather than private firms) were key sites for both economic and socialist development. Rather than drawing on the GDR's history, however, these views were informed by other examples from the Global South. In East Africa, FDGB functionaries saw "what we have also seen in Cuba etc.: the process of reorienting workers to their new responsibility," that is, producing without making economic or political demands.[72] Lamprecht was instructed to stifle discussions about the introduction of practices such as employee profit sharing, though he should do so carefully, by referring to the GDR's experiences rather than appearing to meddle in internal affairs.

As in Zanzibar, plans for GDR trade unionists to travel the country as lecturers were never implemented. The equipment was used only once, when the tents, vehicles, and equipment were put on display next to the NUTA headquarters at Mnazi Mmoja, a central square in Dar es Salaam. Thereafter, the equipment was transferred to a farm that belonged to NUTA and put to other uses.[73] The display in central Dar es Salaam showed, however, that material support sent from the GDR was used to demonstrate the union's strength. Lamprecht found that Marxist-Leninist classics sent by the GDR, as requested by NUTA functionaries, were kept behind glass, untouched, like

---

[67] Paul Bjerk, *Building a Peaceful Nation: Julius Nyerere and the Establishment of Sovereignty in Tanzania, 1960–1964* (Woodbridge, 2015), 131, 150–5.
[68] Wilbert B. L. Kapinga, "State Control of the Working Class through Labour Legislation," in Issa G. Shivji (ed.), *The State and the Working People in Tanzania* (Dakar, 1985), 89–90.
[69] Lamprecht to FDGB, Dar es Salaam, April 9, 1964, SAPMO-BArch, DY 30/98133.
[70] Work report Eberhard [Fröhlich?], Zanzibar, December 8, 1964, SAPMO-BArch, DY 34/3283.
[71] The AATUF had been founded as a pan-African, non-aligned organization in Casablanca in May 1961.
[72] Köhler and Franke (FDGB) to Lamprecht, January 28, 1966, SAPMO-BArch, DY 34/7296.
[73] Lamprecht, Report about NUTA and Its Role in the Arusha Declaration, Dar es Salaam, May 1967, SAPMO-BArch, DY 30/98132.

representative trophies, while the FDGB's own periodicals ended up in the union headquarters' dust bins.[74]

Lamprecht's reports framed NUTA as a micro-battleground of global struggles between progressive and reactionary forces. His main intention within NUTA was to turn the educational department to which he had offered his advisory services into a propaganda department. In this, Lamprecht wrote, he was backed by one of his Tanzanian colleagues trained in Moscow, but faced stiff opposition from another colleague who had attended trade union courses in Denmark. The latter, Collins Siame, was "always in opposition to me because I'm pushing back his trade unionist proposals." Such reports also confirmed the convenient distinction between reactionary "trade unionism," as denounced by Lenin, and Marxist-Leninist labor unionism.[75] Lamprecht saw it as a personal success that the department's director, Utukulu, now readily studied the literature Lamprecht recommended because he had recognized the usefulness of Marxist arguments in discussions with other functionaries.[76] The usefulness of Marxist analysis thus lay primarily in its potential to discredit internal ("trade-unionist") rivals, not in its theoretical soundness or applicability to Tanzanian conditions at large. Overall, Lamprecht found wanting the theoretical grasp of Tanzanian functionaries and employed rhetoric common to all advisors, regardless of origin and creed: the capabilities of the ameliorating expert conveniently dovetailed with the incompetence of their local counterparts.

At a seminar for workers' committees on topics such as self-reliance and productivity, Lamprecht identified "Chinese" and "nationalist tendencies" among party functionaries. Both workers and trade union officials, he wrote to East Berlin, had a merely "intuitive" understanding of class relations. This intuition seemed to be both right and wrong: workers were "in healthy opposition" to businessmen and even hated entrepreneurs of different backgrounds (Indians in particular). The demands for full-fledged "Africanization" were not wrong per se, but all of this, Lamprecht argued, lacked "theoretical saturation."[77] To him, any resort to racial strategies of emancipation was essentially a dead end; genuine solutions would have to be color-blind. Lamprecht was not the only one to hold such views. One of the speakers at the seminar was Abdulrahman Mohamed Babu, one of the most influential and brilliant Marxists in the country who had founded the country's only Leninist-style "party of a new type," the Zanzibari Umma, in 1963. Babu spoke about the tasks of workers under "scientific socialism" and strongly opposed a Norwegian ILO advisor who had spoken earlier on workers under capitalism. Lamprecht lauded Babu for having debunked the "myth" of Scandinavian socialism that was then widely revered in NUTA circles.[78]

During another seminar, a ten-day course for high-level union administrators, Tanzanian leaders promoted their respective views of socialism. Amon Nsekela, chairman and managing director of the National Bank of Commerce, articulated his

[74] Lamprecht to FDGB International Department, Report no. 4, no date [February/March 1966], Dar es Salaam, SAPMO-BArch, DY 34/7296.
[75] Lamprecht, Report September 1967, September 22, 1967, SAPMO-BArch, DY 34/7296.
[76] Lamprecht, Report January 1968, January 16, 1968, SAPMO-BArch, DY 30/98133.
[77] Lamprecht, Report January 1968, January 16, 1968, SAPMO-BArch, DY 30/98133.
[78] Lamprecht, Report January 1968, January 16, 1968, SAPMO-BArch, DY 30/98133.

vision of a socialism along the lines of British and US liberal democracy. Lamprecht was advised by his NUTA associates not to oppose these claims himself; instead, he was asked to present his views to his Tanzanian colleague Mlangwa over lunch so that the latter could inject the arguments thus relayed to him into the broader discussions. Tanzanians knew that the East German presence stirred anxieties and could create the impression that NUTA functionaries were the puppets of communist advisers. In his reports, Lamprecht framed his advisory function as a mixture of effectiveness in promoting East German views and invisibility in front of broader audiences. The invisibility clearly accorded with the preferences of Lamprecht's NUTA associates, whom he portrayed as mouthpieces rather than individuals with their own opinions. A high-ranking representative of the pan-African trade union federation, the AATUF—Zimbihile—was also "sent" by Lamprecht to attack Nsekela with arguments about US democracy and the Vietnam War.[79] Lamprecht thus assigned central importance to his own agency, portraying the actions of African colleagues as the result of his actions. In general, however, the reports suggest a limited impact. This was also because other communist trade unions were hardly involved, and because Western social democrats, some of whom still held leading positions in Tanzanian institutions, had enough power to act as anti-communist gatekeepers.

In July 1968, Lamprecht deplored the fact that the socialist countries had failed to "occupy" another three vacant advisory posts that were then filled by Scandinavians. FDGB allies such as Utukulu promoted the applications of GDR unionists to teach at Kivukoni College, an important training site for party representatives as well as union cadres.[80] Yet no inroads were made. An East German trade unionist with excellent credentials was rejected for a lecturer post in trade unionism, for instance, in 1968, despite a profile that could have hardly been more fitting. Lecturers from non-aligned states like Yugoslavia or those with social democratic traditions were preferred, perhaps also because—in the case of Western organizations—these appointments came with additional resources such as teaching materials and technical equipment.

It is also clear that Western expatriate staff at the college made recommendations shaped by anti-communism and worked to push NUTA further toward Western agencies. The Canadian democratic socialist Griffiths Cunningham, who had joined the college as a lecturer at its opening and later served as its principal until 1969, advised NUTA's leaders to avoid dependence on the FDGB and turn westwards.[81] Cunningham also criticized Lamprecht's final report on workers' education in Tanzania for excessively reflecting "certain European experience [sic] and, in particular, that of the GDR."[82] Yet Tanzanian union leaders did not share the exclusive and dichotomous understanding of either Lamprecht or Cunningham, whereby it was a matter of "choosing" between East and West. When NUTA accepted the offer of the US American

---

[79] Lamprecht, Report January 1968, January 16, 1968, SAPMO-BArch, DY 34/7296.
[80] Lamprecht to FDGB, Report April 1968, April 9, 1968, Dar es Salaam, SAPMO-BArch, DY 34/7296.
[81] Griffiths Cunningham and David Bleakley, Comments on a Report on Workers' Education written by Mr. Max Lemprecht [sic], August 20, 1968, Chama cha Mapinduzi Archives (CCMA, Dodoma), 1003—Chuo cha Chama cha Kivukoni.
[82] Griffiths Cunningham and David Bleakley, Comments on a Report on Workers' Education written by Mr. Max Lemprecht [sic].

Peace Corps to send two volunteers to run NUTA's evening literacy classes in 1966, Lamprecht's argument that there were always "two sides" to such offers and strings attached found little resonance. NUTA secretary C. P. Kapungu told him that the Peace Corps was to be seen as a non-political organization that pursued exclusively altruistic motives.[83] Of course, many Tanzanians were well aware that the acceptance of volunteer agencies was a deeply political act; in 1968, the government even expelled the Peace Corps because of US involvement in the Vietnam War.[84] In the case of NUTA, however, even Lamprecht had problems conceiving the young Peace Corps volunteers as adversaries; they did "not provoke," as he put it in one report, seeming almost surprised.[85] More serious opponents were Tanzanians who promoted non-communist versions of socialism, and Western socialists such as Cunningham who held positions in Tanzanian institutions.

By 1970, however, almost all of these posts were occupied by Tanzanian citizens. Throughout the 1970s, NUTA continued to attract Western advisors but criticized moderate trade unions for their non-committal stand regarding anti-colonial liberation struggles. West German social democrats failed to establish contacts with NUTA and assumed that this was due to East German influence, implying that African actors had no agency and opinions themselves.[86] FDGB reports, speaking a very different language, show that they did. A successor to Lamprecht lamented in his final report from 1976 that "NUTA has done everything to keep me away from political-ideological work among its members."[87] FDGB "propagandists" sent to East Africa to spread the principles of union work were always dependent on the interests of their counterparts; they could never get their feet firmly on the ground. Into the 1970s, GDR actors considered NUTA deficient: just like Tanzania's governing party, it was seen as failing to produce a cohort of dedicated and ideologically reliable functionaries. Still, the FDGB's continued presence until 1989 moved away from education and mainly consisted of supporting the NUTA-run hospital.

Already in the late 1960s, Cold War competition over African labor had gradually died down—and so too had several previously thriving branches of transregional trade unionist education. The FDGB's long-term courses for students in Bernau were discontinued, in part because East Germans saw a mismatch between their efforts to equip experienced activists with theoretical knowledge, on the one hand, and the career-mindedness of white-collar course functionaries who came to make up the majority of course participants, on the other.[88]

---

[83] Lamprecht to FDGB International Department, Report no. 4, Dar es Salaam, no date [February/March 1966], SAPMO-BArch, DY 34/7296.
[84] Elizabeth Hoffman, *All You Need is Love: The Peace Corps and the Spirit of the 1960s* (Cambridge, MA, 1998), 119.
[85] Lamprecht, Report No. 3, Dar es Salaam, January 7, 1966, SAPMO-BArch, DY 34/7296.
[86] Volker Vinnai, "Die Arbeit der Friedrich-Ebert-Stiftung in Tansania—40 Jahre Zusammenarbeit mit Parteien, Gewerkschaften, Zivilgesellschaft und Regierung," in Norbert v. Hofmann et al. (eds.), *Die Arbeit der Friedrich-Ebert-Stiftung in Indonesien, Tansania und Zentralamerika seit den 1960er Jahren* (Bonn, 2010), 112–22, 158.
[87] J. Schindler, Abschlußbericht über den Einsatz als Berater beim Gewerkschaftsbund Tansania (NUTA), February 1976, SAPMO-BArch, DY 34/11454.
[88] Thanks to Immanuel Harisch for sharing this information.

Studying the union as a space of interaction shows that trade union functionaries and activists operated in several arenas at once. They were a part of global circuits of anti-imperialist and pan-African exchanges; they navigated the bipolar world of trade union congregations; and they found themselves sandwiched between workers' interests and governments' demands for increased productivity. Moreover, they also had to situate themselves in racially charged conflicts that were a result of imperial entanglements and histories of structural racism. In these arenas, East African trade unionists mobilized resources and adopted concepts from different sources, and devised these strategically in internal, national, and international struggles. The relations between the trade unions are thus not primarily interesting because of their historical impact, however such an impact might be measured, but because a close look at the encounters opens up vistas to shared and diverging interests. The space of the trade union was enlarged and co-constructed by an array of institutions and individuals that invested in transnational networks to further their visions of anti-colonialism, development, and shared geographies.

African trade unions had established connections with the trade unions of communist Europe during the anti-colonial struggles and continued to sustain international relations under conditions of co-optation and suppression after independence. In East German theories, the affinity between trade unions of the communist camp and labor organizations in the decolonizing world seemed quasi-automatic and natural. Indeed, both had experienced a productionist turn imposed upon the trade unions from above; both promoted an agenda of anti-imperialism and tried to educate workers. In reality, however, it was not an alliance based on a shared position in global struggles; rather, the two had been kindred by choice. Different understandings of socioeconomic and racial inequalities assigned different roles to trade unionism. Demand in East Africa for the East German interpretation of Leninist workers' education was limited because some functionaries preferred a liberal model of autonomous trade unions, while others valued the concept of workers' education in terms of nationalist unity and racial uplift more than Marxist-Leninist conceptions of class struggle that claimed to be color-blind. This mixture of varying priorities and postcolonial elites' suppression of trade union autonomy, more than competition from the West or material shortcomings, constrained the impact of anti-imperialist forms of proletarian internationalism between East Germany, Zanzibar, and Tanganyika that had been built up in the late 1950s and 1960s.

11

The Everyday Space: The Hostel, the Pub, and the Prison—Vietnamese and Cuban Workers in 1980s Czechoslovakia

Alena Alamgir

Above the sink, there is a little shelf. The wall between the door and the sink is covered in white tiles, up to the height of 1 meter. Above the mirror, there is a lighting unit. On the right of the sink, there is a blue-grey carton box (0.4 by 0.5 m) with four pairs of men's winter boots. Another 0.4 meters to the right, there is an armchair upholstered in a mixed-material fabric. Next to the armchair, there is a coffee table (0.6 by 0.6 m) with cups, plates, teaspoons, sugar, and a half-liter beer mug. Behind the coffee table on the right, there is another armchair, on top of which there is a pair of women's shoes, two tank tops, one t-shirt, and a pair of men's pants. In front of this chair, 0.3 meters in the direction of the center of the room, on the floor, there is evidence #1, which consists in a puddle of blood of oval shape with the dimensions of 0.15 by 0.25 m and a pool of coagulated blood with the diameter of 6 cm.[1]

The quotation above is a description of a space in which a crime was committed. It is also a description of a room in which an interpreter and the head of a group of Vietnamese workers in Czechoslovakia lived and was stabbed by one of his charges. The description comes from a criminal case file, numbering some 150 pages, compiled by Czechoslovak police investigators. Its purpose was to capture, and thus freeze in time, the space in which the crime took place so that it could be used later to corroborate, or contradict, statements made by the suspect, the victim, and the witnesses. Since a thorough investigation requires that all details be treated as potentially pertinent and because evidence needs to be situated in a full spatial context, criminal investigation police files turn out to be also windows into the lives of people touched by the investigation. These people include not just the victims and the perpetrators, but, thanks to the informational voraciousness of the investigators, also characters only

---

[1] Archive of the Interior Ministry of the Czech Republic (henceforth ABS), acquisition number [č. př.] 2571/4, package number [balík] 1, KS SNB České Budějovice, 1982.

tangentially related to the case at hand (just as the description of the room above includes also a little shelf above the sink, not just the oval-shaped puddle of blood). For a historian, acting as an anthropologist of things past (in contrast to the police officers who compiled the reports and statements) it is these characters, objects, and encounters, occurring and existing in the margins of the file, though often ultimately irrelevant to the investigation itself, that are a treasure-trove of information.

In this chapter, I examine how foreign workers in state-socialist Czechoslovakia navigated three spaces: the hostel, the pub, and the prison. The spaces are located on a continuum in terms of the extent to which the workers were likely to move through them. The hostel was a universal touchstone, a place that practically all foreign workers, regardless of sex, job, or age, experienced daily and intimately. The pub, a site of after-shift relaxation, was a slightly less universal milieu, frequented more by men than by women, and then mainly by those who enjoyed what pubs had to offer: beer. Prison was a locale that only a tiny fraction of foreign workers experienced personally, yet, because of the reverberations of criminal cases involving foreign workers within and without the migrant communities, the prison was an important space mentally even for those who did not experience it physically.

Spaces, to the extent that people produce them and imbue them with meaning, are inherently social.[2] One consequence of the social nature of spaces is that they structure the interactions and relationships that unfold in them. In the first instance, spaces (or more precisely the rules attached to them) often determine which encounters are even possible within them and which aren't. No less importantly, spaces differ in who is allowed, explicitly or implicitly, to enter and dwell in them, and who is excluded.[3] Here, I examine two issues: (1) the different ways in which each of the three spaces—the hostel, the pub, and the prison—structured the relationships between the migrant socialist workers and the local population; and (2) the ways in which the migrant workers made the spaces—which had originally not been constructed with them in mind—their own,[4] an effort that succeeded to different degrees, depending on the space.

A Methodological Prologue

To investigate these issues, I use dossiers of forty-three criminal cases, amounting to some 4,200 pages altogether, in which foreign workers in Czechoslovakia in the 1980s were involved as the suspects. Most—thirty—feature Vietnamese suspects; thirteen revolve around alleged perpetrators who were Cuban, and three include Poles (in some cases, foreign workers of several nationalities were involved, which is why the total of

---

[2] Henri Lefebvre, *The Production of Space* (Hoboken, NJ, 1991).
[3] Setha Low, "Spatializing Culture: An Engaged Anthropological Approach to Space and Place," in Jen Jack Gieseking and William Mangold (eds.), *The People, Place, and Space Reader* (New York, 2014), 34–8.
[4] I wish to thank Steffi Marung and Kristin Roth-Ey for nudging me toward using these conceptual lenses as I was processing the rich empirical material at my disposal.

the breakdown is higher than the total number of cases). The cases range from the heartbreakingly tragic (the stabbing to death of a roommate in a moment of rage,[5] a suicide[6]) through the mundane (the theft of costume jewellery[7] or the pushing on to the ground of a bus ticket inspector by a free rider),[8] to the almost amusing (an attempted theft of fifty kg of vitamin C, a plot uncovered before it could be carried out).[9] These are clearly not all the cases featuring suspected foreign workers in 1980s Czechoslovakia. For one thing, they come from several but not all regions of the country (for instance, the Central Bohemian and the Prague regions are missing).[10] However, they are a complete set of cases that was housed at the time of my fieldwork (2010–11) in the Czech Interior Ministry Archive in Brno-Kanice.

One may wonder what crime files can tell us about the quotidian lives of migrant workers. While there is some ambivalence to be overcome in using felons as "informants," the records of interrogations, depositions, and witness statements "leak out," as Carlo Ginzburg[11] put it, cultural reality that is otherwise not easily accessible. The first thing we learn from these documents about the everyday existence of foreign workers in state-socialist Czechoslovakia in the 1980s is that—in addition to the workplace[12]—their lives revolved primarily around two spaces: the hostels and the pubs.

The Hostel

In East-Central Europe, the institution of the hostel was closely associated with the figure of the vrátný/á, a word that does not have a straightforward translation in American English. In the UK context, perhaps "porter" in the lodge of a college comes close. These would usually be men or women in their sixties or older, supplementing their pensions by sitting in glass booths giving out room keys. In studies of foreign workers in state-socialist societies, these men and women are generally mentioned as an important part of the surveillance apparatus. They were, after all, supposed to keep

---

[5] ABS, acquisition number [č. př.] 2758-2768/95, package number [balík] 10, KS SNB Ústí nad Labem, 1983.
[6] ABS, acquisition number [č. př.] 3112-3129/98, package number [balík] 101, SNB Olomouc, 1987.
[7] ABS, acquisition number [č. př.] 3060-3071/97, package number [balík] 121, KS SNB Jablonec nad Nisou, 1986.
[8] ABS, acquisition number [č. př.] 2665-2675/95, package number [balík] 47, OS SNB Frýdek Místek, 1984.
[9] ABS, acquisition number [č. př.] 3700-3716/02, package number [balík] 244, OS SNB Olomouc, 1988.
[10] As is all of Slovakia, due to the division of the archives in the wake of the division of the country in 1993.
[11] Carlo Ginzburg, *Clues, Myths, and the Historical Method* (Baltimore, 2013).
[12] I have investigated the workplace in several other pieces: "Socialist Internationalism at Work: Changes in the Czechoslovak-Vietnamese Labor Exchange Program, 1967–1989," Ph.D. dissertation, Rutgers University (2014); "From the Field to the Factory Floor: Vietnamese Government's Defence of Migrant Workers' Interests in State-Socialist Czechoslovakia," *Journal of Vietnamese Studies* 12.1 (2017): 10–41; "'Inappropriate Behavior': Labor Control and the Polish, Cuban, and Vietnamese Workers in Czechoslovakia," in Marsha Seifert (ed.), *Labor in State-Socialist Europe, 1945–1989: Contributions to a History of Work* (Budapest, 2020).

an eye on the comings and goings of the lodgers, as well as ensuring that any outsiders signed in. However, the police files (as well as various reports submitted to the Labor Ministry) make it clear that if surveillance and control was part of their job description, the vrátný were not very reliable cogs in the state machinery. Or, conversely, foreign workers were diligently and successfully resisting this attempt at having their lives controlled. One police memo noted, "At the STAVOSERVIS hostel in Prague's 4th district ... Vietnamese workers constantly behave in undisciplined ways, there are instances of breaking the hostel rules, disturbances [výtržnosti], and verbal and physical assaults on the hostel staff."[13] Another memo stated, "According to the manager of the hostel, there are no problems with [foreign workers] that would be of interest to the police. The only problems are with observing hostel rules since Vietnamese citizens, who live in various places all over the country, visit each other and sleep over at this hostel. The management of the hostel tolerates this."[14] Regulations required visitors to check in with the "porter," sign the guest book, and sleep in guest rooms. However, at this hostel and many others, these rules were regularly broken. There are mentions of Vietnamese workers sleeping over at their friends' in the police files. The hostel managers would thus seem to have been either unwilling or unable to enforce the rules.

Hostels, then, appear to have been spaces of constant, low-level resistance on the part of foreign workers. Or else spaces that made visible the Czechoslovak authorities' incompetence, indifference, or perhaps readiness to tolerate the personal space demanded by foreign workers. At the same time, the frequent unauthorized sleepovers were also a consequence of the Vietnamese workers' intense mobility. As a Czechoslovak manager who was in charge of the Vietnamese workers in his company recalled, "It became clear at the very beginning how clever the Vietnamese were. They figured out train and bus schedules and traveled all around the country on the weekends to see their friends."[15] The manager was astounded at the rapidity with which the Vietnamese workers learned how to orient themselves in a foreign country. The criminal files show that their travels extended beyond the state borders. In one case, a Vietnamese suspect scrambles, upon his arrest, to make sure that a friend of his employed as a foreign worker in the Soviet Union and scheduled to visit him in Czechoslovakia is taken care of by his friends upon arrival, since he himself is in jail and cannot receive him. We learn from a subsequent letter written by friends of the imprisoned man that the Vietnamese friend did indeed arrive from the USSR but ended up staying in Slovakia with yet other Vietnamese friends, and not in the small Czech town where the arrested man lived.[16] We do not know how the arrested man's friends learned of this, but the fact that they did shows just how vibrant and wide-ranging the social networks were among Vietnamese workers, certainly within Czechoslovakia but apparently even beyond.

---

[13] ABS, "Přehled o událostech týkajících se občanů VSR dočasně žijících na území hl.m. Prahy a Středočeského kraje," appendix to file number [č.j.] KS-00235/01-81, report from the Prague chief of police [náčelník Správy SNB] to the deputy interior minister, dated October 20, 1982.
[14] ABS, "Ubytovna občanů VSR—zpráva," memo written by the chief of the Bohnice police precinct to the Prague 8 police district, dated October 8, 1980.
[15] Written narrative by Mr. B., January 2011.
[16] ABS, KS SNB Ostrava, Investigation file [Vyšetřovací spis] VV-17/10-82, case: Vuong Dinh Hoa and company, 1983.

There was an additional regulation in regard to hostel visitors: each hostel had to have one guest room for every thirty dwellers of each nationality. This was fairly straightforward if workers of only one nationality occupied a hostel. However, hostels often housed workers of two or even more nationalities (Vietnamese, Cubans, and Poles, as well as Czechs and Slovaks on temporary assignments). This meant that if a hostel housed, say, sixty Vietnamese and ten Cubans (a fairly realistic scenario), the Cubans would have been far better placed to secure a room for their guests, and hence more privacy. Thus, this policy, which reflected the importance of the category of "nationality" in the Czechoslovak political-social thinking of the period (in line with the more general nationality policy of state socialism),[17] created structural conditions for tensions between the groups of foreign (and domestic migrant) workers.

One thing that contributed to the inefficacy of "porters" when it came to surveillance and control of the movement, and thus the lives, of foreign workers was the language barrier. Repeatedly, porters questioned as witnesses in various cases, when asked about details, mention that they did not know what was going on since they could not understand the hostel dwellers' language. The relationship between the foreign workers and the hostel porters was in this way marked out by a combination of physical proximity and social distance. This is clear from the following porter's statement to the police: when asked why he did not do anything when he heard loud noises, the porter replied, "When [Vietnamese workers] return from work, there is always some banging because they use the kitchenette, which is close to the reception area [where he sits], to chop meat, and those are really loud bangs so I don't pay attention to them anymore... So, if there was some banging in the lobby, then I did not pay any attention to it because I probably thought that they were just chopping meat again."[18] Given that the case involved a stabbing with a knife, the statement is rather disturbing.

Finally, though most did, not every foreign worker lived in a hostel. For instance, the files contain a mention of a male Cuban worker, who, in 1987, lived with his Czech female partner in her apartment, listing the address of the apartment in police records as his residence in Czechoslovakia.[19] The files mention others who, while they didn't officially move out of hostels, spent a lot of time away. For instance, another case speaks briefly of a Vietnamese worker who has a lover in another town and so barely stays in his room. People like this, living with Czechoslovak partners in private apartments or houses, were, obviously, entirely out of reach of the hostel porters and could not be surveilled by them.

The physical organization of the hostels reflected how the Czechoslovak state conceptualized foreign workers' wellbeing. The hostels were required to carry two to three periodicals in the workers' mother tongues, of which there had to be at least one copy per fifteen to twenty people; one TV set, record player, and reel-to-reel or cassette player per forty people; a ping-pong table with accessories and one sewing machine

---

[17] Roger Brubaker, "Nationhood and the National Question in the Soviet Union and Post-Soviet Eurasia: An Institutionalist Account," *Theory and Society* 23.1 (1994): 47–78.
[18] ABS, acquisition number [č. př.] 3475-3487/01], package number [balík] 60, OS SNB Ústí nad Labem, 1981.
[19] ABS, acquisition number [č. př.] 3112-3129/98], package number [balík] 101, SNB Olomouc, 1987.

Figure 11.1 Two Vietnamese workers using a record player in their hostel's lounge. ČTK Photobank | Multimedia.[23]

per thirty women, but none were required for men's hostels.[20] These requirements show how the Czechoslovak imagined that foreign workers spent their free time, or how it wished that they would spend it. Figure 11.1 shows two Vietnamese workers listening to vinyl records. The camera angle makes it easy to identify the singer on one of the covers: Karel Gott, a mega-star of Czechoslovak pop music from the early 1960s till his death in 2019, and at the height of his career in the early 1980s when the photograph was taken. The photo, taken by a journalist working for the country's press agency, ČTK, potentially evokes a lot of messages: that the workers were well taken care of and enjoyed leisure time, that they were familiar with Czechoslovak (pop) culture—perhaps

---

[20] Document provided by the Ministry of Labor and Social Affairs, uncataloged, "Metodický pokyn pro pobyt a ubytování zahraničních občanů dočasně zaměstnaných a odborně připravovaných v ČSSR na základě mezivládních dohod a ujednání," dated February 15, 1988.

even fully immersed in it—and in that regard, not much different from Czechoslovak youth (rather than being wholly at odds with local culture, as post-socialist racist discourses would have it).[21] Ethnographic interviews show that migrant socialist workers did engage with Czechoslovak culture at least to some extent, but also that they made the hostels their own by devising their own forms of entertainment. Cuban workers, for instance, were known to play dominoes in the hostel lobby.[22]

The physical organization of the hostels also showed that the Czechoslovak state's conceptualizations of migrant workers were gendered. We do not know how much use the record players and ping-pong tables got in reality (or whether they were, indeed, present in every hostel, which is unlikely, although TVs would seem to have been ubiquitous). We do know, however, that Vietnamese workers resolutely subverted gender roles in at least one respect: although the state ordered only the hostels housing women to provide sewing machines, both female and male Vietnamese became famous (among the general population) or notorious (in police files) for using sewing machines to produce jeans and other clothing items for sale in the "grey market."

Hostels were also the places where foreign workers stored all their possessions. The regulations regarding hostel equipment reflected this reality, as common areas included storage rooms for suitcases and purchased goods. For goods that could not be kept in hostels, such as mopeds, Czechoslovak employers had to secure additional space for their storage. Due to the inconvertibility of socialist currencies, purchased goods were used as remittances-in-kind and thus played a vital role in migrant workers' lives.[24] While the larger goods were safe, the money that the foreign workers were saving up to make these large purchases (of mopeds, bicycles, and sewing machines) often was not. Files for several cases contain mentions of money, as well as luxury goods such as stereo sets, being stolen from their hiding places in rooms.[25] For instance, in one case, a Vietnamese witness states that the victim, his friend, carried money with him at all times "since there have been two instances of money having been stolen at the hostel."[26] Although, as we learn from another case, the workers were supposed to keep their valuables and larger sums of money with the hostel management, according to one worker's statement, "no one did that,"[27] a fact perhaps explicable in terms of the physical proximity–social distance relationship model outlined above. It also seems that a lot of lending and borrowing took place at the hostel as mentions of such transactions crop up regularly. We get the most detailed information about this from several letters sent

---

[21] Alena K. Alamgir, "Race is elsewhere: state-socialist ideology and the racialisation of Vietnamese workers in Czechoslovakia," *Race & Class* 54.4 (2013): 67–85.
[22] ABS, acquisition number [č. př.] 3700-3716/02], package number [balík] 240, SNB Olomouc, 1987.
[23] [ČTK ID number: 202_550_18; November 1981; original caption: "Pham-thi-Vui (left) and Luu-kim-Chi in the hostel's lounge."
[24] Alena Alamgir, "The Moped Diaries: Remittances in the Czechoslovak–Vietnamese Labor Migration Scheme," in Mahua Sarkar (ed.), *New Directions in Labour and Migration: Historical Legacies, Present Predicaments and Futures Trends* (Berlin, 2017).
[25] ABS, acquisition number [č. př.] 4664/09, package number [balík] 6, 1989.
[26] ABS, Investigative file [vyšetřovací spis] VV-11/10-84, Nguyen Van An, KS SNB Ostrava, Investigative Unit, 1984.
[27] ABS, acquisition number [č. př.] 3700-3716/02/09, package number [balík] 113, MS SNB Ostrava, 1988.

by Vietnamese suspects awaiting trial to their friends in the hostel. Here is one example from 1985:

> I am very sorry that I did not settle my debts. Perhaps you know that I owe Son in [the town of] Most 2,000.-Kcs; to Chung (who is a police officer in Vietnam) 1,300.- and a sewing machine in the locker; to Hung (the crane operator) from the 6th floor 1,000.-Kcs. [On the other hand] Truong from Most owes me 500.- and Huan and Luat in [the Slovak town of] Trnava owe me 1,000.-. In the locker, I have 700.- and one pair of jeans, brand name Levi's, from Luang, they are in a nylon bag.[28]

The list suggests a remarkably complex network of borrowing and lending, one more reminiscent of entries in a business accounting ledger than of a private exchange. The transactions are evidently tied to black- and grey-market dealings (the sewing machine, the Levi's), and the author seems to be alternately on the seller/lender and customer/borrower ends. The network operated on several levels: starting at the local level of the specific hostel (Hung from the 6th floor), it extended to nearby towns (Most), and from there all the way to remote towns hundreds of kilometres away (Trnava). The sewing machine would have been either a remittance-in-kind to be individually exported to Vietnam at the end of a worker's stay, or a tool used to carry out small business activity in Czechoslovakia. The purpose of the latter was, again, the creation of savings to be exported to Vietnam in the form of in-kind remittances. These remittances, in turn, would be either consumed by the worker and their family in Vietnam or else resold. The proceeds from the sale would then be used either for family consumption or as investment (perhaps capital to fund a small business in Vietnam).

Thus, it turns out that a financial network whose one node was located on the sixth floor of a migrant worker hostel in a small Czechoslovak town was, in fact, transnational in scope. The core routes of this network shadowed the official circuits forged by socialist government officials and inter-governmental treaties, but, as the pair of Levi's in the locker shows, the network was not confined to the state-socialist orbit; instead, it contained offshoots connecting it with global capitalist networks. Throughout the 1980s, Vietnamese workers and apprentices became known as sources for coveted but not widely available merchandise: the Levi's (or any jeans), digital watches, or silk scarves with metallic threads. The Vietnamese purveyors found their customers among their co-workers, and, once that market was saturated, among the co-workers' acquaintances, and so on. For instance, in the mid-1980s, a class of Vietnamese apprentices went to help out with the potato harvest on an agricultural cooperative. Commenting on her former students' business acumen, their teacher noted, "I do not know how and when [the Vietnamese apprentices] did it, but when we were leaving at the end of the day, all the co-op's female employees were sporting silk scarves around their necks and digital watches on their wrists."[29] In state-socialist Eastern Europe,

---

[28] ABS, acquisition number [č. př.] 2849-2860, package number [balík] 68, KS SNB Ústí nad Labem, 1985.
[29] Interview, Southern Bohemia, February 1, 2011.

Western consumer goods were imbued with much social and cultural meaning; they increased the owner's status and were a tacit rebuke to the deficiencies of the state-socialist economy.[30] Being supplied by migrant workers, as they oftentimes were, meant that these fragments of the West, or the First World, were being furnished to the denizens of the Second World by the sojourners from newly decolonized countries, or the Third World.

The physical organization of hostel life also reflected and simultaneously cemented hierarchies within the groups of foreign workers. Records show that group leaders and interpreters did not have to share rooms, while regular workers were three to a room. The private rooms occupied by the group leaders would also seem to have had phones, symbolizing and embodying the power that the group leaders held: it could be used in the service of surveillance, that is, to report to the embassy misbehavior by the workers, as well as, one imagines, to hand out favors in the guise of allowing workers to use the phone.

Thus, the physical organization of the hostels shaped the workers' lives in several ways: it emphasized the primacy and non-interchangeability of national belonging through the guest room policy; cemented existing hierarchies in the group through the housing of the group leaders; instructed workers on desirable ways of spending their leisure time; and conveyed to them the Czechoslovak state's notion of gender roles (besides the sewing machines rule, women's hostels also had to have more laundry facilities).

From the point of view of law enforcement, the very existence of hostels meant that perpetrators of crimes among foreign workers were much easier to identify and locate than perpetrators from the population at large. Since foreign workers were readily identifiable, through language and appearance, to Czechoslovak witnesses, and since each town only had a finite number of hostels (in smaller towns, the number would be just one), as soon as an incident happened outside of hostels, even if suspects were not known, the police would know where to begin their search. This is evident from most of the crime files in the collection. This, then, made the criminality of foreign workers far more visible than the criminality of the local, ethnically unmarked, populations.

The Pub

While hostels, along with the workplace, were the sites where most of the quotidian life of foreign workers took place, in the crime files, pubs feature most prominently. This is because the most frequent type of crime—a brawl, usually classified as "disorderly behavior" or "assault and battery/bodily injury"—took place there. Brawls (seven of which involved the hurling of a beer mug at someone) between foreign workers and Czechoslovak citizens constitute almost half, specifically eighteen, cases in this set. While the other crimes seem to be often contingent, context- or personal history-dependent, the pub brawls seem almost generic: the same scenario plays out over and

[30] Alenka Švab, "Consuming Western Image of Well-Being—Shopping Tourism in Socialist Slovenia," *Cultural Studies* 16.1 (2002): 63–79.

over again, only in different towns, pubs, and with different actors. Importantly, despite the fact that only the Cubans are popularly remembered in the former Czechoslovakia as "hot-headed" and always up for a fight, the Vietnamese were no strangers to these encounters—they were party to nine of the eighteen reported fights.[31]

However, more interesting from the point of view of social history than the numbers are the common circumstances in which these brawls erupted. The pattern went something like this: a group of foreign workers went to the pub to have a few beers. The Czechs at the table next to them started telling them to keep it down, that they were being too loud,[32] and/or started to make racist comments. At some point, one of the foreign workers hit a Czech or threw a beer mug at him, after which his or the Czech man's friends joined in and everybody was fighting with everybody else. For example, this is how a Cuban recounted part of one story:[33] the Czechs at the next table were being offensive, "they called us darkies, and were insulting Fidel Castro and communism. He [also] said that Cubans are shit, and so is communism. In the meantime, the waitress was refusing to serve the Cubans beer, at which point one drunk Czech pushed a Cuban, who then, involuntarily, pushed beer off the counter." His friend remembered the invectives in the following way: a Czech man reportedly told him, "'You have no business being here, Cubans here are worth shit' ... we ignored him."[34] A Vietnamese worker in another case reported a similar interaction: at one point, a Czech man came to the table at which he and his friend sat and started calling them whores and monkeys. In his deposition, his friend confirmed this and added, "Why this man was insulting us I don't know, but it is not unusual for drunks to insult us for no reason."[35]

Czech witnesses who observed but did not take part in the brawls often corroborated the racist taunts. For example, a Czech woman who was friends with the Vietnamese who ended up in a pub brawl testified that, as she was sitting with the Vietnamese, "after a while, [Czech men] Roman and Jarek came to my table and told me not to waste my time [zahazovat se] with the Vietnamese and go sit with them."[36] In another case, a Czechoslovak citizen (a Slovak in this case), testified that he heard a Czech man yell at a Vietnamese at a neighboring table, "You Chinese whore, you should go home."[37] Unsurprisingly, in practically every case, all of the participants in the brawls were drunk, sometimes blind drunk (the police files include blood alcohol content levels). However, the persistence of the interaction pattern suggests that it would be a mistake to see the alcohol consumption as the cause of the clashes. Rather, alcohol seems to have functioned as an inhibition-remover, one that made it possible for simmering resentments and racial hostility to erupt.

---

[31] Though there were many more Vietnamese than Cuban workers.
[32] ABS, acquisition number [č. př.] 4730-4740/09, package number [balík] 94, MS SNB Ostrava, 1987.
[33] ABS, acquisition number [č. př.] 2085-2105/91, package number [balík] 45, OS SNB Jindřichův Hradec, 1979.
[34] ABS, acquisition number [č. př.] 2085-2105/91, package number [balík] 45, OS SNB Jindřichův Hradec, 1979.
[35] ABS, acquisition number [č. př.] 2917-2927/96, package number [balík] 43, SNB Karviná, 1985.
[36] ABS, acquisition number [č. př.] 2917-2927/96, package number [balík] 42, SNB Karviná, 1985.
[37] ABS, acquisition number [č. př.] 2665-2675/95, package number [balík] 47, OS SNB Frýdek Místek, 1984.

Contemporary statements made by both the sending countries' officials and Czechoslovak administrators framed the brawls as antithetical to the labor exchange programs' spirit, which was supposed to be the spirit of socialist internationalism.[38] However, perhaps, rather than an aberration, these clashes may be more usefully read as another, if less pleasant, facet of what Gertrud Hüwelmeier called socialist cosmopolitanism, which she described as "a relative plasticity and ethnic egalitarianism that characterized the mobility and interaction, trade and migrant labor networks in ex-COMECON countries."[39] This mobility, for the most part, generated "a kind of global socialist life and ... forms of a cosmopolitan sociability by creating overseas friendship relations, economic ties and networks of exchange and reciprocity." In the best cases, these relationships resembled those of a Vietnamese female professor educated in the Soviet Union and later working in Algeria, for whom, when feeling homesick, "what made all the difference were her Russian-speaking colleagues, especially two Poles, with whom she discussed books and music, and visited local archaeological sites. Thanks to them, she says, she was able to carry on living a proper intellectual's life."[40] The drunk Polish and Cuban factory workers punching each other in a Czechoslovak pub[41] are, arguably, less pleasant analogs of those more noble connections.

While the friendly and nurturing bonds were made possible by the shared cultural references, the hostile ones reflected the tensions between peoples hailing from different parts of the world. The tensions, brought to the fore by the co-presence in space, revolved mainly around different conceptions of socialism and race. We have already seen an illustration of both ("they called us darkies and were insulting Fidel Castro and communism. He [also] said that Cubans are shit, and so is communism"). This account from a Czechoslovak pub is quite similar to that of a conflict in a Hungarian factory: "Things [in the Dunai Vasmü metallurgical plant] started to go wrong since 1983. We [Cubans] could not get on with the Poles. They criticized Castro and we criticized Solidarity. Both groups frequented the same place to go out and drink: 108-as bisztró. Brawls were frequent."[42] Racism not only rose to the surface after one too many drinks; it could be quite overt and manifest itself even before a first drink was served in the "misjudgement [with regard] to black [Cuban] individuals who were denied access to a luxury bar facility."[43]

Examining the verdicts shows that the courts took the racist taunting into consideration.[44] However, they only did so at sentencing when they treated the verbal

---

[38] Alamgir, "Socialist Internationalism at Work."
[39] Gertrud Hüwelmeier, "Socialist Cosmopolitanism Meets Global Pentecostalism: Charismatic Christianity among Vietnamese Migrants after the Fall of the Berlin Wall," *Ethnic and Racial Studies* 34.3 (2011): 436–53, 440.
[40] Susan Bayly, "Vietnamese Intellectuals in Revolutionary and Postcolonial Times," *Critique of Anthropology* 24.3 (2004): 320–44.
[41] See ABS, acquisition number [č. př.] 2410-2419/94], package number [balík] 27, OS SNB Louny, 1979.
[42] Cited in Hana Bortlová-Vondráková and Mónika Szente-Varga, "Labor Migration Programs Within the Socialist Bloc. Cuban Guestworkers in Late Socialist Czechoslovakia and Hungary," *Labor History* (April 2021), DOI: 10.1080/0023656X.2021.1908972.
[43] Bortlová-Vondráková and Szente-Varga, "Labor Migration Programs Within the Socialist Bloc."
[44] The court consisted of several judges, there being no jury in the local legal tradition.

racism that preceded the physical altercations as a mitigating circumstance that justified a lowering of the sentence. But in none of the cases under consideration was the verbal racism enough for a not-guilty verdict. From the judges' perspective, the physical harm resulting from the clashes took precedence and was always at the core of the process of allocating guilt and deciding on the seriousness of the crime. Since it was the foreign workers who, as a rule, were the first to take the altercation from a verbal to a physical level, it was they whom the courts judged to be the initiators of the conflict; verbal abuse was not viewed as initiating the fight. This approach was consistent with the state-socialist approach to race and racism, which was anchored in the insistence that racism was foreign to socialist societies and only existed elsewhere.[45] In connection with the foreign workers, this notion of racism existing elsewhere was connected with the conceptualization of the migrant labor program as a socialist civilizing mission.[46] This is evident in the verdict in the case of a fight between Cuban and Polish workers, where the judge justified the sentences imposed in this way: "Even though the reason for the fight was not established, this way of resolving disagreements is wholly incompatible with a civilized society. The accused behaved aggressively and in a way that grossly contradicts the principles of socialist coexistence of citizens in a socialist society."[47] In other words, the accused foreign workers failed to use the labor exchange program as a vehicle for becoming civilized.

That said, in many cases, foreign workers received sentences in the lowest ranges codified for the crime in question due to another mitigating factor: the fact that they would be serving the sentences far from home. The language used in the verdicts indicates that foreign workers convicted of crimes and sentenced by Czechoslovak courts served the sentences in Czechoslovak prisons and were deported only upon the completion of their sentences (deportations were listed in the verdicts as part of the imposed punishment). In two cases, the judges explicitly cited this fact as a reason for imposing sentences in the lower part of the prescribed range. In one case, the judge wrote, "The court, however, took into consideration that the defendant has no criminal past and serving his sentence will affect him, as a foreign national, more severely [than it would Czechoslovak citizens] and it will have an appreciable impact on him given the fact that he will serve it in an environment foreign to him."[48]

We do not know whether foreign workers served out their entire sentences in Czechoslovak prisons, only that the verdicts suggested that they would. In some of the cases, the foreign governments (Vietnamese, Cuban, and Polish) whisked their citizens under investigation back to their home countries without the knowledge of Czechoslovak authorities before the investigations were concluded. In these cases, the investigations were suspended and no trial took place in Czechoslovakia. The foreign governments also likely intervened in an official way while the trial was underway.

---

[45] Alamgir, "Race is elsewhere."
[46] Alamgir, "Race is elsewhere."
[47] ABS, acquisition number [č. př.] 2410-2419/94, package number [balík] 27, OS SNB Louny, 1979.
[48] ABS, acquisition number [č. př.] 3212-3223/99, package number [balík] 21, KS SNB Ústí nad Labem, 1986.

The Prison

Discussing verdicts and sentences brings into focus one more space that appears in the crime investigation files, if at times only as a nebulous possibility hovering in the background, a space in which a very small minority of foreign workers found themselves: the prison. The source base for this topic, though modest, is exceptionally valuable given the total absence of this facet of state-socialist migrant workers' experience from the literature, which makes it well worth exploring despite its fragmentary nature. The empirical evidence comes from twenty-nine letters written either by or to Vietnamese suspects, all of whom were in jail awaiting their trials. No fewer than twenty-seven of the letters come from the same case, and the remaining two are each from a different case. Hence, the first twenty-seven letters are written by the same set of people, and thus somewhat repetitive. The repetition is due, in part, to the fact that the letters had to be approved by the prison authorities before they were mailed, and this, in turn, necessitated that they be translated. This meant that the letters sometimes took so long to reach the addressees that the imprisoned writers thought the letters had been lost and thus they rewrote and resent them. In other cases, the writers repeated what they wrote previously because the original letter, indeed, had not been delivered since it violated the communication rules, chiefly the proscription on discussing the facts of their cases.

The letters offer us at least a tentative glimpse into the lives of detained foreign workers (in this case, all Vietnamese). The letters are deeply affecting as they convey poignantly the sense of profound loneliness that the imprisoned Vietnamese suffered. They were lonely, first of all (as even the judges intuited) due to their limited, and sometimes almost non-existent, ability to converse with their fellow inmates:

> During the past few days, I have been very sad. I live here with other Czechoslovak prisoners. I have not met any of our compatriots [the incident involved a group of Vietnamese and several were arrested], nor do I have any news from any of them, each of us is in a different place. That's why I am so terribly sad, I am completely alone here, I have no one to talk to. I am remembering you, my family, my faraway motherland, my childhood friends.[49]

Others wrote similar letters: "I am sharing the cell with Czech prisoners. I would like to talk with them, but I don't speak much Czech, it's boring." Another wrote, "I don't know what to do. I can't just sit in the cell the whole time, so I walk back and forth and I count the steps, meters, kilometers. Sometimes I cover more than ten, and even twenty km." Or again, "If I were imprisoned in Vietnam, it would be much better. I would share the cell with compatriots and I would have someone to talk to. Here, in a Czechoslovak prison, we just look at each other silently or play chess or some game with matches."[50]

---

[49] ABS, KS SNB Ostrava, Investigation file [Vyšetřovací spis] VV-17/10-82, case: Vuong Dinh Hoa and company, 1983.
[50] All quotes from ABS, KS SNB Ostrava, Investigation file [Vyšetřovací spis] VV-17/10-82, case: Vuong Dinh Hoa and company, 1983.

However, there was an additional aspect that made the Vietnamese prisoners even lonelier, putting them in a situation that appears almost unbearable: the intense concern that their families back in Vietnam do not learn about their predicament. The anxiety stemmed from the fear that their transgression would bring upon their family a great shame. Every one of the imprisoned letter writers writing to his Vietnamese colleagues in Czechoslovakia included in their letters, sometimes repeatedly, an admonition along the following lines: "I ask you and all our other friends to please not write anything about this affair in your letters to Vietnam." The fact that the imprisoned Vietnamese were determined to do whatever it took to keep their loved ones back in Vietnam in the dark about what was happening to them meant that they were deprived of the comfort of both writing to and receiving letters from their parents and other relatives. This was because, to quote from another letter, "I wanted to write to my parents, but they only let us use pencils here, and what would my parents say if they received a letter from me written in pencil?" Since a pencil-written letter would have blown their cover, the prisoners resorted to asking their friends in the hostels to open whatever letters they received from home, convey the contents to the prisoners, and write in their stead to their families, informing them that the prisoner in question was healthy and doing well, without ever mentioning that he was in prison. At the same time, the workers, of course, realized that eventually the families would learn, and this was a source of immense anguish for them: "What will I say to my parents, my friends when they deport me, and I arrive in Vietnam? The festivities that accompanied me when I was departing for a foreign country will be matched by the disgrace that will accompany me when I return from abroad. I keep thinking about it all the time." A rare letter from an uncle not yet aware that his nephew was reading his dispatch in a Czechoslovak prison, gives us an idea of the pressure the workers were under:

> I know that [it] is not cheerful to be spending the [Lunar] New Year holiday in a foreign country, far from the motherland and from parents, but don't be sad, you have to hang in there, study hard, work hard, and in a few years' time, you'll return and be with us again. You must also lead a proper life to become a good citizen of your motherland and a good son to your parents ... I have heard that some young men committed crimes that do not bring a good name to the motherland. I am sure that you condemn such acts and do not maintain contacts with bad people. All of us Vietnamese are proud to belong to the nation that for years fought for independence of our motherland under the leadership of President Ho Chi Minh, and one that is in the process of building a happy life for future generations. You have been sent abroad to study and work well ... I know [unreadable] that your behavior is exemplary, in accordance with my and your parents' wishes.[51]

One can only imagine what feelings a letter like that might have stirred up in a Vietnamese worker jailed in Czechoslovakia on charges of assault and causing serious

---

[51] ABS, KS SNB Ostrava, Investigation file [Vyšetřovací spis] VV-17/10-82, case: Vuong Dinh Hoa and company, 1983.

bodily harm. It is difficult to interpret the meaning and significance of the patriotic and political references in the letter. There is a realistic possibility that the uncle anticipated that his letter might be intercepted and vetted by authorities somewhere along the way and made sure to include these references to increase the odds that the news of a more private character—for example, "Vinh is healthy and will be getting married. He met a girl who went to the same primary school as him. I have yet to meet her"—will reach the addressee. At the same time, there are multiple ethnographic reports documenting the authenticity of similar attitudes among Vietnamese workers toward their spells in state-socialist European countries.[52] That is to say, while the motivations and experiences of the migrant workers (and their families back home) were complex and varied, and stemmed in part from economic necessity or self-interest, political-ideological convictions were part of the mix too.

Unsurprisingly, the stay in the space that is the prison often meant that the prisoners went to other places in their heads. As was only to be expected, that place was often their home country: "One of my fellow prisoners gave me a piece of orange peel; I ate just a tiny piece, but it strongly reminded me of our faraway motherland and tears started flowing from my eyes."[53] Somewhat unexpectedly, some of the prisoners also remembered (or imagined) fondly the Czechoslovak landscape, one such only in passing, writing to a friend on the outside, still working for a Czechoslovak company: "In these winter days, it is beautiful outside, is there a lot of snow where you are?"[54] Another one is much more extensive and poetic:

> Dear Thang, during these winter days, it's probably beautiful outside, isn't it? I can imagine how beautiful the whole landscape is under the white cover of snow: hills, trees, meadows, roofs, all under snow. Nature in this country is very beautiful in winter. And on top of that, they have winter sports here: skating, skiing, ice hockey. But I cannot enjoy this beauty.[55]

And he reprised the theme in a letter to another friend: "Dear Hoan ... are you taking pictures of the Czechoslovak landscape covered by snow? I can imagine how beautiful the conifers are with their branches covered by snow, how beautiful the whole country is under the white blanket, our native country doesn't have this kind of natural beauty."[56] These letters suggest that, despite the imprisonment and the exceedingly difficult

---

[52] Tereza Kušníráková, "Vztah vietnamských navrátilců předlistopadové imigrace k československému státu a jeho společnosti," *Český lid* 99.1 (2012): 45–66; Chrisitna Schwenkel, "Rethinking Asian Mobilities: Socialist Migration and Post-Socialist Repatriation of Vietnamese Contract Workers in East Germany," *Critical Asian Studies* 46.2 (2014): 235–58; Alamgir, "Socialist Internationalism at Work."
[53] ABS, KS SNB Ostrava, Investigation file [Vyšetřovací spis] VV-17/10-82, case: Vuong Dinh Hoa and company, 1983.
[54] ABS, KS SNB Ostrava, Investigation file [Vyšetřovací spis] VV-17/10-82, case: Vuong Dinh Hoa and company, 1983.
[55] ABS, KS SNB Ostrava, Investigation file [Vyšetřovací spis] VV-17/10-82, case: Vuong Dinh Hoa and company, 1983.
[56] ABS, KS SNB Ostrava, Investigation file [Vyšetřovací spis] VV-17/10-82, case: Vuong Dinh Hoa and company, 1983.

circumstances in which the workers found themselves, they maintained a positive relationship to the Czechoslovak landscape. One of the imprisoned workers also maintained a positive relationship with a Czechoslovak colleague, to whom he wrote from prison, "Here, as in Vietnam, we welcome the arrival of the new year as the arrival of the spring. Each of us is one year older, or, as we Vietnamese say, we will be one spring older. On the occasion of the [Lunar] New Year, I am sending you and your family wishes of good health, happiness, contentment and success at work."[57] He then proceeded to enquire about his friend's life and asked him to write, for "even though [the Vietnamese prisoner's] Czech is not good, [he] hopes that he will be able to understand the content of the [Czech friend's] letter."[58]

This brings up the question of relationships that foreign workers maintained with the local population, an important issue given that the general portrayal in the literature and popular memory of these groups, especially the Vietnamese, is one of living in isolation. There certainly was an aspect of isolation, or more specifically, the phenomenon of physical proximity and social distance, as I argued above. However, as the letter indicates, there indubitably were social contacts and relationships between the foreign workers and local people. Even in most files concerning the pub brawls, there are mentions of Czechoslovak friends or acquaintances talking and interacting with the foreign workers before the mayhem (initiated by third parties) erupted. Many of these relationships seems to have been fairly superficial: the Vietnamese as well as the Czechoslovaks would often say they knew the other(s) only by sight or by first name, that they occasionally chatted, or worked together in the same shop or department. In one case, a Czech co-worker living in the same hostel gave rides to and from work to his Vietnamese colleagues but charged money for it. At other times, however, these relationships were more substantial. In the context of the pub brawls, the Czechoslovak citizens would stand up for their foreign friends or try to prevent what was swiftly degenerating into a clash by trying to talk both sides out of it.

A special category is constituted by romantic and sexual relationships. Once again, some of them appear to be somewhat shallow, others rather deep, including the fathering of children,[59] or, as we saw above with a Cuban worker, moving in and living together. Some came into being in the workplace: one male Vietnamese worker dated a Czechoslovak female crane operator he had met on the job.[60] There are also mentions of marriages between Vietnamese men and Czechoslovak women in oral history interviews. For instance, a Czechoslovak manager in charge of a Vietnamese group in a particular factory remembered four mixed weddings. He gave more details about two of the cases: "One, a nice, well-built guy, Hung, courted a hairdresser, a single mother of a girl, and married her." As for the other one, it "was an odd case. He was a guy about

---

[57] ABS, KS SNB Ostrava, Investigation file [Vyšetřovací spis] VV-17/10-82, case: Vuong Dinh Hoa and company, 1983.
[58] ABS, KS SNB Ostrava, Investigation file [Vyšetřovací spis] VV-17/10-82, case: Vuong Dinh Hoa and company, 1983.
[59] ABS, acquisition number [č. př.] 3212-3223/99, package number [balík] 21, KS SNB Ústí nad Labem, 1986.
[60] ABS, Investigative file [vyšetřovací spis] VV-11/10-84, Nguyen Van An, KS SNB Ostrava, Investigative Unit, 1984.

forty years old and knocked up a cleaning lady from the hostel, a lady of ample proportions, also around forty. After the baby was born, he married her." Both the women the Czechoslovak manager described seemed to have occupied somewhat marginal social positions: one was a single mother and the other one was overweight. The partner of the Vietnamese worker who had a child by him is referred to in the investigation files as "Gypsy," that is, a member of the Roma ethnic minority.[61] The Roma, both men and women, appear as marginal characters with some connections to foreign workers, both Vietnamese and Cuban, in several other cases in the files. So, it appears that the relationships, sexual and otherwise, between foreign workers and local citizens more frequently involved locals who occupied some sort of marginalized social position.

Finally, there was one special relationship that arose within the criminal justice system between Vietnamese interpreters, who were, as a rule, recruited from among Vietnamese group leaders (who tended to be the graduates of Czechoslovak universities or trade schools) and Czechoslovak psychiatrists. These relationships came about because in the cases of murder or attempted murder, the prosecutors, in keeping with the usual practice, requested that mental health professionals examine and evaluate defendants. This was not a straightforward affair when defendants happened to be Vietnamese and the Czechoslovak medical experts found themselves practicing cross-cultural forensic psychiatry. In standard practice, what is valued and desired is the interpreter's inconspicuousness, almost invisibility: "a good translator (who is accurate and unobtrusive) can greatly facilitate the clinical interview, primarily by being less visible or prominent in the interview process."[62] In the Australian context, judges have expressed the desire that "[a]n interpreter really only acts as a transmission belt or telephone," or again that "[t]he interpreter should look upon himself rather as an electric transformer, whatever is fed into him is to be fed out again, duly transformed."[63] This was far from what took place in the cases under consideration here. Rather than serving only as language translators, they were called upon to be cultural translators. One of the files states this explicitly: "Since the [Czechoslovak] experts had no information about the prevalent disposition/mentality of the Vietnamese, the interpreter was asked to share with the experts some facts in regard to current norms among the Vietnamese population, especially in those areas that can be expected to differ from our European culture."[64] The cultural brokerage that was asked of the interpreter was astoundingly broad:

> [T]he interpreter shared with the Czechoslovak psychiatrists that the use of a knife is very common in conflict situations in Vietnam, almost equivalent to our slap in

---

[61] ABS, Investigative file [č. př.] 3212-3223/99, package number [balík] 21, KS SNB Ústí nad Labem, 1986.]
[62] Virginia Barber Rioja and Barry Rosenfeld, "Addressing Linguistic and Cultural Differences in the Forensic Interview," *International Journal of Forensic Mental Health* 17.4 (2018): 377–86, 383.
[63] Sandra Hale, "The Challenges of Court Interpreting: Intricacies, responsibilities and ramifications," *Alternative Law Journal* 32.4 (2007): 198–202.
[64] ABS, acquisition number [č. př.] 2849-2860, package number [balík] 68, KS SNB Ústí nad Labem, 1985.

the face. So is the absence of outward emotional expression in daily contact. Further, the interpreter informed the experts about the basic features of the educational system, the process of work placement, compulsory military service, and the rank of the social group corresponding to the status of the defendant's family. The interpreter told the [Czechoslovak] experts that the accused showed a substantially higher ability to express himself during the psychiatric and psychological examinations than during police interrogation … at which time, his overall communication gave the impression of lower intellectual capabilities. [By contrast] during the expert examinations, the interpreter assessed the defendant's intellectual capabilities as average, that is to say corresponding to average IQ levels.[65]

The above passage shows that the interpreter was a source of a breathtaking amount of information on a wide range of topics concerning Vietnamese cultural practices. Two of the items on the long list of the topics managed by the interpreter seem of particular importance: (1) the assertion that knife assaults are "almost equivalent to our slap in the face," and (2) his comparison of the accused man's communicative competence during the police interview versus during the psychiatric assessment. The first mattered because, in the Czechoslovak legal system, the sanctions attached to assaulting someone with a knife were rather different from those imposed on someone for slapping another in the face. Such reframing (along with the reframing of the meaning of facial expression) would have profoundly changed both the meaning and the implications of the crime with which the man was being charged. The second one mattered because it spoke to the sincerity of the accused, and hence to the presumed veracity of his statements, which, again, would have had implications for both charges and potential punishment. In a sense, in the first instance, the interpreter momentarily assumed the role of a police officer, and, in the second one, that of a medical expert. Even if the idea that interpreters are mere "transmission belts" is naïve, the role played by the interpreter here goes far beyond even that of acting "as gatekeepers and/or manager[s] of the exchange as they have more control over allocation of turns of talk."[66] What we see here, instead, is a stunning degree of both autonomy and authority conferred upon the interpreter by the Czechoslovak medical and justice system experts. Indeed, so extensive seems to have been the power of the interpreter in this case that he is cited several times in the file as an authority on the truthfulness of the defendant's statements. This was an exercise in very real and very important power.

We see the same dynamics in another case featuring a different defendant and a different interpreter. Here, the interpreter is quoted as saying that "[the defendant's mode of] expression is not very coherent; it is marked by poor vocabulary, a-grammatical structures, and is sometimes difficult to understand. The interpreter assesses him as a simple person with little education."[67] While these evaluations were

---

[65] ABS, acquisition number [č. př.] 2849-2860, package number [balík] 68, KS SNB Ústí nad Labem, 1985.
[66] Fabrizio Gallai, "Pragmatic Competence and Interpreter-Mediated Police Investigative Interviews," *The Translator* 23.2 (2017): 177–96.
[67] ABS, acquisition number [č. př.] 3475-3487/01, package number [balík] 60, KS SNB Ústí nad Labem, 1989.

still tied fairly closely to the linguistic competence of the accused, and hence, arguably within the interpreter's purview, the translator also offered his opinion on the fact that the defendant deserted while conscripted (during the American War), saying that "that probably doesn't indicate anything special about the accused, since, at the time, everyone was reportedly deserting their units."[68] Thus, we see a pattern of the Czechoslovak medical and law enforcement authorities ceding to Vietnamese interpreters a not negligible amount of freedom and power to frame the meaning and the seriousness of the crimes that their compatriots were accused of.

Conclusion

Hostels were the workers' homes away from home. As such, the migrant workers used various means of making these spaces, which had not originally been built for them, their own. The most obvious method for doing this relied on populating the hostels with various objects like the wall decorations that we can see in Figure 11.1. Another means of making these spaces their own was through using the kitchenettes to cook their own meals, an activity through which they ushered into the hearts of the hostels one of the most intimate and most deeply meaningful cultural artifacts: their national cuisines. Yet another kind of object that marked the hostels as the migrant workers' own spaces were the goods that they stored there, which they could then use as remittances-in-kind. These goods, just like the informal economic activities the workers engaged in, not only made the hostels more their own, but also directly connected their two homes[69]—the faraway family home and their temporary work assignment home—thus creating transnational networks spanning thousands of miles and all three (First, Second, and Third) Worlds. The migrants also remade the hostels into their spaces through activities. Besides cooking, they also pursued their own leisure activities, such as dominoes, and most radically by converting the living space partly into a workspace. This workspace was very different from their official workplace: here they fully controlled both the process of their work and its results (for example, the sewing of jeans and other clothing). These activities, through their link to remittances, once again connected the workers both with their family homes and global economic networks.

Although the receiving state tried to formally insert itself and its power into the migrant workers' hostels, the dwellings ended up being spaces almost entirely controlled by those workers. The workers defied and flaunted the hostels' (and thus the state's) rules, severely curtailing the ability of "porters" to surveil them, much less to regulate their lives. With the exception of the porters, with whom the workers were locked in a relationship of physical proximity and social distance, locals made only occasional forays into hostels—girlfriends and co-conspirators, many members of socially marginal groups, such as the Roma, make brief appearances in the crime files. Thus,

[68] ABS, acquisition number [č. př.] 3475-3487/01, package number [balík] 60, KS SNB Ústí nad Labem, 1989.
[69] Vietnamese who worked or studied in state-socialist Europe often refer to the countries as their second homes: see Tereza Kušníráková, "Vztah vietnamských navrátilců předlistopadové imigrace k československému státu a jeho společnosti," *Český lid* 99.1 (2012): 45–66.

hostels turned out to be the spaces that the foreign workers were able make their own to a significant degree.

By contrast, the most salient characteristic of the pubs was that they were the sites where the locals and the migrant workers interacted frequently. While these interactions and encounters sometimes led to lifelong friendships,[70] they also frequently sparked hostilities. The pubs were places in which fierce clashes over the control of space and who rightfully belonged in it took place. The clashes tended to follow a strikingly uniform pattern in which first, (drunk) locals started taunting migrant workers with racist insults, often laced with derisions of the form that socialism took in the migrant workers' countries of origin. The verbal put-downs then led to physical altercations, which, finally, pulled the state—embodied by the police officers called to the scene— into the space from which it had originally been largely absent. Judges, also direct representatives of the state, were keenly aware of the role that place played in these situations. This was reflected in the fact that they routinely treated the fact that the convicted foreign workers would be serving their sentences far from home as a mitigating circumstance and imposed lower sentences on them.

Finally, the prisons were spaces thoroughly permeated by the Czechoslovak state's power. They were also the spaces that were the hardest for the migrant workers to "make their own." The prisons were not part of the transnational networks that encompassed the hostels. This was due to the intensely felt need to conceal the carceral situation from the families back home, which led many imprisoned Vietnamese to choose to abstain from the most important transnational communication channel: letters to their families in Vietnam. All that remained to connect them with home was memories, sometimes assisted by momentary sensations, such as the smell of orange peel. Yet, the solitude of the prison also made visible the attachments that the workers had made to the Czechoslovak landscape and nature.

While the imprisoned foreign workers lived among Czechoslovak inmates, their limited linguistic competence often prevented them from cultivating relationships with them. For the same reason, the migrant worker prisoners could not directly communicate with either the police or the forensic psychiatrists. This limitation, however, opened the door to a unique relationship between the Czechoslovak criminal justice system authorities and medical experts on the one hand, and other members of the migrant community, the interpreters, on the other. Far from functioning as "information transmission belts," the Vietnamese translators were invited by the Czechoslovak authorities, cognizant of their ignorance of Vietnamese cultural norms, to interpret the meaning of the actions of the workers accused of crimes. This gave the interpreters the power to frame their compatriots' actions, in effect granting them the powers normally reserved for either police officers or medical experts, and thus contributing significantly to how the meaning, and hence the seriousness, of the committed crimes would be eventually assessed and adjudicated.

---

[70] Kušníráková, "Vztah vietnamských navrátilců"; Alamgir, "Socialist Internationalism at Work"; Hüwelmeier, "Socialist Cosmopolitanism"; Bayly, "Vietnamese Intellectuals."

12

The Travelogue: Imagining Spaces of Encounter—Travel Writing Between the Colonial and the Anti-Colonial in Socialist Eastern Europe, 1949–1989

Eric Burton, Zoltán Ginelli, James Mark, and Nemanja Radonjić

From the mid-1950s, as anti-colonial struggles intensified and decolonization accelerated, travel writing became a key genre through which to educate populations in state socialist Eastern Europe about the new world that was emerging beyond direct empire. In the GDR, for instance, of the thirty-three book-length travelogues published between 1955 and 1962, only eight dealt with Western countries; the rest witnessed the progress of "fraternal socialist nations" such as China, as well as other countries in Africa, Asia, and Latin America.[1] Whereas the former provided first-hand accounts of the dark sides of capitalism in ways designed to stifle admiration and wanderlust, the latter sought to inspire national readerships to feel solidarity with this epochal transformation. Publishing houses across the region intiated book series: in Hungary, Globetrotters (*Világjárók*) by Gondolat and Travel Adventures (*Útikalandok*) by Táncsics were the most important. In Poland, the series Continents (*Kontynenty*) led the way. The largest ever Yugoslav travel writing compendium, *Travels Round the World*, was published in 1961.[2]

This significant form of postcolonial travel writing has been long forgotten.[3] It was seldom internationalized: the majority of texts remained in one language, and were not

---

[1] Jean Mortier, "Reiseliteratur," in Michael Opitz, Michael Hofmann, and Julian Kanning (eds.), *Metzler Lexikon DDR-Literatur: Autoren–Institutionen–Debatten* (Stuttgart, 2009), 270.
[2] Fadil Hadžić (ed.), *Put oko svijeta* (Zagreb, 1961). It contains thirty-five accounts on Europe, ten on North America, six on Australia, ten on South America, eighteen on Asia, and eight on Africa.
[3] The vast majority of academic work concerns Western travelers and the colonial experience. See Carl Thompson, "Introduction," in Carl Thompson (ed.), *The Routledge Companion to Travel Writing* (New York, 2016). Where Eastern Europeans appear, it is usually through their travels in the West, e.g. Wendy Bracewell and Alex Drace-Francis (eds.), *Under Eastern Eyes: A Comparative Introduction to East European Travel Writing on Europe* (Budapest and New York, 2008). During the socialist era, writers constructed accounts of progressive Eastern European explorers; interest in this encounter has revived in the last decade: Alex Drace-Francis, "Travel Writing from Eastern Europe," in Nandini Das and Tim Youngs (eds.), *The Cambridge History of Travel Writing* (Cambridge, 2013), 198–9; Jiřina Šmejkalová, "Command Celebrities: The Rise and Fall of Hanzelka and Zikmund," *Central*

promoted for markets beyond the region. Accounts of African or Asian travelers to the bloc were translated and published in the "Third World" by Soviet publishers, but accounts of Eastern Bloc travelers to Africa and Asia were not.[4] When the expansion of the socialist world provided travel opportunities to a select few, such texts made sense of this opening for *national readerships*. Commonly issued by either state-supported youth publishers, or state organs, such as the Ministry of National Defense in Poland, they sought to convince a younger generation to see their own country's socialist projects as part of a global transformation.

Whilst new writing encouraged socialist citizens to look beyond exoticizing and Orientalizing discourses on the extra-European world, fantasies of global power, domination, and mobility were often not far from the surface. Moreover, earlier travel accounts, steeped in the region's colonial fantasies, were (re)published after the publishing restrictions of the Stalinist period were lifted, satisfying markets for such material that had already been established before the communist takeovers.[5] Hunting traveloges and adventure stories, which positioned their protagonists as "heroic Europeans" in imperial territories, sold more than those which superficially declared themselves *anti-colonial* travelogues. Focusing on the GDR, Yugoslavia, and Hungary, but also drawing on examples from Poland, Czechoslovakia, and Romania, we explore how the choice to put a predominantly colonial genre in the service of anti-colonialism was illustrative of the many ideological tensions, and ambiguous and shifting commitments, at the heart of Eastern European state socialism.

Bringing a Distant World Close: The Anti-colonial Travelogue

The creation of a new, specifically anti-colonial travelogue rested on the belief that a colonial gaze did not naturally adhere to the genre. Colonial travel books were critiqued as remnants of the past, and the region's interwar iterations blamed for misleading Eastern Europeans to ally themselves culturally with a colonial West.[6] Nevertheless, a reformed travelogue, the work of a new type of traveler, was possible. Whereas journeys

---

Europe 13 (2015); Martin Slobodniak, "Socialist Anti Orientalism: Perceptions of China in Czechoslovak Travelogues from the 1950s," and Róbert Gáfrik, "Representations of India in Slovak Travel Writing during the Communist Regime (1948–1989)," both in Dobrota Pucherová and Róbert Gáfrik (eds.), *Postcolonial Europe? Essays on Post-Communist Literatures and Cultures* (Amsterdam, 2015). For some Polish work on travel writing that touches on the socialist era, see Elżbieta Malinowska and Dariusz Rott (eds.), *Wokół reportażu podróżniczego* (Katowice, 2004); Krzysztof Podemski, *Socjologia podróży* (Poznań, 2005).

[4] Rossen Djagalov, *From Internationalism to Postcolonialism: Literature and Cinema between the Second and the Third Worlds* (Montreal, 2020), 99–100.

[5] See Péter Mándi, *A könyv és közönsége* (Budapest, 1968); on the Soviet case, Stephen Lovell, *The Russian Reading Revolution: Print Culture in the Soviet and Post-Soviet Eras* (Basingstoke, 2000), chapter 3.

[6] See Zoran Milutinović, "Oh, to be a European! What Rastko Petrović Learnt in Africa," in Wendy Bracewell and Alex Drace-Francis (eds.), *Under Eastern Eyes: A Comparative Introduction to East European Travel Writing on Europe* (Budapest and New York, 2008), 286; Milutin Milenković, "Libija više nije zemlja pjeska i kamena," in Dragoslav Adamović (ed.), *Afrička putovanja bez kolonijalnog pasoša* (Zagreb, 1964), 255–9; Oskar Davičo, *Crno na belo* (Belgrade, 1969), 156.

to the South had once been the preserve of the aristocratic explorer or leisured bourgeois, socialist-era texts emphasized the role of the "curious wanderer," the "enlightened professional," and the "common person." Often their staged innocence concealed the special permissions necessary to undertake such travel: Hungarian writer Rózsa Ignácz presented herself simply deciding to take off to visit a long-lost friend in East Africa she had know from her Transylvanian hometown.[7] The Yugoslav writer, journalist, film director, and painter Fadil Hadžić described the mission of what he called the "new travel writer" as to "politically orient us and paint the world—still not free of colonialism and discrimination."[8] Oskar Davičo, the former surrealist whose reportages were published to parallel Tito's trip to West Africa in 1961, saw his work as the renunciation of "colonial baggage" and the rejection of the work of interwar modernist Rastko Petrović, whose widely-read travelogue "Afrika"—a central reference point in the Yugoslav tradition—had been strongly influenced by Joseph Conrad's writing.[9] Davičo spent his days with like-minded guerrillas and syndicalists, pioneers and peasants. In his anti-colonial text, the "other" becomes the Western imperialists themselves—Belgian soldiers, French clerks, and British officers.[10]

The envisaged readership for these new anti-colonial travelogues was primarily national and young. Most sought to educate youth to see the amazing changes in the world as an extension of their own specific national histories and traditions.[11] In Poland, *Spark* (*Iskry*), which had previously published mainly children's and teenage literature, became the main outlet of foreign travelogues. In Yugoslavia, the first travelogues were commisioned by publishing houses such as New Youth (Novo pokoljenje), while in Hungary they appered in magazines such as *Young Communist* (*Ifjú Kommunista*) or *Pal* (*Pajtás*). Many East German travelogues appeared with the Verlag Neues Leben, a publishing house controlled by the East German youth organization FDJ, for the younger reader. Yugoslav Nikola Vitorović's *The Black Tears of the Congo*, which addressed the Congo Crisis and murder of Patrice Lumumba, and Hungarian Endre Barát's 1962 novel *Burning Spear*, a fictionalized account of Kenyan liberation, were given as prizes to the best school students.[12] Such works were chosen because they focused on dynamic contemporary events and thus helped students reject images of Africa as exotic societies "stuck in the past." Socialist media often presented the desire for travel writing as stemming from citizens themselves: in the GDR, a reader of *Neues Deutschland* remarked in a letter to the editor in 1956 that more books about changes in the world beyond Europe were needed;[13] Yugoslav readers were presented in the press as demanding that popular travel newspaper serials be published in book form.[14]

Some writers encouraged readers to critique the colonial lenses through which they viewed the world. The Hungarian poet Lajos Kónya, in his *Chinese October*, sought to

---

[7] Rózsa Ignácz, *Zebradob-híradó. Kelet-afrikai útinapló* (Budapest, 1968).
[8] Hadžić, "Predgovor," *Put oko svijeta*, 5.
[9] Davičo, *Crno na belo*, 79.
[10] Davičo, *Crno na belo*, 122, 142, 221, 223, 235, 237, 300, 331, 334.
[11] Aleš Bebler, *Putovanja po sunčanim zemljama* (Belgrade, 1954) 5.
[12] Nikola Vitorović, *Crne suze Konga* (Belgrade, 1961); Endre Barát, *Égő Lándzsa* (Budapest, 1962).
[13] "Warum so wenig Reiseberichte aus dem Ausland?" *Neues Deutschland*, January 21, 1956.
[14] Bebler, *Putovanje po sunčanim zemljama*, 5.

erase what he referred to as the "exotic bourgeois images" of the East that European imperialism had created, and proposed a "secularized image" of communist China that would allow his readership to see it closer to socialist Europe.[15] Famous Hungarian graphic artist Lajos Vincze criticized Eurocentric "chauvinism," and in his *Sunrise on the Yangtze Shore* employed culturally sensitive accounts of the everyday life of the Chinese under communism to evoke a favorable comparison with what he called "white civilization."[16] Following the Sino-Soviet split, some writers shifted their focus to Southeast Asia, most notably Vietnam. Others used the travelogue to explore their struggle to shake off upbringings in countries that—despite having only few or no extra-European colonies—had still been shaped by a pan-European imperial culture. The Polish author Wiesław Górnicki, who traveled to India in the early 1960s, drew on the rituals of socialist self-criticism. He castigated himself for being a European Orientalist who framed the world in terms of civilization and backwardness, viewing rural India through the lens of Rudyard Kipling's *The Jungle Book*. The struggle to purge the imperial lens was the key lesson for his audience.[17]

In Yugoslavia, where Franz Fanon's challenge to Eurocentric thinking was published earlier than elsewhere in the region, travel writers such as Dušan Miklja took up his call to question the tenets of European superiority over African backwardness.[18] Yugoslavs, he claimed, were well equipped to assist in creating a positive, anti-colonial image of Africa: their own history of liberation from the Ottoman and Austro-Hungarian empires rendered them more informed and sensitive travelers.[19] Boža Milačić was critical of the way in which globally-influential Western books, such as John Gunther's *Inside Africa* (1955, Yugoslav translation, 1966), attributed to the continent child-like characteristics.[20] Aleš Bebler explored the inability of "Western writers" to adequately represent Africa and Asia—and demonstrated how Yugoslavs could do it by not adopting the "colonizers' voice."[21] In Dušan Miklja's *Black Sisyphus*, the stories of local African porters on Mt. Kilimanjaro were used to criticize what he called "Victorian and post-Victorian" images of white men conquering high mountains with the assistance of colored peoples. Instead, he reversed the trope to show Europeans merely discovering

---

[15] Lajos Kónya, *Kínai október* (Budapest, 1952).
[16] Lajos Vincze, *Napkelte a Jangce partján* (Budapest, 1959), 272; Mária Dutka, "Műteremlátogatás a Kínába induló Hincz Gyulánál," *Magyar Nemzet*, October 9, 1957, 7.
[17] Wiesław Górnicki, *Podróż po garść ryżu* (Warsaw, 1964). Edward W. Said's *Orientalism* did not appear until 1981 in Yugoslavia and was published only after the collapse of communism in Hungary and Poland (1991).
[18] The first Fanon translation was Slovenian: *Les Damnés de la Terre/Upor prekletih* (Ljubljana, 1963). The 1973 Serbo-Croatian translation (*Prezreni na svijetu*, Zagreb, 1973) became the most circulated one. The year 1977 saw the publication of a collection of Fanon's other famous works, including parts of *Black Skin, White Masks*. Franz Fanon, *Sociologija revolucije. Ogledi o alžirskoj i afričkoj revoluciji* (Belgrade, 1977); Dušan Miklja, *Crni Sizif. Zapisi iz Afrike* (Belgrade,1985); Aleksandra S. Lazarević, "Black Sisyphus—Notes from Africa," *Razvoj=Development International* 1 (1986): 239–42; Nemanja Radonjić and Emilia Epštajn, interview with Dušan Miklja, Belgrade, 2018 (audio file available at the Museum of African Art, Belgrade).
[19] Many travelogues emphasize this contrast, e.g. Landolf Scherzer, *Bom dia, weißer Bruder: Erlebnisse am Sambesi*. Second edition (Rudolstadt, 1986), 146; Vitorović, *Crne suze Konga*.
[20] Božo Milačić, *Sunčana putovanja i bijele noći. Zapisi sa putovanja od Islanda do Sahare* (Zagreb, 1963), 45.
[21] Bebler, *Putovanje po sunčanim zemljama*, 151.

what the Africans already knew, the African sherpas who live under Mt. Kilimanjaro becoming his knowledgeable "true heroes."²² Such statements stood in a longer-term tradition of Eastern European claims that due to their own experiences of being colonized they were free of the rapacious colonial desires that marked the West.²³

Most of the region's travelogues in fact exhibited a far more complex relationship with European colonialism. Whilst globalizing socialist projects did give meaningful frameworks to represent new forms of interconnection and solidarity that to some degree dissolved the high borders around European civilization, they were also still marked by the Eurocentrism of Marxist timelines in which development that had happened *here* might be exported *there*. Mutual recognition did not necessarily mean mutual learning.

Such was the tension in the accounts of Jiří Baum, a Czechoslovak natural scientist and author of both contemporary African travelogues and progressive histories of Czech exploration. Baum's work reflected the post-Stalinist impulse to throw off the conception of Africa as a static backwater, and to celebrate the European socialist expert—distinct from the earlier conquerer—who could help knit together a new "humane ecumene":

[The socialist traveler] was no longer a discoverer and conqueror, or a concocter of adventurous expeditions to foreign lands. He was an expert, a zoologist, driving through the whole world in cars, and collecting experiences, observations and research for a great zoological work ... in a world that has already converged and become united in a single human ecumene ... The Africa of Holub, Vráz, Machulka, and Šebesta [nineteenth-century Czech explorers] has disappeared. The nature of wild Africa is moving to reservations, the rivers, once mysterious, are rising up in artificial lakes behind dams, the sands of the deserts can be quickly driven across on automobile roads, and planes land anywhere in the savannahs and forest clearings. The African (hu)man creates a new society in the changed landscape.²⁴

Socialist experts published travelogues that established parallels between the two countries' developmental histories.²⁵ Presenting modernization as a familiar process that could be achieved with the right kind of ideas and global alliances, such writers encouraged in their home populations the faith that solidarity was effective—while also demonstrating that their own models of development suited postcolonial societies better than Western ones. Although promoted in socialist travel literature as the polar opposite of Western models, socialist development in fact embodied Eurocentric modernization theory, reproducing a chronopolitics familiar from Western imperialism, joining their "liberal counterpart in a denigration of the inferior times, the obsolete

---

²² Miklja, *Crni Sizif*, 108.
²³ Ulrich E. Bach, *Tropics of Vienna: Colonial Utopias of the Habsburg Empire* (New York, 2016), 2.
²⁴ Foreword by Josef Kunský in Jiří Baum, *Afrikou divočinou* (Prague, 1957). See also Jiří Baum, *Holub a Mašukulumbové* (Prague, 1955).
²⁵ See Bogdan Šekler, *Džambo Afriko!* (Belgrade, 1976); Dušan Sekulić, *Putokaz za jug* (Belgrade, 1982); Slobodan Nešović, *Svitanja i sutoni. Lutanja Evropom, Azijom, Afrikom i Amerikom* (Zagreb, 1976).

soon-to-be-superseded times, of the non-West."²⁶ Tribalism, traditionalism, polygamy, and "primitive" life would be banished by modernity, industrialization, rational planning, state welfare, and the nuclear family. The media contrasted images of the newly built, modern infrastructure—schools, libraries, hospitals—and production facilities with both tropical landscapes and "the prejudices, superstitions, and narrow tribal nationalisms" that had to be overcome.²⁷

Nevertheless, writers occasionally saw in folk heritage and tradition connections that transcended this Eurocentric developmental timeline. Experts from interwar ethnographic movements that had championed the rural fight against feudal society and mass poverty expanded their interests in the postwar to advocate for an uplift of rural peripheries globally.²⁸ These writers sought to find commonality across peasant traditions, to reject their exoticization by other Western travelers, and to advocate for cultural sensitivity in the modernization of the countryside.²⁹ A Yugoslav automobile expedition to Kilimanjaro demonstrated to their Sudanese hosts, through participation in a ceremony called "the dance of knives," that their folklore might contain the same motifs. Both the Yugoslavs and Sudanese were surprised and thrilled, since the only connection was Ottoman rule: mutual recognition in each other's folk art became the central point.³⁰ Yet these accounts had a nostalgic edge for a dying Europe eroded by socialist modernization: contemporary Africa once again became Eastern Europe's past. Hungarian Rózsa Ignácz related how the strong community life she experienced in East Africa had been lost at home under state socialism, and was moved to recount how contemporary Ugandan folk tales evoked in her vibrant "flashbacks" to Transylvanian landscapes and prewar rural Sekler folk culture.³¹

The experience of Nazi occupation was key in establishing commonality: Yugoslavs presented guerrilla fighting in Africa and East Asia as echoes of their own wartime "National Liberation Struggle."³² Polish travelogues related shared suffering: Górnicki's Indian travelogue presented the peasant revolt in Telangana and the brutal suppression of the Nizam after independence as echoes of Nazi cruelty: "maybe only the liquidation of [the] Warsaw ghetto or the events of [the] Zamojszczyzna region [in south-eastern Poland] can be compared with what happened then in Telangana."³³ Neverthless, such interconnections were, again, frequently structured through a Eurocentric conception of time. Reflecting too the essential bilateralism of most socialist internationalism, the

---

[26] Charles Mills, "The Chronopolitics of Racial Time," *Time & Society* 29.2 (2020): 313.
[27] Tamás Bácskai, "Ghana a tegnap és holnap között," *Élet és Tudomány* 17.44 (November 16, 1962): 1379–83, 1452–8 (HU OSA 300-40-1: 848) 1383.
[28] András Róna-Tas, *Nomádok nyomában: Etnográfus szemmel Mongóliában*, Világjárók 21 (Budapest, 1961); Vilma Ligeti, *Indiai arcképek*, Világjárók 114 (Budapest, 1977).
[29] See Paul Betts, "Culture," in James Mark and Paul Betts (co-ords.), *Socialism Goes Global: The Soviet Union and Eastern Europe in the Age of Decolonisation* (Oxford, 2022), 160–72.
[30] Šekler, *Džambo Afriko*, 41.
[31] Ignácz, *Zebradob-híradó*, 202. See also Zdenko Štambuk, *Od Zanzibara do Mjesečevih planina* (Zagreb, 1957); Zdenko Štambuk, *Afrički zapisi* (Zagreb, 1961).
[32] Concerning Algeria in the 1950s and Vietnam in the 1960s, see Zdravko Pečar, *Alžir* (Belgrade, 1959); Milutin Milenković, *Sa alžirskim ustanicima* (Belgrade, 1960).
[33] Wiesław Górnicki, *Podróż po garść ryżu* (1964), 127, quoted in Agnieszka Sadecka, "Exotic Others or Fellow Travellers? Representations of India in Polish Travel Writing during Communist Era," Ph.D. thesis, Eberhard Karls Universität Tübingen (2016), 68.

postcolonial present in Caribbean, Asian, or African nations became a replay of a particular European nation's revolutionary history. Writers found immense political pleasure in imagining themselves transported into their nation's past through travel. Sándor Csoóri was a young populist intellectual from a peasant background whose account of his 1961 trip to Cuba, printed in the popular press, and eventually published as *Cuban Diary* in 1965, would be influential in shaping a broader cult of the Cuban revolution in Hungary in the early to mid-1960s. Csoóri in Cuba was transported to Hungary in 1848 and its struggle for independence from the Habsburgs:[34]

> Fidel Castro and Che Guevara were in my eyes the relatives of the young revolutionaries of 1848 ... I met twice with Che, once in our hotel [and] another time during the march on José Martí square. It was like being in a Jókai [nineteenth-century Hungarian romantic nationalist] novel in which I was the main character.[35]

Caribbean and Latin American revolutionaries often rejected this framing, preferring to relate the growing relationship in terms of entangled revolutionary traditions rather than through a Eurocentric Marxist timeline; after all, as some observed, one might more convincingly claim that Latin American independence in the nineteenth century established a pathway that Eastern Europe had followed.[36]

Yet Eastern European populations were seldom exposed to such voices. Strikingly, very few contemporary travel accounts were published by authors from outside socialist Europe whose various ideological frameworks might challenge orthodox national accounts. Che Guevara's Bolivian diary was available in non-aligned Yugoslavia[37] (in general more open to radical Third Worldist and Western culture than neighboring bloc countries). A 1968 Hungarian version of the diary appeared in a restricted circulation of 300 copies for party members: the political elite feared its radicalizing effects.[38] Some Hungarian cultural and literature journals, such as *Helikon* (established 1955) and *Wide World* (*Nagyvilág*) (1956) did introduce "Third World" writers in other genres, but travel was recounted only by Eastern European—and occasionally politically acceptable Western—writers. Travelogues from the distant past were translated as part of broader academic efforts to construct an anti-Eurocentric historiography, but only as long as they did not speak directly to the Eastern European present: for instance, Hungarians published some of the travels of medieval Arab scholars Ibn Battuta or Ibn Khaldūn, and texts on the contemporary Arabic perceptions of Hungarians.[39]

---

[34] Sándor Csoóri, *Kubai napló* (Budapest, 1965); *Kubai útinapló*, published as three part series in *Új Írás* in 1963.
[35] Sándor Csoóri, "Közel a szülőföldhöz," *Kortárs* 4 (2004): 17–24.
[36] See, e.g., Roberto Fernández Retamar, "Martí in His (Third) World," trans. John Beverley, with Miguel Llinas, *boundary 2* 36.1 (2009): 68–9.
[37] Ernesto Če Guevara, *Dnevnik iz Bolivije (7.11 1966–7.10.1966)* (Belgrade, 1968); Ernesto Če Guevara, *Partizansko ratovanje i revolucija: izabrani radovi* (Belgrade, 1974).
[38] Miklós Haraszti's satirical poem about this incident led to political punishment. Miklós Haraszti, "Che hibái," *Új Írás* 9.12 (1969): 63. The book only gained wider publicity when György Moldova "rehabilitated" it in the 1980s: György Moldova, *A napló* (Budapest, 1983).
[39] Vilmos Benczik, *Arabok: Irodalmi és politikai antológia* (Budapest, 1976); Ibn Battúta, *Ibn Battúta zarándokútja és vándorlásai*, ed. István Boga, Világjárók: Klasszikus Útleírások (Budapest, 1964); István Boga, Tamás Katona, and László Várady (eds.), *Mai arab elbeszélők* (Budapest, 1960).

Moreover, communist regimes publicized a long tradition of enlightened and humane travel by Eastern Europeans in Africa that reinforced a Eurocentric timeline.[40] In this they drew on nationalist texts from the late nineteenth century onwards that fantasized about being the more enlightened and humane developers of an extra-European world, who had been denied their chance.[41] Communists developed this genre, reviving accounts of travelers whose life stories anticipated the political and moral values of socialist nations in novels, biographies, and film. Despite the official denunciation of imperialism, there was only a marginal critique of the Eurocentric and colonial history of expeditions and expansion. Instead, the "progressive" aspects of spreading an enlightened European modernity and civilization across the globe were now reclaimed where its "instinctual" Marxism or a more scientific, socialist, and humanist engagement could be discerned.[42] Each socialist nation had its own set of national explorer-heroes remade in this vein.[43] Socialist Czechoslovakia promoted Emil Holub, a progressive 1848-er who supposedly wanted to be an "anti-colonial David Livingstone." According to a 1953 account, Holub was invited by Belgian King Leopold II to help oversee the colonization of the Congo along with explorer Henry Stanley, but refused to take part in such ruthless exploitation: "Holub saw his mission in entirely different terms! He prepared for and conducted his expedition motivated by genuine scientific interest, not so that, serving colonisers, he could help them enslave natives and exploit their country..."[44]

Romanian communists likewise promoted Mihai Tican-Rumano as the compassionate white explorer of interwar Africa whose humanism led him to criticize the ruthless exploitation of those who claimed to represent civilization.[45] Similarly, in Hungary, the explorer János Xántus, the 1848-er refugee national hero and anti-imperialist, was promoted in schools and universities, whilst the memory of wealthy aristocrat Sámuel Teleki, whose expedition in northern Kenya encountered local resistance and resulted in hundreds of deaths, was repressed until the mid-1980s.

Coloniality in an Anti-Colonial Era

Socialist-era travel literature was still marked by European imperial culture. Although socialist states presented Eastern Europe as a region free of colonial desires, their national readerships had long been part of an enthusiastic pan-European audience for colonial adventure narratives. The internationalization of socialist culture spurred

---

[40] Wendy Bracewell, "Travels Through the Slav World," in Wendy Bracewell and Alex Drace-Francis (eds.), *Under Eastern Eyes: A Comparative Introduction to East European Travel Writing on Europe* (Budapest and New York, 2008), 170–2.

[41] James Mark and Steffi Marung, "Origins," in James Mark and Paul Betts (co-ords.), *Socialism Goes Global: The Soviet Union and Eastern Europe in the Age of Decolonisation* (Oxford, 2022), 31–4.

[42] László Vajda, *Nagy magyar utazók: 19. század* (Budapest, 1951).

[43] For the humane pre-Yugoslav explorer, see Aleksandra S. Lazarević's description of Dragutin Lerman, a Belgian Congo official of South Slav origin, in the review of Dushan Miklja's *Black Sisyphus* (Belgrade, 1985) in *Razvoj / Development-International* 1.1 (1986): 242.

[44] "Our Science, Technology, Art and their Representatives (Materials for Bulletin Boards)," March 1953. See also Baum, *Holub*.

[45] Dominica Filimon, "Foreword," in Mihai Tican-Rumano, *Peste mari si tari* (Bucharest:, 1973), 11.

both the creation of new hybrid anti-colonial adventure literature and the republication of older colonial travelogues and adventure stories set in "exotic" locations—which sold in much greater numbers than the politically orthodox accounts.

Some Eastern European countries had their own series of colonial adventure stories featuring their compatriots. P. Howard (Jenő Rejtő) was one of the most popular writers of mass-market "pulp" fiction in 1930s Hungary. His humorous stories, set in French colonial Africa and Southeast Asia, detailed marginal Eastern European figures, such as petty criminals or declassed intellectuals who had escaped the social hierarchies and over-regulated materialism of Europe to find freedom and meaning in the colonial world, as adventurers or legionnaires, fighting side by side with colonial troops. Rejtő's novels were republished and had a huge readership in Hungary from the late 1950s. In Poland, nobleman Henryk Sienkiewicz's frequently racist story *In Desert and Wilderness* (1911), which encapsulated the idea that Poles could be humane colonizers due to a sensitivity derived from their own experience of occupation, remained on the postwar national school syllabus. The well-known reporter Marian Brandys wrote a follow-up travel account *Śladami Stasia I Nel* ("In the Footsteps of Stas and Nel"—protagonists of the novel) in 1962.[46] And its popularity only increased when the action-adventure film version was released in 1973. Whilst travel and revolutionary literature from the contemporary "Third World" was restricted, Western colonial-era literature was still published in sizable quantity. Stories of the white "lord of the jungle" Tarzan, first published in the 1920s, were still popular in the 1960s: in Yugoslavia they were sold in weekly installments alongside classics, such as Dostoevsky novels.[47] Russian translations aside, two of the bestselling foreign authors in Hungary were Jules Verne (three million copies sold between 1945 and 1970) and Rudyard Kipling (half a million).[48]

Socialist-era authors developed this tradition of extra-European adventure stories, remade in an anti-colonial mode and offering new aesthetics, narratives, and rhetoric.[49] Ferdinand May's 1962 *Storm over Southwest Africa: A Story from the Days of the Herero Tribe*, later described by the Africanist and travel writer Alfred Babing as the young GDR's "first Africa book," evoked empathy with the military struggle of the Herero people against German settlers' encroachment on their territory in the early twentieth century—a plot that suited the GDR's support for Namibian freedom fighters in the early 1960s.[50] Such works provided an alternative to the work of Karl May, whose fanciful late nineteenth-century tales of the Wild West had long been incredibly

---

[46] The status of this book on the school curriculum is an ongoing discussion in Poland. Thanks to Agnieszka Sadecka for this information. Anna Klobucka, "Desert and Wilderness Revisited: Sienkiewicz's Africa in the Polish National Imagination," *Slavic and East European Journal* 45.2 (2001): 243–59.

[47] Wladimir Fischer, "Of Crescents and Essence, or: Why Migrants' History Matters to the Question of 'Central European Colonialism,'" in Andrew Colin Gow (ed.), *Hyphenated Histories. Articulations of Central European Bildung and Slavic Studies in the Contemporary Academy* (Leiden, 2007), 84; Radina Vučetić, *Koka kola socijalizam. Amerikanizacija popularne kulture u socijalističkoj Jugoslaviji šezdesetih godina XX veka* (Belgrade, 2011), 319.

[48] Ferenc Erdei (ed.), *Hazánk, Magyarország* (Budapest, 1970), 591.

[49] Christine Bürger, *Deutsche Kolonialgeschichte(n): Der Genozid in Namibia und die Geschichtsschreibung der DDR und BRD* (Bielefeld, 2017), 109.

[50] Ferdinand May, *Sturm über Südwest-Afrika. Eine Erzählung aus den Tagen des Hereroaufstandes* (Berlin, 1962).

successful. Postwar elites considered them ideologically suspect: officially, the "Karl May chapter was definitely closed in the GDR years ago," as the publishing industry's organ *Börsenblatt* wrote in 1958.[51] In non-aligned Yugoslavia, by contrast, one of the most read novels amongst 1960s Yugoslav youth was once again Karl May's *Winnetou* (*Vinettu*), the story of a fictive Native American hero—according to a poll in the party newspaper *Borba*.[52] This was in large part due to the West German–Yugoslav cinematic co-productions based on May's novels. In the GDR, by contrast, May's writing was still considered insufficiently progressive, and the struggles of Native Americans or Africans had to be foregrounded in new works in line with the state's anti-imperialist position. Liselotte Welskopf-Henrich, particularly her six-part novel *The Sons of Great Bear*, turned the ethos of the anti-fascist struggle into an identification with Native American resistance.[53] When new stories skirted too near to May's Wild West tales, publications were rejected. Only in 1983 did Karl May's work re-enter GDR book stores and libraries, with over sixty of his titles republished (some printed with a run of 100,000 books). May himself had to be reinvented, now cast as the son of a proletarian and an upright anti-imperialist "fighter against the US policy of looting and extermination."[54]

Travelogues were no exception to this colonial revival within an anti-colonial frame, often written by those whose ideological formation had long preceded the communist takeovers. The widely-known Hungarian Arabist Gyula Germanus gained celebrity status after successfully taking the Muslim Hajj in secret, which he wrote up in *Allah Akbar!* (1936). During the Stalinist period, he received political protection as a former teacher of Communist Secretary General Mátyás Rákosi, and after 1956 he helped restore the regime's international prestige amongst ideologically friendly Arab countries.[55] Germanus wrote several successful works about his Middle Eastern travels between 1955 and 1965, while *Allah Akbar!* was republished five times between 1968 and 1984.[56] His work continued a nineteenth-century tradition of Hungarian Orientalism which combined a mystical East with a nostalgia for the Habsburg monarchy—a position which evaded public criticism even under state socialism.[57] His bestselling work (published under his wife's name) was *Bengal Fire* (1943), republished ten times during the socialist period.[58] The novel gained popularity with the "rediscovery" of Bengali poet, painter, writer, and "anti-imperialist hero" Rabindranath Tagore in the mid-1950s: the centenary of his birth in 1961 was a major event. Yet at the book's core was a celebration of the efficiency of the British Empire in a Bengal beset by "eastern lethargy," mysticism, and sensuality. The reader could most easily identify

---

[51] Cited in "Wildwest im Osten," *Neues Deutschland*, June 13, 2015.
[52] Quoted in Irena Šentevska, "Kako je vestern osvojio Istok," *Moderna Vremena* 2 (2018).
[53] Thomas Kramer, "Abenteuerliteratur," in Michael Opitz et al. (eds.), *Metzlerlexikon DDR-Literatur: Autoren–Institutionen–Debatten* (Stuttgart: Metzler, 2009), 1.
[54] Cited in "Wildwest im Osten," *Neues Deutschland*, June 13, 2015; "Der Ritt durch die Zensur. Karl May in der DDR," *Der Spiegel*, January 28, 2009.
[55] Ádám Mestyán, "Materials for a History of Hungarian Academic Orientalism: The Case of Gyula Germanus," *Die Welt des Islams* 54.4 (2014): 33.
[56] Gyula Germanus, *A félhold fakó fényében* (Budapest, 1957); Gyula Germanus, *A Kelet fényei felé* (Budapest, 1966). *Allah Akbar!* was published in 1968, 1973, 1976, 1979, and 1984.
[57] For Yugoslav Orientalist visions, see, e.g., Zulfikar Džumhur, *Pisma iz Afrike i Evrope* (Sarajevo, 1991).
[58] Rózsa Hajnóczy and Gyula Germanus, *Bengáli tűz. Három év története* (Budapest, 1957).

Figure 12.1 Members of the Hungarian hunting expedition to Africa before the trip in Budapest, 1959. MVTA Budapest.

with the main characters who were bourgeois, white Europeans living in a villa with servants, depicted as justified in their complaints about Indian hygiene and the perils of the "tropics," whilst also delighting in a forbidden love triangle which an exoticized Indian environment seemed only to encourage.

Accounts which celebrated hunting, safaris, and the white colonial "good life" made a comeback too. To a degree, this reflected the importance of hunting to communist elites' political and social networking (see Figure 12.1).[59] In the GDR, visting leaders from Zambia, Afghanistan, North Korea, Cuba, and the PLO were taken on animal shoots.[60] In Romania, hunts with foreign leaders and diplomats, which began in 1969,

---

[59] Helmut Suter, *Honeckers letzter Hirsch: Jagd und Macht in der DDR* (Berlin, 2018); György Majtényi, "Between Tradition and Change: Hunting as Metaphor and Symbol in State Socialist Hungary," *Cultural and Social History* 13.2 (2016): 231–48.

[60] Thomas Fleischman, *Communist Pigs: An Animal History of East Germany's Rise and Fall* (Seattle, 2020), 156.

were stopped by Ceaușescu in 1981 when, during one of Gaddafi's visits to Romania, the Libyan leader's stepbrother, head of the personal guard, was accidentally shot.[61] In most of the region, given its aristocratic and imperialist associations, hunting was hidden from public view: in Yugoslavia, pictures of Tito posing with animal trophies in Africa were not allowed in the press, and books about hunting were discouraged for publication.[62] GDR diplomats tried to hush up the hunting trip of the country's head of the State Planning Commission in 1981 after it was publicized in a Tanzanian newspaper.[63]

Hungary was quite different in this regard: publishing houses brought out reissues of colonial travel accounts and aristocratic hunting novels as early as 1951. Stalinist bans on "reactionary" imperialist literature were very brief.[64] Exoticized images of hunting in savannahs or jungles were vividly depicted by Gábor Molnár, Hungary's most read novelist. Molnár began writing in the 1930s and grew famous by the late 1950s: his many expedition and hunting novels sold several hundred thousands copies each in Hungarian and were translated into Portuguese, Mongolian, Russian, English, and German.[65] Hungarian aristocrats' travel within Western empires made its mark on the socialist era: former noble Baron Zsigmond Széchenyi's African hunting stories, first published in 1930 under the title *Csui!*, reappeared in 1955 and was subsequently reprinted twelve times under state socialism, eventually selling 360,650 copies.[66] From the late 1950s, contacts with the Hungarian diaspora in North and East Africa were mobilized to help Széchenyi embark on a new hunting expedition to gather animal specimens to replace the Natural History Museum's African collection that had burned down during the 1956 Revolution. His *African Campfires*, based on his 1930s hunting expeditions, sold almost 200,000 copies in 1959 alone—much larger numbers than the more explicitly anti-colonial travelogues.[67] The works of the famed hunter Kálmán Kittenberger, whose vast animal collection was consumed by the museum fire, proved incredibly popular as well, especially among youth.[68] The stable boy to safari-socialist

---

[61] Vasile Crișan, *La vânătoare cu Ceaușescu* (București, 2010), 168.
[62] Archive of the Museum of African Art in Belgrade, Documentation of Zdravko Pečar and Veda Zagorac, box 43, Beleške u vezi sa knjigama Zdravka Pečara. See also Radina Vučetić and Paul Betts, *Tito in Africa: Picturing Solidarity* (Belgrade, 2017), 40–4.
[63] Eric Burton, interview with former GDR diplomat, Königs-Wusterhausen, September 18, 2015.
[64] László Vajda, "Az útleírás-irodalom és az olvasó," *Magyar Nemzet*, April 15, 1954, 5; László Vajda, *Nagy magyar utazók: 19. század* (Budapest, 1951).
[65] See his autobiography: Gábor Molnár, *A Bakonytól Amazóniáig* (Budapest, 1978).
[66] "Széchenyi Zsigmond | 50," *Hungarian Natural History Museum*, http://www.nhmus.hu/szechenyi50/.
[67] Zsigmond Széchenyi, *Afrikai tábortüzek: Vadásznapló kivonatok 1932–1934* (Budapest, 1959). István Dénes's trips to Egypt (1958) and East Africa (1959) bore several travelogues, accounts of game hunting, and a film documentary directed by Imre Schuller, which were all very well received in the press. István Dénes, *Így láttam Afrikát* (Budapest, 1961); László Horváth, *Háromezer kilométer Afrikában* (Budapest, 1963); János Szunyoghy, *Egy év Tanganyikában* (Budapest, 1968).
[68] Kálmán Kittenberger, *Kelet-Afrika vadonjaiban* (Budapest, 1955); Kálmán Kittenberger, *Vadászkalandok Afrikában* (Budapest, 1955); Kálmán Kittenberger, *A Kilimandzsárótól Nagymarosig* (Budapest, 1964); Kálmán Kittenberger, *Utolsó afrikai vadászatom* (Budapest, 1969); Kálmán Kittenberger and Kálmán Mészáros, *Afrikai vadászemlékek: Válogatás Kittenberger Kálmán, Mészáros Kálmán írásaiból* (Budapest, 1970).

playboy Endre Nagy, who married into aristocracy, but briefly became the "chief hunter" of communist dictator Mátyás Rákosi only to adventurously flee communist persecution in 1952, established an estate—bought from the reclaimed family fortune stolen by the Germans during the war—near Mount Meru in Tanzania that later became a hub of important socialist trade and diplomatic networks, where socialist attachés could meet for hunting safaris and sexual excess. He assisted socialist travel writers in East Africa and would later organize the 1971 World Hunting Expo in Budapest.[69] Even the State Secretary of Agriculture, László Földes, wrote in 1967 about his hunting experiences with Nagy, but he felt compelled to use a pseudonym, István Szuhai, to protect his political reputation.[70]

Celebrations of a leisure culture steeped in colonial fantasy were not present in GDR publishing. Indeed, safaris were condemned as the "bloody nonsense" of Germany's former colonial officers, and the immoral profit-making of Europeans and white Southern Africans.[71] Wolfgang Ullrich, the Director of Dresden's Zoological Garden and advocate of wildlife conservation, condemned the individualized pleasure of trophy hunting and the desire to see Africa through "notch and bead sighter" (*Kimme und Korn*).[72] Yet even here former colonial writers made a comeback. Hans Schomburgk, who had once produced colonial propaganda for the German colonies in South West Africa, wrote some of the most popular work on Africa in the late 1950s. Public biographies omitted his role in settler colonialism and the openly racist imagery of his earlier works. According to one commentator, Schomburgk was "honored as a colonial pioneer who became more progressive with increasing age." GDR citizens learned that he was said to have been deported to a Polish concentration camp and had a Jewish grandmother.[73] As he gained a reputation as *the* German expert on Africa, Schomburgk managed to get his 1956-7 expedition financed by both East and West Germany, and the film he produced was shown in both states (albeit in different versions).[74] Schomburgk's more than twenty books sold millions of copies in both Germanies, and were translated throughout the Eastern bloc. Nationalist liberation struggles were absent: his was a nostalgic vision of a "traditional" Africa of tribes and wildlife threatened not by colonial violence per se, but rather by the creeping influence of European modernity and civilization, whether of the capitalist or socialist variant. In the 1960s and 1970s, however, Schomburgk's nostalgia became increasingly rare in the GDR, as most works took an optimistic view of progress through decolonization and modernization.

---

[69] See György Majtényi, "Keresztező életutak," *Beszélő online* 13.7 (2008), http://beszelo.c3.hu/cikkek/keresztezo-eletutak; István Matúz, "A Merutól Balatoneredicsig—Egy világcsavargó hazatér," *Kárpáti Igaz Szó*, May 4, 2020, https://kiszo.net/2020/05/04/a-merutol-balatonedericsig-egy-vilagcsavargo-hazater/.
[70] István Szuhai, *Piga, Piga! Vadászkalandok három világrészen* (Budapest, 1967); István Szuhai, *Szimba, a király* (Budapest, 1971). For other hunting travelogues connected to Nagy, see Éva Tomai and János Zoltán, *Ketten az afrikai őserdőben* (Budapest, 1975).
[71] Fritz Rudolph and Percy Stulz, *Jambo, Afrika! DDR-Afrika-Expedition zwischen Kongo und Sansibar* (Leipzig, 1970), 224.
[72] Wolfgang Ullrich, *Afrika einmal nicht über Kimme und Korn gesehen* (Radebeul, n.d. [c. 1958]).
[73] Rolf Baldus, "Hans Schomburgk—Per Fahrrad unterwegs zum Wild und zu den Wilden," *Wild und Hund* 14 (2014): 43.
[74] "Schomburgk aus Afrika zurück," *Neues Deutschland*, January 10, 1957.

The revival of hunting travelogues, alongside accounts of longing for lost African tradition, encapsulated the desire for escape from the bureaucratic structures of socialist modernity into a romanticized past. Endre Szokoly's travelogue *Seven Years in Bolivia*, though written about his experiences in 1939–46, was published in 1958.[75] Official reviews positioned his book as revealing social inequalities, class war, and the necessity of anti-imperialist racial solidarity and agrarian revolution.[76] But the dominant discourse in the book was one of exotic lands of adventure—a frontier society inhabited by heroes, villains, or fallen idols. Central to Szokoly's travelogue, too, were naturalized class distinctions based on inherited traits or merit, depicting a world of order and tradition, and a richness of culture, lost in socialist Europe. The historical setting made it possible for the reader to identify with ideological and classed positions otherwise prohibited under state socialism.

The Colonial in the Anti-colonial: Escaping a Frustrated Globality

The attractiveness of hunting and frontier stories lay in their suggestion that Eastern Europeans could become mobile travelers in this new world where Western European empires no longer dominated. Presenting a world of rugged individualism and adventurous competition, they offered a fantasy of status and escape for those Europeans whose global reach had been long frustrated outside imperial systems. Mobility, in a world now opening up, thus sometimes became a very explicit longing for white, aristocratic, and patriarchal privilege. It was not only that a culture nostalgic for a past of European dominance existed alongside an official commitment to liberation movements: colonial culture supplied a fantasy that underpinned it. Even writings that rejected the revival of colonial tropes and declared themselves committed to anti-colonialism framed their excitement for the status and mobility that socialist solidarity had enabled through familiar scripts of expedition, conquest, and mastery. Yugoslav writer Fadil Hadžić celebrated how non-alignment enabled their countrymen to enter spaces they had previously been denied. Travelogues could impress home populations by showing

> ... in the remnants of colonial, the new global position of socialist states ... The Yugoslav travel writer enters forbidden zones of international politics and exits with a fat notebook which quite often has the tragic history of some small, backward people ... he brings the pen of his young socialist homeland ... from the little African village to the biggest metropolis ... against those who consider the war of the blocs the only possible future.[77]

---

[75] Endre Szokoly, *Hét év Bolíviában*, Világjárók 10 (Budapest, 1958).
[76] See, e.g., the review in *Ország-Világ* 2.39 (October 1, 1958): 5.
[77] Hadžić, "Predgovor," 4–7. See also Pečar, *Afrička kretanja* (Zagreb, 1965); Dara Janeković, *Kad mora uzavriju* (Zagreb, 1985).

The new access to formerly colonial territory was powerfully illustrated in the most popular of postwar travel genres: the anti-colonial road trip. Presented as celebrations of the benefits of socialist modernization and technology, these writings nevertheless invoked a genre forged in the interwar promise of development to colonies over which Europeans had weakening holds. Drawing on the example of earlier trips by Citroën (1920s) and Škoda (1940s) in Africa, Czechoslovak journalists and explorers Miroslav Hanzelka and Jiří Zikmund drove Tatra cars across Africa, South and Central America, Asia, Indonesia, and Central Asia during 1947–9 and 1959–64.[78] Their exploits generated some of the few travel texts to be widely translated across the bloc.[79] They used their trips not only to sell the benefits of socialist modernization, but also to show how anti-colonialism had brought Eastern Europeans a new global status. The Yugoslav travel expedition Kragujevac–Kilimanjaro (1975) produced two travelogues and many other shorter pieces based around driving from the Zastava car factory in Kragujevac to the highest mountain in Africa.[80] The five newest Zastava 101 cars were shown passing "thousands" in Cairo driving older Zastava models.[81] The expedition ended at a site of conquest long used in accounts of Western explorers—with the raising of the "red banner of self-management."[82] It shared many of the features of older expeditionary literature. Africa was presented as unspoilt nature: jungles, deserts, and wild lands were there for machines to conquer, updated for a world of non-alignment and socialist modernization.

Even the celebration of a post-imperial promise of racial equality and diversity could be scripted—amongst male writers—as offering new opportunities for sexual conquest. Sándor Csoóri, whose *Cuban Diary* was so influential in promoting the Cuban revolution in Hungary, was also one of the writers most responsible for the sexualization of the island's women in his nation's imagination. In *Cuban Diary*, a celebration of equality in ethnic diversity quickly turned into a lascivious male fantasy of access and conquest. Echoing older conceptions of Cuba as a sexual playground for Europeans and Americans, Csoóri seemingly wrote himself into the very imperialist tradition that his state warned him against:

> Gy. was unenthusiastic. He was disappointed with the legend [i.e. of Cuban women] ... there weren't as many beautiful women as they said. The first was too black, the second too fat in the mouth, the third had eyes whose corners were pulled too far down, the tenth's ankles weren't quite thin enough ... I would say that he is blind ... if you sit in the hotel lobby, as it unexpectedly quietens ... and one [woman] comes in, in their presence everything else falls away ... the dark

---

[78] Šmejkalová, "Command Celebrities," 72–3.
[79] On its reception in German and Russian, see Šmejkalová, "Command Celebrities," 81–2.
[80] Nemanja Radonjić, "'From Kragujevac to Kilimanjaro': Imagining and Re-Imagining Africa and the Self-Perception of Yugoslavia in the Travelogues from Socialist Yugoslavia," *Annual for Social History* 23.2 (2016): 55–89.
[81] Šekler, *Džambo Afriko*, 15.
[82] Šekler, *Džambo Afriko*, 151. GDR travelogues were firmly rooted in working environments and camps of liberation movements and seldom reproduced the spontaneous wanderer of pre-socialist travelogues.

complexion, gleaming hair on a bare shoulder, such that she conceals a raging fire inside herself... Spanish? Black? Mulatto or Indian? Or some sort of mix?... This is scarcely an exception; in this country there is a kind of wonder in the variety of races ... the "concept" of "Cuban women," as with all sorts of concepts, slides into mythology at certain points. About their beauty and specialness there is no kind of exaggeration ... These male mental associations—the looseness, sensuality, this modern paradisiacal vision of sexual lasciviousness springs forth. The most demure fantasy becomes a turn-on and suddenly one imagines oneself wandering with a "love amongst the gleaming lemon trees."[83]

Csoóri experienced great difficulties in publishing his travel report from Cuba as a book, though it eventually appeared in 1965. Later, he claimed this was not due to his idiosyncratic political readings of the Cuban revolution, which were tolerated, but rather to authorities' concerns at his over-sexualization of Cuban women. Yet censors objected not to the echoes of colonial male conquest, but rather to excessive displays of desire that endangered socialist morals.[84]

In the late 1960s, an emerging women's socialist travel literature in Hungary provided alternative perspectives and often critiqued the socially retrograde effects of the colonial fantasies of their male counterparts. Éva Szilágyi went to Ethiopia and Tanzania in 1969–70 on an UNESCO-funded commission by the National Council of Hungarian Women and reported on a range of stories, all from women's perspectives of postcolonial transformation.[85] Rózsa Ignácz, in her East African travelogue *Zebra Drum News* (1968), emphasized how her male compatriots' travel writing reproduced a will to dominance in their sexualized depictions of "Third World" women, and highlighted how this was connected to the stalled transformation of gender relations at home.[86] Ignácz idealized the newly liberated African woman and sought out lessons for the ongoing domestic struggle for female equality. The cult of the white male upper-class explorer was targeted for attack too.[87] Macho safari tales were extensively criticized by the Telegraph Office reporter Ágnes Galla-Kovács, whose 1976 travelogue was pointedly titled *I did not hunt in Tanzania*.[88] The focus on the position of women was also characteristic of Ágnes al-Kurayshi (née Vályi), a Hungarian teacher who married an Iraqi engineer and moved to the Middle East. Her resulting book, *Continuing the One Thousand and One Nights* (1979), explored not simply the "glories" of Iraqi socialist modernization, but combined both Orientalist and feminist lenses in her in-depth explorations of the challenges of everyday lives for poor nomad Bedouin, workers

---

[83] Sándor Csoóri, "Kubai útinapló (III. rész)," *Új Írás* 3.12 (December 1963): 1458–72, 1468–9.
[84] András Görömbei, *Csoóri Sándor* (Budapest, 2010), 47. Similar sexualized imagery of black women occurred in GDR accounts: Makosch, *Das Mädchen vom Sambesi*; Jürgen Leskien, *Shilumbu, was will er in Afrika!* (Berlin, 1988).
[85] Éva Szilágyi, *Asszonysorsok Afrikában* (Budapest, 1972).
[86] Ignácz, *Zebradob-híradó*, 62.
[87] See Wendy Bracewell, "New Men, Old Europe: Being a Man in Balkan Travel Writing," in Wendy Bracewell and Alex Drace-Francis (eds.), *Balkan Departures: Travel Writing from Southeastern Europe* (Oxford and New York, 2009).
[88] Ágnes Galla-Kovács, *Nem vadásztam Tanzániában* (Budapest, 1976).

and students. Although her work mostly remained within a framework of socialist solidarity, she used her hybrid position to draw on personal situations of women to highlight cultural difference: she detailed meetings with her gynecologist in Saudi Arabia (where she gave birth) to explore the increasingly subordinated place of women under fundamentalist Islamic patriarchy.[89]

A good number of male travel writers fantasized that their anti-colonialism would help them transcend a former identity as those less powerful Europeans who had never held colonies. They indulged in the fantasy of becoming a new type of white man whose progressive commitments would confer them privileges once confined to high-class Western colonials. István Kende, Hungarian foreign policy expert, reporter, and columnist of the main state newspaper *Népszabadság*, who later edited a huge encyclopaedia on developing countries (1973), was commissioned in 1958 to report on newly independent Guinea, then aligning itself with the Soviet bloc.[90] In the resulting travelogue, *Good Morning, Africa!*, he transformed himself into the new European who, by dint of his modesty and supposed lack of lust for power, could access spaces unavailable to Westerners. As the pioneering anti-colonial explorer, he joins a local party meeting in Bokaria where "a white friend has never spoken to them before."[91] He is then invited to visit diamond mines with four Bulgarian filmmakers. A centerpiece of the narrative is Kende's meeting with an old African storyteller who confirms his status as a new kind of white man:

> You are a white man who wanted to hear my homeland's history. So far I only knew white men like the ones I had business with in Poré Daka! I am happy ... This word [*tubabu*, meaning white man] felt inappropriate. Since this word denoted the concept that for him until now had only represented the oppressor, the hated alien, equipped with whips and intrigue, and not the sons of those countries, who establish contracts with independent Guinea based on equality and mutual assistance ... In a few hours, warm friendship developed between the diamond miners and the Hungarian journalist. He [Kende, referring to himself] was the first white man—the first *tubabu*—who came here, into the Kuankan diamond field barefoot, with rolled up trousers, wading right into the mud where they work all day long. He was a *tubabu*, but not one who came to make a good deal on diamonds, but one to observe the life and work of the black diamond miners.[92]

The importance of the performance of humility in the service of gaining a long-denied power, of employing anti-colonialism to gain status as the more enlightened type of Europeans, was powerfully illustrated in instances of its frustration. Exclusion on the basis of white skin was commonly related, presented as a painful awakening: the

---

[89] Ágnes al-Kurayshi, *Az ezeregyéjszaka folytatása* (Budapest, 1979); Eszter Szakács, "Propaganda, Mon Amour: An Arab 'World' Through Hungarian Publications (1957–1989)," in Eszter Szakács and Naeem Mohaiemen (eds.), *Solidarity Must Be Defended* (Budapest, 2020).
[90] István Kende, *Jóreggelt, Afrika! Guineai útirajz*, Világjárók 24 (Budapest, 1961).
[91] Kende, *Jóreggelt, Afrika!*, 157.
[92] Kende, *Jóreggelt, Afrika!*, 69, 73, 75.

anti-colonial desire that should have guaranteed the superior socialist traveler mobility into the world's expanding post-colonial spaces could not be realized. Writers regularly related their encounters with communities who refused to let them embody anything beyond Western racism. The globally renowned Polish travel writer Ryszard Kapuściński presented himself as the offspring of a rural village in the poor eastern Polish borderlands (*kresy*), where nationalist conflicts echoed the problems of nation-building in Africa. Despite a self-fashioning that emphasized non-racialized proximity, Kapuściński registered his profound disappointment when, visiting the slums in Kenya, black Africans refused to treat him as anything else other than a white European.[93] Yugoslav Oskar Davičo related how travel in Africa led him to want to shed his white skin and thus throw off the marker of the heritage of racism which stuck bodily to him. Yet he quickly realized that anti-racist self-fashioning was in practice an impossible fantasy. He could not escape the political implications of his epidermal phenotype:

> It's pointless, but what can I do, I feel ashamed. My people and my class never tortured, enslaved, killed. For centuries we were slaves ourselves. Yes, but I am white, this is all that passers-by can see. If only I could carry a digested history of my country on my sleeves! ... But to them I look like a Frenchman, Belgian, English, Boer, a lyncher from Little Rock. And it's embarrassing to think that in the eyes of an African I can be equalized with them, with "those." If I could change the color of my skin, I would do it without hesitation.[94]

Their white skin, they discovered, bore the mark of European imperialism they thought only Western Europeans should really have to bear. It could thus become a source of resentment that Africans, supposedly seduced by an exclusionary *négritude*, would not consummate their fantasy through deeming them "a better kind of white." In the 1980s, the well-known GDR writer Jürgen Leskien explored how his work in the SWAPO exile camps in Angola was unfairly hindered by the association of his white skin with the former German Empire. Unlike Davičo's 1960s undiminished fantasy of racialized transformation, Leskien's failure was now resentfully turned back against Africans whom he blamed for racializing difference and hence unraveling socialist solidarity:

> Why do I wonder when the three-year-olds call me SHILUMBU [white man], they who are born in the camp, who do not know their homeland and not the Boers and not the Germans living here in their third generation. They got it from the mothers: how they look, the white farmers, the white policemen, the white officials ... But why did Botswana [a SWAPO member and co-worker of Leskien] insult me? Can't I expect him to differentiate? Who gives him the right to lump me together with the twenty thousand ethnic Germans in today's Namibia? After

---

[93] Ryszard Kapuściński, *Shadow of the Sun* (London, 2002), 40. See similar reflections in Josef Nesvadba, *Dialog s doktorem Dongem: neskutečný cestopis* (Prague, 1965). Translated Franz Peter Künzel, *Vinh Linh oder Die Entdeckung des Dr. Dong*; in French: *La découverte du docteur Dong*.
[94] Davičo, *Crno na belo*, 20. For similar shame, see Štambuk, *Od Zanzibara do Mjesečevih planina*, 86.

weeks of working together, now that he knows the calluses on my hands, now that we drink the same water, live through the same fears?[95]

By contrast, some female writers were critical of these unrealistic anti-colonial dreams that provided cover for men to fantasize about gaining power. Rather, they were prepared to address explicitly the much longer-term embeddedness of privilege derived from settler colonialism that enabled them to wander as white Europeans. The Hungarian traveler Vilma Ligeti, on her stay in India during 1961–4, wrote about how she sometimes benefited from the privilege of her skin color, while simultaneously distancing herself from the racially superior attitudes of the British she met.[96] Rózsa Ignácz in her *Zebra Drum News* emphasized Easterners' moral superiority as anti-colonial travelers, contrasting her own presence in Africa with that of Roberta Blacksmith, a wealthy contemporary British "world traveler," who epitomized the ignorant imperialist lady of leisure.[97] Ignácz saw herself as a poor, lone traveler originating from rural Transylvania, a region detached from a wider Hungarian "Empire" by the Treaty of Trianon in 1920. She presented herself as embodying a peripheral post-imperial identity that might, however ambiguously, fit into an expanding postcolonial world:

> I want to be a world traveler, who settles nowhere for sure, always wanders further, doesn't take the same road twice, and after going around the "whole world," returns home again on a road never seen before, to arrive at the same age as on departure. I imagined all this in the back of our garden in Kovászna [Covasna]. The world started a few steps from the garden, where a small parcel of pinewood stretched from the vast forests of the South Carpathians ... But honestly, how should I introduce myself, if not as such: a world wanderer? ... I am a moneyless guest. I go where my friends take me. I learn about East Africa through what I have access to. But I don't have a prepaid hunting ticket to a big safari.[98]

However, Ignácz recognized her privilege, explicitly reflecting on her own position by asking is she a world traveler? She acknowledged that her mobility is a result of white émigré networks.[99] Writers continued to rely not only on colonial-era infrastructure, but also on their anti-communist national diaspora, which they always mentioned. In Hungarian accounts in particular, it was still acceptable to present the national bond as stronger than Cold War ideological divides once one found oneself outside Europe. Travelers reported on making pilgrim-like visits to the "legendary" doctor and natural scientist László Sáska or the exotic anti-communist "hunter celebrity" Endre Nagy in Tanzania, or they visited the memorials to Orientalists Sándor Kőrösi Csoma or Ármin Vámbéry in Asia.

[95] Leskien, *Shilumbu*, 87–9.
[96] Vilma Ligeti, *Síva árnyékában*, Világjárók 50 (Budapest, 1966).
[97] Ignácz, *Zebradob-híradó*.
[98] Ignácz, *Zebradob-híradó*, 12–13, 85.
[99] Ignácz, *Zebradob-híradó*, 12.

The End of Anti-colonial Solidarity? Distancing and Bordering

Slobodan Nešović's 1976 *Sunrise and Sunset: Wandering around Europe, Africa, Asia, and America* was one of the first Afropessimist accounts available to Yugoslav readers. He sails into a "dirty" and "unkempt" Conakry—a place whose "dilapidation" confirmed the impossibility of modernization.[100] Postcolonial spaces that travel writing had once brought into tempered proximity with their Eastern European reading publics were now increasingly being made distant. Late Cold War hunting travelogues revived older tenets of environmental determinism on racial issues: Ferenc Ignácz's *Habub over Sudan* (1976) cited tribal customs to reinforce the differences between Europeans and Africans, emphasizing their wildness and traditionalism.[101] Such texts reinforced Europe as a region separate from an Africa unable to break from rural backwardness. Seven years later, Dušan Sekulić in *A Road Sign Pointing South*, the very title of which suggested the newly emerging Global North–Global South divide, provided even bleaker images: "A shadow of a Tuareg ... on an undernourished camel."[102] Happiness was associated with access to material goods, so the more developed areas of the world were referred to as "happier places."[103] Writers increasingly portrayed the fortune of one's civilization as "predestined," just like the fate of African children: "It is their misfortune that they are born on a black continent, black not because it is the home of the blacks; but because their destiny is black."[104]

Yugoslav travelogues were still ambiguous. They highlighted despair whilst also asserting that non-alignment could still provide a "geography of hope." Such sentiments continued until the collapse of state-socialism. The journalist Dara Janeković resisted these newly emergent geographies—North–South, developed–underdeveloped—and placed Yugoslavia within a space that included Asian, African, and Latin American countries as part of a common non-aligned world within which the Yugoslav reader would feel comfortable.[105] In the GDR, too, travelogues on Africa were still written to bolster support for liberation movements such as Namibia's SWAPO and the South African ANC.[106] Nevertheless, even in those socialist states that remained committed to anti-colonialism, Africans were no longer represented as mythical anti-colonial heroes. Anthropology and ethnography had formerly been used to explore the commonalities between Eastern European and extra-European tradition and culture; now their methods were used to emphasize how mentalities and ways of life were fundamentally different. GDR writer Landolf Scherzer wrote *Bom dia* about Mozambique in part to counteract what he saw as a decline in solidarity. More GDR

---

[100] Nešović, *Svitanja i sutoni*, 96.
[101] Ferenc Ignácz, *Habub Szudán felett* (Budapest, 1976).
[102] Sekulić, *Putokaz za jug*, 78.
[103] Sekulić, *Putokaz za jug*, 66.
[104] Sekulić, *Putokaz za jug*, 89.
[105] Janeković, *Kad mora uzavriju*, 180–3, 185, 99–144, 329, 333, 336, 340, 342.
[106] Leskien, *Shilumbu*; Jürgen Leskien, "Schreiben über das nahe Fremde," in Ulrich van der Heyden, Ilona Schleicher, and Hans-Georg Schleicher (eds.), *Engagiert für Afrika: Die DDR und Afrika II* (Münster, 1994).

workers had to be mobilized, he argued, as now only "church people" and "jazz musicians" still volunteered to go abroad without material incentives.[107] For Scherzer, Mozambique was still worthy of solidarity; nevertheless, he focused on everyday micro-environments in order to make sense of why Mozambican contract workers who came to the GDR seemed so culturally distinct. He explored what they ate, how they thought and lived out gender relations, and the religious rituals they performed: in sum, how their behavior emerged from a certain historical, social, and environmental context that was different from what could now be called the "European way of life."

Whereas accounts of Africa now articulated distance, newly emerging travelogues on the economic miracle of East Asian Tigers presented these countries as a future to which Eastern Europeans might aspire. Socialist travel writing had by and large abandoned East Asia after the Sino-Soviet split, but rediscovered it in the 1980s. In the chapter "A Ticket for Tomorrow," the Yugoslav Aleksandar Vitorović described Singapore as being like "a leap from a tropical shack into an iron-clad skyscraper."[108] György Kalmár, who had reported on socialist revolutions in Africa, was sent to Seoul in 1987. In a popular travelogue, he presented South Korea and Hungary as common victims of wartime occupation and the postwar settlement. Nevertheless, he claimed, South Korea's openness, dynamism, and powerful export industries had created an economic model that demanded attention from a similarly peripheralized region. Focusing on the organization of everyday life and work, the anthropological eye that elsewhere was being used to distance Africa from Europe was here employed to critique, through a Far Eastern mirror, those communist cultures that had failed to produce sufficiently dynamic mentalities to prosper.[109] This new breed of travelogues no longer celebrated Eastern Europe's leading role in a postcolonial world, but rather used such success stories as an argument for fundamental political and economic transformation at home.

Once socialist states had carefully selected national explorers whose commitments could framed as progressive, humane, and anti-colonial. In Hungary, in 1986, on the occasion of the 100th anniversary of Count Sámuel Teleki's violent expedition to Eastern Africa, an interdisciplinary team of scientists took the same route and shot a film. Such initiatives marked an important ideological turn: the anti-colonial lens was removed and imperial-style narratives revived—now national greatness was to be found in the recovery of the nation's proximity to a European imperial past. This continued after the collapse of state socialism in 1989: a "Sahara expedition" to North Africa in 1993 was organized by the Hungarian Geographical Museum, following the 1933 route of the "English Patient," László Almássy, to commemorate its sixtieth anniversary. The rehabilitation of colonial-era travels underpinned a robust anti-communist culture: such revivals, often led by physical geographers and historians, were justified on the (mistaken) understanding that such explorers had been forgotten before 1989. They also reproduced socialist-era assertions that Eastern Europe was free

---

[107] Scherzer, *Bom dia*.
[108] Aleksandar Vitorović, *Putopisi i susreti* (Belgrade, 2004), 253. See also Vaso Popović, *Priče iz belog sveta* (Zagreb, 1980); Branko Rakočević, *Putopisi 4* (Belgrade, 1983).
[109] György Kalmár, *Szöulból jelentem* (Budapest, 1988).

of colonial guilt, and hence could unproblematically promote histories of explorers and scientific advances in education, museums, popular magazines, and youth festivals such as "Explorers' Day," without critiquing their colonial heritage.[110]

Conclusion

As decolonization accelerated, state-supported publishing houses, alongside major state institutions, published travelogues of the extra-European world in ever greater numbers. In them, writers adopted an impressive variety of roles: not only as anti-colonial travelers, war reporters, technocratic experts, socialist modernizers, and activists, but also as leisured adventurers, explorers, or hunters. This seemingly strange mixture of anti-colonial commitment and colonial aesthetics was not accidental: the travelogues of such a varied cast of characters allowed writers and readers to make sense, in varying ideological keys, of their region's expanding global role. Travelogues were publicly justified in that they "collapsed the distance" between Eastern Europe and an anti-colonial world through, for example, parallel histories or rural ethnographies of mutual recognition. Yet many texts simultaneously crafted a deeply appealing fantasy of global status that had once been conferred on a privileged class of mainly upper-class Western European men.

This assemblage was the result of a long tradition of regional self-definition. Since the mid-nineteenth century, a variety of writers had defined Europe's East through its absence of extra-European territories: their peoples' civility had resulted in an insufficient rapaciousness necessary to conquer, which in turn had meant their denial of a (fantasy) role as the humane and solidaristic propagators of the European Enlightenment abroad, rescuing a global project besmirched by the violence of Western Europeans. State socialism revived, remade, and institutionalized this long-standing perspective, but did not create it. Most Eastern Europeans could not travel to the postcolonial spaces these travelogues publicized. This constrained condition further propelled a fantasy of motion and status—with their stories of crossing borders and rapturous welcomes—that anti-colonialism and a commitment to socialism at last conferred on them. Travelogues made powerful the realization of a longer-term Eastern European dream of overcoming their marginalization as Europeans, now surprisingly realized in an anti-colonial form in the postcolonial world's "peripheral" spaces. It was their own distance from imperial violence that in large part enabled them to recover the travelogue from its former colonial associations, whilst continuing to employ the travelogue's aesthetics to sell a dream of global power. The only sustained criticism of the will to power in socialist-era travelogues came from women's travel writing in the 1970s, which rejected what they saw as the hyper-masculine colonial fantasies of their male compatriots.

---

[110] See Zoltán Ginelli, "The Contested Post-Socialist Rehabilitation of the Past: Dual Narratives in the Republishing of Tibor Mendöl's *Introduction to Geography*," *Hungarian Cultural Studies: e-Journal of the American Hungarian Educators Association* 7 (2014): 242–73.

The varying combinations of commitment to the positive representation of the postcolonial world on one hand, with implicit or explicit fantasies of gaining status as Europeans on the other, defined the genre of European socialist-era travel writing—at least until the mid-1970s. Nevertheless, there were differences between countries. Although a few travelogues were translated and shared within the Eastern bloc, they were predominantly produced for national reading markets. All were concerned with the projection of national power. In the more industrialized Czechoslovakia and GDR, travelogues sought to bolster national standing through an emphasis on the technological progress their country brought. In Hungary, celebratory accounts of national liberations outside Europe were accompanied by widely-read accounts of hunting and aristocratic, masculine leisure, which uncritically evoked colonial fantasies of global mobility finally realized. Yugoslav travelers were often more attuned to the questions of race, and were frustrated when the mobility that non-alignment was expected to confer was impeded by African and Asian perceptions of them simply as inheritors of a colonialism associated with white Europeanness. By the last decade of state socialism, however, as the potential status to be gained from an anti-colonial orientation subsided, distance replaced a desire for proximity. Travelogues that had once imagined connections now detached the region from a broader anti-colonial world, confirming their place in an ever more bordered European civilization.

Select Bibliography

Abreu, Laurinda and Sally Sheard. *Hospital Life: Theory and Practice from the Medieval to the Modern*. Frankfurt am Main: Peter Lang, 2013.
Abu Al-Hajjaj, Yousef. *al-Sadd al-'Aaly wa al-tanmiat al'iqtisadia*. Cairo: Dar al-Ma'arif, 1964.
Agbodeka, Francis. *A History of University of Ghana: Half a Century of Higher Education (1948-1998)*. Accra: Woeli Publishing Services, 1998.
Alamgir, Alena K. "Race is elsewhere: state-socialist ideology and the racialisation of Vietnamese workers in Czechoslovakia." *Race & Class* 54.4 (2013): 67–85.
Alamgir, Alena K. "'Inappropriate Behavior': Labor Control and the Polish, Cuban, and Vietnamese Workers in Czechoslovakia," in Marsha Seifert (Ed.), *Labor in State-Socialist Europe, 1945-1989: Contributions to a History of Work*. Budapest: CEU Press, 2020.
Alexander, Jocelyn and JoAnn McGregor. "African Soldiers in the USSR: Oral Histories of Zapu Intelligence Cadres' Soviet Training, 1964-1979," *Journal of African History* 43.1 (2017): 49–66.
Allman, Jean. "Between the Present and History: African Nationalism and Decolonization," in John Parker and Richard Reid (eds.), *The Oxford Handbook of Modern African History*. New York: Oxford University Press, 2013.
Allman, Jean. "Phantoms of the Archive: Kwame Nkrumah, a Nazi Pilot named Hanna, and the Contingencies of Postcolonial History-Writing," *American Historical Review* 118.1 (2013): 104–29.
Anderson, Warwick. *Colonial Pathologies: American Tropical Medicine, Race and Hygiene in the Philippines*. Durham, NC: Duke University Press, 2006.
Armstrong, Charles K. *Tyranny of the Weak: North Korea and the World, 1950-1992*. Ithaca, NY: Cornell University Press, 2013.
Autio-Sarasmo, Sari and Katalin Miklóssy (eds.), *Reassessing Cold War Europe*. London and New York: Routledge, 2013.
Banks, Elizabeth. "Socialist Internationalism between the Soviet Union and Mozambique, 1962-91." Ph.D. dissertation, New York University, 2019.
Barnett, Thomas. *Romanian and East German Policies in the Third World: Comparing Strategies of Ceaușescu and Honecker*. London: Praeger, 1992.
Bishop, Elizabeth. "Talking Shop: Egyptian Engineers and Soviet Specialist at Aswan High Dam." Ph.D. dissertation, University of Chicago, 1997.
Bishop, Elizabeth. "Control Room: Visible and Concealed Spaces of the Aswan High Dam," in Panayiota Pyla (ed.), *Landscapes of Development: Modernization and the Physical Environment in the Eastern Mediterranean*. Cambridge, MA: Harvard Graduate School of Design, 2013.
Bodie, George. "Global GDR? Sovereignty, Legitimacy, and Decolonisation in the German Democratic Republic, 1960-1989." Ph.D. dissertation, University College London, 2020.
Borowy, Iris. "Medical Aid, Repression, and International Relations: The East German Hospital at Metema," *Journal of the History of Medicine and Allied Sciences* 71.1 (2015): 64–92.

Bortlová, Hana. *Československo a Kuba v letech 1959–1963*. Praha: Univerzita Karlova v Praze, Filozofická fakulta, 2011.

Bortlová-Vondráková, Hana and Mónika Szente-Varga. "Labor migration programs within the socialist bloc: Cuban guestworkers in late socialist Czechoslovakia and Hungary," *Labor History* 62.3 (2021): 297–315.

Burgess, G. Thomas. "Mao in Zanzibar: Nationalism, Discipline, and the (De)Construction of Afro-Asian Solidarities," in Christopher J. Lee (ed.), *Making a World after Empire: The Bandung Moment and Its Political Afterlives*. Athens: Ohio University Press, 2010.

Burton, Eric. "Diverging Visions in Revolutionary Spaces: East German Advisers and Revolution from Above in Zanzibar, 1964–1970," in Anna Calori, Bence Kovsev, Anne-Kristin Hartmetz, James Mark, and Jan Zofka (eds.), *Between East and South: Spaces of Interaction in the Globalizing Economy of the Cold War*. Berlin and Boston: De Gruyter, 2019.

Burton, Eric. "Hubs of Decolonization: African Liberation Movements and Eastern Connections in Cairo, Accra and Dar es Salaam," in Lena Dallywater, Helder A. Fonseca and Chris Saunders (eds.), *Southern African Liberation Movements and the Global Cold War "East": Transnational Activism 1960–1990*. Berlin, Boston: De Gruyter, 2019.

Chakrabarty, Dipesh. "Postcoloniality and the artifice of history: who speaks for 'Indian' pasts?" *Representations* 37 (1992): 1–26.

Cooper, Frederick. "The Dialectics of Decolonization: Nationalism and Labor Movements in Postwar French Africa," in Frederick Cooper and Ann L. Stoler (eds.), *Tensions of Empire: Colonial Cultures in a Bourgeois World*. Berkeley, Los Angeles, and London: University of California Press, 1997.

Csoma, Mózes. *Koreaiak Magyarországon az 1950-es években*. Budapest: L'Harmattan, 2012.

de Haan, Francisca (ed.), "Forum: Ten Years After: Communism and Feminism Revisited," Special issue, *Aspasia* 10 (2016).

Derr, Jennifer. *The Lived Nile: Environment, Disease, and Material Colonial Economy in Egypt*. Palo Alto, CA: Stanford University Press, 2019.

Djagalov, Rossen. *From Internationalism to Postcolonialism: Literature and Cinema between the Second and the Third Worlds*. Montreal: McGill-Queen's Press-MQUP, 2020.

Donert, Celia. "Femmes, Communisme et Internationalisme: La Fédération Démocratique Internationale des Femmes en Europe Centrale (1945–1979)," *Vingtième Siecle* 126 (April–June 2015): 119–31.

Drace-Francis, Alex. "Travel Writing from Eastern Europe," in Nandini Das and Tim Youngs (eds.), *The Cambridge History of Travel Writing*. Cambridge: Cambridge University Press, 2013.

Edwards, Justin D. and Rune Grauland (eds.), *Postcolonial Travel Writing: Critical Explorations*. New York: Palgrave, 2011.

Engerman, David C. "Learning from the East: Soviet Experts and India in the Era of Competitive Coexistence," *Comparative Studies in South Asia, Africa, and the Middle East* 33.2 (2013): 227–38.

Fabian, Johannes. *Time and the Other: How Anthropology Makes Its Object*. New York: Columbia University Press, 1983.

Franey, Laura. *Victorian Travel Writing and Imperial Violence: British Writing on Africa 1855–1902*. New York: Palgrave Macmillan, 2003.

Friedland, William H. "Basic Social Trends," in William H. Friedland and Carl G. Rosberg (eds.), *African Socialism*. Stanford, CA: Stanford University Press, 1964.

Ghodsee, Kristen. *Second World, Second Sex: Socialist Women's Activism and Global Solidarity during the Cold War*. Durham, NC: Duke University Press, 2018.

Goldwin, Adam J. and Renee M. Silverman (eds.), *Mediterranean Modernism: Intercultural Exchange and Aesthetic Development*. London: Palgrave Macmillan, 2016.
Gradskova, Yulia. "Women's International Democratic Federation, the 'Third World' and the Global Cold War from the late-1950s to the mid-1960s," *Women's History Review* 29.2 (2020): 270–88.
Gregory, Derek. *The Colonial Present: Afghanistan, Palestine, Iraq*. Hoboken, NJ: Wiley-Blackwell, 2004.
Harisch, Immanuel. "'Mit gewerkschaftlichem Gruß!' Afrikanische GewerkschafterInnen an der FDGB-Gewerkschaftshochschule Fritz Heckert in der DDR," *Stichproben. Wiener Zeitschrift für kritische Afrikastudien* 17.34 (2018).
Holečková, Marta Edith. *Příběh zapomenuté university Univerzita 17 listopadu (1961–1974) a její místo v československém vzdělávacím systému a společnosti*. Praha: Nakladatelství FF UK, 2019.
Hong, Young-Sun. *Cold War Germany, The Third World, and the Global Humanitarian Regime*. Cambridge: Cambridge University Press, 2015.
Hughes, Celia. "Left Activism, Succour and Selfhood: The Epistolary Friendship of Two Revolutionary Mothers in 1970s Britain," *Women's History Review* 23.6 (2014): 874–902.
Iacob, Bogdan C. "Sozialistische Transfers im Gesundheitswesen in Afrika in den 1970er-Jahren: Geografische Verschiebung und Wertewandel," in *Jahrbuch für Historische Kommunismusforschung*, 139–57. Berlin: Metropol Verlag, 2019.
Iandolo, Alessandro. "The Rise and Fall of the 'Soviet Model of Development' in West Africa, 1958–1964," *Cold War History* 12.4 (2012): 683–704.
Jolly, Margaretta. "Confidantes, Co-workers and Correspondents: Feminist Discourses of Letter-writing from 1970 to the Present," *Journal of European Studies* 32.2–3 (2002): 267–82.
Kalinovsky, Artemy M., *Laboratory of Socialist Development: Cold War Politics and Decolonization in Soviet Tajikistan*. Ithaca, NY, and London: Cornell University Press, 2018.
Kalinovsky, Artemy M. et. al. *Missionaries of Modernity: Advisory Missions and the Struggle for Hegemony in Afghanistan and Beyond*. London: C.W. Hurst, 2016.
Katz, Elihu et al. *Broadcasting in the Third World: Promise and Performance*. Cambridge, MA: Harvard University Press, 1977
Komzin, I. V. *Svet Asuana*. Moscow: Molodaya Gvardiya, 1964.
Kozlov, Denis and Eleonory Gilburd (eds.), *The Thaw: Soviet Society and Culture during the 1950s and 1960s*. Toronto: University of Toronto Press, 2013.
Krysowata, Jolanta. *Skrzydło anioła: historia tajnego ośrodka dla koreańskich sierot*. Warsaw: Świat Książki, 2013.
Kuli, Vladimir, Timothy Parker, and Monica Penick. *Sanctioning Modernism: Architecture and the Making of Postwar Identities*. Austin: University of Texas Press, 2014.
Lal, Priya. "Tanzanian Ujamaa in a world of peripheral socialisms," in *The Routledge Handbook of the Global Sixties*, 367–380. London and New York: Routledge, 2018.
Levin, Ayala. "Exporting Zionism: Architectural Modernism in Israeli-African Technical Cooperation." Ph.D. thesis, Columbia University, 2015.
Lisle, Debbie. *Global Politics of Contemporary Travel Writing*. Cambridge: Cambridge University Press, 2006.
Livsey, Tim. *Nigeria's University Age: Reframing Decolonization and Development*. London: Palgrave Macmillan, 2017.
Lorenzini, Sara. *Global Development: A Cold War History*. Princeton, NJ: Princeton University Press, 2019.

Macekura, Stephen J. and Erez Manela (eds.), *The Development Century: A Global History.* Cambridge: Cambridge University Press, 2018.
Mark, James, and Paul Betts (eds.), *Socialism Goes Global: The Soviet Union and Eastern Europe in the Age of Decolonisation.* Oxford: Oxford University Press, 2022.
Mark, James, Artemy M. Kalinovsky, and Steffi Marung (eds.), *Alternative Globalizations: Eastern Europe and the Postcolonial World.* Bloomington: Indiana University Press, 2020.
Massino, Jill. *Ambiguous Transitions: Gender, the State, and Everyday Life in Socialist and Postsocialist Romania.* Oxford: Berghahn Books, 2019.
McCann, Gerard. "Possibility and Peril: Trade Unionism, African Cold War, and the Global Strands of Kenyan Decolonization," *Journal of Social History* 53.2 (2019).
McClintock, Anne. *Imperial Leather: Race, Gender, and Sexuality in the Colonial Context.* London: Routledge, 1995.
Mikkonen, Simo. "To control the world's information flows: Soviet Cold War broadcasting," in A. Badenoch, A. Fickers, and C. Henrich-Franke (eds.), *Airy Curtains in the European Ether,* 241–70. Baden-Baden: Nomos, 2013.
Mossallam, Alia. "We Were the Ones Who Made This Dam High," *Water History* 6.4 (2014): 297–314.
Pratt, Mary Louise. *Imperial Eyes: Travel Writing and Transculturation.* London and New York: Routledge, 1992.
Pucherová, Dobrota and Róbert Gáfrik (eds.), *Postcolonial Europe? Essays on Post-Communist Literatures and Cultures.* Amsterdam: Brill-Rodopi, 2015.
Rashid, Ibrahim. *al-Sadd al-'Aaly: hadiruhu wa mustaqbaluhu.* Cairo: Dar al-Ma'arif, 1969.
Regulska, Joanna and Bonnie G. Smith (eds.), *Women and Gender in Postwar Europe: From Cold War to European Union.* London and New York: Routledge, 2012.
Reichardt, Achim. *Nie Vergessen! Solidarität üben.* Berlin: Kai Homillius Verlag, 2006.
Richterova, Daniela, Mikuláš Pešta, and Natalia Telepneva. "Banking on Military Assistance: Czechoslovakia's Struggle for Influence and Profit in the Third World 1955–1968," *International History Review* 43.1 (2021): 90–108.
Roubal, Petr. *Československé spartakiády.* Prague: Academia, 2016.
Rupprecht, Tobias. *Soviet Internationalism after Stalin: Interaction and Exchange between the USSR and Latin America during the Cold War.* Cambridge: Cambridge University Press, 2015.
Sanchez-Sibony, Oscar. *Red Globalization: The Political Economy of the Soviet Cold War from Stalin to Khrushchev.* Cambridge: Cambridge University Press, 2014
Schwenkel, Christina. "Rethinking Asian Mobilities: Socialist Migration and Post-Socialist Repatriation of Vietnamese Contract Workers in East Germany," *Critical Asian Studies* 46.2 (2014): 235–58.
Serra, Gerardo. "From Scattered Data to Ideological Education: Economics, Statistics and the State in Ghana, 1948–1966." Ph.D. thesis, London School of Economics, 2015.
Silina, Lada. *Vneshnepoliticheskaia propaganda v SSSR v 1945–1985 gg.* Moscow: n.p., 2011.
Sladojević, Ana. *Muzej afričke umetnosti. Konteksti i reprezentacije.* Belgrade: Muzej afričke umetnosti, 2014.
Sladojević, Ana and Emilija Epštajn (eds.), *Nympakorndzidzi: one man, no chop. The (re)conceptualization of the Museum of African Art—The Veda and Dr. Zdravko Pečar Collection.* Belgrade: Museum of African Art, 2017.
Sołtysik, Łukasz. "North Korean children and youth in Lower Silesia and Masovia in 1951–1959," *Śląski Kwartalnik Historyczny Sobótka* 65.1 (2010): 57–95.
Sretenović, Dejan. *Crno telo, bele maske.* Belgrade: Muzej afričke umetnosti, 2004.

Stanek, Łukasz. *Architecture in Global Socialism: Eastern Europe, West Africa, and the Middle East in the Cold War*. Princeton, NJ: Princeton University Press, 2020.
Stanley, Liz, Andrea Salter, and Helen Dampier. "The Epistolary Pact, Letterness, and the Schreiner Epistolarium," *a/b: Auto-Biography Studies* 27.2 (Winter 2012): 262–93.
Stierli, Martino and Vladinmir Kulić. *Toward a Concrete Utopia: Architecture in Yugoslavia, 1948–1980*. New York: Museum of Modern Art, 2018.
Stoler, Anne Laura. *Duress: Imperial Durabilities in Our Times*. Durham, NC: Duke University Press, 2015.
Storkmann, Klaus. *Geheime Solidarität. Militärbeziehungen und Militärhilfen der DDR in die "Dritte Welt."* Berlin: Christoph Links Verlag, 2012.
Struck, Bernhard, Kate Ferris, and Jacques Revel. "Introduction: Space and Scale in Transnational History," *International History Review* 33.4 (2011): 573–84.
Telepneva, Natalia. "Saving Ghana's Revolution: The Demise of Kwame Nkrumah and the Evolution of Soviet Policy in Africa, 1966–1972," *Journal of Cold War Studies* 20.4 (2018): 4–25.
Tignor, Robert. *Arthur Lewis and the Birth of Development Economics*. Princeton, NJ: Princeton University Press, 2006.
Tignor, Robert. *Capitalism and Nationalism at the End of Empire: State and Business in Decolonizing Egypt, Nigeria, and Kenya, 1945–1963*. Princeton, NJ: Princeton University Press, 2015.
Tudorancea, Radu. *Ipostazele "ajutorului frățesc". RPR și războiul din Coreea (1950–1953)*. Cluj-Napoca: Eikon, 2014.
Vandewalle, Dirk. *A History of Modern Libya*. Cambridge: Cambridge University Press, 2012.
Van Genugten, Saskia. *Libya in Western Foreign Policies, 1911–2011*. London: Palgrave Macmillan, 2016.
Vargha, Dora. "Technical Assistance and Socialist International Health: Hungary, the WHO and the Korean War," *History and Technology* 36.3-4 (2020): 400–17.
von Puttkamer, Joachim. *Schulalltag und nationale Integration in Ungarn. Slowaken, Rumänen und Siebenbürger Sachsen in der Auseinandersetzung mit der ungarischen Staatsidee 1867–1914*. Munich: Oldenbourg, 2003.
Vučetić, Radina and Paul Betts (eds.), *Tito in Africa: Picturing Solidarity*. Belgrade: Museum of Yugoslavia, 2017.
Vyhlídal, Milan. *Činnost československých intruktorů v egyptských ozbrojených silách. Účast na egyptském vojenském školství v letech 1956–1977*. Praha: Carter Reproplus, 2016.
Webb, Alban. "A Leap of Imagination: BBC Audience Research over the Iron Curtain," *Participations* 8.1 (2011): 154–72.
Weis, Toni. "The politics machine: On the concept of 'solidarity' in East German support for SWAPO," *Journal of Southern African Studies* 37.02 (2011): 351–67.
Westad, Odd Arne. *Global Cold War: The Third World Interventions and the Making of Our Times*. Cambridge: Cambridge University Press, 2005.
Zeleza, Tiyambe. "Pan-African Trade Unionism: Unity and Discord," *Transafrican Journal of History* 15 (1986).
Zídek, Petr and Karel Sieber. *Československo a subsaharská Afrika v letech 1948–1989*. Praha: Ústav mezinárodních vztahů, 2007.
Zídek, Petr and Karel Sieber. *Československo a Blízký východ v letech 1948–1989*. Praha: Ústav mezinárodních vztahů, 2009.

Index

Entries followed by the letter *f* indicate a page with a figure.

AATUF (All-African Trade Union Federation) 212, 214
abortion 192
Abraham, William 132, 133
Achimota School 123
Adelman, Jeremy 3
adoption 32
adventure stories 244–6
Afghanistan, expatriate communities in 152, 155
AFKSZh (*Anti-Fashistskii Komitet Sovetskikh Zhenshchin* [Anti-Fascist Committee of Soviet Women]) 98, 100
Africa 79 *see also under individual countries*
   archives 198
   art 10, 80, 81, 85–96
   art in Yugoslavia 85–96
   colonialism 80–1
   culture 80–4, 94–5
   decolonization 119
   East Africa 6, 198, 199, 200–1, 202–16
   exoticism 80, 85, 88, 89–90
   FDGB 197, 198, 199
   "Josip Broz Tito" Art Gallery of the Non-Aligned Countries 94
   négritude 86, 88, 89
   Soviet military training 161
   sub-Saharan 85, 88, 89
   theater 81
   trade unions 197, 198, 199–216
   travel writing 238, 239, 240–1, 245, 247–9, 251, 252, 253–5, 256–7
   Yugoslav art in 82–5, 95
"African Bronze" exhibition 94
African Campfires (Széchenyi, Zsigmond) 248

Africanization 120, 121, 122, 123–6, 137, 208
"Afrika" (Petrović, Rastko) 239
Afro-Shirazi Party (ASP) 204, 209
aid *see also* development aid *and* military aid
   humanitarian 159
AIWC (All-Indian Women's Conference) 117
Alexandria Biennale for Mediterranean Countries 84, 95
All-African Trade Union Federation (AATUF) 212, 214
All-Indian Women's Conference (AIWC) 117
Allah Akbar! (Germanus, Gyula) 246
Almássy, László 257
"Among Arab Friends" (Koroteev, V.) 71–2
anti-colonialism *see also* decolonization
   adventure stories 245–6
   Aswan High Dam project 63–6
   road trips 242, 251
   Soviet training 169–70
   trade unions 200, 201, 204, 215, 216
   travel writing. *See* travel writing
   travelogues 238–44, 250–1, 253–5, 257, 258, 259
   Yugoslavia 91, 92
Anti-Fashistskii Komitet Sovetskikh Zhenshchin (Anti-Fascist Committee of Soviet Women; AFKSZh) 98, 100
anti-imperialism 202–4
antisemitism 150
Antonín Zápotocký Military Academy (Vojenská akademie Antonína Zápotockého; VAAZ) 139
Apor, Péter 14–15
architecture 70, 122–3, 132

art 77–80
  African 10, 80, 81, 85–90
  modernism 77–9, 86–8
  Yugoslav 82–5
"Art of West Africa, The" exhibition
  88–9, 90
ASP (Afro-Shirazi Party) 204, 209
"Assuan High Dam" (Galochkin, N.) 71–2
Aswan High Dam project 59, 60–3, 75*f*
  as anti-colonial project 63–6
  architecture 70
  Egyptian engineers 65, 71, 75, 76
  journalism 71–3
  production crisis 73–6
  salaries 71
  Soviet production culture 67–8, 76
  women 72
Ayensu, Grace 111

Babu, Abdulrahman Mohamed 213
Badganny, Afonso Manga 160, 162, 173
Balakhovskaya, Liudmila 97, 102, 114
Balme, David 123, 124, 131
Barát, Endre 239
Barghoorn, Frederick 47
Baum, Jiří 241
BBC, audience research 50
Bebler, Aleš 240
Belgrade International Theater festival
  (BITEF) 81
Bengal Fire (Germanus, Gyula) 246–7
bilateralism 14–16
BITEF (Belgrade International Theater
  festival) 81
Black Sisyphus (Miklja, Dušan) 240–1
Black Tears of the Congo, The (Vitorović,
  Nikola) 239
body, the 30–1
Bom dia (Scherzer, Landolf) 256–7
Bondarenko, Olga 101–2, 105, 107, 108,
  111, 114–15
Brandys, Marian 245
broadcasting 39–41, 47 *see also* Moscow
  Radio
  surrogate 42
  transnational 39, 40–2, 47, 49
brokers 9–10
Broz, Josip 78
Bulgaria 21–2

Burning Spear (Barát, Endre) 239
Burton, Eric 6, 13, 16

Cabral, Amíl Lopes da Costa 159, 160, 164,
  165, 166, 167–9, 173, 174
Cameroon 109–10
Cape Verde 164–5
Carvalho, Júlio 160, 161, 165, 166, 167, 171,
  173
Cassama, Fode 160, 164, 168, 170
Ceaușescu, Nicolae 177
Césaire, Aimé 1, 16, 86
Ceylon 108–9
Chakraborty, A. K. 106
Chapaev (Vasilyev, Georgi and Vasilyev,
  Sergei) 170
childhood 28–9
China 16, 206, 239–40
Chinese October (Kónya, Lajos) 239–40
Cissé, Fatou 107, 113
civilization 26, 29–31, 38, 228
Cold War, the 8, 100, 101, 117
colonialism 1, 16, 31 *see also* anti-
    colonialism *and* decolonization
  Africa 80–1
  architecture 122–3
  art 79–80
  Aswan High Dam project 63–6
  colonial adventure stories 244–6
  Egypt 61–2, 63–6, 67
  exoticism 80, 85
  Ghana 120, 122–6, 128–9
  India 246–7
  "Josip Broz Tito" Art Gallery of the
    Non-Aligned Countries 94
  KSZh 111
  Museum of African Art 91–2
  Portugal 159
  Soviet training 170
  Tanganyika 208
  trade unions 199–200
  travel writing 238–9
  World's Fairs 79, 80
  writing 16
common humanity concept 98–9, 117
communism 1 *see also* socialism
  threat of 8
Communist Party 1, 16
Congo, the 244

Index

connectivity 6
consumption 189–90, 223–5
contact zones 4–5
"Contemporary Art from Ghana" exhibition 87–8
"Contemporary Sculpture of Makonde" exhibition 87
Continuing the One Thousand and One Nights (al-Kurayshi, Ágnes) 252–3
correspondence 97–8, 101–18
  censorship 152
  information sharing 106–7
  object sharing by post 107–8
Csiu! (Széchenyi, Zsigmond) 248
Csoma, Sándor Kőrösi 255
Csoóri, Sándor 243, 251–2
Cuba 164–5, 167, 172, 173
  Cuban workers in Czechoslovakia 218, 221, 226, 227, 228
  Cuban workers in Hungary 227
  travel writing 243
  women, sexualization of 251–2
Cuban Diary (Csoóri, Sándor) 243, 251–2
cultural difference 25–30, 31, 38
cultural diplomacy 78–9, 81–2, 83
culture 33, 77
  African 80–4, 94–5
  broadcasting 47
  cross-cultural exchange 107
  differences in 256–7
  Egypt 82, 83–4, 148–50, 154
  hierarchy 93, 95
  language 46
  monoculture 47
  North Korean 33
  socialist 43
  Soviet Union 46
  translating 233–5, 236
  Vietnamese 233–5, 236
  Yugoslavia 77–9, 81–5
Cunningham, Griffiths 214, 215
Czechoslovakia
  anti-colonial road trips 251
  black/grey-market 223–5
  consumerism 223–5
  criminal cases 217, 218–19, 220, 223–4, 225–6, 227–8, 229–32, 233–5, 236
  Cuban workers in 218, 221, 226, 227, 228

defection 153
Egypt 140–1 *see also* MTC
expatriate communities 140–1, 150–5
experts 139–41, 150–5, 157–8
experts and dissatisfaction 155–7
experts as instrument of business and solidarity 141–3
experts and MTC construction 143–7
experts and racial and cultural tension 148–50
explorers 244
gender 222, 223
hostels 218, 219–25, 235
image 151–2
invasion 156
military aid/training 9, 139–41 *see also* MTC
North Korean refugee children 21–2, 23–4, 25, 26, 27, 29–32, 34, 36
Polish workers in 227, 228, 221, 227, 228
Prague Spring 155–7
prisons 218, 229–35, 236
pubs 218, 225–8, 232, 236
racism 226, 227–8
Roma workers in 233
socialism 156, 226, 227, 228
spaces 140–1, 158, 217–36
travel writing 241, 259
Vietnamese workers in 217, 218, 220, 221, 222f–4, 226, 229–35, 236

Davičo, Oskar 239, 254
"Days of African cultures" festival 81, 82–3, 95
decolonization 1–2, 40, 82, 98, 119, 199–201 *see also* anti-colonialism
East Africa 198, 202
education 119
Ghana 119, 120, 121, 122, 123–6, 130–2, 138
of mind 82, 86
through internationalization 130–2
travel writing. *See* travel writing
development aid 61, 108–11
  Ghana 108, 130–1, 133
Devi, Sumitra 108, 111, 114, 115–16
diplomacy 105
  cultural diplomacy 78–9, 81–2, 83

Dizdarević, Raif 93
Dneprostroi Dam 62, 63
Dove, Mabel 101–2, 104, 108, 117
Drewnowski, Jan 121, 126–8, 129–30, 131

East Africa 6, 198, 199
   trade unions 198, 199, 200–1, 202–16
East Asia 257
East German Confederation of Free German Trade Unions (Freier Deutscher Gewerkschaftsbund [FDGB]). *See* FDGB
East Germany. *See* GDR
Eastern Europe/Europeans 1, 3, 5, 6–7, 9, 11 *see also under individual countries*
   in Ghana 120–2, 126–8, 129–30, 131, 132–3, 137
   health 24–6
   internationalist education programs 21–38
   North Korean refugee children 14, 15, 21–35
   race/racism 16, 17, 18
   socialist youth organisations 35
   trade unions 199, 201–2, 206
   travel writing. *See* travel writing
   white privilege 253–5
   women 13
education 119, 122–3 *see also* MTC *and* schools
   internationalist education programs 21–38
   itinerant trade union schools 209–11, 212–13
   socialism 146, 147
   trade union 204–15
   US American Peace Corps 214–15
Egypt 59, 60, 61–2, 67, 158 *see also* Aswan High Dam project *and* MTC
   culture 82, 83–4
   Czechoslovakian military aid 140–1 *see also* MTC
   economy 143
   engineers 66–7, 75, 76
   expatriate communities in 140–1, 150–5
   modern art 87
   nationalism 150

   religion/religious attack 149
   war 155
   workforce 69, 74, 75*f*
   Yugoslavia 82, 83–4, 86–7
Eighth Non-Aligned Conference 94
Engerman, David 3, 4
"Exhibition of African Masks, The" 88, 89
"Exhibition of Egyptian Contemporary Art" 87
"Exhibition of Ethiopian Paintings" 87
exhibitions 79–80
exoticism 80, 85, 88, 89–90
expatriate communities 10, 139–41, 150–5
explorers 244

FDGB (East German Confederation of Free German Trade Unions [Freier Deutscher Gewerkschaftsbund]) 197, 198–9, 201
   archives 198–9
   education 204–15
   gender 208
   itinerant trade union schools 209–11, 212–13
   Lamprecht, Max 211, 212–15
   production 212
   Tanzania, Republic of 211–15
   TFL 207–8
   Zanzibar 202–3, 204, 209, 210–11
Federation of Progressive Trade Unions (FPTU) 203–4, 209
Fëdorova, Zinaida 104, 106, 111, 113–14
feminism 100–1, 111–12, 116–17
Földes, László 249
folklore 242
Foreign Broadcasting Bulletin 46
FPTU (Federation of Progressive Trade Unions) 203–4, 209

al-Gaddafi, Muammar 178, 180
Galla-Kovács, Ágnes 252
Galochkin, N. 71–2
GDR (German Democratic Republic) 21–2, 31–2, 33, 35
   anti-colonial adventure stories 245–6
   colonial adventure stories 245–6
   hunting accounts/expeditions 247, 248, 249
   TFL 207–8

trade unions 197, 202, 209, 216 see also
    FDGB
travel writing 237, 239, 245–6, 254–5,
    256–7, 259
gender 12–13 see also men *and* women
    Czechoslovakia 222, 223
    FDGB 208
    Gharyan hospital 187, 188
    North Korean refugee children 27
Gerakan Wanita Indonesia (Gerwani) 102,
    113
German Democratic Republic (GDR). See
    GDR
Germanus, Gyula 246
Gerwani (Gerakan Wanita Indonesia) 102,
    113
Ghana 87–8, 111, 119–21, 136 see also
    University College of the Gold
    Coast/University of Ghana 168
    Achimota School 123
    Africanization 120, 121, 122, 123–6,
      137
    aid 108, 130–1, 133
    decolonization 119, 120, 121, 122,
      123–6, 130–2, 138
    nationalism 135
    Soviet presence 132–3
    Western presence 133, 134
Gharyan hospital 179–80, 196
    abortion 192
    care malfunctions 191–5
    consumption 189–90
    family dynamics 187–8, 189
    gender 187, 188
    leadership 192–3
    sexuality 188–9
    socialism 187–91
    space 181–6
    staff/staff concerns 182–6, 187–92, 195
Giri R.K.M. 102–3
global history 3–4, 6
Global South. See Third World
globalization 7–8
    radio broadcasting 39, 40–1, 43
Good Morning, Africa! (Kende, István) 253
Gorbunov, Iurii 170, 172
Górnicki, Wiesław 240, 242
Great Britain 61–2
    Ghana 120, 121, 122–6, 128

India 246–7
Guevara, Che 165, 243
Guinea 253, 256
    expatriate communities in 152, 154
Guinea-Bissau 159–60, 170
    guerrillas, training. See PAIGC
    independence politics 168–9
    nationalism 173, 174
Gunther, John 240
gymnastics 30–1

Habub over Sudan (Ignácz, Ferenc) 256
Hadžić, Fadil 239, 250
Hanzelka, Miroslav 251
Harrison, Austen St. Barbe 123
health 24–6, 29, 30
healthcare 178–9 see also Gharyan
    hospital
history 2–4
    global history 3–4, 6
Holub, Emil 244
hostels 218, 219–25, 235
Howard, P. 245
humanitarian aid 159
humanity 98–9, 117
Hungary 21, 22, 26, 28, 29, 31, 32–3, 34–5,
    37
    bestselling authors in 245
    colonial adventure stories 245
    explorers 244
    foreign workers in 227
    hunting accounts/expeditions 247*f*,
      248–9, 257
    travel writing 237, 239–40, 242, 243,
      246, 252, 253, 255, 257, 259
    hunting accounts/expeditions 247*f*–50 ,
      252, 256, 257

I did not hunt in Tanzania (Galla-Kovács,
    Ágnes) 252
Iacob, Bogdan 10, 11, 13
Ibrahim, Son'allah 70
ICFTU (International Confederation
    of Free Trade Unions) 202,
    207, 210
identity 23
    national identity 23, 33–6
Ignácz, Ferenc 256
Ignácz, Rózsa 239, 242, 252, 255

imperialism 79, 121, 253–5 *see also* colonialism
anti-imperialism 202–4
architecture 122–3
in Ghana 120, 122–6, 128–9
Great Britain 246–7
travel writing 244, 257–8
In Desert and Wilderness (Sienkiewicz, Henryk) 245
India 111, 113
expatriate communities in 151, 152, 154, 155
travel writing 240, 242, 246–7, 255
Indonesia 102, 113
expatriate communities in 151, 154, 155
influence 61
Insan al-Sadd al-'Ali (*Man of the High Dam*) (Ibrahim, Son'allah; al-Qilish, Kamal; Mus'ad, Ra'uf) 70
Inside Africa (Gunther, John) 240
integration 22–3, 26–7, 28–31, 32, 33–7
International Confederation of Free Trade Unions (ICFTU) 202, 207, 210
internationalism 33, 35, 37–8, 41–4
internationalist education programs 21–34
civilization 26, 29–31, 38
curricula 35
difference 25–30, 31, 38
integration 22–3, 26–7, 28–31, 32, 33–37
internationalism 33, 35, 37–8
national identity 23, 33–6
secrecy 36
socialism 35
spaces 23–5, 31–2, 35, 37
internationalization 130–2
Islam 149, 150, 253
Issa, Ali Sultan 202–3, 204, 206, 209

Janeković, Dara 256
Jentoft, Morten 45
"Josip Broz Tito" Art Gallery of the Non-Aligned Countries 90, 93–5
Jungle Book, The (Kipling, Rudyard) 240

Kalecki, Michal 134
Kalmár, György 257
Kapuściński, Ryszard 254

Kende, István 253
Kenya 200, 208, 244, 254
Khandvala, Kapila 108
Khrushchev, Nikita 2, 59, 112
Aswan High Dam project 61
Kipling, Rudyard 240
Kittenberger, Kálmán 248
Kivukoni College 214
Komitet Sovetskikh Zhenshchin (Committee of Soviet Women; KSZh). *See* KSZh
Komzin, I. V. 67–8, 71
Kónya, Lajos 239–40
Korea *see also* North Korea
war 29
Koroteev, V. 71
Kossou, Basile 95
Kragujevac–Kilimanjaro expedition 251
Kremenchuk 64–6
KSZh (*Komitet Sovetskikh Zhenshchin* [Committee of Soviet Women]) 97–101
aid 108–11
epistolarium 98, 99, 100, 101–18
propaganda 104, 109, 114
Kuibyshev hydroelectric station 62, 63
kul'turnost' 169
al-Kurayshi, Ágnes 252–3
Kwapong, Alexander 136–7

Lal, Priya 3
Lamprecht, Max 211, 212–15
language
correspondence 103
Czechoslovakia, foreign workers in 221, 233–5, 236
language skills 26–7
MTC 145–6, 148
Perevalnoe military training camp 162, 173
radio 43, 44–5, 46, 47, 51, 53, 56
Soviet Union 46–7, 104
translation 103, 233–5, 236
Latin America 243, 250 *see also* Cuba
Leite, António 160
Lenin, Vladimir 201
Leninism 213
Lerner, David 40
Leskien, Jürgen 254–5

Index

Lesnik, Renata 54
Libya 11, 178–9, 194 *see also* Gharyan hospital
Ligeti, Vilma 255
Luz, Silvino da 160, 161, 165, 167, 173

M.S.T. 104
Magnitogorsk 62–3
Majoedin, D. 107
Mali 85
Mane, Arafan 160, 162, 163, 171, 172–3
Martei, Margaret 108
Marxism 213
"Mask and African Wooden Sculpture" exhibition 94
Materials for Final Engineering Report f the High Aswan Dam Project, Bulletin 10, "Organization of Construction" 66
Matta, Brandão Bull da 160, 162, 170, 173
May, Ferdinand 245
May, Karl 245–6
media ethnography 50
men
   North Korean refugee children 27
   radio audience 56
   white 253–5
Mensah, Joseph 125, 135
Mesiatsev, Nikolai 43, 48
mid-level actors 10, 11
Mikkonen, Simo 49–50
Miklja, Dušan 240–1
Milačić, Boža 240
military aid 8–9, 15, 19, 139–41, 159 *see also* MTC
military sector 8–9, 12, 15, 19
Military Technical College (MTC), Cairo. *See* MTC
military training *see also* MTC
   kul'turnost' 169
   Soviet 159–60, 161–6, 169–72, 174–5
Mind of Africa, The (Abraham, William) 133
mobility 7–8
modernism 77–9, 86–8
modernity 169, 241–2
"Modernization as a Global Project" (Engerman, David and Unger, Corinna) 3–4

Molnár, Gábor 248
monoculture 47
Moyo, Hassan Nassor 203–4
Mozambique 256–7
MTC (Military Technical College), Cairo 140, 141, 142–7
   curricula 144–6
   discipline 146–7, 148
   expatriate community 151, 153
   faculty 144, 145, 147, 150
   language 145–6, 148
   politics 145–7, 155–7, 158
   Prague Spring 155–7
   propaganda 146–7
   racial and cultural stereotypes 148–50
   religion/religious attack 149
   staff discontent 155–6, 158
Museum of African Art 90, 91–3, 95
museums 80, 90, 92

Nadler, Michael 132
Nadler, Shulamit 132
Nagy, Endre 249, 255
Nasser, Gamal Abdel 60, 145
national culture 33, 34–5
national identity 23, 33–6
   Soviet Union 46
National Union of Tanganyika Workers (NUTA) 212–13, 214–15
national voices 41–5
nationalism 198, 199, 200, 201, 202
Native Americans 246
Nazi occupation 242
négritude 86, 88, 89
Nešović, Slobodan 256
neurasthenia 191
New World Information and Communication Order (NWICO) 48–9
Niculescu, Barbu 129
Nikitin, A. P. 64 n. 27
Nkrumah, Kwame 119, 120, 121, 125, 130, 136, 138, 168 *see also* Nkrumahism
Nkrumahism 132–7
North Korea
   integration 35–6
   national identity 23, 33, 35–6
   war 29, 33–4

North Korean refugee children 14–15, 21–34
  civilization 26, 29–31, 38
  difference 25–30, 31, 38
  integration 22–3, 26–7, 28–31, 32, 33–7
  internationalism 33, 35, 37–8
  national identity 23, 33–6
  secrecy 36
  spaces 23–5, 31–2, 35, 37
Nsekela, Amon 213, 214
NUTA (National Union of Tanganyika Workers) 212–13, 214–15
NWICO (New World Information and Communication Order) 48–9

O'Brien, Conor Cruise 133, 135
Omog, Gertrude 109–11, 112
one nation hospitals 179 *see also* Gharyan hospital
Orientalism 246–7
Osende, Elise 112
othering 80

PAIGC (Party for Independence of Guinea and Cape Verde [Partido Africano da Independência da Guiné e Cabo Verde]) 159, 175
  cultural program 170–2
  film screenings 170–1
  political instruction 168–9, 170, 172–4
  Soviet military training 160, 162–6, 169–72, 174–5
  Soviet political training 169–70, 171–2
  Soviet weapons technology and training 166–8
participatory development 178
Party for Independence of Guinea and Cape Verde (Partido Africano da Independência da Guiné e Cabo Verde; PAIGC). *See* PAIGC
Patel, D. G. 114–15
peace movements 98–9, 101, 109, 113–14, 117
Pearson, Drew 59, 60
Pečar, Stravko 10
Pečar, Veda 10, 88, 90–1
Pečar, Zdravko 88, 90, 91, 95
Perera, Mrs 108–9

Perevalnoe military training camp 161–3, 164, 166, 167, 168, 175
  cultural program 170, 171
  political training 169, 170, 172, 173, 174
Pešta, Mikuláš 9, 11, 13
Petrova, Lydia 102, 107, 108, 109, 111–12, 114
Petrović, Rastko 239
Pires, Olívio 160, 165, 167
Pires, Pedro 160, 161, 165, 167, 168, 173, 175
Piroja Wadia, D. R. 114
Poland 128
  colonial adventure stories 245
  Nazi occupation 242
  North Korean refugee children 21, 22, 24–5, 26, 27–8, 33–4, 35, 36
  Polish academics in Ghana 121, 126–8, 129–30, 131, 134–6, 137
  Polish workers in Czechoslovakia 227, 228, 221, 227, 228
  Polish workers in Hungary 227
  travel writing 237, 239, 240, 242, 254
popular entertainment 17–18 *see also* radio
Portugal 159
postcolonialism 80, 81–2, 95 *see also* colonialism
Prague Spring 155–7
Pratt, Mary 4–5
prisons 218, 229–35, 236
Private Alexander Matrosov (Lukov, Leonid) 171
production culture 65, 66, 67–70, 76
productionism 198, 199–202
propaganda 41, 42, 104, 109, 114, 146–7, 213
pubs 218, 225–8, 232, 236

Quallatein, Ahmed Badawi 206–7, 209
Quartey-Papafio, Ruby 115, 116*f*

race/racism 16–18, 79, 190, 196
  Czechoslovakia 226, 227–8
  neurasthenia 191
  sexuality 189
  stereotypes 148–50

travel writing 245, 249
white privilege 253–5
radio 39–40 *see also* Radio Moscow
   language 43, 44–5, 46, 47, 51, 53, 56
   Radio Peace and Progress 43
   Zambia 55
Radio Moscow 40–2
   archives 49, 54
   audience 47–8, 49–57
   broadcasting plans 47–8
   criticism 42–3
   foreigners, dependence on 41–2
   internationalism 41–4
   language 43, 44–5, 46, 47, 51, 53, 56
   music 53
   Punjabi service 41–2
   as social space 55, 56, 57
   socialist culture 43
   state control 42, 46
   voices 41–5, 47
   worldwide survey program 51–4, 55, 56–7
Radio Peace and Progress 43
Reflections on the Revolution in France (Burke, Edmund) 133
Rejtő, Jenő 245
religion 115–16, 149, 150, 253
   healthcare 194
Republic of the Congo 111
RFE/RL 42
Richter, Vjenceslav 78
Rim Zang Dong 29, 30
Road Sign Pointing South, A (Sekulić, Dušan) 256
Roma, the 233
Romania 10, 11, 177–9, 180, 189 *see also* Gharyan hospital
   abortion 192
   defections 186
   economy 186, 195
   explorers 244
   healthcare 192, 195–6
   hunting accounts/expeditions 247–8
   North Korean refugee children 21, 22, 23, 25f, 26–7, 28, 32, 34, 36
   women 13
Rubenstein, Alvin 61, 76
Rupprecht, Tobias 85
Russian Revolution 113

S.R.S. 105
Sadowski, Zbigniew 121, 134–6, 137
"Sahara expedition" 257
Said, Edward 96
Sanghi, K. 97, 102, 104
Sáska, László 255
Sauvy, Albert 1, 2
Scherzer, Landolf 256–7
Schomburgk, Hans 249
schools 21–34
   civilization 26, 29–31, 38
   curricula 35
   difference 25–30, 31, 38
   expatriate community 153
   integration 22–3, 26–7, 28–31, 32, 33–37
   internationalism 33, 35, 37–8
   national identity 23, 33–6
   secrecy 36
   socialism 35
   spaces 23–5, 31–2, 35, 37
Second-Third World encounters 9–10, 11, 13, 15–16, 18–20
   common goals 19
   race/racism 18
Second World 3, 6–7 *see also* Eastern Europe/Europeans
   expatriate communities 10, 139–41, 150–5
   globalization 7–8, 11
   military aid 8–9, 19
   mobility 7–8
   race/racism 17, 18
   Second-Third World encounters 9–10, 11, 13, 15–16, 18–20
   solidarity work 12
   spaces 5–6
   women 12–13
Second World War 242
Sekulić, Dušan 256
self-regulation 32
Senghor, Léopold 86
Seven Years in Bolivia (Szokoly, Endre) 250
sexuality 13, 188–9
Shah, Kamal 111–12
Sienkiewicz, Henryk 245
Silva, João Pereira da 160, 161, 163, 164, 166, 171
Silva, Osvaldo Lopes da 160, 161, 165

Singapore 257
Skhodnia military training camp 164–6, 167, 171, 173–4, 175
Śladami Stasia I Nel ("In the Footsteps of Stas and Nel") (Brandys, Marian) 245
Sladojević, Ana 92
Snows of Kilimanjaro, The (King, Henry) 85
socialism 5, 11
　correspondence 103–4
　culture 43
　Czechoslovakia 156, 226, 227, 228
　education 146, 147
　Egypt 145
　FDGB 205
　Gharyan hospital 187–91, 193, 195
　morality 189–90
　North Korean refugee children 35
　race/racism 16
　radio 47–8
　spaces 5
　trade unions 199, 201–2, 203–4, 205, 207, 209, 213–14
　travel writing. *See* travel writing
　women 12
socialist cosmopolitanism 227
socialist internationalism 99–100, 101, 105–6, 118
socialist modernism 78
socialist youth organisations 35
Soedjanti, Miss 106
solidarity 11, 12, 13, 33–4, 37, 111
　FDGB 201–2
　travel writing 256–7
Sons of the Great Bear, The (Welskopf-Henrich, Liselotte) 246
South Korea 257
"South of Sahara" exhibition 89
Soviet Union 1–2, 59 *see also* Moscow Radio
　AFKSZh 98, 100
　Aswan High Dam project 59, 60–1, 62–5, 67–76
　audience research 50–1
　development aid 61, 108–11
　engineers 68, 774, 7
　films 170–1
　globalization 7

　identity 169
　influence 61
　KSZh 97–118
　kul'turnost' 169
　language 46–7
　military aid 8–9, 15, 159
　military hierarchy 162, 163, 164, 166
　military sector 8
　military training 159–60, 161–6, 169–72, 174–5
　national identity 46
　NWICO 48–9
　PAIGC 159, 161–6, 169–72, 174–5
　political training 169–70
　production culture 65, 66, 67–70, 76
　propaganda 104, 109, 114
　race/racism 16
　Radio Peace and Progress 43
　religion 115–16
　secrecy 162–4, 165
　space race 112, 113
　spaces 5, 63
　stamps 114–15
　support for 112–13
　weapons technology and training 166–8
　WIDF 99, 100–1
　women 12–13, 72–3, 97–8, 99, 100–18
　workforce 69, 71, 74, 75–6
　Zanzibar 203
Soviet Woman 101, 102, 104, 108, 109, 114, 115
space race 112, 113
spaces 4–6, 59, 60 *see also* Second-Third World encounters
　art 79, 80
　Aswan High Dam project 63–4, 65, 70–1
　brokers 9–10
　Czechoslovakia 140–1, 158, 217–36
　exhibition 79, 80
　expatriate communities 10, 139–41, 150–5
　expert communities 11
　financial imperatives 11
　gender 12–13
　Gharyan hospital 181–6
　global 6–8
　hostels 218, 219–25, 235

military 8–9
military training camps 174
museums 80, 90, 92
North Korean refugee children 23–5, 31–2, 35, 37
prisons 218, 229–35, 236
pubs 218, 225–8, 232, 236
race/racism 16–18
radio 40, 41, 43, 47, 49
radio as social space 55, 56, 57
schools 23–5, 31–2, 35, 37
social 55, 56, 57
socialist 5
solidarity 11, 12, 13
Soviet 5, 63
writing 9
Spitulnik, Debra 55
state control 35, 36
radio 40, 42, 43
Stoler, Ann 121
Storm over Southwest Africa: A Story from the Days of the Herero Tribe (May, Ferdinand) 245
Story of a Real Man, The (Stolper, Aleksandr) 171
Strela-2 anti-aircraft system 167–8
sub-Saharan Africa 85, 88, 89
Sudan 242
Suharti, Mrs 113
Sukhorukhov, Vladimir 162–3
Sulayman, Sidqi 66
Sumanagara, E. 112
Sunantaria 102, 103, 104
Sunrise and Sunset: Wandering around Europe, Africa, Asia and America (Nešović, Slobodan) 256
Sunrise on the Yangtze Shore (Vincze, Lajos) 240
surrogate broadcasting 42
surveillance 219–20, 221
Syria 150
Széchenyi, Zsigmond 248
Szilágyi, Éva 252
Szokoly, Endre 250
Szuhai, István 249

Tanganyika 197, 198, 199, 200, 207–8 *see also* Tanzania, United Republic of
NUTA 212–13

TANU 200
TFL 200, 207–8, 211–12
Tanganyika African National Union (TANU) 200
Tanganyika Federation of Labour (TFL) 200, 207–8, 211–12
TANU (Tanganyika African National Union) 200
Tanzania, United Republic of 87, 197, 205, 211–12
AATUF 212, 21
FDGB 211–15
itinerant trade union school 211, 212–13
Kivukoni College 214
NUTA 212–13, 215–16
US American Peace Corps 214–15
Tarzan 245
Teleki, Sámuel 244, 257
Telepneva, Natalia 9, 15
Tereshkova, Valentina 112
TFL (Tanganyika Federation of Labour) 200, 207–8, 211–12
Third World 1, 2, 6–7, 39 n. 1 *see also under individual countries*
audience research 50, 53, 54
communist threat 8
correspondence with KSZh 97–8, 101–18
economy 177
expatriate communities in 10, 139–41, 150–5
FDGB 197, 198
global mobility 8
history 2–3
military aid 8–9, 19, 139, 140–1
NWICO 48–9
participatory development 178
Radio Moscow in the 41, 44–5, 48, 50, 53, 54, 56
Romania 177–9 *see also* Gharyan hospital
Second-Third World encounters 9–10, 11, 13, 15–16, 18–20
Soviet development aid 61, 108–11
Soviet military training 160, 162–6, 169–72, 174–5
spaces 6
travel writing. *See* travel writing

women 97-8, 101-18
Yugoslavian art 84-5
Tican-Rumano, Mihai 244
"Ticket for Tomorrow, A" (Vitorović, Aleksandar) 257
Tito, Josip Broz 78, 83, 90, 94
Tjoa, Effie 113-14
trade unions 6, 197, 216 *see also* FDGB
   Africa 197, 198, 199-216
   anti-imperialism 202-4
   Eastern Europe 201-2
   education 204-15
   productionism 198, 199-202
   socialism 199, 201-2, 203-4, 205, 207, 209, 213-14
tradition 242
translation 103, 233-5, 236
transnational broadcasting 39, 40-2, 47, 49 *see also* Moscow Radio
   audience research 50
travel 107
travel writing 237-8, 258-9
   anti-colonial adventure stories 245-6
   anti-colonial road trips 242, 251
   anti-colonial travelogues 238-44, 250-1, 253-5, 257, 258, 259
   colonial adventure stories 244-6
   cultural differences 256-7
   East Asia 257
   historical 243-4
   hope/pessimism 256
   hunting accounts/expeditions 247*f*-50, 252, 256, 257
   imperialism 244, 257-8
   readership 239-40
   romanticized 250
   white privilege 253-5
   women 251-3, 255, 258

Uganda
   expatriate communities in 154
   trade unions 200
Ullrich, Wolfgang 249
Umma Party 209
Unger, Corinna 4
United States of America 60
   Aswan High Dam project 60
   Native Americans 246
   US American Peace Corps 214-15

universalism 1
University College of the Gold Coast / University of Ghana 119-24*f*, 137-8
   academic freedom 136-7
   Africanization 120, 121, 122, 123-6, 137
   architecture 122-3, 132
   ceremony 131
   criticism 128
   Department of Economics 128-30, 134-5
   faculty 124, 125, 126-30, 131, 132-3, 134-8
   foreign aid 130-1, 133
   internationalization 120, 121
   Kwapong, Alexander 136-7
   Nkrumah, Kwame 119, 120, 122, 123, 125, 132-7, 138
   Soviet bloc academics 132-3, 137
   student protests 137
   syllabi 128-30

VAAZ (Antonín Zápotocký Military Academy [Vojenská akademie Antonína Zápotockého]) 139
Vámbéry, Ármin 255
Videkanić, Bojana 78, 79
Vietnamese workers in Czechoslovakia 217, 218, 220, 221, 222*f*-4, 226, 229-35, 236
Vimla, K. 113
Vincze, Lajos 240
Vitorović, Aleksandar 257
Vitorović, Nikola 239
voices 41-5, 47
Voronina, Nina 102, 103, 108, 111
vrátný/á (porter) 219-20, 221
Vučetić, Radina 10

Wanita Demokrat 112
Wasu, Pritpal Kaur 108
Welskopf-Henrich, Liselotte 246
West, the
   education 215
   media domination of 48-9
white privilege 253-5
WIDF (Women's International Democratic Federation) 99, 100-1
Winnetou (*Vinettu*) (May, Karl) 246

women 12–13
　abortion 192
　AFKSZh 98, 100
　AIWC 117
　correspondence between 97–8, 99, 100, 101–18
　Cuban 251–2
　Czechoslovakia 222, 223
　Egyptian 72
　expatriate communities 151–2
　Gharyan hospital 187, 188
　healthcare 191–2, 193
　Indonesia 102, 113
　KSZh 97–118
　morality/sexuality 13, 188–9
　North Korean refugee children 27
　politics 117
　sexualization of 251–2
　Soviet 12–13, 72–3, 97–8, 99, 100–18
　space race 112
　Third World 97–8, 101–18, 252
　trade unions 208
　travel 107, 112, 115, 116f
　travel writing 251–3, 255, 258
　white 255
　WIDF 99, 100–1
Women's International Democratic Federation (WIDF) 99, 100–1
World's Fairs 79
　Brussels World's Fair (1958) 78, 80
　Montreal World's Fair (1967) 80
　Seattle World's Fair (1962) 80

Xántus, János 244

Yemen
　expatriate communities in 154
Yugoslavia 10, 77, 94
　African art in 85–96
　African art/culture 80, 81–2, 94–6
　anti-colonial road trips 242, 251
　art/culture in African spaces 82–5, 95

　art/culture in Third World spaces 84–5
　BITEF 81
　colonial adventure stories 245, 246
　cultural diplomacy 78–9, 81–2, 83
　Egypt 82, 83–4, 86–7
　folklore 242
　hunting accounts/expeditions 248
　institutionalization of African art in 90–6
　"Josip Broz Tito" Art Gallery of the Non-Aligned Countries 90, 93–5
　Kragujevac–Kilimanjaro expedition 251
　Museum of African Art 90, 91–3, 95
　Nazi occupation 242
　négritude 86, 88, 89
　socialist modernism 78–9
　travel writing 237, 239, 240–1, 242, 250, 254, 256, 257, 259

Zaki, Hassan 66, 67
Zambia 55
Zanzibar 197, 198, 199, 200, 202–4 see also Tanzania, United Republic of
　ASP 204, 209
　Department of Worker's Organisations 211
　FPTU 203–4, 209
　independence/revolution 209, 211
　Issa, Ali Sultan 202–3, 204, 206, 209
　itinerant trade union school 210–11
　Quallatein, Ahmed Badawi 206–7, 209
　trade union education 206–7, 208
　Umma Party 209
　ZPFL 202–4, 209
Zanzibar and Pemba Trade Unions (ZPFL) 202–4, 209
Zebra Drum News (Ignácz, Rózsa) 252, 255
Zikmund, Jiří 251
ZPFL (Zanzibar and Pemba Trade Unions) 202–4, 209

www.ingramcontent.com/pod-product-compliance
Lightning Source LLC
Chambersburg PA
CBHW052215300426
44115CB00011B/1702